PATTERNS OF CHRISTIAN ACCEPTANCE

Patterns of Christian Acceptance

Individual Response to the Missionary Impact
1550-1950

Martin Jarrett-Kerr, C.R.

LONDON
Oxford University Press
NEW YORK · TORONTO
1972

Oxford University Press, Ely House, London W.1

GLASGOW   NEW YORK   TORONTO   MELBOURNE   WELLINGTON
CAPE TOWN   SALISBURY   IBADAN   NAIROBI   DAR ES SALAAM   LUSAKA   ADDIS ABABA
BOMBAY   CALCUTTA   MADRAS   KARACHI   LAHORE   DACCA
KUALA LUMPUR   SINGAPORE   HONG KONG   TOKYO

ISBN 0 19 213946 0

© Oxford University Press 1972

Printed in Great Britain at the Pitman Press, Bath

IN MEMORIAM

an unknown number of Jamaican slaves
'owned' by my West Indian forebears

The voice of my brothers'
blood crieth unto me
from the ground

CONTENTS

Preface   *page* xi
Acknowledgements   xvii
PROLOGUE
CHAPTER 1
The Fateful Impact   1

PART ONE
Early 'Group Dynamics'
CHAPTER 2   10
i. Japan   12
ii. Madagascar   16
iii. Buganda   22
iv. China   30

PART TWO
Absolute Beginners
CHAPTER 3
Japanese   37
i. Grace Hosakawa   37
ii. Gotô Juan   44

CHAPTER 4
Chinese   50
i. Hsü Kuang-ch'i   50
ii. Candida Hsü   58

CHAPTER 5
Indians   65
i. Devasagayam Pillay   66
ii. Sattianaden   71

CHAPTER 6
Africans   77
Queen Mokwaë   78

CHAPTER 7
North American Indians   86
i. Japheth Hannit   89
ii. Kateri Tegaquitha   91

PART THREE
Towards Maturity   100

CHAPTER 8
André Kim (Korea)   101

CHAPTER 9
André Ly (China)   115

CHAPTER 10
Joseph Vaz (Ceylon)   130

CHAPTER 11
Sergei Seodzi (Japan)   142

CHAPTER 12
Miao-Chi (China/Japan)   153

CHAPTER 13
George I ('Siosi') Tupou (Tonga)   171

PART FOUR
In Open Sea   189
Section A: Reproductions

CHAPTER 14
Various   189

CHAPTER 15
i. Paul Mulla (Turkey)   196
ii. Paul Takahashi Nagaï (Japan)   201

Section B: Transpositions   210
CHAPTER 16
Upadhyay Brahmabandhav (India)   211

CHAPTER 17
i. Lu Cheng-hsiang (Dom Pierre-Célestin Lou, O.S.B.)
    (China)   222
ii. Samuel Adjayi Crowther (Nigeria)   226
iii. Ini Kopuria   232

PART FIVE
Improvisations 238

CHAPTER 18
a. Latin America 238
i. DONA MARÍA ANGEL 238
ii. ANTONIO CONSELHEIRO 240
iii. HIDALGO Y COSTILLA AND JOSÉ MARÍA MORELOS Y PAVAN 241
b. The Philippines 245
iv. JOSÉ RIZAL 245
c. Africa 251
v. JOHN CHILEMBWE 251
vi. SIMON KIMBANGU 254
d. Maoriland 260
vii. T. W. RATANA 260
e. China 266
viii. HUNG HSIU-CH'ÜAN AND THE TAIPING REBELLION 266
ix. GENERAL FENG YÜ-HSIANG 275

Conclusion
CHAPTER 19
The Widening Lens 282

Notes 295
Appendixes 315
Bibliography 325
Index 337

PREFACE

The hardest facts to contemplate are those which are obvious, deplorable, and yet (apparently) inescapable. One of these facts today seems to be the widening gap between the 'Third World' and the rest: not merely, though most patently, an economic gap, but also a cultural gap and an 'expectations gap'. Meetings are held, conferences are called, papers and books are written —but the gap quietly widens. This is so partly because common beliefs and commitments, in terms of which it might be possible to bridge this widening gap, are still to seek.

So far as one can see, there are four, and only four, possible bridges.* The first, and the one with the clearest outlines, is Marxism. This really might have been an encouraging option at a time when it inspired whole populations in the Second as well as in the Third World (i.e. on both sides of the gap which lies between the first two and the third). But we have seen this hope shattered with the total break between the Russian and the Chinese versions of Marxism. The second is pragmatic scientific secularism, the dominant philosophy of the First World (the world sometimes known as Euramerica). This might now seem to be the most hopeful: the mathematical formulae of physics ignore distinctions of colour, class, and race more successfully than any of the religions of man have managed to do. But the criteria for deciding the use to which these mathematical formulae should be put cannot be (or at any rate so far have not yet been) satisfactorily deduced from within science itself. The third is Islam. This is a force which has unified many varied nations and cultural heritages in the past; but it has been a unification achieved at the expense of alternative hostilities. The fourth is Christianity. Empirically and statistically this might not seem to offer very concrete hope, in spite of its theoretical— indeed, cosmic—claims. However, disparity between promise and performance is common to all human movements, and in the case of Christianity is allowed for within the system itself.

* But see note on p. xv.

But if this fourth possibility is to be a genuine bridge, then the most important part of that bridge at the present moment is on the far side: it is those Christians who are not only in but of the Third World who will be the test case for the possibility of bridge-building.

One way of assessing the possibilities is by looking at the history of Third World Christianity. There are several different methods by which this might be done: the most thorough and illuminating would be that of the social anthropologist, who might try to collate the studies of cultures in many areas, and the mutual interaction of those cultures and the Christian faith accepted into them.

I have not the competence for this method, though I have tried to use some of the findings of individual studies in different areas. The approach in this book is more modest, and therefore both more arbitrary and more impressionistic. I have tried to look at modes of acceptance at different stages in different countries, as seen through the lives of individuals. The result is bound to be arbitrary, since the representativeness of any of the *dramatis personae* could be challenged.

I have nevertheless chosen this method partly because it is the only one within my compass; but also because it makes easier one absolutely essential element in the process—I mean, trying to survey the field from the receivers' end. This is absolutely essential, to obtain a fair picture. But more, it is absolutely essential because until very recently almost the whole material for such a study has been purveyed from the givers' point of view. This is no doubt why so much 'missionary history' is given short shrift by the professionals. Yet today it is at last possible to make the imaginative attempt to see through the receivers' eyes, because the receivers themselves, or their descendants, are writing about it. As we shall have reason to state a number of times when speaking of individual characters, recent studies by historians from the Third World correct the traditional Western history books in many important details. The life of the Korean, André Kim, for instance, can be told against a quite new background now that a Korean scholar has studied the sociological and political forces around the government which condemned Kim's predecessors;[1] several recent scholarly works by West African historians show us the 'missionary' successes in Nigeria

in a very different light;[2] use of original Chinese material, of
Congolese witnesses, or of Malawian vernacular memoirs has
enabled experts within the last ten years or so to give us a quite
fresh account of such episodes as the Taiping rebellion,[3] Kim-
bangism,[4] or the revolt of John Chilembwe.[5]

Indeed, in so far as this book is original it is so for these reasons.
First, so far as I am aware no other book (at the time of writing)
brings together these individuals from so wide a geographical
area and so long a time-span. Second, though this does not
claim to be a work of original scholarship, it draws on much
original (and often inaccessible) scholarship of others. Third, it
makes available some lives which have in fact never been told
as such before: e.g. there is no life in English of Paul Hsü
Kuang-ch'i, and the one life of his granddaughter Candida has
never been translated from the French; the life of Queen
Mokwaë has had to be dug out from scattered references in
missionary journals; similarly, the life of André Ly, the Chinese
priest in the little-known mid-eighteenth-century China, can
only be studied by working through the three-volume French
history of the Paris *Missions Étrangères,* and through the 900-
page-long Latin diary which he kept; again, it is a safe bet that
no student has even heard of Sergei Seodzi of Japan, since the
brief sketch of him, in an obscure collection of Russian pamphlets, has been specially translated from the Russian for this book
by a friend whose labours I hope I have adequately acknowledged; the earlier Japanese layman and engineer, Gotô Juan,
too, can only be discovered by delving into a little-known
German periodical published in Switzerland; there is, so far as
I have been able to discover, no full life of King George Tupou
I, of Tonga, and this has been therefore reconstructed from a
number of studies; Paul Mulla, the Turk, is known to a few
French students, but hardly beyond that; there is no extant life
of Upadhyay Brahmabandhav; and though there have been
plenty of accounts of Bishop Samuel Crowther, including one
full-length biography, they were all written before the new
work on Nigerian history that has been appearing in the last
decade. . . . And so on.

And the fourth claim this book might make to originality is
that there is no other that brings together various Christian
traditions; Catholic, Protestant, Anglican, Orthodox, etc. True,

for much of the time it has to show these in opposition, indeed rivalry, with each other: though there were (we shall see) exceptions—the friendship gradually formed between White Fathers and some early C.M.S. missionaries and their African companions in Buganda; the kindness of Dutch Protestants to Jesuit priests in Canada tortured by Amerindians, etc. Today certainly the ecumenical climate is right for joint study of the kind this book attempts.

It may be helpful to summarize the shape of the book.

Part I, to meet the objection that it is not outstanding in-dividuals who are the most representative of movements, con-tains a sketch of some communal incidents of Christian witness. One of the complaints most often brought against the white missionary is that by 'converting' individuals he detached them from their culture; therefore biographies of distinguished non-European Christians will in fact be biographies of distinguished eccentrics. Part I is meant as a reminder that the strongest force in the lives of early Third World Christians was the Christian family.

Part II gives samples of 'first receivers'. Here the possible range is vast: I have deliberately selected the least known and least accessible.

In Part III the children and grandchildren of those in Part II are beginning to shake off some of their early dependence.

In Part IV they are 'on their own', more or less. But there are two ways of being on your own: *reproducing* (often, alas, in trivial detail) the faith once delivered to you; or *transposing* it into the natural key of your heritage.

But there is also a more radical transformation. In Part V we look at a variegated sample of 'theme and variations', or improvising upon a given melody. These are the people who would be described by main-stream Christians as 'deviants'; but it should be obvious from the shape of this book that their significance is absolutely crucial for the future.

Part VI therefore looks cursorily back over the book, notes the importance of Part V, and throws out a few hints for the future.

I have had frequently to use the terms 'non-Western' or 'non-European'. They are obviously odd: the Sioux from the mid-West may be 'non-European', but so is his white American neighbour, and he can hardly be called 'non-Western'; a mestizo from Paraguay may be 'non-Western' but he is hardly 'non-European' except by the bizarre pigment-measuring notions of the Republic of South Africa. And worse, by singling out the 'coloured' world for treatment, is the book not guilty of racialism in reverse? My only reply is: read on, and then you can judge.

There may be surprise that Abyssinia should be absent from this collection since it is, with the possible exception of the Indian Christians of St. Thomas, the oldest example of 'Third World Christianity', as well as the inspirer and day-dream of many African independent churches. The reason for its absence is, first, ignorance; and second, that the only personality I could find who would provide a suitable biography, Ghebre Michael Amlak (1791–1855) died as a martyr,[6] not for Christianity at the hands of 'heathen', but for Latin Christianity at the hands of Ethiopian Christians. Though I have not (I hope) tried to dodge the unhappy significance of this type of Christian in-fighting, it is hardly illustrative material for what this book is about.   M. J.-K

Hostel of the Resurrection
Leeds
1970

NOTE

To the four possible bridges mentioned at the beginning of the Preface some would wish to add a fifth: Buddhism. It is my view, however, that the most widespread form of Buddhism, Mahayana (or 'The Greater Vehicle'), is too absorbent and amorphous to offer a firm foothold.* Strict Theravada ('The Lesser Vehicle') Buddhism is a different matter: here might be a genuine candidate. But it is, I believe, a form of 'naturalism' which to some extent aligns it with the second of the four alternatives above—pragmatic secularism. Buddhist thought in general, however, certainly has and will have an important contribution.

* See, for instance, the section on Miao-Chi, Part III, chapter 12, below.

ACKNOWLEDGEMENTS

My first debt is to the U.S.P.G. and its magnificent library: especially to the Librarian, Miss Holland, whose wide knowledge and experience has been so readily available. I hope I have occasionally been able to repay her assistance by being able to give her the welcome information that this or that volume in her library is not in the British Museum.

To my friend, Jean Bruls, of the Société des Auxiliaires du Mission (S.A.M.) and till recently Editor of *Dieu Vivant*, I owe much information and the loan of a number of books. I am grateful to Bishop Stephen Neill and Bishop Richard Rutt of Taejon (Korea) for information about books I had never heard of; and to my old friend David Paton whose wide knowledge and caustic criticism have been equally helpful.

To the Rev. Eric Rowland for immense pains in translating some twenty to thirty pages of Russian solely for the purposes of this book.

To Hilde Tod who stood in for my almost non-existent German and elucidated the life of Gotô Juan.

To the Librarians of the following Libraries, for help with tracking down rare books: the Jesuit Library, Farm Street; the C.M.S. Library, Waterloo Rd.; Selly Oak Colleges Library, Birmingham; the India Office Library, London; the Catholic Central Library, Westminster; the Kensington Public Library; Cardiff and Leeds City Libraries; the Brotherton Library in the University of Leeds; the Library of Rhodes House, Oxford; and the Manchester Public Library.

Thanks are due to the following publishers for permission to reproduce copyright material from their publications:

The Japan Society of London: *Japanese Society Transactions and Proceedings* (C. R. Boxer, 'Hosakawa Tadaoki and the Jesuits'; vol. XXXII, 1934–5).

Lutterworth Press: K. Reichelt, *The transformed Abbot, Miao-Chi* (1954).

Other works which I have consulted and drawn upon considerably for information are given special mention in the Notes, Appendixes, and Bibliography.

If any other copyright material has been used without acknowledgement, owing to inability to trace the source, I trust that the owners will exercise indulgence. I shall be glad to have my attention drawn to any such.

PROLOGUE

CHAPTER 1 | THE FATEFUL IMPACT

A. Do you believe in God?
B. Yes, when I go to church.
A. What do you believe in when you aren't in church?
B. I believe in self-interest, whatever happens.
A. What is justification by faith?
B. To believe—each one for himself.
A. What is justification by works?
B. To put money in one's pocket.
A. What is heaven?
B. Heaven is to be able to live at Bubbling Wel Road [*sic*] and to drive round in a Victoria.
A. What is hell?
B. Hell is to fail.

This is part of a comic catechism for modern Chinese youth based on the impression of Anglo-Saxons formed by Chinese visitors to the West. It was written by Ku Hing-ming and published in English in 1915.[1] It expresses graphically what the more educated Chinese thought of Western culture in the early part of this century. Even the Western-educated Sun Yat-sen held that Occidentals were less civilized than Orientals if only because they are so much more hairy.[2]

If such was the impact of Western Christianity on the cosmopolitan Chinese as recently as three-quarters of a century ago, it is understandable that the impact was even more unfavourable three hundred years earlier, and much more unfavourable still among people less advanced than the Chinese. Indeed almost the first effect of Western Christianity among island- or forest-people was quite simply disease. One of the saddening elements in the dramatic story of how the missionaries first reached the Auca people, in primitive Ecuador, was the development of a 'flu epidemic among the forest-folk, who had no immunity to Western germs.[3] Precisely the same thing had happened to the Polynesian people a hundred and fifty years earlier.[4] Indeed there was one hideous incident in which a schooner, in 1861, *deliberately* landed some measles-infected

Tann Islanders on Erromango Island, promptly causing the death of a third of the population.[5] Neither the accidental nor the deliberate bringing of foreign illness should, of course, be blamed on Christian mission as such: though it must be admitted frankly that some missionaries saw it as, literally, providential. On 22 May 1634 the Puritan, John Winthrop, wrote to an English friend, Sir Nathaniel Rich, about the Amerindians, and their land (coveted by the Whites):

They [the natives] are neere all dead of the small Poxe, so as the Lord hathe cleared our title to what we possess.[6]

The other most obvious impact, arriving either with, before, or soon after the missionaries, was that of the cannon and the gunboat. There has seldom been a more complacent, indeed, delighted expression of this than in the remarks of an army chaplain (temporary) in South Africa towards the end of the last century. The Rev. Colin Rae, an Anglican clergyman, was asked by the Bishop of Bloemfontein to accompany an expedition in 1894, as chaplain, against an obscure Tsoana chief, Malaboch, of the Blaauberg District of Zoutpansberg. Malaboch had been refusing to pay taxes, on the plea that the land the Europeans were taking belonged to his people. So the Boer Campaign was mounted, under General Joubert. The chief's caves, where he and his people went into hiding, were blown up and Malaboch was captured. There is a tragic picture printed in Rae's book of this once proud chief, dressed in prison slacks in Pretoria Gaol. Mr. Rae describes the whole Campaign with evident satisfaction. On the Campaign he visited a missionary who worked among Malaboch's own people. He discussed the work of missionaries with this lonely minister in Middelburg (the Rev. C. Sonntag), and afterwards observed that, though he had some sympathy with them for their self-denying work, yet

I do not altogether agree with their *modus operandi*, for I am in entire sympathy with the policy of the Government with regard to the native tribes. In bringing the natives out from their strongholds, and thus dispossessing the petty chiefs of their powers, the Government is doing a much better work than any Christian missionary has yet accomplished. When in his kraal the native lives an idle, useless life; he struts and squats about like a little demi-god smoking *isangu* and drinking *utyala*, and otherwise satisfying his animal passions. . . . The missionary's one object should be . . . to teach them that great lesson which was practised and taught by the Great Master Himself, and of which the greatest of His apostles commanded, 'That if any would not work, neither should he eat.' . . . The Kafir when driven from his kraal is not left to starve, but may always find employment in the various mines. . . . When the native is taught to *want*, then he will work; it is no use setting him a good example, which he will not follow; something more forcible must be done. He must be kept under control, and subjected to discipline, and the keynote must be work! work! work![7]

This expression of racial superiority seems characteristically British. The assumption that not merely white civilization but Great Britain, and not merely Great Britain but London, is at the centre of the universe, is implied in the educational syllabus which the English missionaries used to prescribe for the schools of their converts. This is charmingly brought out in a report of inspection of a Mr. Young to a school in Tonga in 1853. He wrote in pleased terms of the pupils:

Their writing on slates was creditable. . . . In spelling they gave the correct orthography of the different countries in America, thus embracing both spelling and geography. They stated the distances of the principal English towns from London with tolerable correctness; repeated the tenth chapter of John, and answered questions in the Second Conference Catechism very satisfactorily.[8]

(A useful piece of research might well be done on 'the assumptions revealed in syllabuses of mission schools of the last century and a half'.)

And, not content with bringing their superiority, these foreigners brought with them their controversies and dissensions. The London Missionary Society and Wesleyan Methodist Society were so alarmed at the arrival of Roman Catholic priests in the Polynesian islands that they protected their young converts in the Training Institution in Tonga by giving them 'The Rev. Dr. Hannah's "Lectures on Popery"'.[9] And they must have been pleased with the result of their teaching, for the following dialogue was reported to have taken place in 1843 between some of the Tonga chiefs and the French priests. They had asked the latter why they had come:

Priests: It is our duty to go and preach the Gospel to every creature.
Chiefs: We have the Gospel preached to us, and the Word of God to read.

Priests: No, you have not. These men who preach to you are leading
you astray; they are of Mr. Wesley's religion, which took its rise
only about a hundred years ago; and Mr. Wesley was no better
than Jovili [an impostor who was in the Navigator's Islands just
before].

Chiefs: Our religion is the religion of the Bible, and took its rise with
the Bible.

Priests: Your Bible is full of errors.

Chiefs: We believe our Bible to be the Word of God and of truth, and
are determined to abide by it. . . . [and so on.][10]

And in some cases the religious differences between Christians
must have seemed to many of the onlookers to have been the
direct cause of some of the factional wars (Tahiti and Tonga,
Uganda, etc.), even though careful historical research has been
able to show later that these differences were at most one factor
among others, and often accidentally associated with social and
cultural and dynastic rivalries which would have led to wars in
any case.

Nevertheless, even if the qualification is admitted, it is also
true that the preaching of the Gospel sometimes had directly
political overtones, which the recipients cannot have missed.
Dr. Charles Chauncy, preaching at the ordination to the
(Amerindian) Mission of Joseph Bowman in 1762, said:

Were our views, in this matter [i.e. the necessity of missions],
confined to this world only, there would not be wanting powerful
inducements to prompt us to liberality. We should hereby attach the
Indians to our interest. . . . The French nation have taught us this
to our sorrow, as well as cost. They have all along made it a point
to support missionaries among the Indians. . . . By the pains they
have taken to convert them, not to the faith of Christ, but to the
religion of Rome, they have been able to use them as instruments in
bringing into effect their mischievous designs against us. . . .[11]

And this is matched with the completest symmetry by the
attitude of some of the French priests themselves, working
among Indians. (Not all: some of the priests in Acadia were
accused of being too favourable to the British.) The Jesuit Fr.
Bigot, and the seminary priest, Fr. Thury, were notorious for
the use of their converts in war against the English. Fr. Thury
certainly instigated attacks on the English frontier before the
war, and had a hand in repeated forays after it began.

The minister Pontchartrain twice wrote him letters of commend-
ation, praising him in the same breath for his care of the souls of the
Indians and his zeal in exciting them to war. . . . The King was
begged to reward him with money; and Pontchartrain wrote to the
bishop of Quebec [16 April 1695] to increase his pay out of the
allowance furnished by the government to the Acadian clergy, because he, Thury, had persuaded the Abenakis to begin the war
anew.[12]

It is true that some of this mutual accusation was based on
guesswork, and has been proved untrue. The Jesuits were, for
instance, accused of instigating every one of the 'Interior Wars'
(the Cayuse War, the Yakima War, the Coeur d'Alène–
Spokane war, and even the Nez-Percé war).

An early pioneer demanded political action against the 'Yesuit'
Indian plots; 'not a robbery has been committed' along the Oregon
Trail 'but was excited by the Yesuits.' In 1848 a bill for the forcible
expulsion of all Jesuits was introduced into the territorial legislature
but failed to pass.[13]

Careful historical study shows these accusations to have been
false; and the Indians themselves certainly were not taken in by
them. The Tahitians were not taken in by similar accusations
made against the missionaries in the South Seas a little earlier.
Count Otto von Kotzebue, son of the famous Russian dramatist
and poet of that name, visited between 1823 and 1826 (for the
second time) some islands in the Pacific, and then published (in
German) an account of his voyage which received considerable
notice among the literati in Europe. In it he spoke of the work
of the London Missionary Society in Tahiti as a 'spark thrown
into a powder magazine . . . followed by a fearful explosion'.

The new religion was introduced by force. . . . Whoever would not
instantly believe the new doctrine was put to death. . . . Streams of
blood flowed—whole races were exterminated; many resolutely met
the death they preferred to the renunciation of their ancient
faith. . . .
    True genuine Christianity, and a liberal government, might have
soon given to this people, endowed by nature with the seeds of every
social virtue, a rank among civilized nations. . . . But the religion
taught by the Missionaries is not true Christianity. . . . It has put
an end to human sacrifices, but infinitely many more human beings
have been sacrificed to it, than ever were to their heathen gods.[14]

This was taken up by the *Westminster Review*, which regarded von Kotzebue as an eminent authority. William Ellis, the Congregationalist missionary historian, was able to show that the elegant traveller was wrong on almost every point, concluding that when there was fighting, and persecution, as indeed there was in 1812, 'the Christians were themselves the victims, not the authors or instruments, of these persecutions; they sustained them with fortitude. . . . When the Christian religion spread more extensively, in 1815, force was used—not by the Christians, to promote it, but by the pagans, to annihilate it'.[15]

Von Kotzebue was on stronger ground when he complained (as other critics have done) that the missionaries suppressed legitimate sport and gave no outlet to the natural ebullience of their converts.

A more convincing gravamen against the missionaries was that they exaggerated the importance of their enterprise—not, of course, judged from the eternal plane (which of us here could do that?), but simply from the empirical level of their own impact. Because their arrival did have a reverberating effect in 'primitive' societies, of island- or forest-people, they assumed it must echo as loudly everywhere. Yet (as I have shown elsewhere) it was possible for a Japanese to write a story about a castle and a battle in early seventeenth-century Japan, the time at which Christians (mostly Jesuits) were making the biggest advance that they ever succeeded in making in Japan, especially in that part of the country, without ever mentioning that some of the participants in the battle were Christians and that there were actually priests in the castle at the time.[16] Persecution is hard enough to bear: to be quietly ignored is far worse. But the reason for taking no notice of the Christians is obvious enough on reflection. One educated Chinese wrote in 1891 that it is common knowledge that 'it is only the worst, the most feeble, the poorest, the most vicious of Chinese who are, or can be, what the missionaries call converted'.[17] And even more discouraging is the passing remark of a recent Chinese historian who has made a detailed study of educated Chinese who studied outside China from 1872 to 1949. Among them, he says, there were a number of Christians who could have been included. 'However these Chinese were mostly Catholic clergy who had little general impact on China; hence they are not part of my study.'[18]

The fact is that many missionaries have taken very literally the words of Christ, 'I will make you fishers of men', and have gone about it sometimes too much with a statistical eye to the catch. Further, fishermen all over the world have proverbially exaggerated the size and quality of their haul. And in presenting their prize specimens to the world they have not always been concerned to retain a critical accuracy. 'Presenting their prize specimens' is not an unfair description, for converts were quite often brought back to Great Britain or France in the eighteenth and nineteenth centuries, as good propaganda for missionary fund-raising. This has always been a problem. The missionaries were always being requested to produce good, dramatic material for home meetings. The Secretary of the Presbyterian Foreign Mission Committee wrote to Hope Waddell in Nigeria in 1850:

It is the Calabar idols, cloths and other things from Africa that have provoked such excitements. I know that you . . . do not favour such things; but you must remember . . . the notice that such things are to be seen packs a large house on a week-day evening and gives one the opportunity of stating to them solemn and important truths. . . . [And to another worker:] You must not abate one iota of your graphic delineations; otherwise *The Record* and with it the interest felt in the mission will go down.[19]

This, indeed, sets a problem for a book which, like this, depends largely on biographies of non-European Christians written by missionaries. These biographies are nearly always 'one-source' books, and the writers were too busy (or too uncritical) to check some of their stories. When—as has rarely happened—historical scholarship has later gone over the material it has often been found that there were serious inaccuracies, or romanticisms, to correct. An instructive case is the life of the fine African missionary, Canon Apolo Kivebalayu; when his recent biographer came to study the events, she found that one particular graphic and melodramatic story about him, which had been repeated in several brief lives, had no basis in fact.[20] (It was not needed, for the authentic episodes of his career were enough to establish Apolo as one of the outstanding nationals of his time, without needing additional legends.)

It is fair, though, to say that not all verbal legends are unreliable. Sir Basil Thomson, who worked in the South Seas, gives us a remarkable and reliable example of 'the durability of tradition'. He conducted a native newspaper in Fiji, and collected fragments of historical poetry still remembered, inviting contributions from the Fijians. At the same time he was printing some fragments published in a missionary book about 1860.

Among the contributions received in response to my appeal was a poem of the murder of Koroitamana [*circa* 1825]. It had been gathered from the mouth of a very old woman of Bau. My native sub-editor recognized it as being the same as one of the fragments from the missionary book, and brought me the printer's proof. Here, then, was an opportunity of comparing versions of the same poem taken thirty-three years apart. The poem contained five or six stanzas of ten to eleven lines, and in all these there were but two differences of one word each.[21]

This accurate oral memory among non-literate people was not, alas, put to much use by the Christian missionaries, except for a few far-sighted ones. Nevertheless, it was usually through the missionaries that oral legend became preserved as written poetry; for it was often they who first reduced spoken languages to grammar, syntax, and ultimately print. It is symbolic that it was in 'a missionary book' of 1860 that Sir Basil found these fragments of pre-Christian poetry. Even the most thorough non-Western critic of the missionaries would have in honesty to say, if he came from an area that was pre-literate before the coming of the Christians, 'you taught me language, and my profit on 't is that I now know how to express my dislike of your motives and methods'.

For whatever may be quite fairly said about so many of the Euramerican purveyors of the Christian faith, there is a cloud of witnesses to speak up for a large number of them: some of these witnesses will be found in the chapters that follow. And sometimes the witness is the more striking for being unconscious. Observers have, for instance, noted the similarities between the reception of Communism by Chinese peasant communities and religious rites, especially rites of purification.

In a Chinese village in South Shansi the Communists arrived in 1945 and 'liberated' the area. Then followed the usual process of *fanshen*: literally, 'turn the body', 'turn over', almost equivalent to 'conversion'—i.e. 'stand up, throw off the landlords' yoke, throw over superstition, study science, abolish word-blindness, *scilicet* introduce education for the masses'. The process in this case is exceptionally well documented, by a sympathetic, Chinese-speaking American who was living there three years later when land-reform was in its second stages. In the first stage, he notes, the revolution was extremely radical. In this village the proportion of Christians happened to be unusually high: 25 per cent (as contrasted with the figures for the whole of China at the time, viz. 2 million Roman Catholics out of 600 million). Most of these, including the Chinese Roman Catholic priest, were accused (in most cases, alas, legitimately) of being associated with 'landlordism' and the Kuomintang. They were expropriated, the Church taken over for a granary-store, the priest driven out; and any Christians still found practising their faith were discriminated against. Within a few years the Church was, as a visible and effective witness, dead. But the *fanshen* process was even more ruthless, and after a time party leaders were sent from headquarters to check the over-enthusiasm of the inexperienced local reformers. In June 1948 a 'County Conference' was called by Secretary Ch'en, Party Leader of Lucheng County. He said that the redistribution of land and goods had been too drastic and violent: the attack had been overdone. 'Many middle peasants [he said] have been injured economically and many commercial and business establishments have been harmed. When it comes to rich peasants and landlords, "sweep-the-floor-out-the-door" tactics have been used. . . .' For there simply was not enough land to redistribute. The local *cadres* had shown a faulty outlook, by adopting what he called 'an ultra-poor peasant' line, and striving for 'absolute egalitarianism'. Land-reform policy cannot be applied mechanically and artificially to post land-reform conditions. 'Marx, Engels, Lenin and Chairman Mao Tse-Tung', he says, 'all oppose absolute egalitarianism.' And then, when he wants to summarize the objection to the excessive radicalism of the village's first attempts at reform he does so by, in effect, accusing them of a spiritual overweeningness, indeed precisely of the theological sin of pride (though no doubt he was unaware of the implications of the language he used). Here are his words: 'So our standard for judging *fanshen* was wrong. . . . We took absolute equality as our banner. . . . We did not look to the further interests of the people and of the Revolution. We tried only to be charitable. We wanted to give everyone what they needed. *We tried to be God.*'[22]

CHAPTER 2

Kenneth Scott Latourette, the monumental historian of Christian expansion, has observed what he regards as a curious feature of missionary work in the Islands of the Pacific during the nineteenth century: that the most widely represented and the most numerically successful of all Christian bodies there were the Congregationalists (London Missionary Society) and the Methodists. But these are denominations which in their origin had been made up of dissenting minorities and with a great stress on personal conversion. It was particularly curious that Congregationalism should have been so prominent. 'Relatively it loomed larger than in any other major non-Anglo-Saxon area except Turkey. Although in its motherlands it stressed the individual more than did most Protestant groups, in the Pacific it came in contact with peoples whose traditional pattern of life was tribal and collective.' He adds, however, that the spread of Congregationalism in the Pacific Islands largely by mass movements may not have been so anomalous after all: the Congregational tradition of the local gathered community, and also the record in Great Britain of the Cromwellian commonwealth where (as later in New Zealand) the attempt was made to mould the entire life of the community in Christian terms, may have prepared the way for a similar approach among Polynesian and Melanesian peoples.[1]

Whether, indeed, the Pacific Islands proved exceptional in this way is doubtful. Any relatively 'primitive' civilization has a strongly-developed group sense, and in one area after another we find the reaction to the coming of the new 'Western' or non-indigenous religion to be: Wait and see, and then we'll all move together if we have to move at all. What is remarkable is that spontaneously and in different areas around the globe this group-acceptance led to a group-martyrdom. Remarkable, because 'group-acceptance' suggests a mere conventional conformism, which one would expect to lack the stamina and conviction called out by the challenge of death. But lack it they certainly did not—perhaps it is fair to say that the stamina was already there in the traditional group loyalty, and that this was merely transferred to the new adherence. But it is not less remarkable for that. And in view of the fact that the rest of this book will be considering individuals, it is well to establish from the outset that it is really the approach via the individual that is anomalous.

It is not surprising that the acceptance of, even desire for, group martyrdom should have been prominent among Roman Catholic converts. Their Western teachers had, after all, taught them that martyrdom not only brought a heavenly reward to the martyr but brought renown and spiritual blessing to the Christians still left. Certainly the zeal with which the relics of the martyrs (European or indigenous) were collected by any Christians lucky enough to survive, their preservation and enshrining in churches, shows that the converts had indeed a very powerful sense that here were riches given them by God. In the case, particularly, of the Japanese martyrdoms in the late sixteenth and early seventeenth centuries, there are striking examples of this. When, for instance, five Japanese were killed together in 1509 (two crucified in the common Japanese manner), the Christians took great risks to obtain the remains. The officers were keeping close watch, so they waited for a dark and stormy night. By this time most of the martyrs' flesh had been consumed (by the weather, wastage, and decay), and—the contemporary account does not flinch at giving the ghoulish details:

there remained on the crosses almost nothing but bare bones. . . . Then they [the Japanese Christians] came up, and took away only a little at a time from the said sacred bones, so that in the morning the theft of them should not be perceived. And they did it in such a way that it might appear that the missing portions were due to damage inflicted by the weather.[2]

And when two or three other martyrs were hacked to death, the Christians managed this time to get permission to collect the remains, which they did

with great joy, leaving nothing, not even a drop of blood. They even cut off the finger-nails; and scraped the very pavement on which the martyrs had lain. The heathen were astonished and praised this care and devotion to the remains.[3]

Unfortunately there was a good deal of dispute between two of the chapels, one of them having obtained the body of a little boy (aged six) who was martyred along with his father, and refusing to give it up to the other which had the rightful claim to it. One is reminded of similar sacred rivalries in Europe in the early Middle Ages.

It is interesting, however, that it is not only the Roman Catholic converts who took care to collect relics. Though the non-Roman Christians had not the same *cultus* of the saints and their remains, they took equal care to give their dead decent burial; and in the case of Madagascar, went out of their way to preserve what can only be called 'relics' of their witness.* And when it comes to the spirit in which suffering and death were borne, even the expressions used to describe this (many of them biblical, of course) scarcely vary between Protestant and Catholic.

i. JAPAN

It is convenient to begin with these mass martyrdoms in Japan, since they were among the earliest of the modern era. The Jesuits kept careful records of these, including the conversations, and in some cases the letters, of their converts (translated, naturally, into Portuguese). Here, for instance, is the opening of a letter written from prison, on 7 January 1609, by Michael 'Ficoyemon' (so they Portuguesed it). It is written to tell the Jesuit Vice-Provincial

of the great favour which God has granted to a miserable sinner—for such I know I am—by no merit of mine: allowing me to be detained for the fourth year in prison for the confession of His Holy Name; and this . . . I endure with such lightness and content that it seems to me as if I had only been imprisoned for one day. . . . Further He has visited me with such a severe illness that I feared I would die in prison: but He has willed to prolong my life, so that I may bear witness to His holy faith.[4]

This is quick work. St. Francis Xavier landed at Satsuma in August 1549. The Jesuits' work had its ups and downs, and began to be threatened, not only by the hostility of the Shogun (military lord) Hideyoshi from 1587, but also by the arrival of Franciscan missionaries, who were less experienced and more

* See below, pp. 20, 21.

brash than the Jesuits. Nevertheless—and largely because Hideyoshi did not at first rigorously enforce his anti-Christian decrees—by 1606, after a bare half-century of labour, the Jesuits could boast of 750,000 Japanese converts, with five or six thousand new ones every year, and Nagasaki, the great Catholic centre, was competing with Manila and Macao for the title of 'Rome of the Far East'.[5]

However, Hideyoshi did not allow his condemnations of 1587 to remain altogether a dead letter: and in 1597 (5 February, 'a cold winter's morning'), twenty-six Christians were crucified in the Japanese mode, after having been paraded round some two to three hundred miles by land, from Kyoto, via Sakai to Nagasaki. The reason for this outburst was that the Franciscans, still newly arrived and with little sense of the delicate political situation, were Spaniards: they believed that they could adopt towards the highly cultured Japanese the same demands for unconditional surrender to the Gospel and total abandonment of native tradition which had proved successful in backward Mexico, Peru, and the Philippines. Further, a Spanish vessel bringing wealth to Japan from Manila had just been wrecked. And, to crown all, the Spanish Pilot-Major of this boat, boasting of Spanish power, had admitted to the Japanese that the Spanish empire had been helped by the pioneer work (the 'fifth column' as the Japanese might have called it) of the Franciscan missionaries.

In spite of all this provocation, Hideyoshi decided not to slaughter all the white missionaries—the Jesuits were still necessary to him for trade with the Portuguese at Macao. So, finally, of these twenty-six victims only six were Europeans (all Franciscans): the rest were Japanese—seventeen converts of the Franciscans and (included in error) three Jesuit lay brothers.[6]

Unfortunately it has to be admitted that both Jesuits and Franciscans—this means both Portuguese and Spaniards— made very little bones about combining spiritual with imperial advance at this time. One Jesuit priest wrote to the King of Portugal in 1555 from Japan claiming credit for introducing prayers for the king of Lusitania to his Japanese converts.[7] And in the Jesuit *Relations* for 1602–3 the Portuguese author (writing actually about the missions in India) entitles it: 'Of the service which the Company [of Jesus] renders in all the aforesaid parts of the Orient, not only to God, but to His Majesty and the

Crown of this Kingdom', and explicitly says that, 'Because as many heathen as are converted to Christ, just so many friends and vassals does His Majesty's service acquire, because they later fight for the State [of India] and Christians against the heathen.'[8]

On the whole, however, in Japan it was the Franciscans who were more open about the Church–State connection, and the Jesuits more secretive about it. This is one of the reasons why the Franciscan converts were mostly among the poor, who would not appreciate the political implications of Christian missionary policy, while it was the Jesuits who were able to reach the nobility and the literati, the *samurai* and the *daimyo*.

Indeed, the Franciscans prided themselves on their attention to the poor, the sick, and the oppressed. They claimed that this was the best argument for Christianity; that the Jesuits' subtlety and dialectic was misplaced, and that, as one Franciscan Father put it, learned Buddhist Bonzes, passing the hospice of Kyoto and seeing the friars washing the lepers' feet, used to say, 'We don't want any more arguments. This is it! There must indeed be salvation.'[9] And it is sad to have to record that the Jesuit hospital, founded in 1557 (the first ever in Japan), was deliberately limited, some twenty years later, to Christians, to *samurai*, and to nobles.

Lepers and sufferers from venereal diseases were on no account to be admitted, since they were so repulsive to the Japanese. . . . The Visitor [Fr. Valignano, in his *Summario* of 1583] explained that they could not help everyone; and if they admitted low-class patients, it gave the hospital and the missionaries a bad name.[10]

Little wonder that the Franciscans claimed that, while over thirty thousand Jesuit converts gave up their faith when Hideyoshi's anti-Christian edict of 1587 was published, the Franciscans' converts had later stayed firm: for the latter owed their faith to the martyrdom of the twenty-six in 1597, whereas the former were mostly converts from selfish motives and could not withstand persecution.[11]

This continued to be so to some extent in the severer persecutions that broke out after Hideyoshi's death. During these persecutions, which continued sporadically from 1613 to 1622 (and beyond), a much higher proportion of *heimin* (peasants, artisans, and merchants) than of *samurai* remained faithful to the death.[12] And it was the Japanese Christians themselves who all the time bore the brunt of it: so much so that in 1617 a Dominican and an Augustinian friar deliberately sought out martyrdom, partly to strengthen the spirit of their flock, and partly because they felt it invidious that so far only converts and none of the European priests had been executed.[13] The distinguishing feature of these mass martyrdoms was that they were public occasions and demonstrations of faith. Three Christian *samurai*, for instance, were burned at the stake in 1613, in the presence of a big crowd of Christians who prayed and sang hymns. In 1622 the martyrdom of two Jesuits and their Japanese companions was witnessed by some thirty thousand spectators. And the 'great martyrdom' at Nagasaki, when, on 22 September 1622, 132 were killed, was also witnessed by a large concourse: so large that at the next execution, in November, the crowd were forbidden to sing or pray aloud.

However, the following year another Jesuit was burned with forty-nine Japanese companions, and preached to the crowd, unhindered—with such effect that two bystanders ran forward and asked (in vain) to be allowed to die too.[14] But from then on the authorities, who had allowed the crowds to be present in the hope that the executions would act as a deterrent, realized that they were having the opposite effect. Indeed, after 1626 the methods of torture and execution were altered; and though the intensified persecution led many Christians to flee to the North, taking the faith up there for the first time, and though for another twenty years or so priests continued to live and work in hiding, the Christian Church was, to all outward appearances, wiped out towards the end of the century. And yet there were extraordinary survivals. In 1657–8, though the Christians there had been deprived for more than ten years of priests, there were more mass arrests in Nagasaki: six hundred Christians were arrested, and of these 411 were executed, and seventy-seven died in prison. (The last, a girl arrested at the age of eleven, lingered in prison till 1722: sixty-four years.) And in 1664–7, in another part of the country—a part untouched by the Jesuits— more than two thousand Christians were arrested, many killed, and hundreds deported.[15] It has been calculated, by comparing a number of sources and divergent figures, that between 1614 and 1640 there were probably five to six thousand Christian martyrs. Of these, less than seventy were Europeans, the rest all

Japanese.[16] And whatever the quality of individuals, and in spite of the (understandably) increasing number of apostates, there is no denying that the 'Christian Century' in Japan has more examples of solid heroism than almost any other era in the history of the Church. And deep-rooted faith survived against all probability. Two hundred years later Japan was again opened to the West, after well-nigh complete isolation. Père Petitjean (of the *Société des Missions Étrangères*) came to Nagasaki in 1865 (19 February). He erected a chapel. On 17 March some Japanese, about fifteen of them, came shyly to the mission. They recited the *Pater*, they remembered Christmas, Lent, Mary, St. Joseph; and three women of between fifty and sixty years of age said to the Father, 'all our hearts here differ no whit from yours'.[17]

We shall see something of the sociological significance of this group witness at the end of this chapter.

ii. MADAGASCAR

There were sporadic persecutions in China during the early missionary period, but very little in the way of 'mass martyrdoms'. For that we have to wait till the 'Boxer' rebellion at the turn of the nineteenth century. In Korea and Indo-China, too, though there were outbreaks of persecution somewhat like the Japanese experiences, they were not on the same scale; and in any case they have nothing fresh to tell us. So we may move to another part of the world, and this time to the effects of Protestant missionary effort.

The first mission here was founded in 1820 by the London Missionary Society. The King of Madagascar, Radama, was favourably disposed towards the visitors, and even decided to send twenty Malagasy youths abroad (ten to Mauritius, ten to England) for education. He must have been a 'progressive' for he is reported to have been sceptical of the diviners with their *sikidy* (spells to avert evil and bring good luck); he once ignored their advice, and once when approached by people of a sacred village for some scarlet cloth for their shrine, replied, 'Surely he [i.e. the spirit of the shrine] must be very poor if he cannot obtain a piece of cloth for himself. If he be a god he can provide his own garments.'[18]

The missionaries soon got a printing press going, and in 1828 the first sheet of St. Luke's Gospel, in translation, was printed.

Radama died in 1828. He had nominated his nephew, Prince Rakotobe, to succeed him. Rakotobe had been sent to the mission school, and continued a friend of the mission until his death. But Queen Ranavalona, one of Radama's wives, offered to make two officers head of the army if they would put her on the throne. The Prince was seized at night and killed; four officers of the late King's bodyguard who opposed the Queen were also killed, and Queen Ranavalona was proclaimed. The mourning for the King forbade all teaching or preaching, so the missionaries worked hard to produce elementary books on religion and a translation of the New Testament.

The Queen was crowned in 1829, and at first, since the French seemed to be threatening her kingdom, she befriended the missionaries as English, i.e. as potential impediments to French advance. The first New Testament was printed in 1830, and the first twenty converts baptized in 1831.

But the Queen believed that it was the 'idols' who had secured her the throne, and began to move against those who undermined their influence. From 1831 no soldier was allowed to be baptized; then Holy Communion was proscribed; finally all slaves were forbidden to learn to read or write. Accusations against Christians for neglecting traditional worship became more frequent. A chief reported to the Queen, after attending a Christian meeting and hearing a converted slave preach:

They hold assemblies in the night and deliver speeches without permission from the Queen. The Christians are exhorted to serve Jehovah, the first King of the English, and then Jesus Christ, the second. These meetings are carried on by slaves . . . we fear these people, who have become so friendly with the English, will attempt to transfer the kingdom of the Queen to them.[19]

The Queen now determined to stamp out Christianity. First she obtained a list of the houses where meetings were held. Then she told the missionaries that they might teach arts and sciences, but worship and baptism must stop. Then prayer was forbidden —but in fact it was said to have increased, and prayers were held in private houses of Christians every evening until midnight. The missionaries went on with their printing, and even single sheets of their translations became valued possessions. Finally when printing was forbidden, the missionaries had to leave the island.

The first Christian to be arrested as such was not a slave but a woman of noble birth, Rafaravavy. Her house was used regularly on Sunday evenings for worship, until three of her servants gave her away (on 17 June 1835). She was warned, and was able to hide her Bible and other books. Her father was furious with the slaves who had betrayed her and had them put in irons; but she ordered them to be freed, and 'spoke to them of the mercy and forgiveness of God through Christ'. Two of them later became Christians and one died for her faith.[20] Rafaravavy refused, at her trial, to give the names of her fellow-Christians, and the Queen violently ordered her death. But others of rank intervened and sentence was deferred. She had with her a tract, treating of martyrdom in very similar terms to the Jesuit *Exhortations to Martyrdom,* issued to Japanese converts from 1615 onwards.[21] Rafaravavy's tract has this passage:

A. I will cast myself at the feet of Jesus, and if I perish, I will perish.
B. If you perish there, you will be the first that ever did. For sooner shall the heavens and the earth pass away than the Saviour reject anyone coming to Him.

When the Queen for a time pardoned her, on account of the services done for her by her father, she bought a house some distance away and there the Christians met. Other Christians travelled twenty miles into the mountains for prayer. They were able to send a message out to the missionary (a Mr. Johns):

It is thought that we shall certainly forget the word of God now that we have no teachers. The Queen does not know that the best Teacher of all, the Holy Spirit, is still with us. . . . We have opportunities of meeting on the mountains to sing and pray on the Sabbath. . . . All the Christians are teaching others to read, there are ten learning with one friend, six with another, and four with another, and the number is increasing. How much does the compassion of the Saviour console us now!

But in the end they were betrayed and arrested. One of them had been a diviner, an old man baptized as 'Paul'. When asked whether he 'prayed' (technical term for being a Christian), he replied,

I have certainly prayed to that God who created me . . . to make me a good man. I prayed that He would bless the Queen, and give her true happiness in this world, and in that which is to come. I asked Him to bless the officers and judges, and all the people, to make them good, so that there might be no more brigands and liars.[22]

The first to die for the faith was not Rafaravavy herself, but another woman, Rasalama. In prison she had been tricked into giving away the names of other Christians, unknowingly; and when she discovered this she was so distressed that she was glad of the death sentence. She sang hymns on the way to execution; when she passed the chapel in which she had been baptized she said, 'There I heard the words of the Saviour'. She was speared to death as she knelt in prayer. Some bystanders said, 'Where is the God she prayed to, that He does not save her now?' But others said, 'There is some charm in the religion of the white people which takes away the fear of death.'[23]

Two hundred Christians were then ordered to be sold into slavery, among them the noblewoman, Rafaravavy. Later she learned that she was to be executed after all, so she and three other women who had been betrayed escaped. They travelled forty miles and were hidden by Christians. They moved on again—once she was hidden behind a mat while soldiers searched the house that gave her shelter—and for three months they lived as fugitives. When it became too dangerous for any-one to hide them they slept among stones, boulders, or in grass on top of old tombs. As they travelled round they found Christian families fifty miles from the capital, and even on the East coast where none could have been expected. Many had portions— even single sheets—of the Scriptures, in one case preserved in a box in the ground, and could read them. Finally Rafaravavy was smuggled out to Mauritius (1838). (She came to England in 1839 and attended a meeting at Exeter Hall.)

These escapes, and the knowledge that 'praying' was still going on, angered the government still more, and persecution increased. Nine people were executed in July 1840; more in 1842. Yet the teaching went on, and above all the copying of those portions of the Bible that had been preserved.

'Most of the educated Christians [wrote the missionary who visited them later] employed themselves in copying out, so far as their materials would allow, portions of Scripture and other books. The eyes of some of them were severely injured by close application to this work, in their places of concealment. I brought home no memorials of the persecutions in Madagascar more deeply affecting than some of these fragments of Scripture, worn, rent, fragile, and soiled by the dust of the earth or the smoke in the thatch, at times when they had been concealed, yet most carefully mended, by drawing the rent pages together with fibres of bark, or having the margins of the leaves covered over with stronger paper.'[24]

There was quiet for two years; but the worst was to come. By now the Queen's only son, the Prince Royal (Rakotond-radama) was favourable to the Christians; her nephew, Prince Ramonja, had actually become one; and the Prime Minister's favourite nephew was helpful to them. In 1849 Prince Ramonja's house was found to be used for worship, and was destroyed. Eleven Christians were arrested at once, and many more soon after. The judge ordered the prisoners to take the oath which recognized the 'idols', and accused them of disloyalty to the Queen. One of them said,

If our enemies say they [i.e. the Malagasy] will not fight, it is not the Christians at all that they speak of, for against the enemies of the queen and her country the Christians will fight. As for stones and wood, and the idols, and the mountains, God has not given them to be prayed unto; for they are things without life. But God is the Lord of heaven and earth and of all things.

All were kept in prison; the other Christians met at 1.0 a.m. to pray for them. The next morning they were bound, gagged to prevent them testifying, and brought out fastened to poles. The Queen condemned four nobles (one a woman) to be burned alive; fourteen to be hurled to death from a famous rock; the rest to various forms of punishment—flogging, chains for life, slavery, etc. Nearly two thousand (some say three thousand) Christians were condemned to one penalty or another. Those condemned to death sang a hymn:

Ary misy tany soa,   (There is a beauteous land,
Mahafinaritra indrina.   Making most blessed.)

The four nobles to be burned sang 'Hod' izahah Zanahary' ('Going home are we to God'). They were fastened to stakes a little above the firewood. As the flames arose they could be heard praying and quoting scripture. One witness said, 'They prayed as long as they had any life. Then they died; but softly, gently. Indeed, gentle was the going forth of their life, and astonished were all the people around that beheld the burning of them there.' The other fourteen were carried up to the escarpment, Ampamarinana. They were stripped (though still bound by the arms and legs) and thrown over, one by one—fifty or sixty feet down to a ledge, then 150 feet to the bottom. Most were lifeless by the time they reached the bottom. Then the bodies were taken and burned where the noblemen had been.[25]

Mr. Ellis, the author of the account given, visited Tamatave in 1853, and found that though the Christians had now been seventeen to eighteen years without foreign teachers, 'their extreme and constant danger, as well as the absence of all earthly encouragement and help, seemed to have bound them together in a holy brotherhood of love, strong and lasting'.

It is interesting that, in the early days of the persecution, the Christians worked out a password, with its appropriate response. If someone said 'Jeremiah 38, 15' to you, you should respond 'Jeremiah 38, 16'—and then he would know you were a friend. ('If I declare it unto thee, wilt thou not surely put me to death?' *Reply:* 'As the Lord liveth, that made us this soul, I will not put thee to death, neither will I give thee into the hand of these men that seek thy life.')[26] There is no doubt that the number of Christians grew during the persecutions. However much the early missionary enthusiasts may have exaggerated the figures, it seems safe to say that there were between one and two thousand believers at the beginning; about two hundred were killed, and many were taken away as slaves. Yet there were seven to ten thousand Christians by the end.[27] And in 1868, eleven years after the last persecution (1857), there were over thirty-seven thousand.[28] It is hard, of course, to judge of the quality of the converts' lives and their understanding of the faith, from the single-source accounts we have. It will have been evident in some of the quotations given above that the Malagasy statements, hymns, and prayers have been translated into flowery and improving Victorian English. There is no doubt that the equating of 'Christianity' with 'school', here as elsewhere, led to what must have been often primarily educational motives for conversion. A hostile critic, too, might say that the preservation of single sheets of the translated Bible shows a superstitious veneration not unlike that which we have seen in the collecting of Japanese martyrs' relics above. What is more, it seems to be clear that Christianity first took root among the Hovà people, the tribal group that not only acquired supremacy in the nineteenth century in the island, but also showed the greatest interest in Western advancement. So, once it had survived persecution, the newly-adopted faith had the best possible impetus for expansion. But when all allowances are made, the original group-witness of the Malagasy Christians reveals an authentic and heroic element at its root: a testimony of life even more than of word.

iii. BUGANDA

The next example we shall take is the best known of all—the 'Uganda Martyrs'. These have been described so often, and so many books have been written about them,[29] that there is no need to go over the story again in detail. But it is worth recounting from one particular angle since it has something to add to the two previous examples.

A journalist once expressed a widely-held view when he wrote that, 'Among the Baganda of East Africa, a ferocious religious war was engineered by Roman Catholics and Protestants who, in Christ's name, tore the six-hundred-year-old civilization oj a once pagan people into shreds.'[30] The necessary corrections to be made to a statement like this provide a good starting-point for the story. The Buganda civilization was already being 'torn to shreds' by Islam, which arrived first on the field; indeed, it is generally now accepted that it was from the Arabs that King Mwanga learned the practice of homosexuality which was responsible for so much of the disaster that marked his reign. Further, this Buganda civilization included such practices as the slaughter of hundreds of innocent victims, at the death of a king, so that he should have a good escort to the world of the ancestors. King Mutesa, influenced by both Roman Catholic and Anglican missionaries, was the first to order that this custom be abandoned at his death (which occurred in October 1884).[31]

In outline the story is simple enough. The first Christian (as distinct from Muslim) missionaries to arrive at the court of Mutesa, the 'Kabaka' (king) of Buganda, were from the Church Missionary Society, and arrived in 1877. The greatest of them was a layman, an engineer, Alexander Mackay, who came in 1878. Rather to their surprise, the Kabaka gave them a comparatively warm welcome, and they soon found many chiefs anxious to 'learn'. Early in 1879, however, they heard to their dismay that a Roman Catholic mission had also just arrived. They assumed that this was by a deliberate policy of the Roman Church to undermine the Protestant mission; but in fact it was only a part of an over-all plan to evangelize the whole of Equatorial Africa, and the first step towards this had been taken more than thirty years before (1846). Mackay tried to persuade the King not to let the Roman missionaries in; but Mutesa seemed rather intrigued by finding two versions of Christianity on his doorstep, and let the missionaries argue with each other. The appearance of Mackay and Père Lourdel at a *baraza* (court), at which the King asked Mackay to 'read' and Lourdel would not join in, must have puzzled Mutesa. Mackay's account of it runs:

The Katikiro and chiefs . . . all knelt, and after opening the Prayer Book I said to M. Lourdel, at my side, that we were going to pray, and perhaps he would kneel with us. He said he did not understand me. . . . So I went on, and was not interrupted by the padres, only I heard one whisper to the other *Pater Noster* when I was reading the Swahili version of it. . . .

Mutesa in his abrupt style, said to Teli (the interpreter), 'Ask the Frenchmen if they do not believe in Jesus Christ? Why don't they kneel down with us when we worship Him every Sabbiti? Don't they worship Him?'

M. Lourdel . . . became all at once excited, and said, 'We do not join in that religion because it is not true. . . . If we joined in that, it would mean we were not Catholics, but Protestants, who have rejected the truth. For hundreds of years they were with us, but now they believe and teach only lies.' Such was the drift of his excited talk, in a mixture of bad Arabic, Swahili, Luganda and French. . . . I endeavoured to give the King a simple account of the history of the Church, and why we had left Rome. . . . I tried to smooth the matter by saying that we had one belief in many things—one God, one Saviour, one Bible, one Heaven, and one law of life. But my friend would have no terms of peace. 'There was one truth, and he came to teach that, and we were liars.'[32]

But Mackay stuck to his guns, and in a later prayer-session at the Court referred again to the Roman claims, but concluded that 'it was a minor point, this one of Pope or no Pope, compared with the all-important one so often discussed—is Jesus the Messiah, the Son of God, or only a prophet? That was the greatest of all questions'.[33]

It seems fairly clear that Mutesa, toying with Islam, Protestantism, and Catholicism, was really seeking a balance of power between the Arabs, the English, and the French. But his appearance of hesitation between the 'three religions' encouraged the young men of his court to follow their own bent and study under the missionaries. The King had four to five hundred pages and it was from these, and the servants of some of the chiefs, that most of the converts, both to the C.M.S. Mission and to the White Fathers (as they became) were drawn. Some of them had reached exalted positions—such as Joseph Mukasa, later martyred, who was chosen as the King's personal attendant. Some became centres of Christian communities; in the case of one (Matthias Kalemba, another of the martyrs) living twelve hours' journey from the Roman Catholic Mission, inquirers were taught at his home, and twice a month a catechumen was sent to the capital to memorize the priests' instruction and bring it back.[34]

Mutesa had flirted with Islam—but had a horror of circumcision. He flirted with Christianity, but said clearly that he could not give up his wives. In 1880 he seemed to be toying with Christianity again; but a month or so later ordered the arbitrary killing of ninety-nine men, cows, goats, sheep, and chickens, to inaugurate a new ornamental hut over the grave of a previous Kabaka. However, Christianity progressed in both missions; and the relationship between Mackay and the French priests improved considerably. Mackay notes, without too much dejection, that some of his 'readers' were also receiving instruction from the Catholics; and Fr. Faupel, the historian of the 'martyrdoms', admits that some of the best Catholic converts, including some of the future martyrs, were using the Scriptures printed in Swahili by the C.M.S.[35]

However, in November 1882 the Fathers withdrew from Buganda, owing to threats from the Muslims and hostility at the court, and set up a new mission across the Lake. In spite of the absence of any priest, the Catholic community continued to grow, and about thirty of the converts, longing for the sacraments, actually left Buganda in 1884, and travelled to the new Mission.

Mutesa died in October 1884, but profited by the missionaries' influence enough to forbid the usual ritual slaughter of subjects at his death. During this year the Catholic leaders were tested, and came out of it well. Above all, Joseph Mukasa, the late King's attendant, looked after the spiritual welfare of the converts at the court; another, Jean-Marie Muzeyi, not only cared for the sick during an epidemic of plague, baptizing the dying, but also used his own savings to buy children from slavery and instruct them in the faith.

The new Kabaka, Mwanga, seemed at first to give the Christians hope, as he appeared to be favourable to the missionaries, attended instructions given by one of the Catholic converts, Andrew Kaggwa, and tried (not very successfully) to learn to read at the C.M.S. Mission. But he had already acquired the habits of homosexual practice (repugnant to the Baganda), of alcoholism, and of *bhang* (hemp-smoking). Mwanga was only eighteen and much under the influence of his advisers, who were turning anti-European (with the growth of the Catholic mission) and especially anti-English, encouraged in this by the Arabs. The first persecution, in fact, was directed against the Protestant converts when early in 1885 three Baganda Christians were burned to death—the first African martyrs.

But some of the chiefs were not satisfied that Mwanga was sufficiently anti-Christian, and plotted his death. The plot was revealed to the young King through the Christians at the court, especially Joseph Mukasa, who still held the high position he had had with the old King; and the Catholics especially were promoted for this service, and the French missionaries were encouraged to return.

The Fathers were greeted with such enthusiasm by the people, and apparent affection by the King, that they thought the future assured. However, they knew that many at Court were still against them; and the C.M.S. missionaries were even less optimistic. All the evidence now shows that it was the refusal by the Christian pages to indulge in sodomy that most annoyed Mwanga. His determination to persecute them was revealed swiftly. First, there was the murder of Bishop Hannington, the new Anglican Bishop, on 29 October 1885, on the ground that his coming the way he did (from the North-East, through Busoga, the 'back door' to Buganda) meant that the English were coming to steal the whole land. The Catholic attendant on the King, Joseph Mukasa, had the courage to urge Mwanga not to kill Hannington—'Your father Mutesa', he said, 'never put a white man to death. Why, then, should you want to kill one?'[36] On 15 November, after Mwanga had been suffering from eye-trouble and sleeplessness, and suspecting (on the hints of one of his counsellors) that Père Lourdel was trying to poison him, he had Joseph Mukasa killed and burned.

Knowing that matters would not stop there, other Catholic pages came to the priests and urgently asked for baptism: more than forty were baptized. Mwanga threatened to kill all Christian pages, but found that so few would then be left that he did not for the moment carry out his threat. He even for a short time seemed to be welcoming the missionaries again, especially the French; and once admitted that Joseph Mukasa was a good example. But Mwanga's homosexuality led directly to the next outburst. When he found that his favourite page, 'a very pretty boy' one of the accounts has it, was absent at a time when he wanted him, and was even being instructed for baptism by one of the Catholic pages, his anger flared up. The next day, 26 May 1886, he ordered all the Christian pages to be arrested, as well as a number of Christians from the servants in the outer court. Five of them were killed within the next two days, and the rest, after being kept waiting in prison for a week, were burned to death at Namugongo on Ascension Day, 3 June 1886. There were thirty-one: twelve Roman Catholics, nine C.M.S., probably six 'readers', and the rest pagans—included more or less by mistake. Altogether twenty-two Roman Catholic martyrs were later beatified.

There were two outstanding features of this mass martyrdom. First, although the missionaries had come a bare ten years before, the knowledge of the Christian faith, and the constancy in it, shown by these Christian Baganda was very remarkable. Even if, as elsewhere, their first motive was the desire to 'read', they knew what they were doing in becoming Christians. Even their choice between the two Missions was often studied and responsible. Here is one of the later martyrs, Matthias Kalemba talking to Père Livinhac:

My father had always believed that the Baganda had not the truth, and he sought it in his heart. . . . Before his death he told me that men would one day come to teach us the right way.

These words made a profound impression on me, and, whenever the arrival of some stranger was reported, I watched him and tried to get in touch with him, saying to myself that here perhaps was the man foretold by my father. Thus I associated with the Arabs who

came first. . . . Their Creed seemed to me superior to our superstitions. I received instructions and, together with a number of
Baganda, I embraced their religion. . . .

When the Protestants arrived . . . I asked myself whether . . .
perhaps, the newcomers were not the true messengers of God. . . .
It seemed to me that their teaching was an improvement on that of
my first masters. I therefore abandoned Islam, without however
asking for baptism.

. . . When Mapèra [Father Lourdel] arrived, my instructor,
Mackay, took care to tell me that the white men who had just
arrived did not know the truth. He called their religion the 'worship
of the woman' [the B.V.M.]. . . . I therefore kept away from
you. . . .

The first time when I saw you nearby, I was very much impressed.
Nevertheless, I continued to watch you closely at your prayers and
in your dealings with the people. Then seeing your goodness, I said
to myself, 'How can people who appear so good be the messengers
of the devil?' . . . God gave me the grace to understand that you
taught the truth, and that you really were the man of God of whom
my father had spoken. Since then, I have never had the slightest
doubt about the truth of your religion, and I feel truly happy.[37]

The second feature is the striking growth in mutual respect
between the two Christian traditions, among the Baganda
converts as well as the missionaries themselves. Mackay continued strongly 'anti-papist', but spoke highly of some of the
Roman Catholic converts. Twice he referred to the future
martyr, Joseph Mukasa, who had deserted his own Anglican
flock:

Mukasa is evidently a better Catholic than Romanist, for he not
only said to-day he daily prayed to God to deliver us from the hands
of wicked men, but we heard from others that he had interceded for
us to the king, telling him that the prime minister was seeking to
kill us.[38]

And after Mukasa's heroic death:

This fine tall lad had been a faithful servant of Mwanga, ever since
he became king. Formerly he read with me a Gospel and the Acts,
along with Mulumba . . . and others. Afterwards the Roman
Catholics got hold of all these. . . . He has, however, continued
friendly to us, and spoke well for us to the king last February when
we were in deep trouble. . . . Brave lad, Mukasa! Thou hast
witnessed faithfully for thy Master here below. Enter into the joy of
thy Lord![39]

And, most impressive of all, there is the tribute by one of the
Anglican converts, James Miti, to a Roman Catholic, Matthew
Kisula, who was persecuted but not actually killed, and who
looked after a number of the Christians:

Of all the hiding places, the most frequently used was the estate of
Matthew Insule, the blacksmith, at Natete, where even before the
persecution days catechumens would turn in at noon, or late in the
evening, on their way from the Natete [C.M.S.] Catechumenate and
put up there for the night. In the early days, especially during the
persecution, there was no distinction of religion or denomination;
we were all Christians, whether one went to Mackay or Père Lourdel
for religious instruction. All Christian converts were one family,
with two internal arbitrary divisions as it were; we loved one another,
and wished one another well. It was only at Kabula, during our
exile, that trouble began, that religious differences sprang up and
culminated in the well-known religious civil wars of the early days.[40]

Roman Catholic theologians, writing about the Uganda
martyrs, have drawn the appropriate conclusions. The first
systematic study, by Father Thoonen, ends:

Since the Protestant victims . . . died for the truth of Christianity,
and in no way in defence of a specifically Protestant doctrine . . .
there is every reason to agree that they laid down their lives with the
special assistance of divine grace, and that, in the eyes of God, they
are truly martyrs, not less than the Catholic victims.[41]

And Father Faupel says that though the judicial inquiry for the
Beatification of the Catholic martyrs did not discuss their
Protestant comrades, 'This does not mean that Catholics should
not give honour (i.e. short of an official *cultus*) . . . where
honour is due, to persons outside the Church's fold.'[42] And this
attitude was given some confirmation at an official level when
in 1964 Pope Paul VI invited the Anglican Archbishop of
Uganda to be present at the canonization in Rome of twenty-
two of the Uganda martyrs.

But there are two other important considerations which do
not occur in the more traditional type of missionary history: it
is, indeed, characteristic of recent studies that they have been
brought forward. They are both concerned to put the story of
the martyrdoms in a wider historical context. As J. A. Rowe, an
African historian, has pointed out: in the missionary books the
—admittedly poignant—story of the martyrdoms has tended to
take up a lot of space, with none left for the rest; so that

historians dealing with Mwanga's reign find 'a richly documented history of a small but important group of Christians on
the road to martyrdom, and on the other side, the barest outline of everything else'.[43]

What is more, as Mr. Rowe again points out, whereas the
missionary historians contrasted the evil Mwanga with his
predecessor, Mutesa, pictured as more favourably inclined to
Christianity, in reality Mutesa (whom the missionaries only
knew in his years of maturity and wisdom) was more ruthlessly
destructive than Mwanga. His persecution of Muslims

leaves Mwanga's 1886 outburst a pale reflexion. It was estimated
that as many as seventy chiefs and pages were burned at Namugongo,
while up to a thousand persons were slain throughout the country.
This may be an overestimate, but there is no doubt that Mutesa's
persecution of the Muslims was far more severe than Mwanga's
against the Christians, which Faupel estimates cost the lives of perhaps a hundred, including non-Christians, throughout the country.[44]

Rowe asks the question why some of the Christian pages were
martyred, whereas others escaped without too much difficulty,
and others were actually pardoned. And he concludes a careful
study of individual cases by suggesting that the rivalry between
Mwanga and his Katikiro (usually translated 'Prime Minister'
by the missionaries), Mukasa, accounts for much of this.
Mukasa was afraid that some of the Christian pages were
obtaining too much power with the King, and indeed one of
them, it was rumoured, might even become Katikiro himself
one day; so Mukasa worked against them. Yet some of these
were the very ones allowed to get away. On the other hand,
Mwanga was also afraid of the independent spirit of some of the
Christians (and their possible assistance to the 'encroaching'
English), so he had some killed. What is clear is that Mwanga
had no consistent and thorough policy of exterminating Christians as such; and indeed, he appointed two of the escaped
martyrs at the head of two newly-formed regiments soon after,
and at the end of his reign, before his deposition, became
decidedly pro-Christian. Thus the martyrdoms can be described as to some extent political rather than religious.[45]

The other consideration is related to this. Another African
historian, Professor Low, has studied the tribal background of
the period, and his conclusion is that a hundred years' development of the Kabaka's authority in Buganda is needed to explain

Mwanga's outburst. The Kabaka had throughout the nineteenth century been building up a central power, with personally-appointed chiefs who could offset the traditional tribal chiefs. Given this power, the Kabaka could increasingly neglect, even defy, the local gods. The tribal chiefs, on the other hand, used the local gods to challenge the Kabaka, with threats of spells and cursings. But the Kabaka could not turn himself into a god —this was against all Baganda tradition. So he was open to entertain the notion of new divinities: first Islam, and then Christianity—the latter complicated by arriving in two versions. These two religious challenges led to a strong reaction among the tribal chiefs, and 'early in 1880 the adherents of the old gods launched a serious counter-attack by bringing the medium of the most important god of all, Mukasa, God of the Lake, to the Kabaka's court, with cheering and drumming crowds'.[46] There were fears that all this would undermine the social order, especially remembering the Egyptian threat in the mid 1870s to annex the kingdom for their Sudanese empire. Mutesa was hesitant: he did not want to give way to the tribal chiefs, but nor did he want to fail in his essential role as Kabaka. He died before he could resolve the issue. But Mwanga was even less certain of his position, and blew hot and cold; the martyrdoms occurred during one of the hot moments. And the heroism of the martyrs themselves can be understood psychologically in this context, for,

in their ranks there were a number who had solved the immense spiritual and intellectual confusion into which the Kabaka's court had been thrown in the last years of the previous reign, by becoming baptised Christians; men who had found great comfort and strength from the assurance which that had given them; and for some of whom at least retreat presented greater problems than advance.[47]

This cool historical appraisal does not in the least derogate from the significance or emotional power of the martyrdoms. On the contrary, by setting them against the background of the social and political rivalries of the time, it makes them more human, more believable, and thus, even at this distance, more accessible.

iv. CHINA

Our last example will have some similarities with the former ones: it includes both Roman Catholic and other Christians. It was the indigenous members, rather than the foreign missionaries who suffered most; and the persecution was part-political, part-religious. But there were distinctive elements, both in the circumstances and in the aftermath, which make it worth recording.

The 'Boxer' uprising of 1898–1901 was very consciously anti-foreign. It is not surprising, then, that the first accounts of it were largely concerned with the white men and women who were killed in the rebellion. Marshall Broomhall's *Martyred Missionaries of the China Inland Mission* (1901) was limited by its title to the European victims; but it has an appendix, 'Concerning the Native Christians', which gives twenty-five pages (out of a book of three hundred pages) to the majority. Later there were popular, 'tear-jerker' books written on the Chinese martyrs of the movement, but nothing scholarly. Yet of the Protestant victims there were 180–90 European men, women, and children, but nearly 2,000 Chinese; and of the Roman Catholics, there were 5 bishops, 31 priests, 9 sisters, and 2 Marist brothers, but probably over 30,000 Chinese either martyred, or dying as a result of starvation.[48] And, though the total number involved was smaller, the highest percentage of martyrs to church members occurred in the Russian Orthodox mission—200 to 400 killed out of a communicant roll of 700.[49]

There is no need to give more than a sample of stories—of ordinary farmers, their wives and children, of non-Christians involved out of pity—for, moving as they are, they are inevitably repetitive. Many are stories of individuals. Yu-lan, for instance, a boy of seventeen at the L.M.S. mission at Yen-shan, who had to take to the fields when the Boxers came and razed the village. He emerged from the grain field, to find them on his tracks; so he sheltered in a Buddhist temple. The priest shaved his head to make him look a Buddhist, and hid him. For some days the Boxers did not find him, but spies discovered him. When they came to take him the priest tried to stop them.

'This boy is under my care. What right have you to molest him? What harm has he done?'

'You defend and protect him, do you?—a boy who is well known in the district as a member of the Jesus sect? Then you shall suffer with him. You, a priest of Buddha—you might be one of the secondary devils.'

So they cut him down in his own temple. Yu-lan they carried

off, tortured for two days to reveal the names of other Christians, then, when he revealed nothing, killed him with their swords.[50] Or, again, Mrs. Li, the widow in Peking. During the notorious Siege of Peking, Colonel Shiba, who commanded the Japanese forces defending the city, saw that it was urgent to get a message through to Tientsin, asking for help. Several messengers tried, but were killed. Mrs. Li, a widow who had five children and a blind mother dependent on her, came forward: 'It is better that one should die,' she said, 'than that all these thousands should perish.' She was disguised as a beggar, with a basket on her arm; and she got through. When she returned, however, after delivering the letter, no one had remembered to give her a passport for readmission to the city, and the soldiers would not let her in. She hid at her old home, six miles off; but she was betrayed, and the Boxers killed her.[51]

Some of the stories were told by the Boxers themselves, impressed by the victims' courage: e.g. that of two boys, aged thirteen or fourteen, captured at Tung-chow, near Peking.

They suspected the children of being Christian scholars, so they asked, 'Are you believers in the foreign faith?'

'Yes,' replied the children . . . 'we are followers of Jesus.'

The Boxers brought out cords to bind them, with a view to dragging them to the Boxer altar. But 'there is no need to bind us,' said the boys; 'we will not try to escape. Every step that we take towards your altar is a step nearer heaven.' In a few moments they were dispatched by the Boxer swords. The persecutors were constantly amazed at the behaviour of the Christian children. They speak of it often, and add—'They must have been bewitched by the foreigners.'[52]

It has to be remembered, however, that the Christians were not the only ones to suffer. Thousands of Muslims died, too, in the same uprising. And to understand the savagery of the persecution the historical background to the Boxers needs to be explained. They were only one in a series of secret, semi-religious societies which appeared at various times to challenge corruption, express land-hunger, and, in the mid nineteenth century, to give vent to nationalist, anti-foreign feelings. They adopted the same kind of ritual and magic formulae, charms, and incantations, measures for invulnerability, etc., as other 'heretical' sects.[53]

The immediate cause of the final uprising was the financial

crisis of 1898. Through foreign loans, the Sino-Japanese war, and the indemnity imposed on China, the country was almost bankrupt. The 'foreigners' were an obvious scapegoat for the troubles: from Chinese 'Source Materials of the Boxer War' we learn their views:

One Boxer placard said, 'When the foreigners are wiped out, rain will fall and visitations will disappear.'. . . And a sacred Edict was issued by the 'Lord of Wealth and Happiness':– 'The Catholic and Protestant religions being insolent to the gods, and extinguishing sanctity, rendering no obedience to Buddha, and enraging Heaven and Earth, the rain-clouds no longer visit us; but eight million Spirit Soldiers will descend from Heaven and sweep the Empire clean of foreigners. Then will the gentle showers once more water our lands: . . . then the Buddhist Patriotic League of Boxers will be able to protect the Empire and bring peace to all its people.'[54]

The main difference between these Boxers and other movements of peasant origin is that they were given tacit support by the Dowager Empress, who saw in them a possible challenge to the European powers. And their adoption of the slogan 'Uphold the Ch'ing [the threatened Manchu régime], Destroy the Foreigner', made them popular—though in fact they were distrustful of the ability of the government to withstand outside influence.[55] There was a strong 'folk' element in the movement, but their reliance on magical powers led to their downfall. They believed that their spells would render them invulnerable, and when this proved not to be so they began to lose support. For instance, on 2 July 1900 a Chinese commander, 'General Ma Yü-k'un relied upon the Boxers to block [i.e. with magic] the foreign big guns for a period of six hours—with the result that his division was put out of action.'[56]

Nevertheless it is important to realize the strength of the Boxers' case, and few of the missionaries' accounts do this. The fact that they were more bitterly opposed to the Roman Catholics than the Protestants reflects the widespread resentment in China that the Roman Church had (in March 1899) obtained a decree that priests should be treated on an equality with mandarins, and bishops with 'viceroys' (Governor-Generals of more than one province); further, it was complained that the Catholics particularly counted on special judicial treatment for their converts. It was even believed, on one occasion (July 1900) that Roman Catholics had conspired with a rival sect, the 'White Lotus Sect', to rebel against the Manchus, as a result of which the Boxers killed a number of each.[57] In spite of the publicity given to the Boxer martyrdoms, the Boxers' activities were not so widespread as has often been thought. 'There were missionaries everywhere, yet only in the provinces of Chihli and Shensi—and in Manchuria—were the attacks serious. The rest of the country was hardly moved by it.'[58] Moreover,

The fatal casualties inflicted on the Chinese by the foreigners were far greater than those inflicted on the foreigners by the Chinese during the uprising. In F.C. 107 [Further Correspondence, published by the Foreign Office] Satow gives the total number of missionaries and other persons of British, French, German, Italian, Belgian and Dutch, American and Swedish nationality, men women and children, murdered during the Boxer troubles as 239. In the Liuchiatien incident of October 1899 alone, the Cossacks killed over 100 Chinese who had come to petition the Russian authorities against the land tax . . . [and] On 17 July 1900 the Russians slaughtered several thousand Chinese in Blagoveshchenk, and many more in Harbin.[59]

None of these facts need diminish our admiration for the heroism of the Chinese Christian victims of the rising, however much we might wish that more allowance for such facts appeared in missionary writing about them. What is most striking, though, in the accounts—and this is the final distinctive element we spoke of—is the absence, time and again, of any attempts at vengeance. The greatest Roman Catholic missionary of the twentieth century, Père Vincent Lebbe, arrived in China soon after the Rebellion, and was sent to an area where there had been many deaths.

'Once,' he says, 'I heard a man's confession, and as I couldn't find any faults in him, I asked him whether he honoured his parents. He burst into tears, and . . . said: "I have neither father nor mother. They were cut to pieces in the time of persecution."—"But at least", I said, "didn't you have hatred in your heart against the persecutors?"—"Never", he replied.'[60]

And in his *Histoires Chinoises*, Père Lebbe tells a striking story about the village of Shwang-Shu-Tze (this is the French form of the Chinese) which was attacked by the Boxers, who killed more than fifty Christians. Only one apostatized—an old woman, who did penance later. One little boy of nine was dragged to the pagoda, after seeing all his family slaughtered. The Boxers said, 'We're sorry for you. Just burn a stick of incense—it doesn't matter what you think: the external act will be enough. It will save your life.' The boy took the burning stick, and with a defiant gesture threw it on one side, then folded his arms and waited for death. He was cut to pieces. Lebbe goes on,

After the war, when the survivors came back to the village, the pagans of the place were forced to hand over the relics. It was horrible! One had only an arm left, one part of a skull, a third only the scalp. A few whole bodies remained—they were the ones that had been buried alive. . . .

The Christians were now so powerful that they could have killed everyone and burned down the whole village, and no one could have resisted them or sent in a complaint. But our Christians never said a word. It is true, when they left . . . their place of refuge to return home, vengeance had boiled up in their hearts, but the priest had called them, calmed them down, and they did nothing—not even a word of reproach. . . .

Père Lebbe gave it out that no Boxer leaders would be punished: but that he could not trust them unless they became Christians; otherwise they must stay away from the village.

Trusting to my word, a *chi-hsiung*, or executioner-in-chief, came back to the village. I shall never forget it, all my life. It was evening. I had just finished prayer and expounding the catechism, and I was peacefully smoking my pipe with my Christians, when a Christian broke in, followed by a stranger. When they saw him, I noticed the Christians shudder with horror. The stranger prostrated himself at my feet, trembling, and then got up, turned towards the assembled people and said, in a strangled voice, 'Christians, forgive me. I have done wrong.' . . .

One of the Christians stepped out of the crowd and said: 'You've got nothing to be afraid of. Our law is a law of love, and we must love our enemies. If you want to become a Christian, there is no more anything between us: you will be our brother.'

It was one of those scenes so striking that you think you must be dreaming. . . . A few steps away some Christians, hiding so as to listen, and trembling more violently than the flame of the candle which made all these shadows shudder. And in the middle, prostrated with his head on the ground, the one who had sowed bereavement in every family, guilty a hundred times of death—and no one touched him or cursed him.[61]

It was 1902, less than two years after the events, and reveals, not merely individual magnanimity, but group acceptance. Perhaps this is a type of *marturia* (witness) more heroic than many of the more spectacular forms of martyrdom with which this chapter has been concerned.

PART TWO | ABSOLUTE BEGINNERS

In Part II we shall take examples of individual Christians who are all 'first generation' products. These were 'early days', not in a universal chronological sense, but relative to the arrival of the mission, or the accessibility of Christianity to the person concerned.

In Part I we spoke of some of the more striking phenomena of 'group witness' to Christianity. In such phenomena individuals do not always stand out; indeed, the very fact of these occurrences being *en masse* might lead a psychologically-minded sceptic to dismiss the phenomena as forms of group-hysteria. To see therefore something of the background to these incidents, it is helpful to single out certain persons whose lives in individual detail have been (however uncritically) preserved for us.

It is convenient to group them, not in historical order of occurrence, but roughly by countries or areas, since it is the distinctiveness of the environment that marks each of them.

CHAPTER 3 | JAPANESE

i. GRACE HOSAKAWA

We have seen that the Jesuits' practice, if not their policy, was to aim at converting the nobility, or at least obtaining their goodwill, so that official local permission would make their work of evangelizing easier. Until the officials themselves turned against Christianity, it was a policy that worked, to judge by the remarkably rapid growth of the Christian communities.

One of the local lords who became extremely favourable to Christianity, though he was never himself converted, was the *daimyo* (lit. 'great name', i.e., a feudal, territorial lord), Hosakawa Tadaoki Sansai (1564–1645). We do not know how he came to adopt the kindly attitude he did; but it is significant that he lived in this period which marked the unification (to a greater extent than ever before) of Japan; and in which the two greatest men in Japanese history, the *shoguns* (military governors), Toyotomi Hideyoshi and Tokugawa Iyeyasu, lived; and the former of these, who was ruling when the Christians arrived, was at first tolerant towards them, which no doubt influenced lesser *daimyos* like Tadaoki.

Fr. Gregorio de Cespedes, who knew Tadaoki well until his death in 1611, describes him thus:

This man's character is naturally very fierce, and he is exceedingly jealous and strict with the members of his household. Having had to accompany Hideyoshi to the war in Kiushu [Saikoku], he left his wife with the most rigorous orders not to leave the house until he returned home; . . . he charged . . . [his two most faithful retainers] most earnestly to watch over his wife and not to let her go outside under any pretext whatsoever.[1]

But Tadaoki was a friend of Takayama Ukon, the most outstanding Christian convert among the *daimyos*, who was always trying to convert his friends—and indeed, Takayama had persuaded Tadaoki to go and hear sermons.

Tadaoki's wife, then, had frequently heard her husband talking about Christianity.

This aforesaid Lady was very learned in the doctrines of the various Japanese sects, being particularly well versed in the beliefs of the Iexus,* which is one of the chiefest in Japan and much followed by the nobility. As she was by nature of a very inquiring and intelligent mind, she conceived the desire of learning what the Christians had in their beliefs, but . . . she remained so straitly confined and guarded by his [*sc.* her husband's] order that she had no opportunity. . . . [Yet] she determined to find some means of obtaining speech with the Fathers.

It happened that at this time one of those Japanese festivals occurred, when the people much frequent the temples. So she

resolved to go disguised amongst her gentlewomen to see our house, under pretext of visiting the shrines, and she . . . did indeed contrive to go with six or seven of her tirewomen, disguised as one of themselves. Arriving at our house in this manner and finding the church

* Iexus = *Zenshu*, i.e. Zen Buddhism: then, as later, the favourite creed of the warrior class.

very clean and beautifully decorated (since it also happened to be our Easter Day), seeing the rich ornaments on the altar and the very fine image of Our Lord thereon, she was greatly pleased with our things, and sent to the Fathers, saying there were some grave gentlewomen who wished to hear a sermon and learn the substance of our faith, wherefore they should send her some good preacher.

The Jesuits sent word, asking what women they were, but getting no reply they suspected it was someone important in disguise. So they sent Brother Cosme to expound the catechism to them and answer questions,

which they heard with great attention. . . . This Lady then began to dispute very vigorously with him, advancing many arguments from the Japanese sects and asking diverse questions about our faith, in such wise that the Brother was amazed, saying that he had never met a woman of such understanding in Japan, nor one who knew so much about the religions.

She left when it was nearly night, and was reported to be very impressed, 'for it seemed to her that our faith was true, sure, and solid, whereas the sects of Japan (as the Brother had shown her) were false and unreliable'.

But now, though she longed to complete her instruction, she could not repeat the risky excursion; nor did she dare invite one of the Fathers to her house; so she decided to use an intermediary, her favourite gentlewoman, who was also a person of learning and repute. This lady had accompanied Grace to the church, and was just as favourably impressed. So she visited the Fathers, taking Grace's questions with her, and bringing back their answers. This lady in the course of the instruction determined to become a Christian as well.

This principal lady of the household was baptised, under the name of Maria, and as both she and her mistress discussed these things with the other tirewomen, these latter were so moved that seventeen of the chiefest among them came one after another to hear the preaching and become Christians.

There remained now only the Lady herself, who was more earnestly desirous of baptism than any, but believing that this could only be done at the hand of the Fathers she lived in great anguish, not being able to carry out her intention.

She continued to communicate with the Jesuits through her women, sent alms, and also asked for books in Japanese, which she studied and about which she asked many questions.

This wrought so great a change in her person that (as Maria sub-sequently said) everyone was astonished thereat, since in everything she behaved like a Christian, telling her beads and commending herself very frequently to Our Lord, distributing various alms, and treating her Christian tirewomen with such charity and love that she seemed more like their companion than their mistress, constantly scheming how she could be a Christian.

The year was 1587, and it was in the course of this very year that Hideyoshi suddenly (or so it seemed to the Jesuits) veered round, turned against Christianity, and issued his edict against the Christians—an edict which, though not rigorously enforced for long, resulted among other things in the deprivation of the Christian *daimyo*, Takayama Ukon, and also in the exiling of the Fathers.

Although these tidings saddened her greatly, yet they did not cool her zeal in the least, but rather confirmed her in her resolve more than ever before; so much so that, knowing the Fathers would have to leave, she resolved at all costs to be baptised before their departure, saying that on no consideration would she remain a gentile. Since she could think of no better way, she was resolved to be concealed in a large willow basket, and carried in this manner to the church, where she would be awaited by some of her gentlewomen, and after being baptised she would return to her house in the same manner.

But the Fathers saw the danger of this and persuaded her to be baptized by Maria, which she was. And Maria herself was no less affected by the incident. Considering that

whosoever had administered so holy a Sacrament . . . should no longer concern herself with carnal and worldly things . . . she made a public profession of perpetual chastity; as evidence of this she shaved her hair on the spot, as is the custom with Japanese women when their husbands die, or when they wish to make a vow to leave the world.

And Fr. de Cespedes concludes: 'In this way, at the very height of the persecution, was baptised *Gratia* Lady of the province of Tango, with seventeen of her principal gentlewomen, all vowing amongst themselves that even if her husband or [Hideyoshi] wished to make them recant, they would sooner die.'

All did not go smoothly with her. She wrote a letter to Fr. de Cespedes describing some of her trials. Her second son fell ill; so Maria baptized him, as John—and he recovered. And her husband, Tadaoki, when he returned from the war, seemed in a stern and touchy mood.

As he is exceedingly severe in his mode of life [she wrote], he took a nurse of one of my sons (who was likewise baptised) and for a very small fault cut off her ears and nose and threw her out of the house. Subsequently he cut the hair off two others, and expelled them, since all three were Christians. . . . Maria and I are prepared for any persecution whencesoever it comes, whether from [Tadaoki] or from [Hideoyoshi], and we would rejoice if on this score we could suffer something for the love of God.

Hideyoshi's persecution was not, however, rigorously enforced everywhere, and soon some of the Jesuits returned from their temporary flight. One of them wrote that Grace was being pestered and ill-treated for her faith by her husband, and had thought of retiring to the low countries (in South-West Japan): but the priest forbade this, and so she persevered where she was. She could never see any priest now, but was, as he wrote, 'confined to her house . . . without ever being able to confess or having received any Sacrament other than her baptismal one . . . yet she received such bountiful grace at her baptism that she entirely changed from what she had been before, being granted that loving patience which she now has to all our things'.

Tadaoki's resentment at her Christianity did not, as a matter of fact, last very long. Indeed, her patience softened him so that he actually became proud of her being a Christian, and when they moved from Fushimi to Osaka he himself went to superintend the building of an oratory and an altar 'wherein she could retire to pray, as she was wont to do'. Now she could be in correspondence with the Fathers, and she actually learned to read and write Portuguese. Her husband even had Fr. Gregorio with him, as a sort of chaplain (though Tadaoki never became a Christian), on the Korean campaign of 1592–8; and kept up a close friendship with the Jesuit till Gregorio's death in 1611.

After the death Hideyoshi, and the end of the Korean campaign, Tadaoki became a devoted adherent of Iyeyasu Tokugawa, and supported him against a rival; indeed, the triumph of the Tokugawa cause was partly due to the support of the Hokagawa family, for Tadaoki was a fine general.

It was during the war for the succession, in which Tadaoki

was away defending Iyeyasu, that Grace died. The incident is well known, but is a moving one and must be told again in Fernão Guerreiro's words:[2]

During the conflict there occurred the tragic case of a Christian Lady called Dona Gracia, wife of Tadaoki, gentile Lord of Tango. This Lord was one of the Princes who accompanied Iyeyasu to the Kwantō war; he left his wife and household entrusted to the care of Ongara-vadono [the major-domo]. . . . As Tadaoki is above all things devoted to honour, he was always accustomed, when leaving his house, to give orders . . . that if in his absence something should happen which would place the honour of his wife in jeopardy, they should kill her, as is the custom in Japan, and then all slit their own bellies and die together with her. . . . Wherefore, when the regents [the leaders of the coalition hostile to Iyeyasu] sent an order to Tadaoki's mansion, on the same day that hostilities began, saying to those who were left on guard there that they should forthwith hand over Gracia, the wife of their Lord, as a hostage for the future behaviour of her husband, it was answered that she would not be given up. As the servants realised that the regents would speedily surround the house and lay hold of their mistress, they determined for her honour's sake to carry out their Lord's command. They therefore went in all haste to tell Dona Gracia of what was toward, who ordered them to do as they were told. She forthwith entered her oratory; . . . and after ordering the candles to be lit, she knelt in prayer, preparing herself for death. After a little while she sallied forth from the oratory very courageously, and calling all her servants and tirewomen, ordered them to leave, saying that she only wished to die since her husband had ordered it so. . . .

Meanwhile the major-domo, Ongaravadono, together with some other servants, had strewed gunpowder in all the rooms; when the women servants had left, Dona Gracia knelt down, and repeating many times the most holy name of JESUS & MARIA, she with her own hands bared her neck, when her head was cut off at one blow. They forthwith covered her body with some silk vestments, and throwing more gunpowder on these, they went into the main hall, since it would have been discourteous for them to presume to die in the same room as their mistress. Then they all ripped up their bellies, at the same time setting fire to the powder . . . and they and the mansion . . . were reduced to ashes. Nothing escaped therefrom save the women whom Dona Gracia had sent outside, and these, all weeping, went to Fr. Organtino and told him what had passed.

This is not quite the end of the story: for her sacrifice had a great effect in swinging popular opinion round to Iyeyasu's side, which was soon successful. In acknowledgement, Tadaoki was given the larger province of Buzen (in North Kiūshū). His wife's heroic death increased his admiration for Christianity, and he became more generous than ever to the Church. He invited Fr. Fernão Guerreiro to sit opposite him at the chief banquet of his great Levee; and when a Buddhist priest tried to persuade him to expel the Fathers, he said, knowing it would reach Iyeyasu himself, that though not a Christian himself, his wife was, and that she had died

sacrificing her life for the honour of her husband and Iyeyasu him-self: therefore he must honour her memory and assure the salvation of her soul, in so far as he could, by supporting and maintaining the Jesuit Fathers whom he kept at Kokura for the express purpose of celebrating memorial services for the repose of her soul on the anniversary of her death.[3]

The first Requiem for Grace was celebrated, at Tadaoki's request, at Ôsaka in 1601. Tadaoki himself attended, and was so impressed with the ceremony that he ordered it annually. He said that

he greatly admired the spirit in which the Fathers came to Japan from so far away, leaving their homes and relations with the resolve never to see them again; . . . and turning to his retainers, he said: 'There is nothing more devout than the way in which the Christians celebrate services for the dead, as who seek salvation and nothing else; whereas the sects of Japan are a matter for jest and cannot be compared with this'; concluding by saying, 'I am not yet a Christ-ian, but I am half converted.'

The Fathers lived in constant hope of his conversion; but when pressed, he frankly said that he could not live up to the Christian standard: that 'as long as he does not feel within him the urge to keep the sixth [Hebrew 7th] commandment, he will not become a Christian, since it is a shameful thing to be a Christian and not live like one'.

And when the severe persecutions of the Christians started, Tadaoki did his best to moderate them in his area, avoiding the hideous cruelties that accompanied the executions of Christians elsewhere. He could even be good-humoured about it. One of his retainers was a fervent Christian, and nothing would induce him to recant. Tadaoki hesitated to execute him, and only did so in obedience to specific orders from above in 1619. One day when he was vainly trying to persuade this retainer (Diego was his baptismal name) to renounce his faith and save his life, Diego said, 'Surely you would not wish me to go to Hell?' 'Why not?' replied Tadaoki; 'If I am to go there, wouldn't you be prepared to accompany me? Do it like a loyal vassal, and for love of me.'[4] And it is significant that Tadaoki's own brother, Okinoto, remained a Christian, unmolested, till his death in 1618; that his two daughters were never compelled to apostatize; and that his two sons, who were baptized in infancy, though they ceased to be professing Christians, yet secretly helped the Catholics during the persecutions. Tadaoki himself retired in 1621, and died at the age of eighty in 1645: and his life was written by a Japanese priest, Abbot Kanyeisō Sōtau, in 1670. So it could almost be said that Grace did more for the Christian cause after her death than before. And the mode of that death itself poses an interesting theological problem: for the code which commanded it, and to which she assented, was a pagan code; and the honour of her husband and the political succession he was defending can hardly be called Christian causes; and yet in form and intent it is difficult to regard her heroic act (if, indeed, it has been accurately reported) as anything but a Christian martyrdom.

ii. GOTÔ JUAN

The Jesuits' aim to reach Japanese of standing, which as we have seen was remarkably successful, whatever its other disadvantages, meant that they also had to stand up to opposition from men of standing. Professor Boxer gives us, for instance, a fascinating account of attacks on Christianity by two educated Japanese—one a lapsed Christian catechist (or *dojuku*, a Japanese term used by Buddhists, lit. 'fellow lodger'), and the other a local commissioner—published respectively in 1620 and 1658. Though they differ somewhat, they are agreed on many of their objections to Christianity: how can God, if He is merciful as well as omnipotent, have allowed the Fall of man, and the eternal punishment of people whose lives are blameless though they deny God? According to Christian doctrine, a righteous monarch, though living as purely as the Pope, will go to hell unless he believes in God; whereas a traitorous parricide can be saved as long as he believes in God. The Christian renegade complains that the European missionaries are arrogant and look down on their Japanese colleagues; the commissioner complains that the missionaries influence Christians to disobey their fief-lords, and this may lead to rebellion. (He also says that an all-wise and all-powerful God would not have created barbarous races like the Hottentots and cannibals—he had heard stories about these from Dutch traders: the Japanese had been amused by the Negro servants whom Fr. Valignano, the Jesuit Visitor, brought with him in 1590.[5]) They also reject the claims of the Jesuits that miracles had occurred at the time of the martyrdoms.[6]

These criticisms of Christianity were not very profound; certainly not at the level which the Jesuits had to meet in China, and later in India. And it was just as well: for there do not seem to have been many Japanese converts who could have replied to intellectual criticisms in the way that Chinese converts (as we shall see) did. Most of the conversions, though among the élite, were of local lords and warriors and their relatives. The main criticism, therefore, was always that of potential disloyalty; and it must be admitted that certain Christian *daimyo* (war-lords) did believe that the Faith could be defended, if not established, by arms; and one of the Jesuit Fathers, Coelho, seriously planned to enlist the help of Christian *daimyo* on Hideyoshi's side in a dispute, even promising to provide two Portuguese ships. Fortunately he got no support from his brethren, to the relief of the Christian *daimyo* who did not in the least want to get implicated.[7] In fact, Christians could be found on both sides in some of the campaigns:[8] it is interesting that in the final battle of 1600 Iyeyasu (who was supported, as we have seen, by the near-Christian Hosakawa Tadaoki) not only captured his rival and put him to death, but among his rival's warriors was one, Konishi, who also had a price on his head: this Konishi was urged by his friends to commit suicide before falling into the hands of the victorious Hideyoshi, but refused, as he was a Christian, and was executed by Hideyoshi's orders.[9]

Among the supporters, both of Hideyoshi and, after his death of Iyeyasu, was a Northern war-lord, Daté Masumane. He had made his submission to Hideyoshi in 1590,[10] and had borne the brunt of the fighting on Iyeyasu's side in the Aidzu campaign of 1600.[11] But the central authorities had always been wary of him, for up in the far North he could afford to take an independent line. And this no doubt accounts for the fact that he gave some support to the Christians even when they were being officially proscribed. When, for instance, Fr. Sotelo was condemned to death (1613), Daté pleaded for him, he was released, and Daté took him to his own capital in the North. Furthermore, in 1614 Daté sent an embassy of more than sixty persons to Spain, with a message for the King, and from there on to the Pope; and Fr. Sotelo was sent with them. Daté's letter to the Pope asked his Holiness to send Franciscan monks for service in his (Daté's) domains, and to appoint 'a great prelate', through whose zeal and under whose guidance 'all the inhabitants might be converted without delay to the Christian religion'; he also asked the Pope to help him enter into friendly relations with the King of Spain and his Christian States.[12]

No doubt behind this curious embassy lay the hope of extending trade with Spain, or rather through Spain's intervention with New Spain (an expedition was sent there in 1617). But in spite of the failure of this plan—Spain refused to help—Daté remained tolerant towards the Christians. He was compelled to issue edicts against them in 1620; but even these were not always strictly enforced. And one of the chief beneficiaries of his tolerance was Gotô, who, though one of his leading vassals, 'was permitted to profess his Christianity publicly together with all his own retainers, while until then Daté, who was blind of one eye, shut the other to the presence of foreign priests in his capital'.[13]

The North was very little known to the missionaries before 1615. Indeed, it was only when Fr. Sotelo was brought up there in Daté's retinue that any missionary work was able to begin. But the edict of 1614 against the Christians had led to many of them fleeing from the South; they, being already used to the system of lay apostles, worked among the people, and this soon led to a demand for priests. Jesuits and Franciscans made their way up there, and worked under great difficulties, mostly in disguise. They were successful especially with the settlers, peasants, and miners; and some villages became entirely Christian.

Gotô's ancestry has never been established[14] but he was probably a member of the Gotô family of Ôshu province, a minor vassal of Daté Masumane's at Miwake, near Mizusawa. He was helpful to Fr. Sotelo, was baptized in 1613 or 1614, and from then was known as Gotô Juan. In 1611 Daté granted religious freedom to his vassals, and though most of the higher orders were reluctant to embrace Christianity, Gotô became the most important Christian *samurai* (knight) of Northern Japan. His subjects followed his example, and Miwake was one of the villages that became entirely Christian. During the early years of the persecutions it became the centre of the Ôshu mission. Some of the old houses still stand today, and Christian medallions have been found in the roof-beams. A memorial to Gotô stands now where his house once stood. Even after the edict of 1614 Daté did not proceed immediately against the Christians, and Miwake could continue to expand its mission work for several years undisturbed, largely through the efforts of catechists and lay apostles, and dependent to a considerable extent on the example and protection of Gotô Juan.

Gotô has left behind a striking and very practical memorial of his existence and his concern for his people. We do not know whether the Juan Canal—*Juan-zeki* (as it is called) is due solely to his personal initiative; but it is certainly important even today for thousands of people, since it irrigates their rice-fields.

It is reported that on being given Miwake as his demesne, Gotô surveyed the land from a nearby hill. On seeing the vast stretches of land he is said to have conceived the idea of using the water of the river Isawa so that the soil could be watered and cultivated. According to local tradition, floods and other natural catastrophes frequently threatened the construction, but instructed by foreign missionaries Juan was able to use a new kind of giant pulley, so that bigger stones could be used and thicker retaining walls built. The canal is 5–6 metres wide and in places equally deep. At its end it spreads out fanwise to water the paddy-fields; one arm passes Miwake and is named 'Juan's drinking water' to the present day. Juan himself was unable to complete his project, as the spread of the persecution of Christians to this area interrupted the work.

Daté Masumane's tolerance for the Christians was looked on with suspicion by the central Government and by some of his vassals. He had always been independent-minded, and it was suggested that he wanted to seize political power for himself with the Christians' aid. Thus pressed, he issued three decrees in 1620:

1) Those who have received the Christian sacraments against the King's will are guilty of offence against his majesty, and must now disavow their Christian allegiance.

2) Those who report Christians will be rewarded.
3) Christians who refuse to recant will be banned from his territory.

To begin with Daté's edict was little more than a gesture to pacify the central Government, and he tried to persuade Gotô simply to desist from practising Christianity in public, from converting others or giving shelter to Christians. Gotô refused to comply with this order, and so did many others. A number of Christians were then martyred.

In 1621 these Christians in the North received at last a letter of indulgence from Pope Paul V, which had been sent in 1617 along with special messages of consolation for the persecuted Japanese Christians. It had taken over three years to reach them, but was received with great joy and proved a source of strength in the fight to come. The letters of thanks sent to the Holy Father are still extant, in Japanese (29 September 1621), and are a moving testimony to the faithfulness of the Church in Japan. Gotô was the first signatory of the letter from the Christians of Dewa and Ôshu. It affirms their faithfulness and asks for the Pope's blessing.

1622 was a period of lull, but in 1623 the Government made a renewed request to Daté Masumane to inquire into the existence of Christians in his dominion. A change of Emperor did not bring the hoped-for relief. The Christians in Miwake were able to celebrate at least Christmas 1623 in peace, and Epiphany brought a letter from the Jesuit Provincial naming Gotô a special Benefactor of the Company of Jesus and a participant in all their spiritual grace. But soon after Daté was in Edo (the seat of the central Government), and from there he sent a succession of messengers to his province with instructions that proceedings against the Christians should be taken without delay. However, even a personal letter from Daté failed to persuade Gotô to renounce his faith; and so did the attempt of one of the governors. The governnor's wife even tried to flatter him by saying that she would cut off her hair and shave her head (which seems to have been the extreme expression in Japan of self-abasement) if only Gotô would give up Christianity. However, Gotô not only refused but talked to them with such power about the truth of the Gospel that the governor gave up trying and even said that 'soon Juan would have won both of them over to his side'. Gotô wrote a letter to Daté (also preserved) which expressed his obligation to him and his readiness to surrender everything except his faith, and also that he was prepared to accept banishment or death without any feeling of hatred or revenge.

Thus Gotô was banished in February 1624 (though the Daté documents speak of his 'flight'). Daté was still intent on saving the life of his vassal, but the priest, Fr. Carvalho, was caught and mercilessly put to death.

It has not been possible to establish reliably how Gotô died. It seems that he made his way further north to the snowy, icy province of Nambu, where persecution was in its early stages. His confiscated property was found to be heavily in debt, partly because he had been lenient to his subjects, and partly because of the expense of building the canal. Some of his subjects moved to neighbouring villages, others went north into banishment with him. Reports continued to come for years of Christians in this Nambu province who were connected with him or who were his followers. It is even possible (since communications between the Christian remnant in Japan and the exiled Jesuits were meagre and spasmodic, and in the end ceased altogether) that Gotô may have come south again later, and then been executed during one of the last persecutions.

And yet Gotô's name has remained in the memory of the people until now. It was during the Tokugawa period (1603–1867) that the digging of canals became so important that, instead of leaving it, as had been done throughout the medieval period, to the initiative of local feudal lords, the government itself had a number of locally important canals dug. On the other hand the central government was not strong enough, until 1867, to eliminate the power of the feudal lords[15]—which may partly account for the fact that Gotô survived so long. At any rate we know that the strange fate befell him that befell Fr. Matteo Ricci in China: after his death he was 'put among the gods', or at least the semi-gods, of the heathen. In 1924 he was elevated by the Emperor to the rank of the Fifth Order. At the site of his dwelling a small park and memorial were erected in 1930, and there is an annual (Buddhist/Shinto) thanksgiving in his honour. On 23 September 1953, a new gravestone was blessed in his memory in Yonekawa village, where he may have spent his last years: the ceremony was broadcast on the Japanese radio, and more than a thousand people (mostly of other faiths) were present at the Solemn High Mass for his day. 'And so even today the apostolic mission of this man has not come to an end.'

CHAPTER 4 | CHINESE

Matteo Ricci, the Jesuit pioneer in China, who went there in 1595, was the first Christian to make an effective entry into that land. He did so by realizing that the only hope of penetration lay in indigenization, and first of all that meant adapting himself to the *mores*, and absorbing the learning, of the mandarin class. As in Japan a little earlier, the Jesuit strength lay in the declining popularity of Buddhism at the time. Ricci was able, by his remarkably close study of classical Confucianism, to show the Chinese of the time, better than many of their own scholars, that Confucius' teaching (as distinct from popular, debased Confucianism in the sixteenth and early seventeenth century) was deeply opposed to Buddhism. This meant two things: first, that he took the risk that Buddhism would not gain the political ascendancy (in which case Christianity would certainly be proscribed); and secondly, that he had to establish the compatibility of Christianity with traditional Confucianism. His most famous work of Christian apologetics, 'The Teaching of the Lord of Heaven' (*T'ien Chu shih I*), was largely a citation of passages from the six Chinese classics, showing how they harmonize with Christian teaching. He had a public debate in Hangchow with a noted Buddhist priest; and his most powerful Chinese convert, Hsü Kuang-ch'i, wrote a treatise, *P'i shih she shu wang*, attacking the Buddhists, which was sufficiently formidable to provoke a reply from the famous scholar, Yun Chun-hsi.[1]

i. HSÜ KUANG-CH'I (1562–1633)

In the spring of 1604 a man called Hsü Kuang-ch'i came to Peking to sit his most important examination. Born in Shanghai in 1562, he became a 'B.A.' at the age of nineteen, and in 1592 became tutor to a family in Shiuchow. It was here that he met, and became friendly with, one of the Jesuits, Fr. Cattaneo, who gave him some instruction; this was continued under Ricci at Nanking. In 1601 he passed his doctorate with honours (he was seventh on the list). But the examiners found that they had awarded 301 degrees, when only 300 were allowed; one name, at random, had to be struck off the list, and it happened to be Hsü's. In 1603 he returned to Nanking, where he had been baptized 'Paul' (a name reserved by the Jesuits for outstanding converts), hoping to find Ricci. But Ricci had gone to Peking, where he welcomed him the next year when he came up for another attempt at the triennial examinations. These were held from 7 to 9 April 1604—as usual, under conditions of very strict surveillance. This time Hsü was successful. But the 300 successful candidates were then collected in a hall, and had to give an extempore discourse on a set theme: this would determine their appointments. Hsü was ranked 121st, so he did not get a post in Peking, but was sent to a provincial appointment. Ricci was disappointed, as he was hoping for his valuable assistance in the capital; so, knowing the rules by now, he urged Hsü to sit yet another examination—open only to Doctors—for the Imperial Academy. These were the highest honours in China: those who gained them composed the Emperor's edicts, wrote official history, law, and statutes, and taught the Emperor's sons. Hsü was reluctant to sit for this exam, as the competition was so fierce—for twenty-four places. But he finally agreed; and was so high (in the first five) that he was sure of success. In June 1604 he was named Bachelor of the Academy. He rented a house near Ricci, and brought his wife, and his old father who was over seventy, to live with him; and there he became the great protector of missions.[2]

Unfortunately we do not know much about Hsü's early background, and what in it prepared him (unlike many others) to be receptive to Fr. Cattaneo's teaching. We have his testimony of faith before his baptism, but it is more revealing of what the Jesuit Fathers had implanted than of what they replaced. It was the custom that before receiving the sacrament of baptism, the catechumen should make some public confession of the sins of his former life. Formulas for this were composed for illiterate people: but others composed their own. Hsü's declaration was preserved by Fr. Trigault (who calls him Ly-Paul):

I, Ly-Paul, a sinful man, desire to embrace with my whole heart and in entire sincerity the very holy law of Jesus Christ; and for that reason, I raise, as far as I can, my soul towards the Lord of Heaven, and conjure him not to disdain my prayer.

I, a sinful man, confess that having been born in the imperial city of Peking,[3] I never, during the past years of my life, heard of the law of the true God, nor met any of the preachers of this holy doctrine. . . . But not long since I became acquainted, for my happiness, with some men of vast renown and high perfection, who were born in the Western countries, and whose names are Mathew Ricci and Didacus Pantoja; from them I received the very holy law of Jesus Christ. . . .

I renounce, then, my depraved course of life. . . . Grant me the grace to reduce to practice all that has been taught me . . . and, when I have received thy law, to proclaim it everywhere. . . .

Pronounced in the Kingdom of the great dynasty of Ming, the 30th year of the reign of Wang-Lié, on the 6th day of the 8th moon.[4]

Paul Hsü (as we shall now call him) not only became a protector of the missionaries, he also urged and helped them in their literary-evangelistic work. He begged Ricci to write more, and even himself copied Ricci's sermons and circulated them in MS. We have seen that he himself wrote a treatise against the Buddhists; and it was he, apparently, who urged the missionaries to abandon their habits, which looked too much like the official dress of the Buddhist monks or 'Bonzes', and to dress as literati and take titles of Masters or Doctors of the Holy Law. In 1604, a year in which the chief magistrates have (triennially) to pay homage to the Emperor, and when therefore there were about forty thousand people in Peking, Paul Hsü, being in a position of eminence in the Academy, was able to introduce Ricci to the chief mandarins of Nanking, Nanchang, and Shiuchow and to commend him to their protection. Ricci was given much honour, maintained at the public expense, and allowed to enter the palace. The next year Ricci wrote a reply to an attack on him by the Buddhists, *Twenty-five Sentences*, using Stoic arguments to prove a Christian conclusion; a Chinese Christian friend wrote a Preface in which he said that the two most famous Confucian scholars in history (Yu and Hsia) would not be able to find any fault in the arguments, and Paul wrote a 'Postface' (which was usual in Chinese compositions) saying of Ricci:

I found him by chance in Nanking and, after a short conversation, realised that he was the most learned man in the whole world. . . . Later his fame spread throughout the Middle Kingdom and the

wisest and most famous men went to visit him. . . . Amidst troubles
and adversity, during conversation or at dinner, it is impossible to
find in a thousand million of his words a single one contrary to the
great principles of loyalty to the Emperor and filial piety, not one
which does not bring peace of mind and strengthen the moral
code. . . . In ancient times, the kiosk where the phoenixes built
their nests was considered by the Court a precious object, ensuring
peace and stability in the Empire. Today we have the True Man,
learned and great, who brings our moral code to completion and
protects our court; is he not a treasure even more precious?[5]

It was Paul, again, who when Ricci decided in 1605 to build a
proper chapel and residence, with other Chinese friends obtained money or loans and bought a big house with forty rooms
in the centre of Peking. It was he, again, who obtained letters
of introduction to leading authorities, and the necessary passport, granting travel at the public expense, for Fr. Valignano,
the Provincial and Visitor of the Jesuits in the Far East, when
he decided on a visitation of all the houses in China in 1605
(though Valignano died in January 1606, before he could make it).

Perhaps the most striking proof of Paul Hsü's intellectual
powers is the help which he gave Ricci in translating the first
six books of Euclid (along with other minor mathematical
works) into Chinese. They worked at it for three or four hours
a day, Ricci translating orally and Paul copying. Paul showed a
great aptitude for mathematics, and wanted Ricci to translate
the whole of Euclid; but Ricci explained that the later books
would not only be beyond most Chinese, but would not further
the missionaries' apostolic work. Only two of Ricci's friends,
Paul and the geographer convert, Li Chih-tsao, managed really
to master Euclid, and the translation, published in 1607, was
'more admired than understood'.[6]

That same year Paul's father died, and Paul had to accompany the coffin, according to Chinese custom, to the family
home, in Shanghai, and to mourn for three years. After a death,
'a mandarin is obliged to quit his post; a minister of state to
give up the administration of affairs, to live in solitude, and
mourn his loss. He must not pay any visits, and his official
relations with the world are entirely interrupted.'[7] However,
the time was not wasted, for Paul invited Fr. Cattaneo to
Shanghai, and gradually a strong Christian community grew
there.

Dr. Paul had earnestly requested Fr. Cataneo to come to his native place and spread the knowledge of the Gospel there; and the family of Hiu was rapidly converted to Christianity. The princely residence of this important personage was situated in the environs of the town, on the banks of an artificial canal communicating with the Blue River, the mouth of which is at Shanghai. . . . Dr. Paul enjoyed, both on account of his exalted position, his scientific knowledge and high moral character, a great influence over his fellow citizens, and his house became the centre of a flourishing Christian community.[8]

Fr. Cattaneo, it seems, baptized over a hundred there; and by this time there seem to have been about 2,500 Christians in China.[9]

Ricci died in 1610, but others followed. There was an out-burst of hostility to the Christians for a spell, in 1615; some Christians were imprisoned and the missionaries expelled. Some of the Jesuits found refuge with converts, except at Nanking and Peking, and

Even at Peking there were two brothers who, being Chinese by birth, were not included in the sentence of banishment, and continued to inhabit the place assigned to them by the Emperor, as a cemetery for the missionaries, where the remains of Fr. Ricci had been laid. And though the Eunuchs and the Bonzes, the former proprietors of the establishment, made every effort to get possession of it, and over-whelmed the brothers with abuse, Dr. Paul [Hsü] was there to protect them, to assert the inviolability of the imperial donation, and especially the respect due to a place of sepulture.[10]

The persecution came to an end, and—even more happily for the Christians—Paul Hsü was promoted to the high rank of *Ko-lao*. And in 1629 Paul memorialized the Throne, protesting against the outworn methods of the astronomers, which had been in use for centuries, and had notoriously led to a gross error in predicting the eclipse of 1610. He suggested that foreign scholars be officially summoned to help in the work of the Bureau of Mathematics of Astrology (*ch'in t'ien chien*). The result was an imperial decree in September 1629, giving Hsü and his Jesuit teacher, Fr. de Ursis, the task of reforming the Calendar. It was opposed strongly by the eunuchs, and it was not until 1630 that the work was undertaken, by the new Jesuit Father, Ricci's most famous successor, Fr. Adam Schall.[11] A little earlier than this Paul Hsü had been involved in a rather more dubious suggestion. The Ming dynasty was near to falling; in 1618 the Tartar tribe (known to the West as the Manchus) had advanced from the North and threatened the capital. The Ming Emperor was so alarmed that two of the Christian officials, Paul and another (Michael Yang), advised him to seek aid from foreign science. Portuguese cannoneers were actually summoned from Macao; but were sent back by the more conservative authorities. There was a further appeal to the Portuguese for help from the new Emperor in 1630, which again was rejected by conservative opinion. That is the background to the notorious (if reluctant) assistance given to the Emperor in 1636 by Fr. Adam Schall, in manufacturing cannon—and even giving them the names of Christian saints, no doubt to prevent their being dedicated to the Chinese God of Fire.[12] It is this, the drastic culmination of a long process, which leads Dr. Panikkar to talk scornfully about the Jesuits' dream 'of smuggling religion into China through mathematics and astronomy',[13] and the process can to some extent be blamed on Christian Chinese converts like Hsü. But before we leave this as the last word, it is worth looking a little longer at Hsü himself.

The best material for this comes from the French life of his granddaughter, 'Candide Hiu' by the contemporary Jesuit, Fr. Phillipus Couplet, written only eight years after her death, and some fifty years after Paul's.[14] We learn from this that when Paul was baptized he only had one wife, and one sickly boy, Jacques Siu, the father of Candide. His relations and friends urged him to take several more wives, according to the Chinese custom, so as to have a numerous progeny.

But he was unmoved, and said he feared the Lord of Heaven who forbids plurality of wives in the Gospel, commands fidelity, and has made this civil contract into a sacrament, to make the marriage-tie more holy, and make marriage a sign of the covenant made with us in His Incarnation.

And God rewarded his faith, says Fr. Couplet, by giving him numerous grandsons and granddaughters, who were his consolation in old age: in fact, Jacques had four sons and four daughters, of whom the last was 'Candide'.[15]

Paul honoured the priests as he would honour an image of Jesus Christ. When the priest who had actually baptized him died, Paul ordered mourning for him as for his own father, saying that this was his Spiritual Father whom he had just lost, and to whom he owed more than to him who had given him life.

Another Father went to see him, to give him a letter from Cardinal Bellarmine, who was writing to the Christians of China, and Paul was their leader. 'Wait, Father,' he said, 'so that I can receive this letter with all the honour that is due to a Prince of the Church.' And he went in to his Dressing-room, put on the head-gear ['Bonnet' in the original] and the dress of his rank, as if he had to pay court to the Emperor, and then, prostrating himself on the ground, made four deep inclinations of the head, and received the letter in both hands, to show greater respect.[16]

Thus was Chinese protocol adapted to Christian occasions. But we need not assume because of this that Paul's Christianity was purely external. Indeed, Fr. Couplet tells us that he

meditated half an hour daily at the foot of a Crucifix in his oratory. And at Mass, when the Fathers, to give him the honour due to him, tried to move away the poor and the children who were around him and crowding too close to him, he said to them, 'My Fathers, do not deprive me of the consolation of mingling my prayers with those of these children, and of my brethren. For I approach the Altar with more confidence, when I have this escort near me. The innocence of the one, and the poverty of the others, are the surest means of obtaining from God the graces I ask.'[17]

The reference to the Crucifix is important: for one of the accusations against the Jesuits in China made by their enemies was that they suppressed the Cross and Passion of Christ to accommodate Christianity to Confucianism.

Paul had not long been *Ko-lao*[18] before he died. He was the first inhabitant of Shanghai (Christian or pagan) who had reached that exalted rank, and so his name honoured the town: his sons and friends erected a Triumphal Arch in the place. His body was taken to Shanghai, and given a magnificent funeral, all the town accompanying it to the ancestral burying-place. Fr. Adam Schall was present at his death, giving him the last sacraments.

He [Paul] did not forget the young Church which, he foresaw would undergo persecution. He commended the Christians to a new convert whom he had got promoted to the rank of President of the Court of Mathematics, so that he could protect the missionaries and show favour to Christianity.[19]

Perhaps Fr. Huc's account is the fittest with which to end:

Though a statesman and a celebrated author, he was remarkable for modesty and sincerity, two virtues that are by no means conspicuous in the character of his countrymen.[20] It was related of him that one day the Emperor asked of his ministers assembled in council some explanation of a difficulty in legislation that perplexed him. No one solved the problem satisfactorily; but when, at the close of the meeting, one of his colleagues asked Dr. Paul what was his opinion on the point in question, he immediately gave him the required answer with the utmost clearness, and with great erudition. Everyone was astonished that he had not made a parade of his knowledge in the presence of the Emperor, and asked him why he had not spoken thus before the council; but he replied, 'As I was not personally interrogated, I wished to leave to others the merit of the reply.'[21]

But the last picture is a sad one. Fr. Huc himself visited Paul's tomb in 1850, two and half centuries after his time. Earlier he described how,

The princely residence of this important personage was situated in the environs of the town, on the banks of an artificial canal communicating with the Blue River, the mouth of which is at Shanghai. A chapel had been constructed in this magnificent house, where divine service was celebrated with much pomp, and attracted all the distinguished Chinese of the town.[22]

But when the abbé and his companions went to visit the tomb they found,

lying on the ground some fragments of a pillar and of sculptures which had formerly constituted a portion of a triumphal arch and of a funeral monument now crumbled to dust. There is not so much as an inscription to indicate the name of him to whom the monument was erected. . . . We knelt down on a mutilated fragment of granite, and whilst we were repeating a prayer for the deceased, we saw passing a little way off some Chinese peasants. . . . They stopped, and gazing at us with an air of half stupid astonishment . . . said, 'See, there is a master of the worshippers of the Lord of Heaven; he is praying for the dead!' The peasants who spoke thus were the descendants of Dr. Paul! The family was still very numerous, but had long fallen into apostasy and the most abject misery. . . .

However, he comforts himself with the thought that when the Jesuits returned to China in 1842, they had built a chapel near this tomb, and, 'if we do not mistake also, they had afterwards the happiness of bringing back to the Christian faith the descendants of him who protected with so much zeal at the commencement of the seventeenth century the apostolic labours of the former children of St. Ignatius.'[23]

ii. CANDIDA HSÜ (1607–80)

This lady, already mentioned above as the granddaughter[24] of Paul Hsü, perhaps belongs rather to Part III ('Maturity'). But I am treating her here partly because her life leads on from the preceding, and partly because even by the time of her death the Church can hardly be regarded as maturely established.

To convert Chinese ladies was not easy: for, as Fr. Couplet points out, they were kept in such seclusion that they could never be seen—their husbands had to be their first preachers, as a rule. With some difficulty a few churches were opened where these ladies could assemble four or five times a year to hear mass and approach the sacraments; but even this had to be done with caution;[25] only the priest and one server lad could enter. If the priests had appeared dressed as Buddhist Bonzes, they could have had access to the women; but the Buddhist dress had been abandoned by them, and they judged it more important to treat with magistrates, literati, and heads of families, than with 'persons who have naturally a greater disposition to piety, and who can be instructed in our mysteries, either by reading books or by their own husbands'.[26]

Mme Hsü, however, was born of Christian parents, and baptized 'Candida' because her baptism fell on St. Candida's day. From the age of ten, we are assured, she put herself under the protection of the Blessed Virgin, and promised her certain daily prayers.

But by a childish lapse, she for a time failed to say the Rosary. However, a few days later she contracted a burning fever, which recalled her to her rule; regarding it as a punishment for her neglect, thereafter she never missed. And indeed her Confessor later had to order her to stop certain exercises when she was gravely ill.

At sixteen she was married to a rich and powerful man called Hsü Yüan-tu, who was not a Christian. (The Popes had permitted this irregularity in China.) But she was not forced to marry him in the pagan fashion.

The custom then was that the wife, never having seen the man she was to marry, is brought to her house enclosed in a litter. The key of this is given to the husband, who then sets free the one who is about to lose that freedom again by marrying him. She comes out . . . into the Hall . . . and there the Idols are exposed . . . to be worshipped. The husband and wife then prostrate themselves for these adorations.

But the Christians who married pagans stood courageously firm, saying that they would renounce marriage if they were forced to worship these idols. . . . And finally a way was found to arrange separate acts of worship: the Christian worshipping the image of Jesus Christ. And this is what Mme Hiu did, with all her family, when she was led to her husband.

She presented her husband with eight children, and they were all brought up as Christians. She was only thirty when her husband died; and her example had been such that two years before his death she had persuaded him to be baptized.

There was then no second marriage for widows in China; so Candida spent the forty-three years of her widowhood devoting herself to God's work. Indeed, compared with marriage, widowhood was a time of freedom for Chinese women. She used her leisure time in many ways. She had skill in embroidery, and woven silks; and with her sisters, daughters, and servants, she amassed much material which, when sold, brought considerable sums which she secretly used for the support of missionaries, for building churches and chapels, relieving the poor, and procuring for new Christians 'all things necessary for the exercises of piety'.

She left a girl called Rosalie to look after the family: a girl who had taken a vow of chastity ('which is rare in China'). This girl was Mme Hsü's confidante in her secret alms-giving, and distributed the same with marvellous address and discretion.

But she had the temperament of those *dévotes* who are very much attached to their own feelings, and who treat the people set under their care with such superiority that she became quite insufferable to all the servants. Mme. Hiu had much to endure from this girl, and often her Directors had advised her to send her back to her own country, so as to disburden herself of the troubles she caused her. 'But,' said Mme. Hiu, 'then who will provide for the needs of the poor, and who will care for the Missionaries and Catechists? Rosalie is faithful, she is precise, she is discreet in the distribution of alms. We must bear with her tantrums, in order to have these advantages. It is a Cross which God wills me to bear.'[27]

(It is perhaps comforting to know that even seventeenth-century Christian Chinese can produce such familiar phenomena.)

The Jesuits besides churches built up local 'congregations' or 'sodalities' of various sorts: Guilds of Our Lady, a 'Congregation of the Angels' for children, and especially a 'Congregation of the Passion of Our Lord', which used to meet on Fridays, when its members meditated on the suffering and death of Christi,[28] and used the discipline (often to the drawing of blood). The women adopted the same devotions at home, and Mme Hsü had later to be restrained by her Director, on account of her age and infirmity: though she expostulated that 'the missionaries do good and valuable work and yet practise these austerities—why, then, should I try to preserve a healthy body which is no use to anyone?'

But more important was the congregation of female catechists (for that was what, in effect, they were): sixty ladies who, under the direction of the Fathers, taught the Catechism to children in the local church; four times a year visited all the Christian houses, and sent a written report to the missionaries, whether there were statues of the Saviour in the houses, whether there were any traces of old superstitious practices left, any children unbaptized, any old men or sick needing the Church's help. Mme Hsü was the 'Mother' of these Congregations, gave them images, pictures, rosaries, etc., and is reported as having given prizes on the Feast of St. Michael to the children from the district who came with the best reports from the Catechists.

Her son Basil married a pagan girl, who was very resistant to Christianity: but with patience Mme Hsü won over her daughter-in-law, and the latter became in her turn an apostle, 'winning two brothers and some other relations, as much by her example as by the good reasons she advanced'.

When her father, Jacques, died he like Paul Hsü was given official honours. Jacques had preferred a retired life to the embarrassment of the Court, and to ambition for high rank; but his reputation for probity was such that the Emperor ordered his name to be placed among those of the 'disciples of Confucius'. These names, along with that of the Master himself, were exposed in the halls of colleges and public schools, on gilded tablets: and the governors of the towns where these schools were established were obliged every year, with the principal magistrates, and the relations of those whose names appear, to prostrate themselves before these names—just as pupils had to do to their masters, and children to their parents. This Jacques, Candida's father, was of course a Christian; but the missionaries did not consider that these honours implied any 'idolatry'—for, after all, children do not regard their parents as gods, yet they offer them the same honours. Literati who went further and sacrificed animals on these 'Name days' could not be baptized, until they had renounced such a cultus. And yet even here there were distinctions: for not all animals slaughtered on the birthdays of princes, etc., were 'sacrifices': they were, as Fr. Couplet points out, merely demonstrations of joy and public veneration—like those in Europe, e.g. in Germany where a whole beast was roasted in the Great Square of Frankfurt at the coronation of an Emperor.[29]

In 1657 eight French Jesuits, newly arrived, fell into the hands of robbers, were stripped and maltreated. Candida took them in, and had them cared for so well that, though badly wounded, all but one were fit for work again in three months. Unlike most Chinese women, who have little freedom, she accompanied her son, Basil, in his travels round the country, when he was taking up different appointments: and wherever she went she built a church or chapel, and obtained a house for the missionaries.

In 1664 the Confucian scholar, Yang Kuang-hsien, started to oppose the Christians. He produced a list of contributors to churches and of the baptized, and argued that Christianity was a conspiracy to overthrow the realm, that medals worn by converts were secret marks of the conspirators, and—producing a picture of Jesus on the cross—that they worshipped a crucified thief who had tried to be King of the Jews. The missionaries were arrested, and 'Seigneur Basil', Mme Hsü's son, who was in the front rank of Doctors, lost his post. The persecution dragged on for some six years, and Mme Hsü did what she could, sending money to help the missionaries on their way to the coast, and to those in exile she sent a servant all the way to Macao, with a generous donation (12,000 *libra*). However, she was sure it would blow over; and in the end it did, Yang Kuang-hsien was degraded, the missionaries returned, and Basil was restored. When the two Fathers returned to Shanghai they were fêted: the Christians filled more than eighty boats, coming from all the villages around, the Fathers were preceded by bands playing, Mme Hsü's three sons met them at the harbour, and the Governor sent the keys of the church and many presents.

Mme Candida was, however, more worried about her son, Basil. He seemed to be failing in his devotion, had supported a dubious political leader, and had even composed a work in several volumes which could have been an occasion of scandal to Christians 'by the fables he had included in it, taken from the books of the Bonzes, and by many other things which smelt of astrology and its figments, although he had in his youth refuted these figments in an excellent treatise he had published'.[30]

As soon as her Director told her of this book, the formidable old lady sent a message to her son, ordering him to send her all the copies of these books, including the plates he had had engraved (which had cost him considerable sums). When she received them, she sent them to the Fathers asking that they be burned at once. She also invited Basil several times to the Church of Our Lady which she had had built, and he heard mass, and in the end made a general confession and returned 'to the practice of piety'. This was the Church where the Ladies' Congregation met, five times a year, and Mme Candida went in spite of age and sickness,

sans que les pluyes, les neiges, les chaleurs, les vents, ni les autres incommoditez des saisons l'en peussent empêcher, ny les instances de son fils qui luy representoit son peu de santé, & les dangers où elle s'exposait de la ruiner entierement par ces sorties si fréquentes en des temps si incommodes.[31]

The Chinese care over ceremony is exhibited in the orders she gave to her ladies about their behaviour in church. After mass was over, she used to

go to the door with all her household and the Christian women, lined up facing the altar, and they began with three little bows in the Chinese manner. The Father, who stood on their left facing the altar, to receive these grateful acts of reverence, bowed himself to the ground and got up again as many times as the Ladies made their bows. After these bows, the Mme Hiu and all her troop knelt, lowering the head profoundly three times—which the Father did after them. They got up, and then the Ladies all together once again made three little curtsies; and the Father, to thank them, knelt and began again the same inclinations of the head; which they also did in their turn, receiving with similar respect the thanks of the Father by these reiterated genuflections and bows.[32]

It is a little difficult to see how they ever got to the end of this vicious circle of homage; but doubtless Fr. Couplet is right in saying that there is no nation so scrupulous and particular about ceremony as the Chinese, and that they would be scandalized 'if we failed to observe their customs'.

However, Mme Candida's Christianity was not confined to ecclesiastical activities. She learned that many babies were abandoned at birth, especially girls, who would be of no use because of the difficulty of finding them work. So she got permission from Soochow to buy a large house in which to place these babies, and to provide nurses for them. The governor and other mandarins contributed to this. In spite of all the care taken there were so many babies exposed that still two hundred died every year. But she at least made sure of their baptism and Christian burial. She also provided for the blind in an original way. Many of the blind, in order to earn a living, used to collect people in public places and practise divination, story-telling, and other ways of exploiting the credulity of the public. Mme Hsü withdrew some of these and promised them an honest living: she had them instructed in the Faith, so that they could go out along the roads and tell the people the truths they had learned, and draw the listeners toward Christianity, exposing the errors of these false divinations.

A pleasant story is recounted of her, that when three of her brothers wasted money and were in need, she helped them out —but gave them strictly what they needed and no more. 'But when she heard that they grumbled at the moderation with which she helped them, she sent word that she had other brothers who touched her more closely and were in greater need—she meant the poor and the missionaries.'[33]

All together Mme Hsü is said to have founded nearly thirty churches in her country. She sent a gold chalice and other ornaments for the Chapel of St. Ignatius Loyola in Rome (her ladies gave their gold hair-pins and bracelets towards the same), also ornaments for St. Francis Xavier's tomb; and she gave money for four hundred books to be presented to the Holy Father (now in the Vatican Library). The Emperor himself, to mark the esteem he had for her, sent her a magnificent dress, 'garni de plaques d'argent & d'une riche broderie, avec une coëffure de perles & de pierres'.[34] But she took off the silver plaques and the pearls, and sold them, to help to clothe the poor, to adorn altars, and to win souls.

She had long hoped, as had her grandfather, Paul Hsü, that Chinese Christians might be prepared for Holy Orders, 'to help the missionaries one day in their work, or to preserve Christianity should it ever happen that the priests from Europe were banished from China, through some persecution, as they were fifty years before in Japan'.[35] In fact the process of ordaining Chinese priests had started in a small way, and even the first Chinese bishop, Gregory Lô, was chosen to be a bishop in 1674. He had been ordained priest in 1654 or 1656[36] before Mme Hsü's death: but under the Foreign Missionary Society of Paris and in a different part of China, and it is likely that she never knew about it. And Mgr. Lô was not actually consecrated till 1685, five years after her death.

For in 1680 Candida Hsü was taken ill. She asked for the priest to come; he did pastoral duties nearby, said the Sunday mass in her domestic chapel, at which she received communion, and then was going to leave the district as she did not seem to be very ill. But, smiling, she said, 'Wait till Thursday, Father; that is the day you will leave.' And that in fact was the day she died (24 October), after receiving the last sacraments, exhorting her son to stand firm in the Faith, and showing great piety. 'All the poor wept for her, as for their mother; the Churches and the Province lost a model of every sort of virtue; and the Missionaries of China lost their only resource in all their needs'—so says Fr. Couplet; and, since his book on Mme Hsü is dedicated to 'Madame la Marquise de . . .' (no name given), he ends with the appeal: 'And they will continue to feel this loss for long, unless God inspires some Lady of Europe to take the place of this illustrious Widow. . . . For we cannot hope to find in all China another person with the same zeal, the same charity, the same assurance and the same authority.'[37]

As everywhere else in the East, the Roman Catholics were the first to reach India. But in spite of the early start, the Portuguese establishment in Goa, the very remarkable ministry of the Jesuit, Robert de Nobili, in Madura, and the invitation in 1579 by Akbar to the Jesuits to come to his court in Āgra and debate the cause of Christianity, there do not seem to have been any outstanding indigenous Christians for a very long time. True, de Nobili made some eminent Brahman converts, but the records do not give us a living picture of them. The earlier treatment of the Indians by the Portuguese, including the missionaries, was something hard to live down.

Valignano's pleas for the Japanese bring out the contrast with the Indians in an interesting way. Alessandro Valignano, sent out in 1579 as Vicar General and Visitor of the Orient to the Jesuit missionary work, says of the Japanese that they are 'proud and bellicose', and cannot be treated like 'the Indian Christians'. 'For we have no jurisdiction whatsoever in Japan, nor can we compel them to do anything which they do not wish to do, other than by pure persuasion and force of argument; they will not suffer being slapped or beaten, nor imprisonment, nor any similar methods commonly used with other Asiatic Christians.'[1] But precisely because of this, they showed themselves to have better qualities and held out therefore the promise of fitness for a native ministry. Indeed, Japan was a popular mission field among the Jesuits since 'living with Japanese was like living with civilized people, whereas with Indians was like living with base and bestial people'. To make Asiatics priests was impossible, 'because all these dusky race are very stupid and vicious, and of the basest spirits, and likewise because the Portuguese treat them with the greatest contempt'.[2] Indeed, the Portuguese, though they had achieved a reputation for an enlightened attitude to the colour bar in Brazil, do not always seem to have lived up to this everywhere. They are said to have 'treated all Asiatic races with contempt, and termed even highly cultivated peoples like the Chinese and Japanese "niggers"'.[3] It appears that the enlightened views were in fact confined to the official policy of the Portuguese monarchs; instructions against the colour bar were in fact protested against by viceroys, and the correspondence of various Counts in the sixteenth and seventeenth centuries reveals frequent use of derogatory expressions —'niggers' etc.—about the local inhabitants. Indeed, when Fr. Valignano pleaded for equal treatment of Europeans and Japanese, and was strongly opposed in this by Fr. Cabral, Fr. de Souza S. J. supported the latter, on the ground that Fr. Cabral 'has an excuse in the Portuguese character, which naturally despised all these Asiatic races'.[4]

And yet, in spite of this, from the mid sixteenth century onwards (the College of St. Paul, Goa, for training Asian missionaries was set up in 1542) the Portuguese Jesuits established themselves firmly, and as we shall see later, expanded east and south. But perhaps it was in the South-East, especially Madura, that the deepest penetration seems to have been made.

i. DEVASAGAYAM PILLAY (1712–52)

It is well known that loss of caste was the greatest deprivation an Indian can undergo. Robert de Nobili tried to overcome the problem this posed to converts by frankly accepting the caste system, being accepted as of Brahman caste himself, and thus, practically for the first time, extending Christian evangelism beyond the paravas, fisherfolk, and outcastes, and reaching the highest ranks of all. But in the long run his methods were not fully acceptable to Church authority, and the experiment was abandoned. It then became extremely difficult for Indians in any but the lowest grades in society to become Christians.

A sad story is told illustrating this from the life of a Christian warrior in the Madura area, in 1716–17. It was a time when there was some persecution of Christians. At a banquet given by one of the 'chief lords' to soldiers of the *rajah* caste (the highest caste of Brahmans), the lord noticed that one of these soldiers refused to eat meat—it was a Friday. When asked why, the soldier said that he was a Christian. The lord (whose name is given in the French account as Ellamanayaken) was furious: 'What, a Christian rajah? We might just allow low-caste people to receive the new doctrine—but rajahs! What a dishonour to their caste!' The other soldiers joined in the abuse, and tried to force meat down the man's throat; but he stood firm. The Christians were then driven out of the town, and only the church was spared.

But the next year the persecution grew more severe. This

same soldier-rajah was returning from church with his wife, when the relatives gathered round. They drew their swords and said,

'Either you abandon the infamous sect of European pariahs, or each one of us will kill himself under your eyes. Then it will be up to you to think out how you'll defend yourself as not guilty of our deaths before the magistrate.'

The soldier, a better soldier than a theologian, replied, 'There is no need that you should die. Better, rather, that I should die myself, since it is I who am the cause of all this turmoil.'

He was about to throw himself on his sword and transfix himself, when one of his relatives stopped him.[5]

But, alas, says the narrator, it is easier for an Indian to shed his blood than to resist the members of his caste. For they argued with him:

They threatened, promised, beseeched him; and then, seeing him shaken, without giving him time to breathe, took him, only half consenting, to the brahmin, the guru of their caste; and though he offered some resistance, they traced on his forehead the mark of the Beast—I mean, the *nâmam*, viz, a red spot between two white spots, in the shape of a perpendicular trident: the sign of the god *Pérouma* [Vishnu].

And this led to the pagan *rajahs* taking heart, and going to other Christians of the same caste, and forbidding them all commerce and even converse with others of their own caste. 'This ostracism for Christians', said père L. N. de Bourzès, 'is worse than death. Up till now they have remained firm, but we must ceaselessly pray to God that they may persevere.'[6]

However, it was about this time that Nilakandam-Pillay (or Pullay) was born, at Parppanadapuram, on the Malabar Coast. He was of Rajahvamsam, or royal caste; and when he came of age he held a high position at the court of the Maharaja of Travancore.

A Belgian officer, Benedict de Lannoy, took service as General of the Maharaja's army—this was not so unusual as it sounds, in the eighteenth century. He had been made prisoner at the battle of Colachel (1741) in which the Dutch army, de Lannoy's army, was defeated by the Maharaja's. He was released to serve in the Maharaja's army, and reorganized it on European lines. (He died in 1777, in the fortress of Udayagiri, and his tomb was still there in 1914.)[7] He was mostly stationed at this fortress and, while there, came to know Nilakandam-Pillay. The latter had married well and was very rich; but through ill-luck lost his fortune. He came to M. de Lannoy to pour out his woes, and the Belgian officer urged him not to trust in riches, and told him the story of Job. He sent him to the nearest priest, Fr. Buttery, of Vadakunkulam; the latter tested him by telling him to go away, and come back in two months. But Nilakandam-Pillay replied: 'Look, Father: nothing compels me to be a Christian. If I have come to you it is because I already have such a strong faith that nothing could tear it out of my heart; and I am ready to sacrifice for it all that still remains of my former wealth, my position, my family, and even my wealth.'[8] Seeing his determination, Fr. Buttery instructed him, and baptized him in 1744, aged thirty-two, giving him the name 'Devasagayam' (Lazarus).

The young soldier now returned home and converted his wife, who was also baptized in due course. In four years the latter established a strong Christian community. One of the leading Brahmans came and argued with him; and when he failed, he threatened to force Devasagayam into silence:

'And if I don't do this, I shall be unworthy of wearing the Brahmin cord.'

'Very well,' said Devasagayam, 'try your best to silence me. But if you don't succeed, then I warn you, I will put your cord to a shameful use.'*

The Brahman reported this to the Devan (the Prime Minister) who was furious at the insult to the cord. From now on they watched him carefully.

Soon Fr. Buttery had to enlarge the church at Vadekenkulam; for this he needed teak (wood). But there was a Government monopoly in teak, so he asked Devasagayam to approach the authorities in Travancore. Devasagayam asked the Prime Minister for permission to cut some trees; but the Devan shouted at him:

'You're teaching the people to despise the Brahmins and to mock our gods. I'll have the Christians persecuted, and have you cut to

---

* It is not clear what this means, unless it is a threat to use the cord to chastise his opponent; or to throw it away and thus desecrate it.

pieces and your bleeding remains thrown into the fields, a prey to wild beasts.'

'Take my blood,' said Devasagayam—'I am their chief.'

Devasagayam returned home and prayed for strength. The Devan and the Brahmans went to the Maharaja, to complain first, of Devasagayam's contempt of the gods and of his threat to pull off the Brahman's cord and abuse it; and secondly, that his preaching was creating divisions among the Maharaja's subjects, and might lead ultimately to rebellion.

He was arrested in 1748—that is, four years after his baptism. General de Lannoy hastily took him along to the priest for confession, communion, and a blessing, and then let him go, urging him to stand firm to his faith. The soldiers took him away. He was loaded with heavy chains and put in prison. General de Lannoy visited him in prison; but when the Maharaja heard this he was angry and told the Belgian soldier to mind his army and not to meddle in other affairs. From now on he could only communicate with Devasagayam in secret.

Next day the sentence of death was announced. Devasagayam was led out, as if to execution; but the sentence was postponed, and he was brought back—he was sad at this, for he thought that it meant that the Lord thought him unworthy of martyrdom. However, in fact, the Devan had persuaded the Maharaja to allow him to be forced into apostasy by torture. This torture went on for some time, and included such items as leading him out and round the town fastened to a buffalo, thirty lashes with a bamboo cane, pepper stuffed in his eyes and nostrils, and finally leaving him out all day in the sun. But the only result was that the bystanders were impressed by his heroism.

The Christians themselves were of course encouraged by this. The Devan then caused Devasagayam to be brought back to the capital, and put back again into the old prison, with chains on. But the Christians from a wide area around came to visit him. So the Devan had him removed to a remote village and there chained to a mango tree in the open, with no shelter except the leaves of the tree: and thus he was kept for seven months, till the gaolers themselves took pity on him, and General de Lannoy persuaded them to build him a shelter of palm leaves.

The Devan was angry that so many people still came to visit him, even in this remote spot; and forbade visitors. He also told the gaolers secretly to starve him to death. But in fact the gaolers were easily bribeable, and they even allowed the priest to come and visit him, to confess him and give him communion. At one point two soldiers offered to let him escape. Not knowing what to do, he wrote to the priest; but the latter urged him to stay at his post, so he refused their offer.

The Devan now fetched him to Fort Aravagmani, and there once again he was chained to a tree, with no shelter, and fixed in such a position that he could neither sit nor lie down. Yet once again, the guards were bribed, and crowds came to visit him, and there was relaxation of the conditions. So finally the Devan persuaded the Maharaja to pass the death sentence once more—and this time in secret.

Devasagayam had a revelation of this, in a dream. He sent for his wife, and urged her to leave the country after his death, for many of their relatives were heathen and she would find it difficult to hold to the faith, with her children, if she continued to live among them. And he concluded, 'Have no fear: God will help and support you; and by His grace we shall be both united in heaven.'

He was taken to Arambuly. And such was his reputation for sanctity by now that the story went round, immediately after his death, that on the way he was so weak with fatigue and thirst that at one point he collapsed; but immediately 'a fountain of clear water sprang from the rock on which he fell, and so his thirst was quenched'. But as soon as he got to his destination the order was carried out: in the night his guards woke him up and told him to follow them. They pretended it was for another purpose but Devasagayam said, 'It's no use pretending: I know where we're going.' He still had heavy fetters on, and could not walk, so the soldiers fastened him to a bamboo pole and carried him on their shoulders to a black rock. When they got there he asked for a few moments to commend his soul to God. Then after a brief moment of recollection, he turned: 'I've done my duty. Now do yours.' Three shots dropped him to the ground, without killing him, but the soldiers finished him off. It was 14 January 1752—seven years since his baptism, and after three years of imprisonment and torture.[9] His bones were (almost certainly) discovered in the nineteenth century, during excavations in the church in Cottar; and the church in Vadekenkulam has, or had, his chains.[10]

ii. SATTIANADEN (1750–1815)

There is no mention in the preceding life, that of Devasagayam, of the factor which preoccupied the Roman Catholic missionaries almost as seriously as the conversion of the heathen: the competition between rival Christians. In 1847 a distinguished Protestant missionary (John Zachariah Kiernander) said that 'The [Danish Protestant] Mission at Madras had begun in 1726. Up to 1740, i.e. in 14 years, they had been joined by upwards of 700 converts; the majority of whom, though natives, had been Papists.'[11] And the Roman Catholic historian who quotes this goes on: 'The pity is that what was true at the beginning of the eighteenth century remains true at the beginning of the twentieth. Part of the activity and resources of the Catholic Missionary has to be spent in defending his flock against the aggression of the Protestant agent.'[12]

It is, of course, possible to find Protestants using similar language of Roman Catholics; but since here, as in most places, it was the latter who were the first to arrive, the accusation of 'poaching' is more justified in this case on their lips. What was true of the Danish mission in Tranquebar was also true of the 'English' mission (in which the 'English Church', i.e. the S.P.C.K., made use of the services of German Lutheran pastors, especially the great Christian Frederick Schwartz) in Trichinopoly, Tanjore, and Tinnevelly. In Tinnevelly, whereas in 1780 the Register showed forty members, by 1791 it showed that '283 souls, men, women, and children, had been converted from heathenism and baptised, and that 120 souls had been received from the Church of Rome'.[13] And the Indian pastor, Sattianaden, of whom we shall write in this section, records with satisfaction in 1792, during a tour in the hills with the European missionary, Jaenicke, that 'I baptised eight persons, and received two Romish Christians'.[14] On the other hand, the next European missionary, Ringeltaube, writes to the S.P.C.K. in 1806, in London, that, 'As a circumstance that will be pleasing to the Society, I beg leave to mention that on the 28th (February), a Romish Missionary who travels in this country, sent me a present of yams by his catechist, with a polite message. Who would not rejoice at such liberal sentiments?'[15]

In 1771 Schwartz first met, at Ureiour, near the fort of Palamcottah, 'a young man from the country'. Schwartz describes how:

He remained with us for several days, heard in silence, and avowed his conviction of the abomination of Heathenism. . . . The young man began to attend to reading, which he had before almost forgotten. At the evening prayer hour . . . he was very attentive. . . . He had to read over to himself, frequently during the day, the chapter to be read at the evening hour of prayer, when he read it aloud before us all distinctly and without hesitation. By this daily exercise, he very soon learned to read. . . . He received the name of Satti-anaden, or Possessor of the Truth. . . . He after this went into the country to bring his wife and mother-in-law back with him. But this was attended with much sorrow, for the wife came in much distress, would listen to nothing, and wept when she was addressed. The aged mother-in-law came likewise from a great distance, but soon returned, for, said she, there is no standing it; every day there are twenty coming to me to converse about Christianity; this is not to be borne: and so she returned to the country.[16]

One has some sympathies with the mother-in-law, suddenly faced with such novelty and so many people trying to convert her at once. Sattianaden had the usual opposition from relations and neighbours: on one occasion he was threatened with violence. He replied

That he had not done any harm; that he had forsaken idols, which from their very nature were not gods, but a work of men's hands, and had given himself to the one true God who had created heaven and earth. Sattianaden's mother-in-law particularly gave full vent to blasphemy. When he would have soothed her, she said, that she needed no other god—she had a whole basket-ful of gods.[17]

Sattianaden was soon appointed as a Catechist.

Schwartz by now was acquiring a reputation in the country for his integrity and his fairness, as well as his knowledge of the language, which more than outweighed the local opposition. In the disturbances at Tanjore, when the Rajah, Haider Ali was in opposition to the Government of Madras, and refused to negotiate, his own people begged him to seek terms of peace, and finally he said, referring to Schwartz, 'Then let them send me the Christian: he will not deceive me.' When peace finally did come, the missionary work was able to proceed, and it developed very rapidly. More clergy were needed, and it was finally decided that Sattianaden, who had by now been given several independent charges as catechist, should be ordained. Schwartz said of him,

I cannot but esteem this Native teacher higher than myself. He has a peculiar talent in conversing with his countrymen. His whole deportment evinces clearly the integrity of his heart. His humble disinterested and believing walk has been made so evident to me and others that I may say with truth that I never met with his equal among the natives of the country. . . . His love to the poor is extraordinary and it is often inconceivable to me how he can manage to subsist on his scanty stipend—three pagodas a month—and yet do so much good. . . .

And he gives a particular example:

Several years ago his eldest daughter, a child between seven and eight years of age, died of the small-pox. She was a very intelligent child, and feared God. . . . At her funeral, I could not myself restrain my tears; but her father united with joy in singing with the schoolchildren the hymn, 'Jesus my hope, etc.', which affected me greatly.[18]

The ordination, according to the Lutheran rite, took place on 26 December 1790, and Sattianaden preached his own 'ordination sermon' at it. This sermon 'in the Tamulian language' (Tamil) was translated into English by one of the missionaries (Kohlhoff), and published with great éclat by the S.P.C.K. in London. The editor of the S.P.C.K. noted:

The Society, deeming a production of so extraordinary a nature worthy of the public eye, having caused this translation to be printed, and published, in order to evince the capacity of the natives for undertaking the office of the ministry, and to show that the efforts of the Missionaries in India have not been exerted in vain. . . .
How long it may be in the power of the Society to maintain Missionaries; how long the fluctuation in the affairs of this world will afford duration to the Mission itself, is beyond our calculation; but if we wish to establish the Gospel in India, we ought to look beyond the casualties of war, or the revolutions of Empires; *we ought in time to give the Natives a Church of their own, independent of our support; we ought to have suffragan Bishops in the country, who might ordain Deacons and Priests and secure a regular succession of truly Apostolical Pastors, even if all communications with their parent Church should be annihilated.*[19]

And a footnote mentions that the controversial passage in italics 'has sometimes been omitted' in quotations. (The first

Bishop for India was not in fact appointed till 1814—the Rt.
Rev. Thomas Fanshaw Middleton, Bishop of Calcutta.)

The sermon itself is of some interest as showing how far both
the mode and divisions of preaching, and the sentiments, have
been assimilated from eighteenth-century Protestant piety into
Tamil, and so back into English again. The Preface (unsigned,
but presumably by Kohlhoff himself) warns us what we are in
for: '. . . How satisfactory must be the reflexion, that a single
soul like Sattianaden, has been rescued from heathen darkness,
and brought to the knowledge of Jesus Christ? A knowledge not
such as too many of the Romish converts attained, but a knowledge unto salvation . . . etc.' Sattianaden's text is Ezekiel
33:11 ('As I live, saith the Lord God, I have no pleasure in the
death of the wicked . . . turn ye from your evil ways . . .'). It
opens in measured tones:

'In treating of [the text], let us consider the following particulars:
I. To whom the offers of divine mercy are made. II. The way and
means of obtaining the blessings offered in this divine promise. III.
What those inestimable blessings are. . . .'

He shows how God's mercy is offered 'Not only to Jews but to
us likewise who are of the Gentiles'. It is His grace, through His
atonement, that alone suffices:

How unaccountable, therefore, is the practice of the Papists, who
introduce the sacrifice of the Mass, and the mediation of saints, as
methods of atonement for sin, besides the sufferings of Jesus, and the
atonement made by him?'

And then we have a little crude 'comparative religion':

The Heathens rest their hopes of pardon and happiness on their
pilgrimage to *Kasi*, to *Ramesuram*, and other places of pretended
great sanctity, and on a number of ceremonies which are painful to
the body. The Mahometans think they shall be accepted on account
of their reciting certain forms of prayer so many times a day, their
fastings, and their going to Mecca: and the Jews hope to merit
heaven at the hand of God on account of their own works, and the
observance of some ceremonies. . . .[20]

Finally we have a paean to God for all blessings, especially that

He has sent his servants to these dark corners of the earth, to make
known unto us the glad tidings of salvation, and by the grace of the
blessed Spirit many of our nation have accepted the offers of God's

grace and mercy . . . [And] God, out of his free grace and mercy, has brought me likewise, a sinful creature, born of heathen parents, to his blessed knowledge. . . .

In the prayers with which he followed the sermon he prayed not only for 'George our King and the royal family', but 'likewise thy blessing on the king of Denmark, and all other kings . . .'; and—with special reference to the contemporary scene in India:

'We beseech thee to be our defence and protection against our enemies, who are now risen against us; and to deliver us from all those evils and dangers with which we are encompassed.'

And a footnote specifies: 'This alludes to the invasion of the *Mysoreans*, which was prevented by the English army entering Mysore, under the command of Lord Cornwallis.'[21]

From the time of his ordination he worked in Palamcottah and other places in the district, and itinerated with the missionaries. It is interesting to see that on occasions he ministered in places where there were no Indian Christians, taking service for the English in Madura and baptizing their children (there was, then, less of a colour bar in that period than later). In some areas there was frequent persecution—though mild by comparison with what the Jesuits had undergone in other countries. In 1803,

Sattianaden seemed to be quite depressed at the cruelties exercised upon the Christians, and the reports daily brought to him from all quarters [i.e. in the Tinnevelly area]. One of the congregations had lately written to Mr. Gericke, that were it not for the fear of hell, and the hope of heaven, such were their sufferings that they should all throw themselves into the sea.[22]

And in 1805 Sattianaden wrote again,

giving an affecting account of the persecutions exercised on the new converts by their heathen neighbours. The head inhabitants and the native public servants, enraged at the conversion of such numbers to Christianity combined to prejudice the Collector against the Christians by many false and unfounded complaints, and to distress and afflict them by the suffering and cruelties which they exercised.[23]

Dr. Claudius Buchanan, then a distinguished Chaplain of the East India Company, visiting the area in 1806, reports hearing a sermon by Sattianaden in Tanjore:

Sattianaden delivered his discourse in the Tamil language, with much natural eloquence and with visible effect. His subject was the 'Marvellous Light'. He first described the pagan darkness, then the light of Ziegenbalg,* then the light of Swartz, and then the heavenly light, 'when there shall be no need of the light of the sun or of the moon'. . . . He concluded with praying for the prosperity and glory of the Church of England.[24]

It was around this time that the 'mass conversions' in the Tinnevelly area started, and Sattianaden was closely connected with them. Later there were unjust criticisms of Sattianaden's 'easy acceptance' of candidates for baptism in the early days of his ministry, many of whom did not stand fast. But Bishop Caldwell replied:

I do not attach any blame to Sattianaden in particular, who acted in accordance with the custom of the time, and what he supposed to be his duty, to baptise in faith all who asked for baptism, and were willing to receive some preliminary instruction, leaving the results to God. . . . I mention the circumstances as tending to explain why the results were often so evanescent.[25]

And Caldwell defends Sattianaden's later work, exemplified by the fact that between 1803 and 1805 several thousand heathen were baptized in Tinnevelly, mostly by Sattianaden himself. He had to meet many criticisms: for instance that the converts were almost all 'rice-Christians'[26]; that they came to get the help of the missionaries against the oppression of the Nawab's government. *Reply:* 'The Nawab's government came to an end, and the country was ceded to the British, in 1801; the conversions were from 1802.' Or that they came to get 'pecuniary help'. *Reply:* 'The missions were very poor.' Or that they came to 'escape oppression'. *Reply:* 'The converts suffered more oppression as Christians than they had done as heathens, and more than their heathen neighbours suffered, so that in a few instances congregations relapsed into heathenism in order to escape oppression.' Or, finally, that they came 'to obtain the Collector's favour'. *Reply:* 'The country priest [i.e. Sattianaden himself] invariably complained that the Collector was so surrounded by Brahmans that it was very difficult to get the wrongs of Christians inquired into, and still more difficult to get their wrongs redressed.'[27]

---

* The German missionary (sent by the Danish King) who arrived at Tranquebar in 1706.

Unfortunately towards the end of his ministry Sattianaden had to be recalled—at his own request—to Tanjore: he and the Tinnevelly people did not always see eye to eye (they regarded him as an 'outsider' from Trichinopoly), and there seem to have been some differences between him and the later missionary, Kohlhoff, in 1805. The records are entirely frank about this—and therefore are the more to be trusted.

It is clear that understandably the converts themselves took over, wholesale, all the ideas, images, and concerns which the white men quite uncritically brought them. Yet, even when the white men were not there the Indian converts' behaviour has a stamp of authenticity which proves that they were genuinely looking for, and found, something which their whole being craved. Jaenicke describes one of Sattianaden's 'missionary journeys' in the Tinnevelly district (1791): 'The Native teacher experienced the same encouragement [i.e. as Jaenicke himself] on his journey and declared that the people would scarcely give him time even to eat.'[28] And later (1802–3) Gericke's journal for his visit, accompanied by Sattianaden, to Tinnevelly on 30 September reads:

Early to-day I examined and confirmed twenty-one persons, who afterwards, with 27 others, received the Lord's Supper. I exhorted the congregation, from the words, 'seek peace and pursue it': the subject made a salutary impression on many; and a catechist who had brought various groundless charges against the native preacher [i.e. Sattianaden], was so moved by it that, as soon as the Service was over, he came and fell down at Sattianaden's feet, begging forgiveness with many tears.[29]

There is no note of falsity in this familiar scene.

CHAPTER 6 | AFRICANS

African colonization, and Africa as a 'missionary land', are commonly thought to be affairs of the nineteenth century. It is therefore astonishing to read that nearly fifty years before St. Francis Xavier's visits to (and death in) the Far East, and sixty years before Akbar's rule in Lahore, the Portuguese had consecrated their first African bishop. This seems to contradict all that was said in the last chapter about Portuguese scorn for black people. A mission to the Congo in 1491 resulted in King Mani being baptized within the year; by 1507 his son, baptized 'Alfonso', had attempted to make Christianity the State religion, sent several young men to Lisbon for education. One of these young men, Alfonso's son, Henry, was ordained priest (probably in 1518); and in 1532 he was consecrated bishop of São Salvador (the new name given to the Congo capital, Badi). Unfortunately he died only seven years later; there seems some doubt whether he ever even returned to the Congo. Certainly the mission died out by the middle of the century.[1] It is startling to find the Portuguese Church willing to make a black bishop at this early date: no doubt his royal blood made all the difference. And perhaps it was the failure of the experiment that led to later Portuguese hesitation.

The failure—not surprising, in view of the Portuguese involvement in the slave trade!—meant that for three hundred years Christian work almost ceased throughout the continent. Then, in 1840 Livingstone started his mission in Kuruman, and this carried further the great blossoming, largely Protestant and Anglican at first, but soon afterwards Roman Catholic too, of Christian missions in South, Central, and East Africa. (West Africa had anticipated them by some fifty years.)

The Africans who could have been chosen to illustrate the first-generation acceptance are so numerous and so varied that none is truly representative, and the choice invidious. I have finally selected one, not very well known, not even very important, but perhaps for that reason a useful, because typical, example of the problems involved in 'change'—change of culture, allegiance, ethic, and religion.

QUEEN MOKWAË (dates not known)

François Coillard, one of the three greatest French Protestant missionaries, led an expedition in 1878 up to the Barotse people of what is now Zambia. For twenty years the L.M.S. had worked among the Matabele, governed by the great King, Lobengula, with no outward success whatever—no school, no church, no single convert.[2] And when Coillard, seeking for an outlet for the missionary enthusiasm of his South African converts from

Basutoland (now Lesotho), tried to open work among the Banyaï folk, Lobengula forbade it. The Barotse were now suggested to him by the Christian King, Khama of Bechuanaland (Botswana), since they, surprisingly, spoke a form of Sesuto (the Lesotho language) which they had picked up from their earlier conquerors. This first expedition, which was largely exploratory, seemed hopeful; so in 1884 a more formal approach was made. The King, Lewanika (who had recently been deposed, then reinstated, within the year), was more encouraging than Lobengula had been, and a mission school was started.

It was in the course of his travels and visits to the various subgroups of the Barotse people that Coillard first met Mokwaë,* Queen of Nalolo. This was the second capital of the kingdom. It was a Barotse custom for the King to place either one of his sisters or his mother as 'associate monarch' (so to speak) in the sub-capital; and Mokwaë was his sister. This associate monarch was treated like the King himself, addressed as masculine, made to govern the *lekhotla* (tribal meeting or court), and approached with prostrations.[3] Coillard visited her, and noted that no one —not even her husband, the *Mokue-Tunga* (equivalent to the 'Son-in-Law' of the nation)—was allowed to sit in her presence. She greeted him courteously, for they had met before she was queen, when she was a prisoner of the rebel chief Mathaha, and Coillard had spoken kind words to her. She might then even have been killed, if it had not been for the interposition of the then Queen of Nalolo. But now that she was not only free, but on the throne, she was triumphant over the defeat of the rivals, Mathaha and his supporters.

As soon as she saw me, [says Coillard] she began to laugh; she held out her hand, and made me sit opposite to her. Still laughing, she looked fixedly at me for a few moments, and at last . . . she cried out in a tone that startled me, 'Mathaha! Mathaha! We have slain him and all his!' . . .

She related to me all the vicissitudes of the revolution—her flight from Mathaha's village, the devotion of her partisans, who . . . brought her by forced marches to . . . [safety]. She continued her tale . . . to the great victory at Lealuyi, which confirmed Lewanika's power, and concluded by exclaiming with loud peals of laughter, 'We have utterly destroyed Mathaha and his gang, and their bones

* The word simply means 'Queen'; her personal name is not recorded.

7

are bleaching in the sun. And the insolence of these sorcerers to beg for mercy! Mercy indeed! We threw them out on the veldt to the vultures. That was our mercy!'[4]

Coillard then remembered the reputation of this formidable lady. Two years earlier her prime minister, Pakalita, had offended her. She arranged for him to be murdered, by inviting him into her hut, giving him beer, and then leaving him alone with a band of men whom she had instructed to finish him off.

But the slaves were intimidated by the presence of this venerable old man, so universally respected. For a long time Mokwaë awaited the execution of her orders in the court, and at last re-entered impatiently. 'What!' she cried; 'you are given orders, and this is the way you carry them out! Seize him!' Then, arming herself with an old Portuguese sabre, she herself, with one stroke, cut the old man's head off. She made them throw the corpse into a neighbouring court, and then seated herself in the *lekhotla* as usual. Towards evening, the public crier announced: 'The queen informs you that she has pulled a troublesome thorn out of her foot.'[5]

The next day Coillard was allowed to preach in the *lekhotla*, and afterwards Mokwaë invited him to her house. She handed him a cracked old accordion (one of the pieces of evidence of early contact with whites), and ordered him to play. After he had done so, she took it and played it herself, with surprising agility, though with what seemed to Coillard considerable cacophony. Later she visited him, on the islet where he was camping. He hid away any objects she might covet, gave her black coffee (which she politely drank), and a pretty, striped blanket, 'which she received with her usual brusquerie'. But then she saw his photographs, and among them that of Mathaha's. 'The infamous wretch!' she shouted; and then added 'these people' (i.e. white men) 'are dreadful: they carry the living and the dead in their pockets.' But she added contentedly that this Mathaha had been destroyed.[6]

There were times when it seemed that King Lewanika was seriously considering Christian acceptance, though he gave no more than vague promises; but Mokwaë never at this stage seemed to be in earnest about it. After a fruitless five-months' war in 1888 against a rival tribe—a war that Coillard had condemned and Lewanika had not really wanted—the army returned, and there was the traditional tribal welcome for it:

The procession slowly advances, and arrives; Mokwaë leading it, garbed in gaily coloured print: she herself performs recitatives, to which the troops of women escorting her respond in chorus. It is the praises of the king that they are singing; and I must say that these chants, mournful though they may be, like all the songs of our poor Africans, are not devoid of harmony. . . . At an order from the king, she retires to the spacious court of her own home. The chants have ceased; and the court now rises in due form. Leawanik invites me to accompany him to his levée. I quickly shake hands with his Majesty, and sit down close to the mat where he is enthroned. Lewanika kneels down; Mokwaë does the same: they kiss each other on the lips, take both each other's hands, and keep spitting upon one another. . . . Then come the children and near relatives who enjoy the privilege of being spat upon by royalty; then the dignitaries, those highly placed personages who have a right to the privilege of kissing the king's and queen's hand, when they visit them; then the middle class, who keep themselves at a distance, and the common people outside the court, clapping hands with the greatest solemnity.[7]

Coillard was allowed to preach the next morning, and took the opportunity to condemn the war—for which neither Lewanika nor his sister rebuked him. Later that same year one of the three little slave girls whom Coillard and his wife were bringing up caused quite a sensation with her silvery soprano voice, rising above the others in a mission hymn. And this impressed the Queen. Coillard notes that 'They are properly dressed; they can sew and read and perform all sorts of little household tasks; they have, in short, acquired a little air of civilisation, which raises them to such a point, that the queen, Mokwaë, when they came to salute her, quite forgot herself, and gave them her hand.'[8] This 'forgetting herself', over a seemingly trivial matter, is significant of a very important change. But there is still far to go. In 1889 Coillard wrote of her 'she may be very amiable and talkative, but I haven't won her confidence yet'.[9] Indeed, in April of that year Mokwaë fell ill, summoned her children, after consulting the diviners, and forbade the African catechists to sing hymns in her village. Her brother, the King, wrote, too, 'Oh my missionary, the Barotsi say I am going mad. They scoff at Seajika [*sc.* one of the African assistants] and his teaching. They ask what good the *Book* has done them. Never have we had so many calamities as since your arrival: never have so many died.'[10] However, she recovered, and was soon all smiles again.

The following year there was a more direct clash which might have developed dangerously. Her son Kaïba fell ill. The next day Mokwaë summoned her nephew, Litia (son of Lewanika) and told him, 'Kaïba is ill, and the divining bones say that you must go and sacrifice at the tombs of our ancestors'.

'Morena,' replied Litia calmly, 'I am no longer in that darkness, and I have forsaken those ways. I no longer pray to the dead.' Mokwaë made remonstrances . . . but finding she gained nothing she said, 'Very well, you need not go in person. Someone will pray in your place, only you must take a handful of grass impregnated with "medicine", and sprinkle the offerings.' 'But, Morena,' replied Litia respectfully, though firmly, 'I cannot even do that, for it would be the same as if I went myself on a pilgrimage to the tombs.' Mokwaë had to yield the point; but, deeply offended, she forbade him to sing hymns in the village.[11]

In 1891 Coillard had to denounce Mokwaë publicly, in a sermon. She—or her chiefs, with her consent—had maltreated a Methodist missionary working near her place, for an unwitting offence against etiquette. Fortunately the King, Lewanika, agreed with Coillard in the matter, and refunded the fine imposed by Mokwaë, though insisting that the Methodists should leave the area for the sake of peace.[12] All must have been forgiven in due course, for when Coillard's wife, Christina, died in 1892 Mokwaë sent 'her principal personages' to the funeral, thus acknowledging the Coillards as part of her 'family'.[13] In 1894 she asked for 'a missionary' for Nalolo, and was very hurt when Coillard had to tell her there was none to spare. He doubted the seriousness of the request. 'Do not imagine that the inhabitants of Nalolo . . . are yearning for the Gospel. No, it is only a question of dignity. Lewanika has his missionary, a European missionary; and why not Mokwaë? In their estimation, a white missionary is a good milch cow!'[14]

But a real advance was made with Lewanika himself that year. Coillard was due to return to Basutoland, and was saying farewell to the King at Lealui. At a service, which included farewell sermons, solos, and testimonies, the King—still himself uncommitted—suddenly turned to one of his young wives, and said, 'Nolianga, why are you silent? You who love the things of God so much, and whose conscience has so long been exercised, why do you remain silent? Say, why do you not

declare yourself for Jesus? What do you fear? I hinder no one from becoming converted and serving God. Speak therefore!'
Nolianga was silent for the moment. But in fact some time before, without Coillard's knowledge, she had said to the King that she wanted to become a Christian, and had asked him for permission not only to leave his harem (as she would have to do), but to be free to marry anyone she wished—not to be disposed of, according to custom, as he wished. Lewanika had agreed. In fact, comments Coillard, 'I think the dear man is very pleased at it. It is what he had long been wishing and expecting. He wished to leave to God the task of dispersing his wives, whom he has not the courage to send away. And then, if only some of his *likomboa* [household officers] . . . were converted first, how easy it would be for him to follow them.'[15]

Mokwaë, too, began to show some of the same signs of at least a desire for conversion by proxy. M. Béguin, who became the missionary for Nalolo, still thought her proud, self-satisfied, and deceitful—though, he commented, 'c'est que mentir est devenu pour elle, comme pour la plupart des Zambésiens, une seconde nature'.[16] However in 1899 she was still attending church regularly; and when her son, Kaïba, who had seemed hopeful for conversion, took a second wife, Mokwaë said, 'I am very sad about it; I blame Kaïba for he is still only a boy; and anyway, if he takes a second wife he'll not be able now to be converted'—implying that that was just what she hoped for him. Slowly she was moving nearer. In 1901 she asked Béguin what the missionaries were saying about her in their letters.

'Many ask whether you've been converted,' said Béguin.

'And what do you reply?'

'I tell them that you usually come to worship on Sundays, but that you aren't converted yet.'

'Yes, that's quite right,' commented Mokwaë. And a few months later he remarked on evidence of an awakening of conscience.

One Sunday evening, about eight, on a dark night, she walked the two kilometers between the village and the mission station to tell me about a crime that had been committed in her court; and she wanted to tell me herself, so that I'd know she had nothing to do with it. There had been a theft, and one of the queen's men had had the culprit strangled for lèse-majesté. She said she was sad about it, and insisted that it had happened without her knowing. I took the opportunity to exhort her to work at the abolition of the terrible custom of strangulation . . . and to punish her over-zealous servant. She promised to do this.[17]

The genuineness of the Queen's hesitation seems to me to illustrate an important, and neglected, fact about these early 'conversions'. For it would not, in fact, have been difficult for her to have become a Christian well before this. Coillard was a highly disinterested supporter of the Barotse; unlike the other missionaries, he did not use his position and influence to acquire estates for his own Paris Evangelical mission. As the official historian of Northern Rhodesia (now Zambia) says, 'Coillard was content to have his stations delimited by the chiefs so that the Barotse would not imagine the missionaries had come to deprive them of their precious land.'[18] His main objective, apart from preaching and abolishing degrading customs, was to strengthen royal authority. What is more, as time went on the Queen must have seen the advantages that went with Christian adhesion. We have seen that her nephew Litia was a Christian; and the Barotse now had a number of literate people like him, and thus could begin to develop an Administration of their own. Indeed, it was precisely this fact that made the British authorities, from about 1900, jealous of their rising ability. Coillard was sure that the British Administrator 'was full of the most bitter aversion for Litia, the king's Christian son, because "Litia is a Christian", that is to say a man of education'.[19] And Coillard refused to sign the treaty to which the British persuaded Lewanika to agree in 1900, because he felt that the Barotse had come off extremely badly through it. The Queen may well have been tempted to 'convert' simply to show her appreciation for Coillard's support. Yet still she held off.

Thus in 1904 Béguin's successor one day preached on the responsibility of chiefs, to whom all look to know what they ought to do. Mokwaë seemed *bouleversée* by this—but once again it was only a passing mood. Two years later it was the same— 'friendly: but no change'. In 1907 the report said that she was the most assiduous at worship, and the best spiritually disposed person in all Nalolo—but still unattached. Then, nearly ten years later, in August 1916, she suddenly asked to speak after the morning service. She 'fit un vrai sermon' to the great astonishment of the congregation (over three hundred people). In summary she said,

I am not a Christian: I don't want to deceive the missionaries. And yet it seems to me that I am coming nearer and nearer to the things of God. And I am distressed that this village of wild beasts [Nalolo] is so indifferent to the Word of God, to whom we owe ourselves and our country. It would be a great misfortune for Nalolo if the Conference of missionaries decide to abandon our village. And if our missionary left here, I should follow him *clopinclopant* [hobbling].[20]

A few months later she went further. Her husband, Ishé Kuandu, was a catechumen, but could not be baptized until their marriage was regularized. She now agreed to this—viz., exchange of promises, respect, and mutual fidelity, till death. 'Her heart seemed touched,' noted M. Lageard, 'but she fears, with good reason, that she may lose her authority if she is converted'—i.e. shows that she has openly broken with tradition.

In 1917 she was asked to press the Prime Minister to marry a pagan. She replied to the messenger, 'You know I have not made profession, but I am myself a believer. Go back. I don't want to hear such things.' Yet the missionaries still feared she would die like her brother, Lewanika, without publicly professing Christianity.

But finally in 1921 her husband Ishé brought a message that she wished to see the missionaries. There she told them:

'For long I have told myself that I must follow Ishé in the road of God, and now I have decided to follow him.' M. Boiteux asked what had led her to the point, and she said, 'Ever since I began to listen to M. Coillard. . . . Will it be difficult?' Boiteux replied that the hardest for all men, who are proud by nature, is to admit themselves to be sinners. . . . Ishé told them that she had thought about it at the beginning of the year, and had meant to tell the missionaries; but he had urged her to think carefully first. Then she had thought of 'making profession' at morning service; but they decided it would be better to let the missionaries and the king know first.

And so finally, after thirty-five years of hesitation, she got up, on Sunday morning (20 February 1921) after the service and said in front of all the congregation, 'It is enough. I believe. I am God's. I am of the Kingdom. May God forgive me my sins, they are many and they are great. And you—believe!'[21] Not that all was completed at once. M. Boiteux began to give intensive instruction to the couple, and one instance will show the depth at which they were learning. He had spoken to them of repentance, both outward and inward, of reparation, and of the revolution in conduct that this brings. They followed closely, leaning forward, and looking disturbed. Then Ishé interrupted him:

'Look, we understand what you say; but for us, we need examples taken from daily life. Then we'll grasp it better.'

So Boiteux told them a parable of a rich, important man who is disliked by you; an accusation is brought against him, he's condemned, and stripped of all. Now he lives, poor, forgotten. But suppose new facts come to light, and you realise he wasn't as guilty as you thought, and at least didn't deserve so severe a sentence. Your duty is to recall him, tell him of the error and that you're sorry; and make reparation as far as you can. . . . Reparation is painful . . . but what joy comes from it. . . .

Their attention was still held, says Boiteux, and their emotion more visible:

'We understand,' said Ishé to me; 'but you see, when we turned to God, we brought all those things to the feet of Jesus; we said to Him: "Look: there's our past life, there are all our sins, take them—we have nothing to do with them any more."' [22]

CHAPTER 7 | NORTH AMERICAN INDIANS

Francis Parkman, the historian of the occupation of North America, was not very sympathetic to Roman Catholic teachings and practice; but he had to admit that the work especially of the Jesuits among the Indians reached heights of heroism which have seldom if ever been paralleled in history. In one of his books, *The Conspiracy of Pontiac* (less well known than his famous *The Jesuits in North America*), he sums up the difference between the Catholic and the Protestant missions thus:

In respect . . . to missionary enterprise, and the political influence resulting from it, the French had every advantage over rivals whose zeal for conversion was neither kindled by fanaticism nor fostered by ambitious government. [John] Eliot laboured within call of Boston, while the heroic Brébeuf faced the ghastly perils of the western wilderness; and the wanderings of Brainerd sink into insignificance compared with those of the devoted Rale. Yet, in judging the relative merits of the Romish and Protestant missionaries, it must not be forgotten that while the former contented themselves with sprinkling a few drops of water on the forehead of the proselyte, the latter sought to wean him from his barbarism and penetrate his savage heart with the truths of Christianity.[1]

Actually, as we shall see, Parkman elsewhere tends to qualify this account of the Roman Catholic missions. But in another of his books he says that the French priests

avoided all that might impair the warlike spirit of the neophyte. . . . They taught temperance, conjugal fidelity, devotion to the rites of their religion, and submission to the priest; but they left the savage a savage still. . . . The mission Indian . . . wore a crucifix, hung wampum on the shrine of the Virgin, told his beads . . . [etc.]; but, with rare exceptions, he murdered, scalped, and tortured like his heathen countrymen.[2]

It is not altogether true even to say that the Protestant missionaries were not 'kindled by fanaticism'. In a curious volume called *Indian Converts* (1727) by Experience Mayhew, which gives some of the results of the Puritan evangelism among the Indians of Massachussetts, there are examples of miraculous intervention which would rival anything from the Jesuit *Relations*. (For instance, the case of the girl Abigail, who died at about the age of twenty, in 1685. As they came to minister to her on her death-bed, it was very dark; they went looking for candles, but it was not necessary, for a light appeared—not a sudden flash, but a steady light—surrounding her, by which all could see to pray with her and bless her, and which lasted several hours until she died.[3]) In the Introduction (or 'Attestation') to this volume the United Ministers of Boston compare their work, as Protestant missionaries, with that of the 'Romanists' who 'have their singular Advantages, in the Circumstances of their Clergy, to go to and fro in the Earth, and walk up and down in it, everywhere seeking whom they may seduce, and bring under their strong delusions'.[4] But one of the later generation of Presbyterian missionaries who followed in the steps of John Eliot (the 'Indian Apostle'), David Brainerd, begins to show something of a new attitude. In spite of the fact that his life was written by the thundering Calvinist, Jonathan Edwards (in whose house he died in 1747), we get one incident which seems to speak against the characteristic 'fanaticism' of the period. Brainerd describes in his diary how in May 1745 he met a religious leader of the Delaware Indians. 'Of all the sights I ever saw among them . . . none appeared so frightful, or so akin to what is usually imagined of *infernal powers* . . . as the appearance of one who was a devout and zealous . . . restorer of what he supposed was the ancient religion of the Indians.' This figure advanced in all his regalia, masks, and instruments, dancing. 'When he came near me, I could not but shrink away from him, although it was then noon-day, I knew who it was, his appearance and gestures were so prodigiously frightful.' However, they then repaired to the diviner's house, and Brainerd spoke to him of Christianity, some elements of which the diviner liked.

He told me [says Brainerd] that God had taught him his religion, and that he never would turn from it, but wanted to find some that would join heartily with him in it; for the Indians, he said, were grown degenerate and corrupt. . . . He had not always, he said, felt as he now did, but had formerly been like the rest of the Indians, until about 4 or 5 years before that time: then he said his heart was very much distressed, so that he could not live among the Indians, but got away into the woods, and lived alone for some months. At length . . . God comforted his heart, and showed him what he should do; and since that time he had known God and tried to serve him; and loved all men, be they who they would, so as he never did before.

Brainerd said that he was most courteous to him; and was so opposed to Indians drinking strong liquor that if he could not stop them 'he would leave them and go crying into the woods'.

It was manifest he had a set of religious notions that he had looked into *for himself*, and not taken for *granted* upon bare tradition. . . . He seemed to be sincere, honest and conscientious in his *own* way, and according to his own religious notions, which was more than I ever saw in any other pagan. I perceived he was looked upon and derided amongst most of the Indians as a *precise zealot*, that made a needless noise about religious matters; but I must say, there was something in his temper and disposition that looked more like true religion than anything I ever observed amongst other heathens.[5]

These are tolerant sentiments which one does not usually associate with Calvinistic missionary certitude.

i. JAPHETH HANNIT (16 ?–1712)

Japheth's father was an 'Indian of prime Quality'. His first five children died within ten days of birth, 'notwithstanding all their Use of the PAWWAWS and Medicine to preserve them'. When the sixth son was born, his Mother was distressed that she would lose this one too; so she took him out into the field.

But while she was there musing on the Insufficiency of human Help, she found it powerfully suggested to her mind, that there is one *Almighty* God who is to be prayed to; that this *God* hath created all things that we see; and . . . was able to preserve and continue his Life.

On this she resolved that she would seek to God for that Mercy, and did accordingly; the Issue was that her Child lived, and her Faith (such as it was) in him who had thus answered her Prayer, was wonderfully strengthened.

And so she dedicated her son to the service of God, and told him about this when still young; and all the more when the Gospel came to be preached in that place, and she and her husband were converted. Japheth went to school in 1651, and learned to read English and Indian 'and also to write a very legible hand'. He became a Captain over an Indian Company, and later a Magistrate to them; and

in the time of that war betwixt them, which began in the Year 1675, and was commonly called *Philip's War*, good Japheth was very serviceable to both those of his *own Nation*, and *ours* on the Island; . . . he was imployed by the *English* to observe and report how things went among the Indians: and to his Faithfulness in this Discharge of this Trust I conceive that the Preservation of the Peace of our Island was very much owing, when the People on the Main were all in *War* and Blood.[6]

'King Philip', son of a Wampanoag *sachem* who had been friendly to the English and given his sons English names, formed a confederation of tribes in 1671 to resist the encroachment of the whites upon Indian land, and war broke out four years later. After some initial success (thirteen towns were overwhelmed and some six hundred colonists slain) he was captured, beheaded, his body drawn and quartered, and his head exposed as a warning at Plymouth (Mass.) for twenty years. Japheth Hannit's siding with the English evidently won him favour with the missionaries hardly less than with the military authorities. In

1684 he was ordained a Minister, and worked among his people for twenty-eight years. 'Though his Sermons were not very accurate, yet they were very serious, and had a great deal of good Matter in them, and he seem'd to me to do best when he did not try to oblige himself to any strict Method in them.'[7] He had further qualifications to commend him to the colonists. It has to be remembered that many of the latter were sceptical (as so often) of the work of the missionaries. A Royal Commission said in 1665 that in Massachusetts

> They convert Indians by hiring them to come and heare Sermons; by teaching them not to obey their Heathen Sachims, and by appointing Rulers amongst them over tens, twenties, fifties, etc. The lives, Manners and habits of those, who they say are converted, cannot be distinguished from those who are not, except it be by being hyred to heare sermons, which the more generous natives scorne.[8]

It is this sort of thing that the author, Experience Mayhew, had in mind in writing his book for 'Some of our English, who will hardly be persuaded that there is any sincere Religion or Godliness among this poor People.'[9] And so he tells us of Japheth

> As he was generally by the *English* esteemed a truly godly Man, so being a person of a very genteel and obliging Conversation, and one who went clean and neat in his Apparel, he was every where courteously received and entertained by them, the best Gentlemen on the Island not scrupling to invite him to sit at their Tables with them. . . . And once a Master of a Vessel discoursing with him, on the Morrow of the Sabbath, facetiously asked him, whether he prayed for him yesterday or not? Japheth readily reply'd, Sir, I prayed for all God's People, and if you be one of them, I consequently prayed for *you*.[10]

Heathen Indians, and the distant rivalry of Roman Catholics, were not the only problems facing an indigenous Minister of the Gospel: divergences and rivalries within Protestantism had also to be met by the newly Christianized minds of Indian clergymen. Japheth, however, seems to have been quite capable of the encounter. Mayhew tells us that a 'godly Englishman' who had actually taught Japheth, 'having unhappily imbibed the Errors of the *Antipaedobaptists*, thought himself obliged to endeavour to bring Mr. *Japheth* over to his Persuasion'. He visited Japheth and tried to argue him into the belief that 'sprinkling in Baptism' is wrong. Japheth was unconvinced, and as the enthusiast was about to leave him, said,

You know, Sir, that we Indians were all in Darkness and Ignorance before the *English* came among us, and instructed us, and that your self are one of those *English* Men by whom we have been taught and illuminated. . . . And when, Sir, you thus instructed us, you told us, that it may be there would shortly false Teachers come among us, and endeavour to pervert us . . . but you then advised us to take heed to our selves, and beware that we were not turned aside by such Teachers, so as to fall in the Errors into which they would lead us. And now, Sir, I find your Prediction true; for you your self are become one of these Teachers you cautioned us against; I am therefore fully resolved to take your good Counsel, and not believe you, but will continue stedfast in the Truths wherein you formerly instructed us.

'This Speech of *Japheth*'s put an end to the Disputation', said Mayhew.[11] He ends with a standard account of a pious death— a death which, apparently, Japheth foresaw:

As I was well acquainted with Japheth in his *Life*, so I frequently visited him in the time of his last Sickness; and on the whole of my Acquaintance with him, I cannot but think, that he was a very serious and godly Man. . . . His Discourse in the time of his last Sickness, when I was with him, was very pious and savoury.[12]

ii. KATERI TEGAQUITHA (*c.* 1656–80)

We have seen Francis Parkman's view that the Roman Catholic missionaries failed to tame the wild spirits of their converts. No one doubts that they were wild: the cruelty of the 'Iroquois' above all (but also of their opponents, the Hurons) is well known. Nor did it disappear with the coming of 'civilization': we read that as late as 1854, up in the North-West, 'the Indians robbed and harassed immigrants on the Oregon Trail. Just east of Fort Boise, the savage Snakes massacred all but two of the Ward wagon train, brutally torturing the women and roasting their babies before their eyes.'[13] But Parkman makes exceptions to his generalization. He says that,

at the Sulpitian mission of the Mountain of Montreal, unlike the rest the converts were taught to speak French and practise the mechanical arts. The absence of such teaching in other missions was the subject of frequent complaint, not only from Frontenac, but from other officers. . . . [Contrast] the conduct of the French priests with that of the English ministers, who have taught many Indians to read and write, and reward them for teaching others in turn.[14]

But even in speaking of the Jesuits' missions Parkman admits that the converts rarely took part in the burning of their prisoners, and sometimes even tried to stop it—citing one such in 1646 who, when his fellow-Hurons were about to burn a captive Iroquois to death, threatened them with eternal damnation, and when they persisted, baptized the unhappy prisoner in the fire.[15] And he refers to the remarkable work of one of the Jesuit Fathers, Druilletes, who, on an expedition in 1645 with a group of Christian Indians, persuaded them to build a chapel and on Good Friday to pray for the forgiveness and conversion of their enemies, the Iroquois. And he generously comments:

Those who know the intensity and tenacity of an Indian's hatred will see this as more than a change from one superstition to another. An idea had been presented to the mind of the savage to which he had previously been an utter stranger. This is the most remarkable record of success in the whole body of the Jesuit *Relations*. . . . The influence of the French and the Jesuits extended far beyond the circle of converts. It eventually modified and softened the manners of many unconverted tribes. In the wars of the next century we do not often find these examples of diabolic atrocity with which the earlier annals are crowded. The savage burned his enemies alive, it is true, but he rarely ate them nor did he torment them with the same deliberation and persistency.[16]

One of their missions was at Caughnawaga on the St. Lawrence river (see page 95). In 1654 a line of missions was established in Iroquois country: it extended all along the Mohawk river from the Hudson to Lake Erie; and Caughnawaga was one of the most settled of them.[17] The Indians there came to be known as the 'Caughnawaga' or the 'Praying' Indians; it was commenced in 1665 as an asylum against their pagan countrymen and against traders' liquor. In 1687 the Bishop of Quebec paid the settlement a visit and praised the 'high virtue' practised among these 'converted savages': 'The French residents at La Prairie [he wrote] are so charmed with what they see, that they come sometimes to join in prayer with these good Christians, and to reanimate their devotion at the sight of the fervour which they admire in people, a while ago barbarians.'[18]

Catherine Tekakwitha (as the name is usually, but in-correctly, spelt)[19] was the daughter of a mixed Indian marriage. Her father was an Iroquois, her mother an 'Algonquin'. The word 'Iroquois' is itself mixed: an Algonkian word meaning 'real adder', with a French suffix added.[20] It is conveniently used to describe a League of Five 'Nations' (or tribes)—the Cayuga, Mohawk, Oneida, Onondaga, and Seneca—since they form a group which is quite distinct from the Algonkian, or Algonquin. The latter is a vaguer term, referring to a common language. But it is clear that throughout the seventeenth century the two groups, Iroquois and Algonquin, were enemies; and that the Iroquois were, on the whole, more deliberately sadistic in their treatment of prisoners—because torture, like cannibalism when it was practised in certain circumstances, had a religious sanction. It is true that, according to Parkman (quoting the Jesuits), there is no Iroquois word which, in its primitive meaning, can be interpreted as 'the Great Spirit' or 'God': some of the early writers, he says, could discover no trace of belief in a supreme spirit of any kind; and he concludes that 'The Creator of the World stood on the level of a bar-barous and degraded humanity. . . . The Indian belief, if developed, would have developed into a system of pantheism.'[21] But this is no doubt to expect too clear a religious system of a people at this stage; the most that can be said is that the Iro-quois did not attach their mythical legends so closely to the supreme Creator Spirit (Hawenneyu, 'Ruler') as the Algon-quins did.

Yet it seems that the Iroquois were more deeply 'religious' than the tribes that surrounded them. Their respect for the dead was so profound that when they moved their village sites (which, for motives of hygiene, they did every ten years or so) they exhumed their relatives and took the bodies with them. This, indeed, seems to have been one of their reasons for found-ing the 'League' of the Five Nations: the Algonquins, around 1630, were pressing them hard, and their attachment to their dead hampered their fighting, so they banded together for better warring. And the 'dedicatory' element in their hideous torture gives it a different aspect. It has even been suggested that they looked upon both the slow killing of victims and the self-torture which was equally prevalent, as modes of self-identification with the suffering of humanity.[22] At least it is not fanciful to say that their extraordinary stoicism was religious in its motivation.

Catherine was born in what the French knew as 'the village of martyrs' (Osernenon), ten years after the heroic Fr. Jogues was killed there. The fact that her father was a Mohawk *sachem* married to an Algonquin prisoner was not so unusual; indeed, it seems often to have happened, since the Iroquois women were imperious, and the Algonquins much more obedient. What was less usual was that his wife was a baptized Christian. This, however, made little difference to Catherine, since both father and mother died when she was four; and she seems to have had no Christian training. She may have learned a little about the Christian faith when the Onondagas (one of the Five Nations) invited the 'blackrobes' (Jesuits) to live among them, not for their religion, but because their presence might encourage French trade, which the Onondagas wanted.

When she was ten a French force appeared (1666) in her village, and she and the rest of the inhabitants fled into the forest—at night, in the autumn cold, with a hailstorm raging. When they returned a peace treaty laid down the condition that they must accept Jesuits in the village. The Jesuits soon won the confidence and affection of the Indians there, and the village became a Christian centre. Christian Hurons and Algonquins, incorporated in the Mohawk nation, were now free openly to practise the Christianity that they had had to keep secret for some years. A Fr. Pierron preached uninhibitedly, even aggressively. For instance, in 1668 at the Feast of the Dead ceremony, when the dead (including Catherine's father and mother) were to be exhumed and reburied, Fr. Pierron appeared publicly at the ceremony, denounced it as pagan superstition, and told them to stop. For some time the people chanted loudly to drown his voice; but he won—with the help of a powerful *sachem* who later became a Christian.

Catherine was eighteen now. She was not among those who had asked to be baptized; but it was at about this age that she had a strange intuition that she was intended for celibacy. Since her parents' death she had been entrusted to an uncle, who had no leanings towards Christianity, and he ridiculed the idea that she should not get married. Most Mohawk girls were betrothed at about seven; but now, when a young man (her future husband, as the relatives proposed) appeared and offered her the usual gift, she fled.

In the spring of 1675 a new Jesuit Father arrived, Fr. Lamberville; by the autumn he knew enough Iroquois to start pastoral work. One day he entered—foolishly—one of the 'Long Houses', characteristic of Iroquois life. When the first French explorer, the sailor Jacques Cartier, came across Indians (1634–5) he thought of them as backward Europeans. And so when he found a Long House full of Iroquois young ladies, he thought it must be a brothel. In fact prostitution was unknown among the Amerindians, and the Long House was carefully and strictly governed. Something of this still survives: a Long House in an Indian Reserve is 'in the form of a wooden rectangular building, usually with doors at each end; wood-burning stoves are near the ends, with each stove serving as the fire for a moiety. Benches are along the walls, and the central area of the room is dominated by neither moiety.'[23] Normally their inhabitants consisted of the females of a matrilineage, their children, and the 'in-marrying' husbands.[24] There is some evidence that there had been a system of 'vestal virgins' among the Iroquois, and even, recently, among the Onondagas; but French merchants when drunk had broken into their place, and they had abandoned the practice.[25] In any case nothing like that obtained at Catherine's little village, and it seemed most unlikely that she could remain unmarried. So when Fr. Lamberville on an impulse entered one of the Long Houses he was surprised to find Catherine there. It was harvest-time, and the house should have been empty. But Catherine had recently hurt her foot at work and could not walk. The priest talked to her, and she confided her resolution to him. She also asked for baptism, which she received eighteen months later. Surprisingly, her uncle raised no objection.

But a year or two later there was a real dispute between them. The Jesuits had founded the Christian village of Caughnawaga, north, on the St. Lawrence, at Sault-Saint-Louis (opposite the present Montreal) in about 1672; here the converted Indians could be simply Christian Indians, and not imitation Frenchmen, as was attempted—with little success— in a large town like Quebec. Here, too, they could keep their own hierarchy of power (the Jesuits were the only white men living there) and such Indian customs as did not conflict with the Faith. Gradually the best Indian Christians from Catherine's village began to move to Caughnawaga; and Catherine decided to go with them—it was hard for those left behind to resist the general demoralization (especially through drink*). But her uncle was strongly opposed to her leaving, and finally she had to make her escape.

And so she arrived (it was 1677), and Frs. Cholenec and Chauchetière (her future biographers) received her. She was put under the care of a Christian widow, Anastasia. Both she and the Jesuits there did not expect much from a fairly recent convert, coming from a more primitive, pagan area into a well-developed island of piety. But she soon outshone them all.

From this moment on, the twentieth-century biographer is embarrassed, as so often in these lives, by the particular emphases of the only sources available. The worthy French Fathers are determined to show that Catherine not only did them credit but qualified in the special ways required in a process for beatification. Thus reading between the lines we can see more merit in what she achieved in spite of them than in the heights she reached according to their expectations. They made much of her mortifications. She, and a companion in spiritual athleticism, flagellated each other with thorn branches; having heard that St. Louis Gonzaga slept on thorns, she spent several sleepless nights on a bed strewn with thorns; and she and her friend tried placing burning coals between their toes. But this last was in fact similar to tests applied by traditional Indian upbringing, and the Fathers soon stopped it when

---

* On one topic Catholic and Protestant missionary were agreed: that the introduction of drink, especially 'fire-water', to the Indians had had wholly disastrous results. And we have seen that the Calvinist preacher, David Brainerd, agreed with the Indian diviner and would-be reformer on the same subject. The Iroquois, especially, threw themselves into intoxicants with the same abandon that they adopted towards war or torture. Some would lie completely unconscious for two or three days after an orgy; drunken Indians would bite, and eat bits out of, each other; they would throw their children into the fire, and women would make their own children intoxicated and lead them gaily through the streets. The Jesuits always had to stay indoors when a 'drink' was on. No wonder Catherine wanted to leave her earlier village and go for safety to Caughnawaga. And no wonder Experience Mayhew, in his introduction to *Indian Christians*, said that the one sorrowful admission he and his fellow-minister had to make was that too many of their converts lapsed from their Christian faith for one simple reason: alcohol.

they heard about it. (They had to stop other Indian women from similar extravagant penances: like the woman who stood, three nights running, in the St. Lawrence up to her neck, at 20° of frost, reciting her rosary; or another who stood in the frozen water of the St. Lawrence with a baby of three, saying, 'It is better for the child to do penance now than later'.) Except as evidence of Christianizing (and moderating) pagan practices, this is the least impressive side of her short life. More impressive is her vow of virginity. The widow, Anastasia, was emphatic in her opposition. Already there had been, on two different occasions, hints, if not accusations, of immorality against Catherine; she had quietly denied the accusations, and they had been withdrawn. But it was tempting critics and enemies to remain in her unmarried state—which was dangerous and cut her off from the community. She went to consult Fr. Cholenec. At first he supported the Indian point of view, till she bluntly said, 'Isn't the state of virginity higher than that of marriage?' 'Yes', said Cholenec (this was, indeed, the teaching of the Church at this time), rather embarrassed; but he pressed her—had she really thought of the difficulties? Why did she think she was called to it? 'Go away and ponder these things.' 'For how long?' asked Catherine. 'For long,' replied the priest; 'perhaps for months.' 'But I have already thought about all these things for a long time.' 'Come back in three days,' said Fr. Cholenec firmly. Catherine left, but came back a quarter of an hour later. 'It is no use trying to deceive you, father,' she said; 'my mind is already made up.' The priest decided to support her. And now he had to meet the anger of Anastasia; which he did with uncompromising firmness.

As an instructed Christian you should know of the perfection of the virgin state consecrated to God. Yet you are turning one of God's disciples away from this. God is doing the honour of choosing a girl from your hut, to raise the standard of virginity among the savages,* and to give them knowledge of this so sublime state which makes men of mud and earth like the angels in heaven.

More interesting again—though it might seem to be a commonplace matter is the fact that Fr. Cholenec decided to admit her, fairly soon after her arrival, to Holy Communion.

* It has to be remembered that the French word 'sauvages' is more neutral than the English 'savages'.

This was extremely rare among Indians. Communion had never been given—only *pain béni*—to Indians in the Iroquois missions: perhaps it was felt that those who had so recently come to Christianity from cannibalism were likely to understand the Real Presence in too literal a way. The Iroquois had, after all, consumed slices of Fr. Jogues' flesh while he was still living; and the Mohawks, after finally killing Fr. Brébeuf, had cut out his heart: a compliment, since this was done to obtain his strength. So Catherine received communion at Christmas 1677, and again the following Easter.

But what is probably the best testimony of all is the attitude of her fellow-Indians. True, she was slandered by some of them; but her quiet denials prevailed, and after the second attempt to discredit her they did not try again. Though only a young woman, she soon began to be consulted by others on spiritual matters. When asked by some whether they could follow her by also taking vows of chastity, she discouraged nearly all of them. She and her friend visited the French nuns across the river; and three of them would have liked to become nuns. Unfortunately it was unthinkable then for Indian girls to join a white religious order—in any case, they did not want to separate themselves from the Iroquois. For a time they planned to live as a little, withdrawn, indigenous community themselves, in a hermitage which they would construct on a deserted island on the St. Louis. But their Jesuit director forbade it—how would they live?—what about the dangers from traders on the river?—would it not be better to stay and bear witness in the Long House? And so they did.

She seemed to be strong—she had joined in the usual spring Hunts, though withdrawing herself from the rougher and more alcoholic episodes involved in them. But she had had smallpox when a child (the early portrait of her shows the marks quite clearly) and her eyes were weak. At twenty-three she started to develop bad headaches, vomiting, and a low fever. For the last four months she was bed-ridden, and left untended in the hut; but Fr. Chauchetière visited her and then brought young children to her bed-side, so that she could instruct them in the Faith. As winter approached, she began to get many more visitors, asking her blessing, for her reputation had begun to spread. It was a tradition among the Iroquois that dying people have the privilege of singing on their death-bed. Catherine used the privilege to preach to her visitors, and there were said to have been a number of conversions. On Tuesday in Holy Week Holy Communion was brought to her in the hut—another exceptional event, since the Long Houses were not over-clean; but the priests felt that her presence had purified hers. After her death, on 17 April 1680, there was yet another remarkable event: the Indians are said to have behaved as never before at a funeral: the women did not indulge in wild laments, the men did not crowd round her; all was peaceful—they kissed her hands, and some secretly tore off pieces of her clothes as a souvenir. It was Maundy Thursday when she was buried, and there were no pagan offerings—nothing but joy.

Sixteen years later a rough, worldly explorer and trader, Daniel Greysolong du Lhut, who did some of the toughest empire-building in the middle-west (the town of Duluth, in Minnesota, is named after him) wrote that the gout, which had troubled him for over twenty-five years (a painful illness which much have severely handicapped his continual expeditions through the forests), was cured 'by the intercession of the Iroquois saint, Catherine Tegakhoita, to whom he had made a vow to that end'.[26] If gout were associated with over-indulgence in alcohol, it would be ironic justice that he should be cured (if only for a time) by the prayers of one who had had to separate herself from her own people because of that indulgence.

PART THREE | TOWARDS MATURITY

In Part III we shall consider those who are beginning to move out on their own. Once more it would not be revealing to follow a chronological sequence; what matters is the individual's relation to the developing Christianity on the one hand, and to his own national background on the other. Each has been chosen for a particular reason which should become clear as we tell his story. In the first we have a Korean who shows some of the weaknesses of having a foreign supportive system behind him, however much one may and must admire his individual courage. In the second we shall see a very remarkable Chinese priest operating in great isolation with a devotion that appears more like doggedness than heroism. In the third we find an Indian priest working creatively in spite of the inhibiting ecclesiastical confusion, owing to rival 'jurisdictions', which he inherited. The fourth is but a brief vignette, of a Japanese Christian who became 'Russian Orthodox'—chosen simply because this phenomenon which, though common enough, is almost totally unrecorded, certainly as good as unknown in the West. The fifth is given because it is the fullest account we have of a Sino-Japanese Buddhist in his slow movement towards Christianity. Finally, in the sixth we move to the Pacific Islands, to find an influential and by no means subservient character making his particular, and his people's general, imprint upon the new religion which he embraced and developed. In all these cases it is possible to fill in much more of the social and cultural background than was possible in Parts I and II.

In Chapter 3 above we saw that a Jesuit priest accompanied a Japanese *daimyo* when he went to fight in the Korean War in 1592. This Fr. Gregorio de Cespedes was thus able to look after the Christian Japanese in the army. He also tried a little preaching of the Gospel to the Koreans on the side; but since he would naturally be identified with the Koreans' enemy, Japan, he was (not surprisingly) unsuccessful. He returned to Japan in 1595, and the war ended soon after. However, the Japanese took a number of Korean prisoners, and these were sent back to Japan as slaves. Some of them heard the Christian Gospel in Japan and were converted; even more, when the persecutions of the early seventeenth century broke out, they stood alongside their Japanese brethren (the very people who had captured them), and were martyred. Nine of them are included in the list of 205 martyrs of Japan whom Pius IX beatified in 1867.[1]

From the tenth to the fifteenth centuries Korea had been dominated by China; up to about 1400 Buddhism predominated, but then there was a reaction against Buddhism and Confucianism triumphed. The Japanese invasion was successful for a time, and Japan occupied the whole of Korea for some years. Later they withdrew and only held on to the port of Fusan in the south-east. In 1636 the Manchu dynasty overthrew the Ming in China, and reasserted China's dominance over Korea. Now the King of Korea had every year to send an embassy to Peking to pay tribute, and to receive the Chinese Calendar.

And this resulted in one of the strangest pieces of Christian 'expansion' that history has seen. It was still impossible for missionaries to go into Korea and preach without being identified with the oppressor—this time, the Chinese. But some of the Korean envoys, on their annual visits to the court of Peking, chanced to meet the Jesuits who resided there. These latter presented them with books both on natural science and on Christianity.

The Korean Annals allude to the fact that as early as 1631 a Korean ambassador was in touch with these famous Jesuits, and at the beginning of the 17th century Fr. Ricci's *True Principles Concerning God* (published in Chinese in 1595) was already known in Korea. Being of an inquisitive nature and eager for science, the Korean scholars were quick to secure some of these books which they passed from one to another.[2]

Indeed, the Korean Court Journal for 1643 shows that Catholicism was already considered *la science de l'Europe*.[3] The famous Jesuit missionary, Adam Schall, with whom one Korean hereditary prince had established close relations in 1644, tried to get a mission sent in to Korea; and 'Paul Hsü'* had earlier planned to evangelize the country. In 1688 the Government decided that 'the doctrine of God' was too flourishing, and must be driven out. There were now few communications between China and Korea, and in any case an anti-Christian persecution broke out in China in 1724; so the only progress Christianity made in Korea now was through reading. A Korean scholar, Yi Ik (1682–1763), for instance, mentions Ricci's *De Deo Vera Ratio*, and another Jesuit book, and writes a commentary on them, comparing Christian doctrine with Buddhism and Confucianism—he thinks the Christians' God is equivalent to Buddha and to the *Siang-tei* (*sc.* the Chinese *Shang-t'i*, 'Lord of Heaven') of scholars.

But in the mid eighteenth century communication suddenly opened. A young scholar, Yi Seung-houn, was about to travel from Korea to Peking in 1783 with his father who had been appointed third ambassador to Peking. A friend of Seung-houn, Yi Piek, was, unknown to him, reading Catholic books. Piek urged: 'At Peking there is a Catholic church, and . . . European scholars who preach religion there. Go and see them, ask for a copy of the Apostles' Creed, and ask for baptism. Then the missionaries will love you very much, and give you many marvellous and interesting things. You won't come back with empty hands.'[4]

So Seung-houn (whose main interest was probably in mathematics, though he seems not to have been insincere about Christianity) found the Jesuits in Peking, and was baptized, aged twenty-seven, in the spring of 1784, and given the name Peter (Pierre). Later he admitted he had been baptized with little knowledge of the Christian Faith.

* See chapter 4, above, pp. 50–8.

On his return he and Yi Piek read the Christian books they had brought back with them, and soon were collecting a body of converts. A persecution broke out in 1785, and Seung-houn says that ten Christians were martyred. Seung deserted his friends, because his family was conspicuous and vulnerable, and anyway his father forbade him to continue to practise Christianity. But he wanted the Faith to continue, so designated two other converts to carry on with baptisms.

By now there seem to have been a thousand Christians, without priests or sacraments. But they knew enough, through Seung-houn's readings and descriptions of church life in Peking, to know that they ought to have more than baptism: and first, the sacrament of penance. Seung-houn later wrote to the missionaries to describe what happened:

Towards the spring of 1786, the Christians assembled to discuss how to confess to each other: it was agreed that Kia should confess to Yi and to Pin, but that Kia and Yi or Yi and Pin need not confess to each other. Towards autumn, the same year, the Christians assembled once more; it was agreed in this assembly that I should say the holy mass and give confirmation; and I not only agreed to what they asked, but even gave the power to say mass to others. As to the ceremonies, I observed them as they are marked in the different books and prayers of hours, though cutting out some and adding others. For prayers, I chose them in our formulas of prayers.[5]

But suddenly he came to realize his presumption. One of the ten whom he had 'ordained',

who believed he was a priest, began towards spring to read with care a book . . . in which he found all the crimes I had fallen into. He wrote at once to tell me, and I enclose a copy of his letter; I shudder to the marrow of my bones at the awful crimes. I've had all the sacraments stopped in different places, and written to warn the Christians of my sacrilege.[6]

According to Fr. Dallet (the standard nineteenth-century historian of Korean church history), Seung-houn had seen the Catholic hierarchy in action in the Peking mission; and he says that one of the Koreans ('François-Xavier Kouen') had been 'named bishop'. But in fact there was no bishop in Peking from 1785–9; and there is no mention in any source of a Korean 'bishop'—Seung-houn was called 'chief', and it was he who wrote to the missionaries asking for a bishop. Dallet says that the Bishop in China was very unsympathetic when he heard of the Korean irregularities—'He reproved them severely for having rashly exercised the functions which only Holy Mother Church could empower them to do through the sacrament of Holy Orders.'

At any rate, promises were made that if possible a missionary would be sent from China. And meanwhile the Christians progressed rapidly; in 1790 there were reports of 4,000 Christians. And this is not impossible; for in that year Seung-houn, who was of noble birth, was honoured by the King and made magistrate of the district of Phyeng-thaik. True, this made it more difficult for him personally to practise his religion, and he asked to be released as leader of the Christian community. But the kingdom of Korea was a sort of feudal state. The central Government and political institutions were Confucian in system; but with much corruption and favouritism. The scholars, disgusted, withdrew to study; and it was at this time that scientific and religious works were arriving from Peking. One scholar said in 1791 that there was not one of the literati who had not seen a Christian book. Dissatisfied with Confucianism, they were ready for new truth from anywhere.

From 1790 onwards requests kept arriving in Peking for a priest. Matters were held up, however, to some extent by the old dispute about jurisdictions. There were three possibilities: Portuguese (and the diocese of Peking belonged to the Portuguese *padroado*,* who were as always jealous of interlopers); Propaganda; and the French *Société des Missions Étrangères*. In the very long run it was the French who got it; but in the meantime there was much uncertainty. And the attempts made to get priests into Korea were constantly blocked, apart from the outbreaks of persecution.

There were three waves of persecution of Christians between 1791 and 1802, and their sociological significance helps us to understand the background. The first two (in 1791 and 1795) were local; the third (1801–2) was general. What sparked off the first was the defiance by certain Christians of the ancestor-cult. Yet in 1758, in the Christian provinces of Whang-hae and Kang-wun, there had been similar acts of iconoclasm and rejection of ancient tradition, but this led to no persecution. Why? The answer is that the Christians here were of the 'plebs'

* See Chapter 10, below p. 131.

and therefore not worth persecuting. But the later incidents were different. Not only did they involve the nobility, but they involved political parties too. In 1791 the mother of a Christian nobleman, Paul Youn Tji-tchoung, died. The relatives arrived for the family funeral sacrifices. In 1790 the Korean Christians had asked Mgr. Gouvea (of Peking) whether they were allowed to erect ancestor tablets or keep the old ones. The Bull of Pope Benedict XIV, *Ex quo Singulari*, of 1742, had condemned the Jesuit compromise, and forbade the rites; so Mgr. Gouvea replied 'no' to both questions. Paul then burnt his family tablets and abstained from offering sacrifices to his deceased mother. This led to the explosion.

But the further political reason was this. The King of Korea and his Prime Minister (Tchai Tjie-kong) found their strongest support in two political parties, one of which happened to be largely composed of Christians. The members of this party, the Tchai-pa, were mostly scholars and very much at the King's service—and the King loved learning. The political party of which he was most afraid was the Hong-pa, who were opposed to the scholars and very strictly Confucian. The King ignored their first complaint against the Christians, thinking it merely a party-political matter. But when the affair of Paul Tji-tchoung flared up, a long petition was sent to the King, complaining that Paul was supported by a number of scholars, eight out of ten of whom had adopted the 'perverse doctrine', that they were destroying the natural relations of men and debauching the people, and were connected with a band of rebels in China who threatened Korea's security. The King had to take note of this, but even now the Prime Minister assured him that it was largely the expression of the Hong-pa's rivalry; so the King merely had Paul and another Christian arrested, and only signed the death warrant for them reluctantly in 1791. This did not content the Opposition, who referred to the importing and printing of Christian books, especially by the Christian mandarin Yi Seung-houn. But all that happened was that Seung-houn was deposed and exiled, and a decree passed forbidding the entry of European or Chinese books from Peking.

There was a second, slightly more severe persecution in 1795 when a Chinese priest (Jacques Vellozo) managed to get into Korea and was hidden by some Christians. But when his whereabouts was not revealed, even after the executing of a number of converts, a third persecution broke out in 1801–2, after the death of the more lenient King. Fr. Vellozo was discovered and beheaded, and others suffered, on the grounds that they were planning for European ships to invade and occupy Korea. There was this amount of substance to the accusation: a letter from a Korean Christian to Mgr. Gouvea was intercepted which suggested four possible courses of action, in view of the sad plight of the Korean Church: (1) A Korean must be sent to Peking to teach the Europeans Korean (for they found the language difficult), and also a Chinese should open an inn on the frontier, where refugees could be concealed for smuggling in or out; (2) the Pope should write to the Emperor of China and persuade him to order the King of Korea to grant liberty to Christians; (3) Korea should be incorporated into the Chinese Empire; and (4) if the first three failed, the Christian nations in Europe should send several hundred warships to enforce religious liberty. It is not surprising that the Christians were accused rebellion, though in fact even the writer of this letter, Alexander Hoang Sa-ieng, had not envisaged the overthrow of the Korean regime, only freedom for Christians. But the new young King published a decree in 1802 proscribing Christianity—though he forbade any fresh persecution and ordered all imprisoned Christians to be freed. It had been embarrassing to him to discover that the priest, Fr. Vellozo, who had been executed, was a Chinese subject.

For more than thirty years the Church in Korea struggled on, writing time and again begging for priests to be sent to them. There were sporadic persecutions—in 1815, in the province of Kieng-san, when more than thirty were killed, and again in 1827 when over 150 were martyred. And all the time the tripartite correspondence was going on between Propaganda, the Portuguese, and the French, arguing about which should be given Korea. Even when in 1831 Rome decided to make Korea an Apostolic Vicariat (i.e. under Propaganda) the matter was not settled: for in 1834 the Vicar Apostolic (who still could not get into Korea) wrote that the Portuguese considered him a usurper and claimed still to have sole rights of religious administration in Korea. Finally it was the French *Missions Étrangères* that became responsible. A missionary managed to get into Korea in 1834, at last, and sent back two Koreans to train for the priesthood at Macao. But a fresh persecution in 1839 resulted in the execution of the missionary Bishop, Imbert, and his two European priests.

This historical survey helps us to see the significance of the life of the first Korean priest. He was one of two men sent to Macao—there were in fact three Koreans training there in 1837. In 1842 this young seminarian, André Kim, was asked to accompany a French frigate captain, as interpreter, in an expedition to find out whether, the Opium War now being over (in which France had taken no part), there were any possibilities of trading treaties with kingdoms near China, especially Korea, by establishing a strategic and commercial base at some island off Southern Japan. A French priest, M. Maistre, also accompanied them. But this Capt. Cécile finally decided not to go further north than the Blue River, and to postpone the Korean expedition indefinitely. M. Maistre wanted to go on, so with another French priest, M. de la Brunière, he and Kim embarked on a Chinese junk, and reached Liao-tung in October. They went ashore quite openly, but were surrounded at the customs post by officers, satellites, and a crowd. Their guides were terrified. M. de la Brunière spoke some Chinese, and tried to reply to the mandarin, 'I am a foreigner; I don't understand you; leave me alone, I don't want to talk to you.' The rest of the Christians in the party were dumb with terror. But Kim, already showing a confidence, even truculence, which we shall see more of later, made a long speech to the assailants, accusing them of 'accosting us like robbers', of 'making us lose caste', of 'disgracefully troubling harmless men who had travelled from the province of Kiang-nan on business', and so forth. Finally they were allowed to go on. M. Maistre went into hiding, and it was agreed that Kim should try to get into Korea to bring back news from the Christians there. Not far from the frontier he was lucky enough to meet a Korean caravanserai of about three hundred, going to Peking, and by chance to find a Christian courier among them, who gave him news of the late persecution (in which the Bishop and two priests had been killed) and of the affairs of the Church. Kim decided to go on and try to get in. He managed to get past the frontier post at Uiju, but after several days without food, and nearly freezing in the snow, he got back to P'yŏng-yang and reported the difficulties to his superiors.

The next year a Christian Korean managed to get out to

report to the new Bishop, Ferréol (consecrated in 1843), in Manchuria: persecution was again threatened; it would be impossible to get a missionary into the country. Again Kim must make the attempt.

This he did in 1844, trying an entry from the north-east. There was a Tartar town on the Korean frontier, near the Sea of Japan, called (in French notation—it is not now identifiable) Houng-tchoung, where every second year a large fair brought together for a few hours a large number of people from both sides. It was agreed that the Christian Koreans should gather here, to explore the passage in and out. Kim wrote the account of his exploration in Chinese, which was translated into French.[7] It is graphic and full of fascinating and observant detail about fauna and flora *en route*; but much too long even to summarize adequately. He and his companions passed through Ki-lin, and worked their way down the Sungari River, which was frozen over,

To right and left rose high mountains, crowned with giant trees, and inhabited by tigers, panthers, bears, wolves and other wild animals. . . . Woe to any rash person who dares to set off alone into this terrifying solitude. . . . We were told that during the winter more than 45 men and over 100 cattle and horses had been devoured by these carnivorous beasts. . . .

There are always some warriors who pay for their bravery with their life. I met one whom his comrades were bringing back to the tomb of his fathers . . . on his bier were proudly displayed his trophies of victory, the antlers of a deer and a tiger-skin. The leader of the funeral procession threw down, at intervals on the main road, paper money which the soul of the dead man must pick up to use in the country beyond the grave. These poor folk, alas, have no idea that faith and good works are the sole valid currency in the other world.

They stayed in a hostelry just before the first day of the Chinese New Year, a great feast day. Kim describes the festivities of the occasion. He was in bed, but the locals kept vigil.

Towards midnight, I saw a master of ceremonies approach the *khang* or stove which served me as a bed; he was decked out in some strange garb or other. I guessed what he wanted, so I pretended to be asleep. He rapped me lightly on the head several times to wake me. So, as if starting out of a deep sleep, I said 'What's the matter? What is it?' 'Get up,' he said: 'look: the gods are approaching; you must go to meet them.' 'The gods are coming! . . . Where from? Who are these gods?'—'Yes, the gods, the gods are coming. Get up. You must go and meet them!' 'Wait a moment, my friend' (I said). 'You see: I am possessed by the god of sleep; are there any gods among those coming who could be as welcome at this hour? Please, do me the favour of letting me quietly enjoy his presence; I don't know the others you're telling me about.' The master of ceremonies went off, grumbling in words I couldn't catch.

He also describes the actual devotions paid to the New Year god.

At the right moment, i.e. at midnight, men, women, children and old folk go out into the court, each dressed in his very best. There, they stand up; the father of the family presiding over the ceremony directs his eyes to the different quarters of the sky. He alone has the privilege of seeing the gods. As soon as they have revealed themselves to him, he cries out 'They've come! Prostrate yourselves! There they are—over here . . . over there!' All prostrate themselves in the direction he points. They also turn the heads of the animals, and the front of the carts, in that direction: everything in nature must receive the gods in its own manner: it would be unseemly that as the heavenly guests arrive their eyes should encounter a horse's hind-quarters. After such a reception of the divinities, everyone goes back into the house, and they all set to and have a good time and a copious feast in their honour.

Finally they got to 'Houng-tchoung'. The 'fair' lasts only a few hours, and 'these few hours of trading are the only contact between the two peoples [Chinese and Korean]. At all other times anyone who crosses the frontier is enslaved or killed.' Kim reflects, as he waits at the frontier for the fair to open,

'Alas,' I thought to myself, 'these people are still in the barbaric state of regarding a foreigner as an enemy . . . to be driven out with horror.' I began fully to understand the truth that man has no abiding city here below, that he is but a few days' traveller on this earth! . . . Oh, when will come the day when the common Father of the whole human family will enable his children to embrace each other with the warmth of a brotherly salutation, in that immense love which Jesus, his Son, came to communicate to all men.

When the fair opened, they mingled with the crowd, carrying a white handkerchief and with a little red tea-bag tied to their belts (the agreed sign). It was some time before they made contact with their Korean Christian friends: they had been waiting there for over a month.

We couldn't have a very long conversation: Chinese and Koreans were on all sides. . . . The air of mystery which hung over our conversation intrigued the pagans. When they seemed not to be listening . . . we slipped in a few words about our religious affairs, and then at once returned to discussing the sale of our animals. 'How much?' 'Eighty *ligatures*.' 'Too much. Here, take these fifty *ligatures* and let me have your beast.' 'Impossible: you won't get it for less.' That's how we put those who were watching us off the scent.

He was able to take back news to the Bishop in Mongolia that it would still be difficult to harbour a European missionary in Korea, and that many families had withdrawn to the south, where they were less conspicuous, but that converts were still being made.

Early in 1845 Kim again managed to get into Korea, and this time got as far as Seoul, where he bought a house for the use of the Church, encouraged the Christians, and made arrangements in case it proved possible to get a European priest into the country. He returned from Korea by boat—a hazardous journey made with a simple compass: hazardous, not only because the boat was almost sunk in a storm, but because a treaty between China and Korea laid down that any Korean crew touching at the Chinese coast would be sent back to Korea, tried, and executed. Kim managed to get to Woosung, towed by a Chinese ship. There the Chinese wanted to send him back (according to the treaty) to Korea; but he was lucky enough to meet some English sailors, and obtained the protection of the British Consul. The mandarins were impressed with his ability to speak English, and let him go on to Shanghai to get his boat repaired. Here again he made friends with the British; and this helped him against further suspicions from the Chinese officials. Emboldened, Kim took a haughty attitude:

I warned the mandarins not to send anyone else to trouble us . . . and I beat off the Chinese whose curiosity pushed them too far, and I gave the rough end of my tongue to certain subordinates who behaved disrespectfully to me: they were punished by the mandarins. . . . The inhabitants of Shanghai fancy I'm a person of some eminence. The mandarins seeing me talking amicably with the English couldn't understand a word and were longing to find out my secret. One day they sent to ask me when we'd be leaving. I told them 'I must stay on to get my boat ship-shape. What's more, I've heard the great French mandarin, Capt. Cécile, is arriving shortly and I want to stay to see him.' The mandarins are impatiently waiting the day of my departure, because they're afraid of being compromised and of losing face. [8]

On 17 August 1845 André Kim was ordained, the first Korean priest. Eight days later he set off again, but this time accompanied by the Bishop, Ferréol, and another European priest. They tried the sea-route he had experimented with, and once again they had a perilous and nearly fatal crossing. They were blown much further south than they had intended, coasting by the island of Quelpaert (Cheju); but this proved to be providential, for if they had landed near the capital they would certainly have been discovered. The Bishop and Père Daveluy had to be disguised in mourning costume, which covered their more prominent European features.

When they did manage secretly to reach Seoul, they found the church in a bad way. Most families had had one or two of their relatives executed; informers and apostates had been busy, and 'one must frankly admit', wrote the Bishop, 'most of them participated in heathen rites so as not to give themselves away'. In spite of this, nearly two hundred new members were under instruction each year, and the Bishop was anxious to get yet another missionary into the country. They tried the northern route, but failed. So Kim was sent to the coast to see if there was some fishing port through which Père Maistre, the other missionary, could be introduced. Unfortunately he got on the wrong side of some mandarins, probably because of his insistence, as we have seen before, on maintaining rank. They came to his boat, unsuspecting, and asked to have temporary use of it to clear some Chinese junks out of the way. But (wrote Kim),

Korean law forbids using nobles' ships for public duties. Among the people I'd been taken—I don't know why—for a *ian-pan*, or high-ranking noble, and if I'd given up my boat to the mandarin I'd have lost my reputation, which would have done damage to our future expeditions. Anyway Véran [*sc.* his servant] had sketched out for me a line of conduct in such circumstances. So I told the mandarin the boat was for my use and that I couldn't let him have it. The satellites swore at me and went off, carrying my pilot with them.

The upshot was, that they started making inquiries; and finally arrested him. The truth now came out. He was imprisoned, and questioned a number of times; two Christians captured with him broke down under torture and revealed their house in the capital. Kim himself was chained with a wooden collar (the *cagne*) round his neck. Finally he was brought to Seoul for trial. He admitted that he was one of the three Koreans sent out to Macao for training a decade earlier.

When they interrogated me about religion, I spoke long to them about the existence and unity of God, creation, the immortality of the soul, hell, the necessity to worship one's creator, the falsity of pagan religions, etc. When I'd finished, the judges said 'Your religion is good, but so is ours, and that's why we practise it.'—'If that's your opinion,' I said, 'then you ought to leave us to live quietly among ourselves. But so far from that, you persecute us. . . . You admit our religion is good, that it is true—and then you persecute it like an abominable doctrine. You are contradicting yourselves.'

They had found letters and maps in his pack, and now brought them. There were letters he had written, and also some written by the Bishop; and though they could not read a word, they saw that the handwriting was different. They asked who had written them, and Kim replied, in a general way, that they were 'his'. They then brought a pen and told him to write, to see if his handwriting was the same as the Bishop's.

They were using a ruse, so I used one too to defeat them. 'These characters', I said, 'have been written with a metal pen; bring me one, and I'll do what you ask.'—'We have no metal pens.'—'If you haven't, then I can't make characters similar to these.' They brought me a quill pen, and the judge gave it me and said, 'Can't you write with this?'—'It's not the same thing.' I replied; 'however I can show you how with European characters one and the same person can write in different ways.' So, cutting the pen very sharp, I wrote a few lines in tiny letters; then, cutting the nib, I made very big letters. 'You see,' I said; 'these characters are not the same.' That satisfied them.

In spite of the rough treatment they gave him in prison they seem to have been impressed with Kim's abilities. He was given an English world atlas to translate into Korean: he made two copies, in bright colours, for the King; and this was so well appreciated that he was ordered by the minister to compose a small handbook of geography. Bishop Ferréol learned later that he had so won the affections of the judges and the Prime

Minister that they pleaded for his life: 'He has committed a crime worthy of death by leaving the kingdom, but expiated it by returning.' The King, pleased with the atlas, was about to issue a pardon, when he received a letter, delivered by Kim's old friend, Cécile (now a rear-admiral):

By order of the Naval Ministry in France, Rear-Admiral Cécile, commanding the French squadron in China, has come to obtain information about an outrage which took place on the 14th of the 8th moon of the year *Kei-hai* [viz., 21 September 1839]. Three Frenchmen, Imbert, Chastain and Maubert, honoured in their country for their learning and virtue, have been, for reasons unknown, put to death in Korea. In these countries of the East the rear-admiral's duty is to protect the people of his nation, and he has come to find out what is the crime for which these people have deserved such a terrible fate. . . . We believed that Korea was a civilized land. . . .
    Conceding that for the moment your ministers can not promptly reply . . . I am leaving. But next year French ships will come again to get the answer. . . . If after this the Koreans practise a similar tyranny towards any of them, Korea will certainly not be able to escape great disasters. . . .

This settled Kim's fate. Earlier he had written that should death come, he would commend his mother (whom he had not even visited on his first return to Korea, and this time had only seen briefly) to the missionaries' care. Now he was led out to execution. In a loud voice he cried, 'I am at my last hour, so hear me carefully. If I have communicated with foreigners, it is for my religion, for God. It is for him I die. An eternal life is beginning for me. Become Christians, if you wish to be happy · after death, for God reserves eternal punishment for those who have denied him.' When fastened to the stake that was to be his gallows, he was calm. He asked the executioners, 'Is this the most convenient position for you? Can you strike easily here?'— 'No, turn yourself a little. That's better'—'Strike then. I'm ready.' About a dozen soldiers ran round him, each striking his neck. His last message to his fellow-believers had been:

All here below is ordained of God . . . persecution itself does not come without his permission, so bear it patiently and for God. . . . No doubt you will be affected by my death and your souls will be distressed at it; but soon God will give you better pastors than I am. So don't be too sad, and force yourselves with great charity to serve God. . . . Remain one in charity, and after death we shall be united for eternity and we shall enjoy God for ever. I hope it, *mille fois, dix mille fois.*

He was twenty-five. In 1857 Pius XI declared him venerable. There is no doubt that he was consciously a martyr to God. Have we to add, though, that he was unconsciously a martyr to European mercantile interests?

For thirty years more persecutions of Christians in Korea continued, the fiercest being in 1866. Unfortunately the French Government then decided on a punitive expedition, which was ill-led and ended in failure; more unfortunately, it seems certain that native Christians and the surviving missionaries acted as spies and guides to the invading forces.[9] No wonder that the strongest religious sect in nineteenth-century Korea called itself *Tong-hak* ('Religion of the East': in fact, a mixture of Taoism, Confucianism, and Buddhism), by contrast with Christianity which it called 'the religion of the West'. Certainly Christianity never made the dramatic impact on Korea that it made on Japan, still less on China: partly because the Jesuit incorporationist approach had been abandoned, partly because it was—except for the brief, spontaneous beginning—identified with enemy aggression, and never appealed to the literati. In any case, Korea's continued subservience to China until the Sino-Japanese war (1895) meant that the—largely French— missionaries operating from outside, and further impeded by persecution in China itself, were almost unable to identify with Korea. Yet somehow Christianity survived, and gradually became rooted—with the highest percentage of Christians in the population anywhere in Asia except the Philippines. Fifteen years after the severest (1866) persecution, the new king (son of the regent who had ordered the persecution) said in a royal edict:

At the time when King Tjyengtjyong reigned, measures were taken against [the Church's] humble beginnings, and it was not allowed to spread. In very truth, the plant was uprooted and its branches cut off. But, contrary to every expectation, a plant sprang up from under the one which had been cut down. It was destroyed and it came to life more flourishing than before. And during this interval many Christians had been executed and this happened not once or twice but many times.[10]

CHAPTER 9

ANDRÉ LY (1692–1775)
'A Chinese Missionary in Szechwan'

We saw in earlier chapters that the European missionaries were divided in their opinions whether 'native' Christians could or should become priests. The Portuguese in Macao (even the Jesuits there) were sure that Chinese never could do so—'they are inferior, corrupt, proud, vicious'. But the Jesuits in Peking were equally sure that they were as capable as Greeks, Romans, or Europeans of becoming priests; indeed, that they were so urgently needed that the Junior Seminary must be skipped, older men taken, Latin dispensed with, and Chinese used in studies, prayer, and liturgy. Fr. Ricci admitted two Chinese to the Jesuit novitiate as early as 1590—eight years after his arrival; and by the end of the seventeenth century thirty or more Chinese were accepted for Jesuit training. Yet none of them was a priest. This was partly because of doubts in Macao, partly because there was, most of the time, no bishop to ordain them. Yet it should have been easy. In 1613 there was the famous letter to Paul V, which was brought before the Congregation of Rites, presided over by Cardinal Bellarmine: and the momentous Brief from the Pope (27 June 1615) granted permission to the Jesuits to translate the Bible into Chinese, and use Chinese for the Mass, Breviary, and Sacraments. Yet the permission was never used. When it reached China (1617) a persecution had driven European missionaries to Macao; from then till 1660 there was no chance of translating books or training Chinese priests. By the time the Jesuits were able to work again on the mainland and consider the use of the vernacular, opinion had changed in Rome—the decision was reversed not only for the occasion but for 'similes instantiae in posterum'.

In 1664 an international seminary was created in Siam (Thailand), and at last the Pope (Clement X) agreed to allow a Chinese to be consecrated. Lô Wen-Tsao became the first Chinese bishop (usually known as Gregory Lô or Lopez)—though he had to be consecrated at Canton, 1685, by an Italian Vicar Apostolic, for fear of disturbing the Portuguese *padroado**

* See Chapter 10, below.

monopoly. Bishop Lô died six years after his consecration, and had no Chinese successor.

It was in this bleak situation that André Ly started his ministry. By the end of the seventeenth century there were probably 300,000 Christians in China, with some 100 missionaries.[1] A hundred years later, after the suppression of the Jesuits (1773), only 30 missionaries were left, and the number of Christians had dropped to 200,000. Yet in another sense the situation was not so bleak: in spite of persecution and suppression there were some 80 Chinese priests—in Ly's own province of Szechwan alone there were, thirty-five years after his death, 25 Chinese priests, and only 5 non-Chinese.[2]

A member of the French *Société des Missions Étrangères*, Fr. Basset, arrived in Szechwan in 1702. He started to train three selected young Chinese as catechists, with the view to the priesthood. One of these was little André Ly, aged eight. Basset wrote, 'Of our three scholars, the first fell dangerously ill. He is of a mental age of twenty; he's a real little angel. It looks as if God is going to draw him away to the land of the angels.' However, he got better; and Basset was able to write of him the next year, 'Little André, who we thought was going to die soon, is better. He and the other . . . seem still to be of a ready will. They are well worth the trouble we're taking to teach them. I don't believe even in Europe we'd easily find such well disposed children as these two. They seem like two angels at mass.'[3]

For a few years the work went on smoothly in Szechwan, the boys learning Latin, the priests making slow progress. Then, in 1706, disaster arrived. The *Société des Missions Étrangères* had followed a more conservative method than the Jesuits—in fact, as we shall see, André Ly had been brought up in hearty contempt of the policy of Ricci and the others. But even this method was too liberal for the new regime in Rome. The Jesuits had been clear that the 'rites' in honour of family ancestors, and especially those in honour of Confucius, were not 'idolatrous'—were equivalent (in twentieth-century terms) to laying a wreath on the Cenotaph; and that if they were forbidden, no educated Chinese, ambitious for an official career could remain, or become a Christian. On this matter the other missions largely agreed. But now Pope Clement XI sent out an emissary, Mgr. de Tournon, who knew nothing about the Far

East, to study the problem of 'the rites'; and, after his report, Clement forbade Chinese ceremonies as superstitious (1704). The Chinese Emperor, K'ang-hsi, warned the Papal Legate: 'The Europeans can not see deeply enough into the meaning of our books. It is to be feared that the Pope may make a ruling which, founded on false information, will inevitably bring about the ruin of Christianity in my empire.' The Legate refused to accept the Emperor's right to discuss the matter, and the Emperor, not unnaturally, replied by a decree (17 December 1706) that any missionary wishing to remain in China must possess a *piao* (certificate) declaring that (a) the Chinese and Christian God were the same; and (b) the Ceremonies in honour of Confucius and homage to the dead, were not incompatible with Christianity.

Ly was fifteen by the time the news arrived in the north-west of China. The French missionaries had to leave in June, and they took four seminarists with them, Ly being one; two of them took vows of perpetual chastity and of stability in the service of the *Missions Étrangères* before they left. In March 1708 they were all ordered out of Canton, and went to Macao. There the young seminarists were introduced to the Pontifical Legate, Mgr. Maillard de Tournon, and Ly (who would not know how disastrous was de Tournon's advice to the Pope) was particularly impressed, especially by comparison with other priests he had met.

When I was a youth, I happened to meet priests from certain countries of Europe whose arrogance contrasted with the openness of the missionaries who were devoting themselves to my education. Some of them, like the great mandarins, haughty and solemn, let themselves be greeted by their Christians prostrating themselves to the ground. What was our surprise to see a prince of the Church, like the Pontifical Legate, getting up at our approach and receiving our humble greetings with grace.[4]

The behaviour of the 'haughty' priests may have in fact simply reflected the Jesuit method of 'adaptation', by which clergy were, in terms of Chinese etiquette, assimilated to mandarin status. And in another context this happened at Macao too. On 17 August 1709 news was received that Mgr. de Tournon had been made a Cardinal; he thereupon ordered homage to be paid to the Pope on St. Clement's Day.

It is a tradition in China [says Ly], that on the emperor's anniversary the dignitaries of the empire collect their subordinates to the great chamber of their residence, around a table on which the emperor's name shines in gold letters. . . . All kneel and nine times in succession touch the ground with their foreheads. . . . I remember, because I took part in it, that on St. Clement's day Mgr. de Tournon called together all the missionaries . . . Italians, Spaniards, French and Portuguese, and asked them to offer, in the Chinese manner, the same honours to the image of the Sovereign Pontiff. This was a great lesson . . . what honours should be given by creatures to their creator. If such great signs of honour should be offered for mortal things to the national Emperor and to the Vicar of Christ on earth, how much more should be shown to the Creator of all?[5]

Tournon now decided to admit Ly and another student (Tang) to minor orders. When he put the suggestion to the assembled missionaries, they unanimously turned it down, stating (as Ly put it, in his fluent Latin) that 'Sinenses superbi, inconstantes, atque ingrati, sacris ordinibus propterea sunt indigni'.[6] But de Tournon, supported by one missionary (Père de la Baluère), went ahead and ordained them.

After three more years in Macao, followed by various travels, Fr. de la Baluère took his four pupils back to Szechwan, in February 1715—having been away eight years. The Vicar Apostolic, visiting them, described the regime:

The four pupils are excellent at explaining holy Scripture from Latin into Chinese. They read Scripture while we have our meals, each taking his week, and they expound it, from Latin into Chinese. In the morning they study Chinese in the classical books, with a Master who lives with us, and in the afternoon they study logic.[7]

When La Baluère died of pneumonia in September, he left his copy of the works of Cicero to Li and Tang.

The Vicar Apostolic now decided to send the pupils to the distant seminary in Siam, at Ayuthia. It was an international seminary, with 50 scholars (14 from Siam, 24 from Tonkin, 7 from China, and 5 from Cochinchina*). Their education was rigorous: the spirituality taught was based on Scupoli's *Spiritual Combat*, the *Imitation*, St. Augustine's *Confessions* and *Meditations*, letters of St. Jerome, and writings of St. Anselm

* Tonkin is roughly the present North Vietnam, and Cochinchina South Vietnam.

and St. Bernard. The bias was discernibly anti-Jesuit; and Ly himself shows this bias in his *Journal*. When he heard, many years later, of the suppression of the Jesuit order (1773), he was not surprised, and recalled a prophecy made by a Franciscan who,

commenting on the Apocalypse of St. John, was not afraid to suggest this interpretation: . . . that the Antichrist will come forth from the Company of Jesus. And here is the future of this Congregation: for 300 years it will know glory; for 300 years more it will decline into opprobrium; after that it will disappear, because it wanted among its numbers only men remarkable for their physical gifts, their riches, their scholarship, or their nobility. [8]

Ly was ordained priest in the seminary in 1725, when he was thirty-three. He could not immediately go back to Szechwan, because the Italians were there, and so was sent to Fukien province. In 1732 there were renewed edicts against the European missionaries; but this did not prevent them, even when working more or less underground, from continuing long-standing disputes about the demarcation of areas among the different Orders. Ly got back into his beloved province of Szechwan at about this time, working inconspicuously in the mountains away from the centres of persecution. But in 1736 the Vicar Apostolic (Mgr. Mullener) received a letter from Propaganda in Rome, ordering that Szechwan be worked by the Italians. He passed the order on to Ly, who replied in a long and subtle letter which distinguishes two kinds of 'order' from the Sacred Congregation—a decision of the Holy See, which is incontestable, and a 'letter' bearing only the authority of the Cardinal who wrote it; clearly the latest directive was of the latter kind, and therefore arguable. Further,

The Sacred Congregation denies all claims of the Messieurs of the Seminary of the *Missions Etrangères* [to the province of Szechwan]. . . . The word 'claim' can be understood in two ways: (1) kings or princes dispute the possession of a province or the paying of taxes; this is a claim of . . . secular princes, but not of . . . apostolic missionaries. (2) Evangelical workers may argue whether in the country where the first missionaries of such-and-such an order . . . have laid the foundations of a Mission, their successors . . . of the same body may continue the work begun . . . [So] I would like to know whether it is in the first or second sense that the Sacred Congregation denies all claims to . . . the Séminaire de Paris. If it is in the first sense, nothing can be more just: but the Messieurs of the Seminary have never made such claims: that would be the height of madness and rebellion. If it is in the second sense, I find it hard to understand how the Sacred Congregation, while in all the other provinces . . . it authorizes the Dominicans to work in Dominican missions, Jesuits in Jesuit, Franciscans in those of their Franciscan predecessors, refuses to our Messieurs of the . . . Missions Étrangères alone . . . the right to continue the work begun by my Fathers in the Lord . . . in the country where they sowed the seed of the faith.

And finally Ly says: 'I've been told to go. But you don't tell me where I can go; and I haven't received any travel-money for two years: how can I journey without the means?'[9] Fortunately for Ly, after further letters had passed between the *Missions Étrangères* and Rome, the decision was reversed, and he was able to stay on.

Ly started on some of his journeys. His health was not good— since the age of forty he had had an ulcer on his leg; but he managed to visit the scattered Christian communities, which had struggled to keep going, often (e.g. from 1706 to 1711) without a priest, and dependent on a simple catechist. In 1740 the first severe testing came. A mandarin was told by a Buddhist Bonze that a bad drought they were having was due to the Christians. They were all taken to the Prefecture at Pong-shan and tried. The French missionary was beaten; and then Ly was called and questioned. The Prefect said:

'The Christian religion is a bad religion, and forbidden by the authorities, and yet you dare to teach it to others . . . ?'

'Our religion is true,' replied Ly; 'it is not bad; I haven't heard anywhere that it is forbidden, and my family have been Christian for three generations.'

Ly was then beaten, more severely than P. de Martillat, and only spared worse because of his bad leg.

They were able to get away and continue their work. But Christianity was coming under a cloud again; in 1746 an edict ordered Christians to be sought out and banished. In 1749 a Jesuit in another province wrote that the faithful were becoming terrified; and many were saying, 'Let the Europeans withdraw, before enveloping us in their own ruin; we have enough Chinese priests—more than we need—and their presence does not expose us to so much danger';[10] though one Chinese Christian who apostatized said, 'The Europeans have cleared off into exile, but the lashes are for us.' One French missionary (Verthamon) was so unpopular that the local Christians wanted him to leave: he delivered a diatribe to poor Fr. Ly. 'I told him', wrote Verthamon,

that anyone could clear off if he wanted to, and that he himself would do well to clear off; but that for myself, when I no longer have a house in Szechwan, I'll clear off too, and that after that the Christians can look for priests wherever they like; that, finally, I have no desire to be caught if I can help it . . . but that I shan't leave till I judge it appropriate, and not when the Christians want me to; that they are quite mistaken if they think they can push me around. . . .

He added,

I don't know whether my little sermon, which I gave with a good deal of vigour and perhaps with a more military than apostolic tone, drove home, but since that time, M. André [Ly] speaks only of dying for the faith, and not of clearing off. . . . Though I respect M. André, esteem and love him much, and he is an excellent missionary, I shall be inexorable. [i.e. about his rights.][11]

Poor Ly; when this unsympathetic missionary Verthamon—a king's officer before he became a priest, which perhaps explains his tone—had to leave China, and complained to Martillat, the Vicar Apostolic, the latter blamed the Chinese. Ly was very upset; he wrote to Martillat that the Europeans always believed the worst of the Chinese. And later (8 December 1734) he wrote in his Journal that Martillat had received a letter from another European priest saying, 'Quidquid scripserit D. Ly Andreas sacerdos sinensis, nihil eorum credam'; and Ly bitterly commented, 'And so it follows that only Europeans are humble, constant, grateful, and perfect without rules.'[12]

Yet in fact from 1745 Ly was the only priest in Szechwan for four years. They had thought of making an old catechist, Lin Chang, a priest: 'They taught him the canon of the Mass . . . but he never managed to pronounce the letters B and D and some others, so that they had to be content with giving him minor orders.'[13] This was the time when Martillat told him to keep a diary, since letters could not always get through, and he was alone; hence the precious Latin Journal, which is our main source for Chinese Christian history in the latter half of the eighteenth century. The Journal tells us of daily events small and great, and gives a graphic picture of the problems to be faced: 'what penance to be given to a family who have apostatized by leaving the ritual tablets in their house?' (Answer: a year's excommunication.) 'On days of fasting and abstinence, will a Christian commit a fault if he disobeys the rule, so as not to attract the attention of his pagan entourage and be denounced before a judge?' Ly's opinion was: a dispensation should be given. '5 Nov. Gave authority to the subdeacon Venant You to exercise the ministry of baptism without ceremonies, for infants and the dying. . . . Dispensed with the nuptial blessing for a marriage, because of the distance.'[14] In 1753 he wrote two long letters to help his fellow-priests, about missionary work. They are full of sound, common-sense advice.

The apostle who really wants to make himself all things to all men must accommodate himself to their poverty, sobriety and frailness. . . . He must know how, when necessary, to relax his fasts and abstinences (as Mgr. Mullener suggested to me one day) so as not to be a charge on Christians of the poorer class who can't prepare two different meals.

Or—a very practical point for the Chinese:

With regard to Extreme Unction, it is better to omit the anointing of the feet for women. There's nothing they conceal with more care; if, then, you make them unwrap their bandages, you'll shock their modesty and that of the company. . . . In general, avoid letting our liturgical practices lead to jokes or slander, which has often happened. Here is a typical example. In the town of Kan-Cheou (province of Kiangsi) a Christian was dying. . . . The missionary of the community . . . had himself brought there, according to the practice of the time, in great state, carried in a chair. An inquisitive neighbour wanted to find out what extraordinary affair was going on. Through the shutters, he saw the anointing of the eyes of the sick man with holy oil, and he spread the news, which was accepted everywhere and passed on, that the Europeans tear out the eyes of the dying for their spells.[15]

He even makes a fairly radical suggestion about marriage. Because of the vagabondage of the husbands an imperial law was passed that if after three to four years' absence the husbands don't return, the woman may, after a guarantee given by parents of both parties to the mandarin, marry again. What of the Christian woman? She can't, by law, live on her parents, except for a brief period. 'Very few are those women who are strong enough, by God's special grace, to live honourably in the absence of their husbands; so when they run out of money for food or clothes, they become prostitutes—or, worse, hang or poison themselves.' It would be preferable, he suggests, for the Church to fix a time at which they might marry again.[16]

Ly not only showed himself a sensible and flexible moralist— unusual for his time, and especially in the indigenous priest-hood, which tended to a rather wooden rigorism; he was the first Chinese priest to start his own seminary. He describes, amusingly, in his Journal how he came to plan this.

This afternoon a Christian from Kiang-si . . . came to see me. In the course of conversation he quoted the case of a young Chinese Jesuit priest . . . baptised at thirty who, after practising medicine, acted as a catechist and, a few years after, was promoted to the priesthood. I was surprised; and it reminded me of the case of a European priest, so ignorant that he could not answer any of the questions put to him by the bishop. The latter indignantly exclaimed 'Who is the fool who ordained you?' 'But,' replied the dunce, naïvely, 'none other than your Lordship.'[17]

The name, catechist, had become an object of derision among pagans and Christians alike; so he was determined to train priests. He was determined to keep Latin, not only because a concession on this point would bring the contempt of the Euro-pean priests, but also because,

How can a Chinese priest, ignorant of Latin, go to the sources of Christian truth, that is, to Holy Scripture, to the Letters of the Apostles, the writings of the Fathers, the decisions of the Church? . . . This is specially important in times of persecution like ours, when this priest, isolated and perhaps all alone, far from his Bishop, will be deprived of contact, sometimes for years, with the European priests from whom he could get advice?[18]

And so he started a little *école presbytérale*. He had many dis-appointments; one of his most promising pupils he decided to send out to his old seminary in Siam—but the lad was drowned in a shipwreck on the way (1756). However, towards the end of his life (in 1764 when he was seventy-two) he retired to a solitary hut in the mountains round Chengtu, and there was really able to teach the twelve boys he accepted—of whom at least four were later ordained.

The Journal shows the results of constant persecutions on the local Christians.

25 June 1754. The Christian cemetery in Chengtu lies waste. The tombstones have been taken away, the graves are in ruins. . . . The Christians not only don't get buried here any longer, but for three years haven't even dared to come there.[19]

15 December 1747. Reconciliation of apostates. Penance: abstinence from wine three days a week, and fast every Friday till Easter. The two guilty ones have asked pardon on their knees, in public and with tears. . . . I trust that my Lord Jesus, who has called them to penitence, will inspire and uphold them in this penitence.[20]

23 April 1748. Alas, the external calamities that fall on us are less grievous than the internal ills which we suffer. Not only do the Christians far away not send to look for me, but they aren't even disposed to receive me when I come to bring them the . . . sacraments. . . . Some continue publicly in their apostasy; others abandon themselves to drunkenness, to lust, to play. . . .

If I write these lines, it is not, certainly, to accuse these poor people: but to show the reader the ravages which persecution has wrought* among the Christian people, since the best and strongest of them totter.[21]

In April 1752 he wrote a letter to the Bishop of Shensi, which he fortunately also transcribed in his Journal:

Looking carefully . . . and trying to see why Christian preaching has in a hundred years thrown down so few roots in souls, I think I can see two reasons.

First, mistaken methods. Instead of imitating the Apostles and founders of the Church, who . . . founded it in suffering and tears, too many of these missionaries have sacrificed more than was reasonable to human prudence and to external success. . . .

Second reason, related to the first: the profound ignorance of religious truths. They have produced deists rather than Christians: it is not unusual to find men who have been baptised for years, or even in infancy, who would be incapable of saying what is the difference between the Christian religion and idolatry. . . . The result is: frequent apostasies and a lamentable corruption of morals.[22]

It is significant that in February 1749 he had a discussion with another Chinese priest, Stephen Siu, about absolving apostates. Stephen had privately absolved a doctor, and claimed that this was allowed since absolution used to be given not in the Church

---

* 'quantam stragam fecerit . . . persequutio'.

or sacristy but in the confessional (*cubiculum*) and *quasi secreto*. André Ly was firm: 'Publica publice et secreta secrete punienda jubet morale principium' (i.e. since apostates deny the faith before the Prefect they must be publicly reconciled).[23] In 1747 he was much occupied with literary work. Characteristically, he revised a three-volume book of Meditations on the Gospel, composed by a Jesuit in 1620, but now needing to be completely rewritten to conform to the Pope's edict about the Chinese rites; he also composed a catechism on the sacraments for beginners, replacing the 'elements' published by Mgr. Mullener, which disappeared in the 1746 persecution; collected into one work all the prayer formulas translated from Latin into Chinese by Fr. Basset, Martillat, or himself. In the following years he produced, in Chinese, the Ritual for baptism; a catechism on the Eucharist and Extreme Unction; and a treatise on the Seven Deadly Sins. In 1753, held up by bad weather, he occupied himself by translating hymns, antiphons, and other liturgical texts. 'I found it difficult, because of the difficulty of reducing Latin metre to the rules of Chinese poetry. Where it was impossible, I had to be content with giving the general sense, rather than sacrificing the exactness of the text to the elegance of the version.' He wrote a critical study of Chinese 'superstitions'; offered to translate a work of moral theology for seminarians; and in 1762 (aged seventy) in twenty days he wrote a *Mirror of the Virtues of good Servants* for domestics.

His Journal reveals occasional human touches. In August 1751 he writes, complaining of the shortage of *tabachi pulverizati*,* which was valuable as currency; and adds that he unfortunately picked up the habit long ago and now finds it difficult to give up:

About the use of *tabachi*, and other such vices, I say: 'The heart unlearns late what early it learns.' Would that our Chinese scholastics, while yet spending their time in the Seminary in Siam, might grasp the meaning of that proverb, and so be content to withdraw themselves from every kind of vice.[24]

And on 5 August 1753, writing to Headquarters, he suddenly lapses from his usual elegant Latin into bad French: he wants to express his extreme gratitude to a M. La Cerre, because the

---

* Is this tobacco, or snuff? The French for snuff is *tabac en poudre*, so perhaps it is the latter.

six 'botles' of wine sent to him (André Ly) this year has 'dissipé tout l'éructation, qui régnoit autrefois dans ma stomach presque cinq ans. . . . Voyez donc, cher Monsieur, que un chinois parler et écrit le françois comme un petit enfant de France.'*25

After a long period of isolation Ly was delighted to learn that a European priest was being sent out to join him. Fr. Lefebvre arrived in April 1754. Alas, their companionship was short-lived. In June they were both arrested and brought before the 'Viceroy'. During the interrogation the mandarin asked Ly to name the Christians in his area; Ly was silent. Then the mandarin said

'You're over sixty, and educated, and yet you're without rank or position. As you see, we are mighty in the Empire: we have honours and degrees; so you must conclude that all your religion promises you is vain and unreasonable.'

'The Christian religion', replied Ly, 'does not promise a passing and earthly happiness, but eternal blessedness to all those who worship the true God. . . . Among men, to disown our parents is a great crime. Isn't it an even more horrible crime to deny my God to escape torture? If I denied God whom I love with all my heart and soul, I should have to suffer torture far more atrocious than those you want to inflict on me. . . .'

The interrogation (we have Fr. Lefebvre's account of it) continued till nightfall; and the next day they were brought out again. This time there was an intriguing passage of arms between Ly and the mandarin. The latter accused Christianity of undermining filial piety, and said

I've read that your religion teaches that children must be, in regard to their parents, as bricks in regard to their moulds. But once a brick has been made, does it depend on its mould any more? Of course not. Where, then, according to your religion is the holy and necessary submission of children towards their parents?

Ly spotted that the mandarin was quoting a book by Fr. Adam Schall, the famous Jesuit mathematician and astronomer; and he pointed out that Schall, on the contrary, had been using the analogy of brick and mould to establish the Chinese thesis:

* 'got rid of the indigestion which I've had in my stomach for nearly five years. . . . Behold, Monsieur, a Chinese speaking and writing French like a small French child.'

'Piety and submission of children towards their parents, Fr. Schall had argued, belong to natural law, since God uses parents to give birth to their children as the labourer uses a mould to make a brick.' This passage of arms is revealing since it shows that even at this late date the works of the Jesuit apologists *were* being read by the Chinese literati. In the end Fr. Ly got off with forty strokes, and then was freed; but Fr. Lefebvre was ordered out of the country, and once more Ly was on his own.[26] 'Poor Mission of Szechwan,' he declared 'so brutally and, in a twinkling of an eye, deprived of a worker of such worth! . . . When I remained alone . . . solitary like a sparrow upon the roof-top, I could only groan at my sad condition and that of all the province.' However, two years later yet another missionary was sent, a Fr. Pottier. He arrived in April 1756, and never left. At first he was horrified with what he saw. A Christian woman, for instance, had let her daughter marry a pagan without a dispensation. ' "Is not this," asked the shocked Fr. Pottier, "to encourage them to despise the precepts of the Church? . . . If they commit a mortal sin and a sacrilege, it seems to me that the priest who absolves them makes himself an accomplice in this sacrilege".' Fr. Ly replied gently to this direct accusation:

'You are right in principle; and as far as I can I apply this rule. But here I am, in the midst of Christians who for fifteen years or more haven't seen a priest. And even those priests who have visited them in those distant days were content to have them taught by catechists. Can we be astonished that poor women don't know the teaching, while men and even catechists continually violate not merely the commandments of the Church but even the commandments of God. It seems to me excessive to accuse a priest of mortal sin when in these circumstances he prefers to leave these poor Christians provisionally in ignorance, rather than take on himself in an excess of zeal to overwhelm the feeble. Christian charity and prudence seem to demand a method of patience and progressive instruction.'[27]

After a little time Fr. Pottier came round to Ly's point of view. Soon, however, more trouble was in store. In 1760 Fr. Pottier was arrested and after imprisonment and torture was sentenced to exile. He managed to bribe the guards on the way, and slipped back to take refuge with Fr. Ly. The latter, however, was himself threatened. At the funeral of one of his flock, several neighbours who were non-Christians noticed that the rites had not been observed. Questioned by the mandarin, the parents said they had used the ceremonies taught them by Fr. Ly. In June 1761 Ly's house was raided; he was away, but decided to give himself up. He was imprisoned for two months.

It was then that my right hand, rubbed and wounded by the iron rust on the chains, swelled, and the wound festered so badly that for a month pus ran out and gave an unbearable stench. My right foot, too, already damaged by the march, got in such a bad state, because of the muddy water and sand which got into the wound, that all the remedies used to heal it were this time useless: the swelling persisted and the pain was very violent.

The old priest was nearly seventy then. He was twice brought before the mandarin, who again (in vain) tried to get the names of his converts out of him, using various threats. But in the end, in view of his age and infirmity, condemned him to seventy days in the pillory, after which he was to receive forty strokes. However in view of a national celebration for the Emperor's mother he was let off.

Twice more, in the next two years, he was arrested and questioned, and Fr. Pottier had to withdraw into hiding in another province. However, from 1764 things became more peaceful, Fr. Pottier was able to return to Szechwan, and Ly started his little seminary up in the mountains not far from Chengtu. It was shortly before this that a suggestion was made to Paris (1762) that Ly should be consecrated bishop, and made Vicar Apostolic. Père Khervé, the man named for the task, wrote:

André Ly would perform this function better than I. This venerable priest is, as everyone admits, the soul and pillar of the Mission. The action of crowning his long labours would re-animate the almost extinct faith of the Christians of Szechwan, would give the greatest hopes to our students, would retain some of our new priests who are thinking of leaving us to become Dominicans, and would make it easier to find young boys for our college. . . . In any case, as he is very advanced in age . . . this would be the marshall's baton *in articulo mortis*.[28]

Nothing came of the suggestion and Ly himself never heard about it. But he was by no means on his death-bed yet. True, the next year he closed his Journal (30 December 1763) with the words,

My superiors can no longer expect much of an old man of 75, exhausted by ordeals, sorrows and sickness. I feel my feeble body is near its end, unless God wishes to preserve me for exercising patience. . . . It remains only for me to ask my readers to pray for me, poor dying sinner, useless labourer, so that till my last breath I may persevere in the love of God, of Jesus Christ and of the blessed Virgin Mary. . . . *Hic finis mei cursûs, haec oratio, hoc votum meum aeternum.*[29]

But in fact he had another ten years to go, looking after the youngsters at the little seminary. In 1769 Fr. Pottier was named Vicar Apostolic, and went to the seminary to make his retreat before his consecration. Alas, even this was disturbed, for mandarins and soldiers came to arrest him, and he (Pottier) had to escape, and receive consecration in Shensi province. Ly himself retired still further into the interior, and from here he wrote his last letter four months before his death. It is a letter full of gratitude for what his Superiors and the Society have done for him; it is gloomy about the present state of affairs— the civil war between Chinese and Tibetans not far away, violent storms and floods, 'the high cost of living', persecution constantly breaking out afresh:

In these ordeals within and without, I can only cry out with our holy Mother the Church: 'Da pacem, Domine, in diebus nostris, quia non est alius qui pugnet pro nobis, nisi tu Deus noster. . . .

For myself, since the beginning of this year, the infirmities and pains of old age have been weighing so heavily upon me that I feel myself very near my end. That is why, most reverend sir, I beg of you to intercede for me that God who is so merciful may give me the grace of final perseverence in His divine service. . . . The very humble, and henceforth useless servant—André Ly, Chinese priest, unworthy apostolic missionary.

He died quietly on 23 January 1775, surrounded by the respect-ful care of his Christian people, and his colleague (another Chinese priest), at Chuang-mong-se. Years before he had dreaded that he might find himself *'in articulo mortis,* as a punishment for my unfaithfulness, deprived of the sacraments of the Church, of the help of a priest, and of all consolations.'[30] This, at least, he was spared. He had worked in an immense province, with Christians scattered among the pagans often thirty days' march away, often as a single priest trying to cope with some eight thousand adherents. As Fr. Launay, who edited his Journal, said of him:

If his [Latin] style is hardly Ciceronian, at least it has two dominant qualities: clarity and correctness—to which one can often add, a certain elegance. . . .

This priest, deprived of all authority except that which came from his own talents, virtues and labours, had almost no resources in men or money. His perseverance, energy, zeal and piety shone all the more brightly in the loneliness and penury in which he lived; yet his skill in managing men and in organisation had few opportunities to display themselves. But, through the advice which he gave to one or two Chinese priests, to catechists, and to the Christians, through the moral problems which he posed and those which he settled, one can read between the lines the general direction which he was able to give to an entire mission-field.[31]

Père Olichon wrote in 1933 that 'his tomb can still be found in the old region of "Chouang-Mong-Tsé", about 60 kilometres from Chengtu'.[32] One wonders whether the Red Guards have by now removed the last visible memorial of one of the most remarkable, if least spectacular, Chinese Christians of the eighteenth century.

CHAPTER 10 | **JOSEPH VAZ** (1651–1711)
'Apostle of Ceylon'

From China we move south-westwards, and back a little in time, to Goa. Indian Catholic converts had from the earliest days paid their teachers the compliment of adopting Portuguese names. (Archbishop Roberts, S.J., sometime Archbishop of Bombay, has said that as recently as in the early 1960s members of Congress have said to him, referring to one of his Indian priests or bishops, 'I don't regard him as an Indian'—simply because, like the present Cardinal Archbishop of Bombay, they had Portuguese names, though now of the purest Indian blood.) So a Brahmin family of Salcete (Goa), being Christians of several generations, had taken the name Vaz (Vaas, or Vas).

The father spoke Portuguese and Konkani (a dialect of Marathi). Though the family had become Christians in the sixteenth century, they still preserved certain rural customs: and so the mother went back to her people for her confinements. A third child was born to them in 1651, at Benaulim, and baptized Joseph by a Jesuit there. In his teens this lad offered himself for the priesthood, and was sent to the Jesuit University of St. Paul at Goa, and then to a Dominican Academy. He spent six years there, and finally was ordained priest in 1676, by the Archbishop of Goa; but as he was only given a licence to preach and hear confessions, but no ecclesiastical charge, he returned to his home village of Sancoale.

About this time a canon of Goa Cathedral brought news which caught Vaz's attention. The Canon had been on a voyage from Macao to Goa, and on the way the boat had called at Colombo, in Ceylon. Some Christians of Ceylon, hearing there was a priest on board, had secretly visited him, and told him their plight. There were many Catholics in Ceylon, but not a single priest. The Portuguese had been the first to preach Christianity in the island, since 1518; there had even been a grandson of a Sinhalese king, Prince Dharmapala, who had become Christian, had been crowned king in Lisbon, and reigned as a Catholic monarch from 1542 to 1597. But when the Dutch drove out the Portuguese, in 1658, they had proscribed Catholicism. The King of Portugal was patron of all Indian Missions, and Ceylon came under the *padroado* regime by which Portugal had the monopoly of preaching; but the Portuguese had now written off Ceylon. The only hope was for a religious Order to take on the fresh evangelization of the island; but any European religious Order entering Ceylon would at once be recognized, and unfortunately no Orders were open to Indians who alone might get in without being observed. Vaz went to the Cathedral Chapter of Goa, and offered himself for Ceylon. They accepted his offer—but not to go to Ceylon: he was to go to Kanara, in South India, as 'Vicar Forane'* for the Archbishop of Goa. Vaz was disappointed, but at least Kanara was on the way to Ceylon, so he accepted.

He set off in 1681. Kanara (in the Deccan, now known as

* A priest appointed by the bishop to exercise his jurisdiction in a limited area—a town, or district.

South Kanara) had been also neglected by the Church, owing to Dutch depredations: there were said to be some six thousand Catholics in 1658, and only one priest. But there was a worse problem than shortage of clergy and preaching to non-Christians: there was the division within the Church itself.

In 1622 the Sacred Congregation De Propaganda Fidei took over the administration of those missionary areas where the Portuguese were failing to keep the terms of their original acceptance of patronage (*padroado*) from the Holy See. Since Portugal was neglecting missionary work in South India, Propaganda appointed a Konkani Brahman of Goa (Matthias de Castro) as Bishop and Vicar Apostolic of Bijapur in 1637. The Portuguese authorities in Goa resented this intrusion on their preserve, and the King of Portugal issued two royal edicts in 1642 and 1652 forbidding officers, ecclesiastical or civil, to recognize any missionary sent by Propaganda or any injunctions, even from the Pope, without the royal signature. So when a second Goan priest, Thomas de Castro, was consecrated Vicar Apostolic of Kanara, by order of Propaganda, Goa refused to acknowledge him, and told the Catholics of Kanara not to receive the sacraments at the hands of his priests. Castro was supported by Rome—and, more usefully, by the local Indian state authority, the Queen of Kanara—and stood firm. When Fr. Vaz offered himself as a missionary, the Goanese thought this a good opportunity to send him, in order to show that they, the Portuguese, were fulfilling their undertaking to do missionary work, and so could justly claim to be the lawful authorities there and continue to defy the Propaganda representatives.

Unfortunately for them they had misjudged their man. Fr. Vaz, being an Indian of pure blood, was more interested in taking the gospel to his fellow-countrymen than in upholding divisions within the Roman Catholic Church. When he arrived at Kanara he saw that 'although the Archbishop [of Goa] had loudly claimed jurisdiction over these people, he had not sent enough priests to minister to them,' and as a result they were spiritually destitute. There were unblessed marriages, unbaptized children. In one town where there was a large Catholic population, the faithful had ignored the Archbishop of Goa's pastoral, and had made their Easter Duties and received sacraments at the hands of the Propaganda priests, since there were no others. Vaz decided to accept this situation. But what was to happen about marriages? Those who had married recently in the presence of one of the Vicar Apostolic's missionaries, when they actually came under the jurisdiction of Goa, had contracted invalid marriages: for they had known that he, Vaz, was on the way from Goa, and they could have waited till he arrived. In that case they were living in sin, and it was his duty to denounce them! On the other hand, as he wrote to his superiors,

If they were really under the jurisdiction of the Vicar Apostolic, he [Vaz] would be doing them a grave injustice by compelling them to remarry in his presence. . . . To refer the matter to Goa and await a decision would mean long delay and it would cause grave scandal as the people were already highly shocked by the situation. Men were asking whether the Church was really one, since one set of priests denounced what the other set did. He must therefore settle the matter according to his own conscience.

He went to visit the Vicar Apostolic in the capital, Mangalore, and he, Thomas de Castro,

. . . showed me the original of that brief [from Propaganda] that gave him jurisdiction in which, besides other places, this land of Kanar and the port of Mangalore are named. He also showed me a letter of our late Vicar General [*sc.* the Goanese], stating that the copy of the brief sent to him was referred to the Chapter of Goa and that the question of jurisdiction would soon be settled. Seeing these documents I was in doubt. Though for the peace of my own conscience it is enough that you sent me here as your Vicar . . . yet in order to secure the effect of the sacraments and for mutal peace, I begged his Lordship the Vicar Apostolic to delegate his jurisdiction to me conditionally, in case it was really his, promising in the meantime to report the matter to you . . . and begging him to withold excommunications. The proposal seemed good to him, and he granted my request.

All this was in a letter Fr. Vaz sent in 1681 (14 September). It should have been enough to placate a Caligula, but the new Archbishop of Goa (Manoel de Souza de Menezes) was furious with Vaz for having, by implication, acknowledged the Vicar Apostolic's jurisdiction. He would have recalled him, but he received reports of his zeal and holiness, so left him there, but sent two other priests to back him up and strengthen his position as representing the true authority. Poor Vaz was distressed at the continued dissension that this meant; but fortunately the new Archbishop died three years later, and Vaz was able to leave Kanara.

He was still determined to get to Ceylon, so he collected, back in Goa, three Indian priests who had already started to form a religious community. As the existing Orders were closed to indigenous priests, this was his only hope. He joined them in 1685, and was chosen Superior at once. They based themselves on the Oratorian rule of St. Philip Neri.

After six months he proposed a missionary visit again to Kanara. In his own mind this was to be the first stage on his venture to Ceylon, but he did not tell the others yet, for everything had to be kept highly secret. He took one priest, one lay brother, and his servant, John, leaving an Acting Superior in charge of the Community in Goa. For nine months he exercised a roving pastoral ministry, before breaking to his companions the news that he was aiming at reaching Ceylon. The other two members of this Indian Oratory left him when they heard his ambitious—and terrifying—plan, and only his servant, John, remained with him. So Vaz and John went further south, to Travancore, and there were able to consult the Jesuits. The latter knew a good deal about Ceylon, and still more about the hostility of the Dutch, who had destroyed their colleges in Cochin, Qukon, Cranganore, and Maganapatam. They told Vaz that his only hope was to go in disguise: he must abandon his priestly clothes and go dressed as a coolie. So Vaz went to Tuticorin in March 1687. He hid with the Jesuits there during Lent; but was foolish enough to conduct Holy Week services. The Dutch thus got to know that the man dressed as a coolie was a priest; the Dutch officer guessed that he was trying to smuggle himself into Ceylon; and so he ordered that no vessel was to take any passenger to Ceylon without his permission. All seemed to be lost—till the official died, only a few days later; and his successor, not knowing the reason for the order, made no difficulties when two 'journeymen labourers' applied for permission to sail to Jaffna to earn an honest living there.

*   *   *

Fr. Vaz, with his faithful servant, John, embarked in April 1687. They had no luggage, and had to hide the mass vessels and altar stone in their clothes. The crossing normally took three or four days, but a bad storm kept them at sea for twenty. They were put off at Mannar on the west coast of Ceylon, and lived there as beggars for several days. Then they sailed on to Jaffna in another boat, and this helped their concealment, as, arriving from another part of the island they were not examined too closely. They found an old shed, and lived for a time by begging their food. Unfortunately they developed dysentery, which was a dreaded disease, and they were made to leave the hut. John nursed Vaz till he himself got dysentery too, and a friendly woman brought them food.

Even this unhappy beginning, however, turned out to their advantage; for strangers were often interrogated, but by now the two were accepted as beggars. Vaz, too, later reflected that this gave him an insight into the condition of the really poor which he might not have got otherwise. As soon as they were well enough to move around, they set out to find out who were Catholics. This had to be done circumspectly. Vaz started wearing his rosary openly and observing people's reactions. Some abused him, but in some cases the sight resulted in good treatment; so then he started, more boldly, to make the sign of the cross. Finally at one home he asked whether there was a Catholic priest in the town; on being told that, alas, there had been no priest in Jaffna for many years, Vaz asked whether they would like a priest. 'Alas, I am unworthy of so great a blessing', said the head of the house. Vaz left, but the man suspected what he was, sought him out, along with another highly respected citizen, who was also a Catholic; and, he and John being taken into the house, they had a mass for the first time since 1658, nearly thirty years before.

But they still had to be wary. Not only might the Dutch find them, but lapsed Catholics might be tempted to betray them. So they were taken to a small village (Sillalai) which was one hundred per cent Catholic. This was rare on the island. The Dutch had been thorough in their attempt to remove traces of Catholicism. A Dutch Reformed Minister (Philip Baldaeus) had accompanied the invading armies, and had set to work to 'introduce the Reformed Religion'. Churches were turned into preaching halls, schools into centres for proselytizing; and the children were made to learn by heart refutations of 'Popish errors concerning Purgatory, the Mass, Indulgences, Auricular Confession, etc.' This was about the extent of the education given at this stage by the Dutch; for, as one of them (John Maetsuyker) said in 1662, 'In my opinion reading and writing are things not so absolutely necessary for the edification of these poor wretches, as that they be instructed in the fundamentals of religion, which consist in a few points. For if we pretend to propagate Christianity by reading and writing, I am afraid it will prove both tedious and chargeable to the Company.'[*][1] It was fairly easy to isolate the Portuguese descendants, although it was admitted that they remained as a class 'firm and resolute' in their faith, 'So that the Dutch subjected them, on the plea of their being Roman Catholics, to social degradation, excluded them from every office of emolument, and effectually shut them out from every pursuit of industry or path of distinction.'[2]

In the country, however, this imposition of Protestantism was less easy. The Jesuits had instituted lay catechists in every Catholic village to read prayers, baptize the young, and protect the morals of the community. They were known as *Muppu* (i.e. in Tamil and Sinhalese, 'elder'; the Portuguese *Mordomo*), and the system survived the expulsion of the priests. The Muppu of Sillalai housed Vaz and John, built Vaz a chapel-cum-priest's room, and used the inner verandah as a Church. Fr. Vaz, during his stay here, began to acquire a reputation for holiness. 'He was known to be a Brahman, and in Jaffna, more perhaps than in any other part of Ceylon, a Brahman was held in the utmost veneration, and . . . a person who never allowed others to forget . . . his superiority over other mortals, and treated them with hauteur.' But here was a Brahman who showed real humility and treated others with deference. As a result even the non-Christians in the area regarded him as a *sannyasi* (holy man).

But after some time the secret was betrayed. Hendrick Adriaan van Rheede was the Dutch Administrator in Jaffna, and had formerly bemoaned that 'many were imbued with the blind superstition of Popery through the emissaries of Portuguese priests from the Coast of Choromandel.' Van Rheede, hearing that a 'Jesuit' (as he thought) was secretly ministering in Jaffna, got a 'tip-off' where Vaz would say one of his three masses at Christmas. The officers swooped on the house, and arrested the whole congregation—but failed to find the priest.

* i.e., the Dutch East India Company.

Eight were kept as ringleaders; one died in a few days as a result of flogging, four more died before the end of the year, and the rest soon after that; but none denied their faith.

Vaz spent two years in Jaffna, and then, having made sure that the people there were firm in their belief, he set off for Ceylon proper. He landed at Puttalam, in the domain of the King of Kandy, in 1690. The Dutch had not been able to persecute the Catholics here, as they were subjects of the King of Kandy; and Vaz found some thousand Catholics at Puttalam—though they had had no priests for even longer than Mannar or Jaffna: for fifty years. Yet they had kept their Faith securely. At first Vaz ministered openly to the Catholics in a district of Puttalam. Many were Catholic emigrants who had fled from Dutch persecution. 'They had no churches, and most of them lived scattered among the non-Christian inhabitants, often unmindful of their religion.'[3] And a seventeenth-century English observer said that, 'Although there be Protestants and Papists, yet here are no differences kept up among them, and they are as good friends, as if there were no such parties. And there is no other distinction of religion there, but only Heathens and Christians: and we usually say, we Christians.'[4] This was an unconscious and unprincipled ecumenism which a Roman Catholic priest of the seventeenth century could hardly leave undisturbed.

The greater number of Catholics, however, were in Kandy itself, so after a time Vaz determined to move on there. The King of Kandy,* though not a Christian, had been influenced by and respected them, but he also disliked foreigners. As an Indian Vaz should have been acceptable, but as coming from Goa he might be suspect. So he set out, with a Portuguese descendent (Antonio Sottomayor) in August 1691. Sottomayor was returning to Kandy with a bullock cart containing cloth, salt, and salt-fish; when they got to his house, outside the town walls, Vaz stayed, while Sottomayor went on to try to obtain permission for the priest to enter. Unfortunately a relative of his, who had become a Protestant, discovered this, and told the King that a Portuguese spy, disguised as a priest, was trying to get into Kandy.

* Vimaladharma Sūrya II, grandson of a Christian mother (Dona Catherina, Queen of Kandy, 1594–1612); his father had been tutored by a Franciscan.

So Vaz, John, and Sottomayor were arrested and gaoled. However, after observation it seemed that they were not behaving like spies. Vaz was first released to 'simple detention'. He could not yet travel round and minister to people, so he filled in time by learning Sinhalese (he already spoke Portuguese and Tamil, in addition to his own language of Marathi). Finally he was able to say mass, for the first time since he left Puttalam four months before, on Christmas night, 1691.

After a time he began to be able to move around freely, and with the positive consent of the King, who even let him visit Dutch towns outside his territory. He had to go disguised— usually as a beggar—because of the hostility not only of the Dutch but also of the Buddhists.

It is a curious fact of Sinhalese history that the Dutch administration was much more favourable to Buddhists than to Roman Catholics. The Reformed predikants, it is true, were anxious to evangelize, and ready, if necessary to force the Buddhists to accept Christianity by law; but the Dutch East India Company was more concerned about trade, and more than once assisted the Buddhists. For instance,

The succession of their [Buddhists'] *upasampadā* ordination had been broken, for the third time, in the reign of Rajasimha [the present King's father] and ordained priests from Arakan were obtained in 1697 through the good offices of the Dutch Company, to restore the continuity of ordained monks in Ceylon. Thirty-three Sinhalese monks were duly ordained, and 120 were made *sāmanēras* to keep up the sequence uninterrupted.[5]

There was then something of a revival of Buddhism, and in this strength they begged the King of Kandy to expel Catholic priests from his realm.

By this time Vaz had been joined by two other priests of his Indian Oratory—and, after much intricate negotiation with Rome, the Order had been given temporary approval, and Vaz had even been made Vicar General in Ceylon. The King was embarrassed by the Buddhists' request, for he could not defy the dominant religious body in the island—and, indeed, as the Buddhists pointed out, his own Christian predecessors had ended up unhappily.* So he ordered one of the priests to leave

* Yamasimha was baptized 'Don Philip', and proclaimed King of Kandy; but lost his life and his throne. His son, Don João, also proclaimed King, had to flee, and afterwards went to Portugal, dying in Lisbon.

the city; but he made no reference to Vaz, whom he admired. Indeed, soon after, he assured Vaz that he was free to stay in Kandy, travel as he wished, and even build a new church. And in 1701 he even asked Vaz to translate a medical work from Portuguese into Sinhalese.

One of the reasons for the respect in which he was held was his work during a smallpox epidemic in 1697. Vaz found many, especially slaves and beggars, abandoned in the woods by their masters. Remembering his own time at Jaffna, he erected round huts for them, brought them medicine and food, himself washed them and tended their sores, and organized the local Catholics into a team for rescue. Some enemies hinted that this was done for the wrong motives. One even went to the King, and said that the Catholics loved funerals because they brought them gain. The King rebuked him. But others then said that the disease was a punishment on the Catholics: and tried to prove it by showing that smallpox attacked Catholics more than others, since more Catholics than non-Catholics were seen being buried. The King asked whether these were baptized before or after they got the disease. 'During the disease', they said, thinking that this was what the King specially objected to. But he replied, with logic: 'In that case you must not say that more Catholics died of small-pox than others, but that many small-pox victims died Catholics, which is quite a different thing.' At least one Buddhist source, on the other hand, describes the epidemic, and singles out Vaz for high praise.[6]

Even when the work became more settled, his problems were not over. Indeed, he was afraid that too much recognition might do harm. Rome became interested in his work, and the papal Legate, Charles Thomas Maillard de Tournon (whom we have seen in Macao*) was told to look into Vaz's work in Ceylon. He told an Indian priest of the Pope's interest, and praise for his virtues; 'he also' the priest wrote to Vaz, 'desires to confer on you full jurisdiction to absolve from all cases reserved to the Apostolic See, and inquires whether you have received that faculty from any Bishop or Archbishop, on which Bishop your mission depends, since, as yours is a new mission, begun by you independently of others, it depends on His Holiness.' Vaz was scared to hear this; it implied that Ceylon would become a Vicariate Apostolic (like Kanara), and he

* See pp. 116–18.

knew what trouble that brought in lands formerly subject to the Portuguese *padroado*. So he managed to evade that issue.

More serious was a problem which came up, not unlike that of the Chinese rites. In Kandy many of the lands inhabited and cultivated by the people, belonged to the temples, and the owners were therefore liable to some service, often trifling, to the temple. Were these equivalent to participating in heathen rites? Yet if not rendered, the holders of lands would be turned off. Vaz wrote to a Jesuit in Pondicherry, who consulted de Tournon. The latter, not surprisingly in view of his reputation in these matters, replied: 'Bearing in mind many of the decisions of the Apostolic See . . . condemning such practices, as it is not licit for us to take even a remote part in the pagan cult of idols because it is intrinsically evil . . . I am constrained to give my opinion that it will be better if your Paternity does not permit such things in the future.'[7] Yet de Tournon was proved mistaken when he similarly pronounced against the 'Malabar Rites'. Fr. Vaz's own influence was in a more eirenic direction.

Indeed, a historian of Ceylon, not a Roman Catholic, describes the Catholicism on the island in the eighteenth century—largely as a result of Vaz's work—thus:

Evidence [for the strength of the Church] . . . is in the munificence with which the natives contribute habitually to its support. . . . It is due, likewise, to its priesthood to declare that, whatever may be their individual feelings towards Protestantism and its agents, they have carried on their operations in Ceylon with an absence of active jealousy, and an abstinence from any direct interference with the ministrations of the clergy of other denominations.[8]

So perhaps after all the casual ecumenism (which some might call indifferentism) mentioned above bore fruit of a sort. The chief reason for the persecution of Catholic by Protestant had, after all, been political. The Dutch could not think of Catholic missionary work as anything but a disguised attempt to recapture the island for Portugal; and this is not surprising, since the Catholics themselves had hardly envisaged the revival of their faith except through the return of the Portuguese. It was the arrival of a pure Indian missionary that turned the scales.

Joseph Vaz himself died on 16 January 1711—after twenty-four years of evangelizing Ceylon. By then his reputation for holiness was such that what in most people would be described as the forgetfulness and abstraction of old age was taken by his hagiographers to be a seraphic condition.

Throughout the day and during part of the night (wrote Fr. Gonçalvez) he has no rest. . . . He is so immersed in God that he often forgets what he is doing outwardly, and thus it happens that he reads his office several times a day and at mass he does not sometimes know the place he has reached; and similarly in the commemorations of the dead; and he goes on till he notices it.

And again,

At night he slept little, and read something of Sinhalese or Tamil every night, even when he was out on tours. He read by candle-light late into the night, and it happened occasionally that sleep overpowered him in his reading and he knocked his head against the candlestick. Once . . . the superior had a wound in his head and when asked what the matter was, he replied that it was the result of a fall when sleep overpowered him in prayer, and that he struck his head against a candlestick, adding that through laziness it often happened that he fell during prayer.[9]

This holy absent-mindedness stood him in good stead one day. There are various miracles of a not unusual variety told of Vaz —he is said to have produced rain by prayer, to have escaped the Dutch through the supernatural appearance of clouds to conceal him, and so on. But the most charming is the story of his encounter with an elephant:

The Father was advancing alone, his companions following him at some distance, on the way from Marip to Vallavalli. The Father . . . was reading a book, which I suppose was his breviary. The elephant came rushing with great fury, the very sight of which made the attendants run for their lives. But when the animal came up to the Father, it stopped, turned and went away, leaving the Father to pursue his way unconscious.[10]

CHAPTER 11   SERGEI SEODZI

The two Asians whom we shall discuss next are not only very different from each other, but might each have been placed in Part II; for in a sense, and from the point of view of individual biography, both were 'absolute beginners'. But I think it will become clear as their experiences unfold that their context puts them in this section of the book.

We have no information when Seodzi was born, but his reminiscences date from 1880. His family lived in Tokyo, and he recalls how he and his sister, two years his senior, were brought up in traditional Buddhist fashion. They would get up at about half past six, when the rest of the family were already up, greet their parents, and then be told to walk in the garden awhile. His sister who was good at school used to question Seodzi about his home-work and, after testing him on it, they would play till breakfast. Breakfast was served at about 7.30 a.m., and before they started to eat it their Mother poured a small portion into a tiny varnished wooden cup for the 'shrine' of the house.

The 'shrine' (or 'temple') stood in the corner of one of our rooms; in form it was rather like the 'chapels' that we see in almost every house in Russia. In the middle of the 'shrine' stood an elegant wooden model of a Buddhist temple, with open doors. Inside the little temple stood an image of the Buddha. Beside it were memorials of our ancestors. On them, in golden ink, were written the names given to the deceased for the life-after-death, at Buddhist funeral rites. My mother, having taken a tray with these little bowls, took them to the 'shrine' and stood them in front of the memorials; then she knelt and said a short prayer. After this breakfast began.

The children were not allowed to laugh or even talk loudly at meals; after breakfast each one had to thank his parents with a low bow. Then their elder brother left for work at about 9.0 a.m.—he taught in the Cadet Corps—and Seodzi and his sister had to accompany him outside to wish him a happy journey.

From the spring of 1881, however, there was an unusual and puzzling atmosphere in the house. The boy began to overhear conversations between his mother and elder brother, which usually included questions such as, 'What is happening to father? As time goes on he keeps changing more and more . . .' and so on. Once when they were drinking evening tea as usual the father had not joined them; he had had his tea taken into his library, where he usually occupied himself in study.

Suddenly we heard father's voice, reading aloud. At first we thought he must be writing some rare Chinese characters as usual. But soon we realized that he was reading something quite new, a book unknown to us, and, in its form and content unlike anything we knew. What this book was soon became evident, because a proper name was frequently repeated during the reading—the name of Jesus Christ. It was the New Testament in Japanese. Father's voice was very serious as he read; you could hear profound attention and reverence in it. He often stopped, thought for a while on what he had read, and then began to read again. I understood practically nothing of what I heard. . . .

All this produced in me that happy, childish state of mind which often makes children laugh unaccountably and irrepressibly at some new and extraordinary impression. My laughing infected my sister, and we both laughed out loud. But my father's reading had quite a different effect on the older ones; mother told us very severely not to laugh, and added, turning to my brother, 'He must have *gone into some church*'—that is how we talk about those who accept the Christian faith.

This conjecture was soon confirmed, for soon after that they saw their father wearing on his chest a large silver cross on a thin red ribbon. From then on there was much serious discusion, and no little tension in the family; for their father had decided that he must leave and go to live nearer to the Christian church, in Surugadai—a hilly district in Tokyo where the Russian Orthodox Mission was situated. They tried to dissuade him, but he was firm, and went off, first for an unspecified period, and finally for good; he became the teacher of Chinese in the 'Spiritual Seminary' there. He came, of course, regularly to visit his family, and his visits were anticipated eagerly, everyone making sure of being at home when they occurred. But

although he loved us as before, and cared for us, he did not belong entirely to us; he now had his own interests, nothing to do with us, which formed the chief element in his life. Although we did not fully realize this, we children felt it, and its effect on me was especially painful and sad. I was staying with relations at the time, and noticed how they tried not to remind me of my father, as if they were afraid of further hurting the wounded heart of a recently orphaned boy.

And so the father of the family embraced Orthodoxy. He was not, actually, the first to become a Christian in the family. Seodzi's eldest brother was a Roman Catholic, and his sister-in-law, the wife of the brother that lived with them, was a Protestant. The eldest brother had become a Catholic when studying at the Military Academy in France, eight years before; but he was living some distance from the family, and was not a very zealous Catholic, so he had little influence on the others. The sister-in-law, who had received Protestant education in the English school in Tokyo, went to Church on Sundays to pray, but otherwise showed no signs of her Christian allegiance even among the close members of the family, and most visitors were quite unaware that they had a Christian living among them. So when the father took his faith seriously, this had a considerable effect on relations and friends. Even Seodzi's brother began to read the Gospel—'and, probably as a result of that, when his son was dangerously ill, he invited a pastor to come and baptize him'.

Seodzi himself had reached the age when he had to think about a profession. He decided that he would like to enter a military academy, like his eldest brother. But before doing so he had to fill in time, so he went to study at a school of English Language. Here he was able to visit his father frequently; for the house of the Orthodox Mission, where the father was now living, was only a quarter of an hour's walk from the English School. The first time he visited him he was surprised, even upset, at the conditions his father was living in. His room was very small, with one window and one table. On the table lay stacks of papers; on the floor books were piled, for there was no room for them in the small book-case. Over everything lay a thick layer of dust. A small cupboard contained all his personal belongings. Near the cupboard was a metal bowl, with water in it, already cold. Seodzi wondered, 'Why does he live in such a tiny room? Surely, too, there are servants who could dust his books?'—comparing it with his comfortable and roomy home. 'But then I noticed the weak flame of a lamp burning before an icon in one corner. "Yes, that's what is necessary to him," I thought, and said nothing to him of my feelings.'

It was on one of these visits to see his father that Seodzi had

an experience which, though it might seem trivial to an outsider, was decisive for his future. He tells of it so graphically
that it is best reproduced in his own words.

He had gone one day to visit his father and, not finding him
in, he did what he would often do when waiting: amused himself on the gymnastic apparatus which was set up in the yard by
the mission house.

Suddenly I heard the sound of a bell coming to me along the
corridor of the stone building of the mission. This sound was a call
to something, I thought, and I noticed that all the residents of the
mission-house were leaving their rooms and going in one direction.
This aroused my interest, and I followed them into the mission-house.
I went along a corridor and came out into the hall at the main
entrance. From there people were going up a big twisting staircase
to the second floor. I followed them and entered an ante-room, with
walls painted blue. There were doors opposite me, to my left and
right. The door on my left, which was very large, was open wide; but
at first I could only see a white ceiling through the door because the
people were crowded near it.

With the curiosity and boldness of a child, he brazenly pushed
his way through the people, and found himself in the next room.
What he saw there was

a spacious room, in which complete silence reigned, in spite of the
large number of people sitting on the floor. On the right, from one
wall to another, stretched a row of portraits and pictures (as it
seemed to me then), and above them yet another row. Behind these
portraits there must, I supposed, be another room, for they did not
reach the ceiling, and it continued behind them.

But then he suddenly noticed a new factor, which was a great
shock, and as he expresses it, 'made my heart shiver with pain'.

For looking round to the left, in the middle of the room I saw a
coffin, in which lay a dead man. It appeared that I had come in to
the domestic chapel of the mission, and that they were preparing
for a funeral. I saw there, for the first time in my life, a dead body.

As I listened to the rapid beating of my heart, I thought to
myself: 'Why have they brought this disgusting corpse here, defiled
by death? And what do they want to do with it?'

I looked with inexpressible horror at the coffin, at the top end of
which the pale profile of the dead man stood out in relief against a
background of greenery and flowers.

But at that moment, some of the pictures which till then had formed a solid wall, unexpectedly divided and drew back; and from behind them a man quietly came, dressed in a golden robe. All present stood up. Then began chanting, singing and reading.

Seodzi could not understand what was going on. He asked himself,

What does this procession round the coffin mean? Surely the dead man does not know that the priest is bowing to him? What is that smoke? Where is the soul, for the salvation of which the priest is praying to God? Does he know that there is a God, who listens to his prayers? What is the meaning of that ungainly movement of his hand? . . .

He felt these questions very oppressive, and it became almost intolerable to him to stay in this room, with the dead man lying there, only a few paces away.

And I would have run out of the room had not my gaze rested on my father, who stood in front of me. At first I did not believe my eyes. I even leaned forward, watching him. When I was sure it was really he, I took a step forward, towards him; but I stopped and began to follow all his movements. The surprising fact was that the moment I saw father, the heavy feeling that had been weighing down on me instantly became lighter, and I began to seek in father's movements the answers to the questions that had possessed my mind. And in spite of the fact that I saw only the stationary figure of my father, and the frequent but slow movement of his right elbow followed by the inclining of his head—simply in the concentrated tranquillity of that figure, in his assured and mysterious movements, I felt the resolution of the questions that had been agonizing me. Neither the ejaculations of the priest, nor the suddenly resounding singing, nor the oft-repeated chanting, which had made me turn round, seemed to attract any attention from my father, nor from any of those present. All without exception stood in deep silence as if their attention was fixed somewhere far away, on a certain point invisible to me. I caught the general mood of those present and I became at ease and even joyful because in it I had a presentiment of the solution to all the questions that had alarmed my spirit. If there is a God, I thought, if the dead man has a soul, they must be there, where all these people so quietly and confidently are directing their attention. Meanwhile I hardly moved, even trying to breathe quietly in order somehow not to destroy the sweet mood that had been cast over my consciousness, that my attention might be directed there where the attention of all nearby was directed, including my father's —although the object of that attention still remained a mystery to me.

At that moment I felt in my spirit an especial warmth; everything I could see seemed good and dear; even the coffin lost its previous repulsiveness; the flowers on it seemed extraordinarily beautiful. Suddenly, at the beginning of a song, all present knelt down: almost unconsciously I did the same. The sound of the prayers produced in me a deep emotion. I raised my head and directed my gaze into the depths of the next room behind the wall of pictures, a feeling of irresistible sweetness possessed me, I wanted somehow to say a prayer, but I could not find the words; and I became sad; I even felt that from my eyes the tears were flowing irresistibly. . . .

This was the beginning of a new outlook, and Seodzi was impatient to explore the new country he had been introduced to. His parents held him back, and even his father said that it would not be right for him to become a Christian so soon—'This matter is too important, and you are so young that you can't fully understand its significance. . . .' But the more they urged caution, the more Seodzi burned with impatience, especially as he suspected that one reason for his family's discouragement was that they feared their plans for his future career would be upset by his embracing Christianity. He persisted, and finally his father introduced him to a Japanese Orthodox priest, Fr. Paul Sato, who began to instruct him in the Faith.

At first, as he admits, he did not fully grasp all that was taught him—he was moved by the account of Christ's suffering, but the rest of the doctrines he swallowed whole—'for a long time', he admits naïvely, 'I failed to memorize names, or even simply the number of Persons in the Divinity. . . .' And, like most Japanese no doubt, he found great difficulty in understanding what the priest told him about the Christian obligation to love one's enemies. This was so contrary to the code of *bushido*, including the duty, sacred to men of noble blood, of revenge for the death of near relatives, especially of parents: how could he, for instance, 'love' someone who killed his father? The priest tried to explain that vengeance only propagates an endless series of enmities; that it is incompatible with belief in God's eternal judgement; and finally that Christ himself not only taught it but showed it when he prayed for his torturers. It was only this last example that shook Seodzi and persuaded him.

He began to go to the mission church frequently for the

liturgy and for vespers, and this was seemingly what entered most deeply and persuasively into his consciousness. 'I remember the first time I was at the Liturgy. A priest gave me the cross to kiss. I bent towards it with an incomprehensible feeling, not of longing and not of fear, and as I went away I experienced a sensation—if I may make so crude a comparison—as if I had tasted some unknown food from another world.'

There were two Russian priests in the seminary, Fr. Nikolai, the superior, who was by then well known in Japan, and his assistant, Fr. Vladimir, who later became Bishop of Ostrogoi and then Head of Missions in America. The latter invited Seodzi to join a group of students from the seminary who were going on holiday that summer to a villa in the hills two days' journey from Tokyo—not far from some famous medicinal springs. Seodzi's father was teaching Fr. Vladimir Japanese, so he easily obtained the family's consent for this holiday. He describes the journey, and the natural surroundings with a charming adolescent enthusiasm. As they ascended higher and higher up the mountain he

suddenly heard the sound of water flowing over stones. I looked out . . . and saw two paces from me a vertical precipice so deep it made one giddy. At the bottom, on the rocky bed, ran a stormy mountain stream flecked with white. On its other bank, at the foot of the mountain, I noticed a stream of smoke, thin as a thread, rising like a blue kite. It was a bonfire burning, lit by charcoal-burners. Our road ran along the edge of this precipice. It began to get dark; and the marvellous silence all round us became full of mystery. Suddenly the way was broken off by a dark gorge, across which was thrown an old, half-rotten bridge. One of the bearers, to amuse me, pushed with his foot a big rock lying on the very edge of the preci-pice. The rock dropped down with incredible speed, striking the cliff-side heavily. At first it sounded loud and terrifying, but it gradually became fainter, finally dying away to a strange sound like that made by a flash of gunpowder; the stone had evidently been smashed into tiny fragments. I was rather frightened then at crossing the gorge by this shaky bridge. But we managed all right, and soon we arrived at Fr. Vladimir's house. It stood almost beside the precipice, on flat ground, surrounded by a splendid, spacious garden, filled with flowers and young trees. In the garden, in a stone bowl, a beautiful fountain played with clear, cold water from a mountain spring. In the bowl swam many goldfish of different kinds. . . .

Fr. Vladimir welcomed them—there were about fifteen young

men in the party. As Seodzi joined them in prayer (though he knew few prayers yet) he remembered his family, asleep at home, and prayed 'Lord, thou art almighty. Take them, for my sake, to thyself, and give them that joy, just as much as I have it now'.

He became close friends with these young men, in the two months' holiday he spent—June and July—with them, and found them lively in discussion and debate. The one topic that absorbed them was the destiny of the Orthodox mission and its spread among the non-Christians. Seodzi came to the clear decision before the end of the holiday that he would not enter a military academy and join the Cadet Corps, but would go to the Spiritual Academy of the Orthodox mission in Tokyo. He pictured himself already, 'travelling along, in sandals, on poor roads, then fearlessly proclaiming the word of God to a crowd of heathen. How I rejoiced, in my imagination, when I thought of managing to convert even one heathen to Christianity . . . I said to myself, "He will be with me; He will help me." '

And so on his return he went to live at Surugadai; his family were still opposed to it, but now his father supported him in his decision. There were some fifty students in the seminary, and Seodzi had to learn Russian. Relations with the staff were surprisingly informal. Though Fr. Nikolai and Fr. Vladimir were officially 'Rector' and 'Inspector', there seemed to be no barriers between them and the students, and such was the warm companionship that none of them was afraid, says Seodzi, to ask either of the priests to adjudicate their little disputes.

One of his closest friends among the students, Nagasaka, was four years older than Seodzi. All his relatives were heathen and he had had practically to run away from home to become a Christian. He was sent off to Russia to complete his training for the priesthood—when, alas, a mysterious illness struck him down on his journey, and he died in the Dardanelles, and was buried by one of the Orthodox churches in Constantinople. Another student died at the seminary itself, and there was a dispute over the funeral: the seminarians naturally wanted the body in the chapel, for Christian burial; but the boy's father, who was a non-Christian, wanted the body brought home. Finally the father reluctantly gave way, and even attended the funeral service in the chapel. He was so impressed (as Seodzi had been on a similar occasion) that not long after that he too was baptized.

*   *   *

There is one interesting effect of Seodzi's adherence to Christianity: how it made him reflect on the relationship of his new belief to Japanese tradition. Even before he himself was baptized he went back, after Christmas, to visit his family. He had attended the Christmas services at Surugadai, and now,

having arrived home, where my relations joyfully met me with greetings and presents, I involuntarily turned to the shrine, which on this day was especially attended and decorated with flowers and offerings. In it a large lamp was lit, and there were two china flasks of wine and various foods in tiny vessels, comprising the New Year offering, and the whole shrine altogether shone with a special brilliance. This did not hold my attention specially, since it was what I had for years been used to when I had been living at home before. But, as I looked at the golden memorials to my grandfather and grandmother, I suddenly felt with particular force a deep thankfulness, not only to these two, whom I had never seen whilst they were alive, but to all my dead ancestors, whose memory was aroused in me by these memorial tablets. This feeling gave me an inner peace. But (I wondered) was this not opposed to Christian teaching? Or, on the contrary, did it not illuminate the Fifth Commandment ('Honour thy father and mother'), and the Christian belief in the immortal soul?

Had he had the chance to read the story of the Korean André Kim* he might also have asked himself another question. Kim (it will be remembered) describes somewhat scornfully the pagan 'greeting of the coming of the gods', in which all look in one direction, but only the father of the family 'sees' the gods' approach. Seodzi is first moved to take Christianity seriously by observing the worshippers looking intently in one direction, where he can see nothing. It is not irrelevant that the Orthodox have a reputation for being those Christians with the most developed sense of the 'numinous'.

However, Seodzi was not given time to solve theological problems like this, for he was at once whisked off to the dining-room and given *toso* (New Year wine) and all the other delights of the festival.

* See chapter 8, above.

Finally Seodzi reached the point he had waited for so long—baptism. One of his sponsors was an elderly Japanese lady, a very enthusiastic Christian, who was in fact an old friend of his family. At the Easter ceremonies, a few days before his baptism,

I met my future godmother in the porch, she having just arrived. She was very old and did not find it easy to climb the stairs. But on her face was written a peaceful joy, and she said to me 'How lovely to-day's festival is. Of course, you're here to-day for the first time: there are still many good things you have yet to see. Do you know,' she continued, 'I am sorry in my heart that your mother is not here with us. However, God is gracious, and one day He will bring her here.'

This was the one thought that still troubled Seodzi on the day of his baptism—that the two people closest to him in the world, his mother and sister, were not on the same road. 'I hasten to add', though, he writes as he concludes his little memoir, 'that to my great joy three years later they became Christians too.'

*   *   *

The Eastern Orthodox Churches have acquired a reputation in the West for an inward-looking, non-missionary attitude. This was not true of their work in Alaska and China, still less in Japan. After trouble with Cossack adventurers crossing the north-western frontier of China as far as the river Amur in the seventeenth century, a treaty was finally concluded with Russia in 1689, acknowledging the country north of the Amur, as far as the Stanavoi Mountains, to be Chinese; and in return Russia, unlike other European countries, was allowed to send trading caravans to Peking; and later to maintain a religious mission in the capital to provide a spiritual ministry to Cossacks captured in frontier clashes who had agreed to serve in the Chinese army. It is curious to learn that a descendant of these Cossacks—now after two centuries of intermarriage with Chinese quite indistinguishable from the Chinese themselves—died in 1966 as the Orthodox Bishop (Simeon) of Shanghai.[1] It will be remembered that the highest percentage of 'Boxer martyrs' in 1901 occurred among the Russian Orthodox Chinese.*

But in Japan the Orthodox mission was much more deliberately launched. Thirty years before Seodzi's experiences there

* See chapter 2, above, p. 31.

had not been one Orthodox in Japan; by the time he wrote there were perhaps some 20,000. Fr. Nikolai, head of the seminary, was the Ivan Kasatkin ('Nikolai' in religion) who came to Japan in 1861. He had determined from the first to do missionary work, though when he arrived Christianity was still a forbidden religion. When in 1873 the penal laws were lifted, he was able to move to Tokyo and build the seminary, and later a Cathedral. From the earliest days he had started to train Japanese catechists, some of whom became priests later.[2] There seem to have been as many as thirty-five Japanese priests by 1912; 26,000 Christians in 1900 and nearly 35,000 in 1914.[3] Nikolai himself, who became a bishop in 1880 and archbishop in 1906, died in 1912. Unfortunately the later history of the Orthodox mission in Japan was very chequered. Not only the unpopularity of Russia, with whom Orthodoxy was naturally associated, among Japanese; but the divisions within Orthodoxy itself from the time of the 1917 Revolution onwards—these told against her influence. And the problem was equally severe from the Russian side. This is illustrated in an incident in the great Russian 'purge' of 1937. Sergius Tikhomirov (1871–1945) was Metropolitan of Tokyo at the time. He was a great Russian patriot, and (unlike the majority outside Russia) never broke off relations with the Moscow Patriarchate, so that his position among ex-patriate Orthodox was almost unique. Indeed, for this very reason he was much criticized by the *émigré* Russians. In spite of this he was denounced in Soviet Russia as 'one of the principal intermediaries between Japanese militarism and the White Guardist scum'. And so, when Sergius, Metropolitan of Moscow (i.e. Sergius Starogorodsky, the Patriarch of Russia) sent a harmless telegram of greetings to Sergius Tikhomirov of Tokyo, he was accused of espionage—of sending what was really 'a message to the Japanese intelligence service'.[4] Yet in spite of all this the 1962 figures for religious affiliation in Japan give Orthodox: 35,293 members—as against, for instance, about 41,000 Anglicans, over 266,000 Roman Catholics, and 630,000 Protestants.[5]

How Sergei Seodzi survived these troubled times, we have no means of knowing. The little booklet, which contains all that we know of him, is limited to his early experiences. It is entitled *How I became a Christian. The Story of Sergei Seodzi*, and was published (in Russian, of course) by the Synodical Printing

House in St. Petersburg (as it was then) in 1892. The preface, by S. Rachinsky, tells us its origin.

The following memoirs of a young Japanese, S. N. Seodzi, now studying at St. Petersburg Spiritual Academy, were copied out by me from the manuscript of the author, correcting errors of grammar and syntax, but carefully preserving the ideas and style. I think that the original Russian style of an Orthodox Japanese will be more interesting than a more or less successful translation of it into trite literary language.

These memoirs, besides their psychological interest, have another interest, profounder and more important. The activity of our Orthodox mission in Japan is one of the brightest aspects of our contemporary church life. But its great work is still too little known to our educated society. [We need] constant close contact between the Russian church and her young daughter, the Japanese church.

With the building of the Siberian railway, the enormous distance separating Japan from the centres of Russian life will be considerably reduced, and personal intercourse will grow more frequent between Christians of Japan and their great Christian mother—Russia.

May the Lord make us worthy to promote the holy work performed on the hills of distant Surugadai.[6]

S. A. Rachinsky had been a professor in Moscow University, but then had developed an interest in village schools in Japan— he had a school of his own there, which Seodzi's father had visited in 1880. It was appropriate, therefore, that, along with the little old Japanese lady, Seodzi's other sponsor at his baptism should have been this Russian academic. This is a little corner of history of which we know so little that we must be grateful even for the tiny, inadequate glimpses afforded by a rare booklet like this.

CHAPTER 12   MIAO-CHI (1895–1930)

The influence of Japan on the nationalist leaders of China, from the end of the nineteenth century right up to the 1920s, was enormous: a very large percentage of the Chinese intelligentsia (almost all those, in fact, who did not go to Europe or

America) did their studies in Japan. This is a well-known piece of twentieth-century history. But what is perhaps not so well known is that this influence of Japan on China had been taking another form for a long time before, even during the days when Japan's xenophobia had closed her frontiers to outside influence: this older influence (and it was mutual) was religio-cultural, the impact of Chinese Buddhism on Japan.

This is one reason why the Chinese figure in this chapter has, like Seodzi in the last, been placed in Part III. From the Christian point of view he died an 'absolute beginner', but he brought to his Christianity a faith matured through study, pain, *Angst*, and contemplation; it was a brief, but incredibly speedy as well as brilliant blossoming.

Miao-Chi[1] was his later name: he was born Tao-Ying ('hero of truth') in 1895 in the village of Ta Hu, Formosa. His family had migrated there from South China. The Japanese took Formosa in 1895, and the Chinese boys had now all to learn Japanese; other subjects, too, were now added to their school curriculum—natural science, mathematics, etc.

In 1901 his mother fell ill. Some years before a Buddhist monastery had been built not far away—called Fa Yün Ssu (Law's Cloud Monastery)—and the Abbot told her that the only hope of her recovery was to offer one of her sons to the monastery. Miao-Chi was the most intelligent and thoughtful so he was chosen, and he became a novice. His mother died six months later, in spite of the Abbot's promise: but Miao-Chi stayed on, and after a year was ordained monk. It was then that he took the name he would be known by for the rest of his life, 'Miao-Chi' ('mysterious joy'). At first he followed the normal daily routine, which was roughly as follows: at 3.0 a.m. drums and bells woke the monks, and they went to the monastery temple for the morning sacrifice, which lasted about an hour and a half; then followed breakfast in the refectory; then practical work in the forenoon; a mid-day meal at 11.0 a.m., followed by a rest, and then attending to private affairs until 3.0 p.m.; a communal meditation preceded the evening sacrifice, which was followed by the final meal. During the night individual monks took prayer-watches in turn, and recited *sotto voce* the *Ti-Ts'ang* Scripture—the special prayers for the release of lost spirits in the Kingdom of Death.

Gradually Miao-Chi rose to be a leader among the young

monks, and soon was given literary work to do for the Abbot, which excused him the night-watch and certain other duties. He began to make contacts with monks visiting the monastery from China and Japan; as he studied more, and as the tensions of World War I began to affect them all, he became restless, and asked to study more abroad.

And so in 1918 he set off for Japan, and soon took up residence at one of the leading monasteries, Kwannon Temple, Asakusa Park, Tokyo. He found that the spiritual tone of the monastery was very poor, however. Miao-Chi discussed the problem with one or two who were more sensitive to the issues, and they agreed with him. 'Yes,' they said, 'it is a great sorrow to us too. The Shintō movement is all-powerful now, and we are forced to follow.' 'But you have come to the wrong place,' they said; 'You should visit our holy Kyoasan, and Kyoto, which is the real heart of Buddhism in Japan.'

And so Miao-Chi moved on to Kyoasan ('The High Mountain in the Wilderness'), and there he found the spirit much improved. He came to know Takahashi, the leader of the Shingon School (Shingon—'The True Word Sect'), and this, in a very indirect way, was his first introduction to Christianity. He had seen Christians at Formosa, of course, going off to their churches; but had paid no attention to them. Shingon, however, had a curious history which linked it, in a way a student could not escape, with the short-lived Christian mission of the seventh century—nearly twelve hundred years earlier.

Shingon had been founded by Kobodaishi, one of the great Japanese masters. He lived from 774 to 835, and in his religious travels in China he had come across the Nestorian Christians, who were strongest in and around Sh'angan (Sian). It was there that the famous Tablet was erected in 781,[2] describing the expansion of Christianity under Λ-lo-pên, a Syrian Christian who arrived in Shensi in 635. Kobadaishi may even have been present at the dedication of this Tablet, and certainly would have known about the movement there. In fact, just as the tablet uses Buddhist and Taoist terms in its (somewhat defective) account of Christianity, so Kobodaishi used expressions reminiscent of the Nestorian Church in his own writings. Takahashi, the head of the Shingon school, had himself been connected with the re-dedication in 1907 of this historic Nestorian tablet, which was rediscovered by the Jesuits in 1623 in Hsianfu, and was placed in the Museum of Antiquities, Peiling, Sian, early this century. Takahashi introduced Miao-Chi to the holy places in this area, and the young Buddhist monk often came to reread the Tablet.

However, for the moment this contact with Christianity was only tangential. Miao-Chi moved on from archaeology to living Buddhism: he came to Kyoto to study under the expert in Zen Buddhism, who taught History of Religion in Otani College there—Professor D. T. Suzuki, well known in the West (he only died recently, in 1966). Miao-Chi mentioned the Nestorian Tablet, and Suzuki said, 'How interesting that you have come into contact with Christianity in this way. Yes, it has much to give us, but remember that only he who has come to a right understanding of Zen Buddhism can receive a full blessing from Christianity as well as from other great religions.' Suzuki in fact told many of his students that they should study the life and character of Jesus; indeed, when he heard that the Norwegian scholar, Karl Reichelt, (later the author of the life of Miao-Chi) was willing to lecture on 'religion in the light of Buddhism and Christianity', he himself arranged the meeting at Otani College, took the chair, and translated Reichelt's lecture into Japanese.

Miao-Chi was already feeling his way towards a more personalistic Buddhist faith, being drawn to the *Amitabha* Buddha ('All-Father'; in Japanese, *Amida*) of the 'Pure-Land' School (Jōdo); but he knew that there was no historical basis for this, that it was pure myth, and so he held back. But perhaps, he thought, a more secure way would be that of *Zen* (*Ch'an* in Chinese), with its stress on meditation as a way to mystical experience. He therefore entered a Zen Buddhist monastery, and, though he did not think much of the themes for meditation, and found the discipline irksome, he appreciated the atmosphere and the quiet.

In 1920, however, just before he was due to return to China, he had a formative experience. He had already made contact—again through Suzuki—with a very remarkable Japanese figure, Tenko Nishida (sometimes known as 'the St. Francis of Japan'). Nishida was a business man who had had no opportunities for profound theological study. He had been influenced by the best elements in Shintō, Buddhism, and Confucianism; he had also studied the New Testament; but it was a book on

St. Francis of Assisi which impressed him most (as it impressed Kagawa*). This had led to a religious awakening, and in 1903 he founded the It-to-en (Society of the Witness to Unity)†—a brotherhood for the uplifting of the needy and for moral improvement. It was a religious community based on simplicity: clothes, houses of worship, and mode of life were all austere; their meeting hall was bare, with no altar, only a tablet with the words 'Not Two' on it (i.e., there is one God behind all); the brothers gathered early for a frugal breakfast, and then went out to look after the sick and poor; they wore no special habit— merely a simple kimono and straw sandals. Nishida himself said of their aims: 'Inwardly our Society lives by penitence; outwardly it lives by service which asks for no recompense. . . . It is reminiscent not so much of a stern father as of the mother. In the life of mankind there is so little of this tender-hearted side, because men in their selfishness continually wage wars of various sorts.' Miao-Chi attended their early morning prayers, and later met Nishida himself. He was so impressed that he wrote to his brother:

I have been visiting the 'Society to Witness and Unity' at night, and I must say that I have never met a more noble and self-sacrificing people. . . . Strange how again and again of late I have come into contact with Christ, the world's greatest *bodhisattva;* first on Kyoasan, then with my master Suzuki, and through the books he lent me about Francis of Assisi, but now in a special way through . . . Tenko Nishida. . . . The moment I saw him, it struck me that here I am face to face with a prophet, a rare and holy man. I was so overcome that I threw myself at his feet, but he immediately came forward and raised me up, saying 'Do not bow down to me but adore the Blessed One who gave his life for us on the Cross in order that we might all become one.'

This contact was followed by another, even more direct, with Christianity. On 25 May 1920 Miao-Chi had a religious experience which he later looked back upon as crucial. During the mid-day break in the Zen monastery he had been reading a Japanese pamphlet (author unknown), *Life in the Light of Eternity*. It was probably Buddhist, but it quoted phrases from the Bible, and one in particular struck Miao-Chi: 'For God hath placed eternity in their hearts.' (Eccles. 3:11). This reminded him of words of Nishida's: 'He who loses his life,

* See p. 210. † See Appendix 6, p. 317.

finds it. He who voluntarily gives up self finds his real self; not in isolation but in fellowship with the divine and with one's fellow men lies the solution.' These two passages seemed to Miao-Chi to throw light on the problem of evil: no one can wish away the tragic side of life, but it can be faced in the light of eternity; eternity, however, cannot be reached by mere words, i.e. by people who talk Buddhist language about 'a pure and enlightened heart' but continue in selfishness. Miao-Chi realized he must devote himself to leading people out of darkness. As he pondered on this the dinner bell went, and later the night bell; but he hardly heard them. The monks dispersed, but he sat on still, meditating, and only returned to his cell late at night. From then on a change came over his life. The monks noticed it, and so did Suzuki. Miao-Chi began to make meditation the centre of his life.

*   *   *

In 1920 he returned to China. His Superior at the Formosa monastery agreed that he should visit the main Buddhist centres for three years' study, to meet some of the chief *fa-shih* (masters), and to find out about Buddhist publications. His first call was to P'u T'o island, near Shanghai, an island with a mountain which was visited by many pilgrims. He was given a cell in one of the two monasteries there, and he had much time for prayer and reading on his own. The pilgrims were chatty and unspiritual; and many of the monks, too, led immoral lives. During the day Miao-Chi began to move among the crowd, looking for the troubled and the mourning. Soon they came to him for help. Monks, too, began to come for counsel.

During the summer months he met several prominent Buddhist scholars in Shanghai, and certain lay movements, some of which he found were deeply sincere. He also began to notice a striking contrast. In one temple where he stayed, there was the *Chin Nieh Shê* (Society for the Accumulation of Merit) which was a centre for (among other things) the cult of the *Amitabha Buddha*, the personalistic cult to which, as we have seen, Miao-Chi had earlier been drawn. In this temple there were lectures during the week, but on Sundays there was a big congregation of lay Buddhists who stayed most of the day. There was a service which lasted all morning, ending with a procession in which the formula, 'Nan-wu, O-mi-t'O-fu' ('I trust thee, O Amitabha') was murmured over and over again. At noon there was a break of three hours, for a meal and discussion. And then the drum sounded for silence and all gathered again in the temple hall. A monk intoned a hymn of praise. And the chorus replied:

I pray to thee to blot out all those shifting and vain lusts that I have carried with me through innumerable *kalpas* [eras, long periods], so that I may not have to wander through limitless aeons before I sense my true *dharmakāyā* [the Body of the Law, here meaning roughly 'the true essence of life']. . . . I vow to share in the salvation of all living beings, numerous as the sand of the Ganges. . . . If I do not first help all creation to attain Buddhahood then may I myself never attain perfection. . . .

Miao-Chi found this moving, though he could not accept it all. But by contrast he met another group of literary men who stood aloof from this popular worship. They were of the Speculative, *Wei Shih*, School which stresses that behind all shifting phenomena there is a continuity: and this is to be attained by thought, not by superstitious devotion. These philosophers were impressed with Miao-Chi's powers of psychological penetration, and invited him up to their room. But he did not feel at home with them. Some of them were genuine; but too many were merely clever. He felt that down below, among the lay folk, there was quite a different spirit; in spite of the naïve ejaculations to Amitabha there was a warm-heartedness and sincerity at the root.

He moved on now to centres of greater austerity: first up the Yangtse Valley, from Shanghai to Chinkiang, to a noted monastery of the Meditation School (*Chin Shan Ssu*). Its regimen was very strict, with acts of devotion from 2.0 a.m. to 5.0 a.m., and also in the afternoon; only two meals; and little sleep. It was very dirty and tuberculosis was rife there. He then moved out to Chiao Shan Island, to visit some hermits living in huts near the Chin Shan monastery. They never joined in public worship nor ate together; they fetched their meals from the common kitchen, and otherwise hardly ever left their cells. The cells themselves were tiny, and furnished with nothing but a bed, table, bench, and little altar with a Buddha image or scriptures on the shelf. Some of the hermits had long hair, were unkempt, and some had taken a vow of total silence. Others talked to

him, especially two lamas—a Mongol and a Tibetan. They
had travelled over mountain ranges, worshipping at all holy
places. They were happy in the certainty of a glorious reincarnation when they should leave this existence. Miao-Chi was
worried about them, for he was sure they had no foundation for
such a hope.

Next, he visited *Pao Hua Shan* monastery ('Precious Flower
Mountain') not far from Nanking. There were, again, many
ascetics here. One monk whom Miao-Chi met, Yuan-Kuang,
had just indulged in an act of self-torture. There was a practice
by which some monks on the anniversary of their ordination
would burn new marks on arms or chest, burn off a finger, or
cut out a piece of muscle from an arm. Yuan-Kuang had been
looking for a spiritual master for long and, failing to find one,
had decided on an act of mortification which would bring him
everlasting merit. A hermit had helped him to do so, by stretch-
ing his long rosary round his neck and along his body; then he
slowly drew a spill of burning paper along the rosary, until the
whole outline, and the character representing Buddha, were
burnt into his skin. Yuan-Kuang had endured this, reciting the
words to Amitabha, 'O-m-t'O-fu' all the time; but had fainted
in the end. It was the very next day that Miao-Chi met him,
and found him still strong enough to go down to the monastery
for food. But the wounds started to suppurate; and the second
day he was in a high fever. Miao-Chi visited him in his hut,
bandaged him daily, nursed him, and improved the hut by the
somewhat obvious expedient of making a window in it to let in
light and air. Yuan-Kuang was in delirium for days, but when
he recovered he said to Miao-Chi 'You are a bodhisattva sent
from heaven. . . . Please take me on as your disciple.' They
became close friends, and when Miao-Chi had to leave, in
November, Yuan-Kuang went some of the way with him.

Not all the ascetics were so sincere. Miao-Chi met one who
hung iron chains from hooks let in to the muscles of his chest,
and dragged them round as he walked. Miao-Chi told him that
such mortification was valueless, and was a misunderstanding
of the *Lotus Sutra* which only said that the disciple must be
willing to endure suffering if it will honour the Buddha and
help men. Later Miao-Chi found that the monk only put on the
chains when people were watching.

Having already met the Speculative School of Wei Shih,

Miao-Chi decided he must give it a closer look before condemning it altogether as he had done. So he went to Nanking in November 1920 to attend a course at the Lay Buddhist Academy. This Academy had been founded by a remarkable man, Yang Wen-Hui, in 1880, who had been Chinese ambassador in Japan, and had had considerable contact with Christians, Evangelical and Catholic, and had actually helped David Hill to translate Buddhist texts into English. He said that he derived benefit from all the varieties of Christianity he had met. 'For they all lead, each in its own way, into the sanctuary of the "unspeakable" where men attain a glimpse of the true pattern of life. Nevertheless I feel that the most direct way for me is the Wei Shih philosophy. . . .' This founder, Yang Wen-Hui, had died in 1912, but his influence was still strong, and Miao-Chi took his successor as his teacher. The course lasted two months; but it only confirmed Miao-Chi's earlier opinion. The Wei Shih movement was very abstract, and closer to Theravada Buddhism (the original, austere version) than most other forms he had met in Japan or China. The stress on pure introspection, on meditation by which man can reach a high level of intuition, the dismissal of religious notions, of theistic concern or of worship—all this failed to satisfy Miao-Chi. He said, 'The only point where the Wei Shih School touches pure religion is in its mention of Nirvana. Here pure thinking and strict logic have come to an end, and one has to talk about "the unspeakable", and "majestic loftiness", vague ideas which only a "perfected Buddha" can fully comprehend.'

His next visit was to a more acceptable type of monastery, Chiu Hua Shan, in the Yangtse Valley, near Tatung, one of the four great Buddhist centres. Its guardian genius was one, Ti-T'sang, 'the merciful *bodhisattva*' who was said to have become incarnate in Korea (or, some say, Thailand), in A.D. 730; and, like Sakyamuni, to have renounced his princely position to wander through China, and in the end had broken into the Kingdom of Death to preach to imprisoned souls there. Hymns were sung to him and to Amitabha; and it was here that Miao-Chi, though he merely came as a pilgrim with other pilgrims, was asked to be a teacher and stay there permanently. He refused, but offered to give some lectures in the seminary and talk to the pilgrims. To the latter he spoke of the need for purification; that man cannot improve himself, but that the

Buddha sent his *bodhisattva* to open the way to faith. To the student-monks he spoke of his own experiences—of Suzuki, of Tenko Nishida, and so of St. Francis, and finally of the great *bodhisattva* of the West, Jesus Christ.

In January 1921 he set off again, this time to Hankow. Here for the first time—out of sheer curiosity—he attended a Roman Catholic service. He of course knew no Latin, but some of the phrases must have stuck, for seven years later he could still remember parts of the Ave Maria. In the High Mass that followed he was specially moved by the ritual and the Agnus Dei. Soon after this he visited two more Christian churches, in one of which, a Chinese church, he met L. H. Roots, Anglican Bishop of Hankow. Here he found the service much simpler, the church barer, but the atmosphere warm. He decided that 'the Roman Catholics are the light, and Protestants are the salt. Both are needed.' Two days later he crossed the Yangtse, and went to the Buddhist Academy at Wuchang. Here he was put under the Rector, T'ai-Hsü, who saw at once that he was a very special visitor, and gave him a single room so that he could study.

This T'ai-Hsü was one of the most remarkable men of his generation, and the most influential Chinese Buddhist of the day. He was born near Hankow in 1888; when he was about fifteen, he came into touch with some of the political radicals, and had to disappear—this was one of his reasons for becoming a monk. He founded a centre for the study of Buddhism, gave lectures in various centres, and finally started what came to be the nation-wide Buddhist Society, which was influenced by Christianity to the extent that it started schools, orphanages, and hospitals.

In 1911 came the great Revolution in China, when T'ai-Hsü was twenty-three. He planned to make one of the Buddhist centres a revolutionary H.Q.; was given a detachment of troops, issued despatches, visited Nanking, where Dr. Sun Yat-Sen was in office as first President of China. But difficulties soon began. The revolutionary students were anti-religious, and regarded Buddhism as reactionary; on the other hand, when Yüan Shih-Kai took over from Sun Yat-Sen, T'ai-Hsü himself was in danger. He fled in disguise to Shanghai, and from there to P'u T'o Island, where a monastery gave him a hermit's cell. Here, from 1913 to 1917 he was, almost literally, dead to the world. In fact, most people thought that he had been liquidated.

During these four years T'ai-Hsü studied, meditated, and reviewed his life. The result was startling, because unexpected. When he was ceremonially released from his cell he was found to be looking like a hermit, with long hair, unkempt; but to be extremely rational and balanced. He had had no mystical 'awakening' as other hermits did; but he had pondered the failure of his revolutionary ideals, had applied the stern kind of Buddhist Wei-Shih principles to it, and accepted its rationalist outlook. He soon became a leading exponent of this form of self-criticism, of submission to the exploration of consciousness. By the end of 1917 T'ai-Hsü was known in Japan, a guest lecturer in Tokyo and Kyoto; and soon he became Rector of Wuchang Academy. Indeed, in 1928 he toured the West, lecturing in Berlin, London, Paris, and New York. This was the man who now took on the spiritual formation of Miao-Chi.

At first the pupil was much impressed by his new master. T'ai-Hsü lectured on the history of Buddhism, and of ethics and religion generally; he emphasized the danger of superstition and corruption in popular, even monastic Buddhism; and though polite about certain Christian tenets, he was clear about its inferiority to Buddhism, both in clear-sightedness, and by reason of its stress on faith and the necessity for atonement, thus neglecting 'the highest faculty of man, understanding'. T'ai-Hsü was also impressed with his new disciple, and was soon employing him to lecture on comparative religion to new arrivals. He was also sent out to preach in the lecture hall and street chapel of lay Buddhists in Hankow; and here he experienced the same conflict he had noticed twice before. For in popular preaching to crowds in the town the image of Amitabha, lit up with electric light bulbs like an Italian madonna, was the centre of devotion, and worship was followed by 'testimonies' from students, for all the world like an evangelistic meeting. T'ai-Hsü did not seem perturbed by the apparent contradiction: he advised his assistants on these occasions to 'concentrate upon the message of the Pure Land School, because that is all that ignorant people can understand. In this way Buddhists will be able to compete better with Christians who have made so much progress in China especially through their evangelism in street chapels.' However, remembering his earlier admiration for St. Francis, Miao-Chi and some friends started a school for poor children, a welfare association for the sick, and, finding that the Christians had got permission to preach to prisoners, he started to do the same.

During the summer of 1921 he was even chosen to accompany T'ai-Hsü on a visit to monasteries and lay Buddhist societies in Central China. When they returned, however, they found a tense atmosphere. The students had become increasingly political and anti-religious. T'ai-Hsü did not mind atheism—after all, his brand of Buddhism was practically non-theistic—but the students were attacking Buddhism itself as superstitious and reactionary. Some of them were not only subversive but loose in their morals; they used to sneak out of the Academy at night, attend political meetings in Wuchang, and then go on to brothels and gambling dens. Miao-Chi was particularly unpopular among these, as both a 'puritan' and an old-fashioned, 'superstitious' Buddhist. When the ring-leaders of this group of students were discovered to be secreting revolutionary writings and obscene pictures in their rooms, they were expelled. They were set on revenge, and one night when they found that Miao-Chi and other senior students would be returning from a meeting at a near-by monastery, they waylaid them. Miao-Chi was knocked to the ground with a club, and a knife struck him in the chest. Fortunately the knife glanced off the bone, and his lung was unimpaired; but he bled severely, and took long to recuperate. He convalesced at a mountain temple at Kuling, with its lovely walks and a clear view over Poyang Lake. On Sunday mornings he was attracted by the 'Union' Protestant Church at Kuling; he dared not go in, in his Buddhist robes, but a friend lent him a long coat, and he slipped in at the back. He did not yet know enough English to follow all, but was impressed with the prayers, hymns, and readings.

In the spring of 1923 the revolutionary ferment was strong again, and Wuchang Academy was thoroughly searched. A few students were imprisoned, but T'ai-Hsü's influence was powerful enough to save them from execution. Miao-Chi himself graduated, and left: his teacher, the Rector, said at his farewell, 'To-day a true *bodhisattva* has left our academy. May fortune and blessing follow him.' All seemed set now for Miao-Chi to become one of the young Buddhist leaders.

He started by giving daily lectures in Shanghai, and here instead of merely expounding Buddhist texts he spoke more generally about the forms of religious life as seen in the light of

Buddhism and other great religions. Thus he included a short exposition of the main Christian ideas, and ended with a challenge to his hearers to opt for a religious life, not as abstract thought but from the depths of the heart. The lectures were very popular, especially with the young and the upper-class folk; but the older Buddhist teachers were perturbed—was this Buddhism? After a month here he moved on to Hangchow, and again lectured to laymen's societies. But he felt he must return to his base, Formosa, and set off. However, he had to stop at Amoy on the way, and there he was strongly pressed to stay on as a teacher in a new Buddhist Academy for Southern China; with all the political disturbances, and the expulsion of fifteen students, they were anxious for a new voice. He refused, but was persuaded to give some lectures. He spoke of the task of young Buddhists today. We have, from his diary, notes of one of his lectures, and this will give us an insight into the current stage of his thinking at that time. He stresses that 'to help people towards an understanding of the inner consciousness of life it is not enough to know the catchwords of New Buddhism. One must lead the religious life in earnest.' Some, he says, have broken through to this by meditation, some by prayer; he himself has been much helped by the comparative study of religion.

I do not mean to imply that one must become an ordained monk in order to enter upon this highest form of life. The greatest man whom I have met on this earth was a layman. He had received much help from his Buddhist studies, but for him the 'break-through' came when he began to study Christianity. I refer to Tenko Nishida in Japan. . . . He radiates a wonderful peace, serenity and love.

And he goes on to speak of Nishida's debt to St. Francis; and ends by saying what a wonderful thing it would be if our Buddhist Academies could produce a generation of youth that has discovered the same secret of life.

*   *   *

At last, at the end of July 1923, after five years of travel and the equivalent of twenty-five years of spiritual exploration, he arrived back home in Formosa. His widowed father was now a monk; his brothers married. On the seventh anniversary of his mother's death Miao-Chi, as an ordained Buddhist monk, was able to conduct the memorial sacrifice. After a short rest with his family he returned to his old monastery, Fa Yün Ssu, and in October he was appointed a regular *fa-shih* (master) giving courses for young monks in Formosa; he started a periodical, *Asia's Light,* and the Abbot made him head of the newly founded Formosa Academy. For his lectures on comparative religion the hall of the Academy was too small, and they had to move into a temple. He began to fulfil the promise he had shown when he first went there.

Less than two years later, in the spring of 1925, the Abbot persuaded the Council of Elders to appoint Miao-Chi Assistant Abbot. This was a responsible post which he had not expected; it involved visiting temples in the area, and he soon found that owing to the economic depression monks had been raising money in dubious ways, so that he had to insist on reforms. He therefore founded the Buddhist Reform Association, with the aims of preaching Mahayana Buddhism in all its purity, of fighting superstition, of eradicating monastic corruption, and of contributing to the economic and social progress of Formosa. Only two monks tacitly opposed the Association, and Miao-Chi showed his courage in insisting that the Abbot—who was hesitant about the matter—expel them from the monastery, even though he knew it would make them his enemies.

For two years he was fully engaged in this work, and was proud to see his own pupils graduate with honour. Yet, unknown to others, he was going through a severe period of doubt. For he knew from his historical studies what his hearers did not, that the teaching about the Amitabha had no historical foundation, and that the concept of the Pure Land, and the prayers and poems associated with it, was a human construction. And so, the more the layfolk showed their gratitude for his help, the more troubled he was that he should be regarded as a spiritual leader when his own convictions were so precarious. He took refuge in popular evangelistic preaching; yet even here there was a doubt—he was trying to lead men upwards, but to what? He began to give more and more time to prayer, and less to sleep. He also found support in two colleagues who had returned from visits to China in 1927; they had paid many visits to a brotherhood in Nanking, the Ching Feng Shan Brotherhood, conducted by Dr. Karl Reichelt, the Norwegian Lutheran, for instructing Buddhist monks in

Christian teaching. These two had brought back a New Testament and with its aid they had long discussions with Miao-Chi about Christianity.

Late in 1927 Miao-Chi took up residence in Taipeh, capital of Formosa, and opened a modern book-shop and reading room. He was installed now as Abbot of the Dragon Mount Temple there (*Lung Shan Ssu*) and this meant that he was near the centre for his work. He started a wider society (the *O-Mi-T'o-Fu*) to spread the light of Amitabha; and he persuaded the Council of Elders to put aside some of the alms given to the monastery for the destitute. Yet his doubts persisted. As a scholar he knew that according to the oldest sources Sakyamuni, the Buddha, rejected the notion of salvation through a heavenly mediator. Yet the two classics of the 'Pure Land' School (the Amitabha Scripture and the Sakyamuni Scripture) proclaimed Amitabha as the Universal Saviour and King of the Western Paradise. Sophisticated Buddhists could only reconcile the two contradictory notions by saying that simple people could be won by the second, and then later could be awoken to see the Amitabha conception as an inspiring symbol of man's initial experience of Nirvana. But Miao-Chi doubted the honesty of this procedure.[3] At one point (in March 1928) he was driven, after a night of struggle, to throw himself on his face and pray, 'O Heaven have mercy, and send a teacher who can lead me to the light.' And it was not before the altar of Buddha that he threw himself but in the middle of his cell.

*   *   *

It was at this point that Dr. Reichelt visited Miao-Chi at his temple. It was Reichelt's first visit to Formosa; and to his surprise Miao-Chi showed him a card of introduction that he had been given him by Bishop Logan H. Roots, when they had met in Hankow seven years before. They 'clicked' at once, and for days they met, sometimes morning and evening, discussing religious truth. Miao-Chi was particularly puzzled by the problem, arising from the most central tenet of the purest type of Buddhism, that, since the 'personal' is inescapably subject to limitation, God cannot be personal or he too would be limited. And yet he admitted that there were other strains in Chinese religious thought.

I have studied our Chinese classics [he said to Reichelt], and often felt that when the sages, such as Confucius, Mencius, Moti and Wang Yang-Ming, reached so far in insight and personal devotion, the reason was that *T'ien* (Heaven) or *Shang Ti* (The Exalted Ruler) to them was really what you Christians mean by speaking to a personal God.

Reichelt was able to add to these other strains by producing indications even in Buddhist thought which point beyond the impersonal.[4]

Miao-Chi struggled, too, with the Christian doctrine of creation, so foreign to a Buddhist. Yet he admitted that the Buddhist doctrine itself did not satisfy him, that matter is *maya* (illusion, or emptiness), and yet is eternal, so that there can be no creation, only evolution and involution, an endless circle of combination and recombination of the four elements (air, fire, water, earth) through the four stages (becoming, stagnation, disintegration, and annihilation), never ceasing till all craving for life and rebirth is overcome. Reichelt suggested to him that the Christian view is more optimistic than the Buddhist— though realistic about the fact of evil and tragedy. Miao-Chi admitted that this was closer to man's deepest instincts than the Buddhist outlook.

Gradually, as Reichelt began to use spontaneous prayer before and after their discussions, Miao-Chi echoed them; and one day prayed himself: 'Holy God, who through Jesus Christ hast revealed thyself to mankind, I thank thee and offer praise to thee because I too am allowed to come under the power of thy Spirit and learn to know thee. . . . Bless us as we now kneel in thy sight, and fulfil thy will and thy work in us'. Soon he arranged for Reichelt to give public lectures for Buddhists and Christians. There was a large audience, and Miao-Chi interpreted him from Mandarin into the local Chinese; Reichelt noticed that, 'when he translated my description of mission work amongst Buddhists, and about our life in the Brotherhood, Miao-Chi always used the "we" form, thus including himself. In other words, he felt that he was already one of us.' Finally it became clear that Miao-Chi had in fact decided to become a Christian. Reichelt warned him of the problems that would follow, and urged him to accept the fellowship and support of the Church, which he promised to do.

Reichelt himself had to leave Formosa in March, but he commended Miao-Chi to the local Christians.

Now followed a time of great trial. When Miao-Chi had made his decision he did not feel it immediately necessary to leave Buddhism, and give up his position as Abbot. But he started at once to make changes. There was, for instance, a popular custom of 'divination' in the temple—casting lots to find favourable omens for the future; this was not approved of by educated monks, but still continued among the simpler followers. Miao-Chi stopped this. He also took a month off to write some articles for his periodical, *Asia's Light*, in which he not only argued the necessity to introduce the concept of God, taken from the ancient religions of China, into contemporary Mahayana Buddhism—and quoted the more theistic passages from classical Hindu and Buddhist writings to support this—but spoke of the New Testament openly, and of Christ as the revealer of God and the unique saviour in whom the *bodhisattva* idea finds complete realization. The articles were very influential, but naturally aroused much protest; so Miao-Chi called a special meeting of his *O-Mi-T'o-Fu* Society to explain his position. Here he was even more explicit, and made a personal appeal that his hearers should study the New Testament.

The opposition grew, and the two monks whom he had had expelled now started to work against him. He was brought before the Council of Elders and charged. The Abbot of the main monastery defended him: Miao-Chi might have been a bit intemperate, he said, but after all Mahayana Buddhism is characterized by tolerance; even the great T'ai-Hsü had announced that, if only Christians would drop the idea of a personal God, Christianity could be regarded as a Western form of Mahayana. And he testified to Miao-Chi's personal example and conduct. One of the witnesses, representing his enemies, got up; seeing that the case seemed to be going in Miao-Chi's favour he said, 'There is nothing to be done now but lay before you another document. From reliable sources we know that Miao-Chi has been in contact with subversive elements at home and abroad; his communistic tendencies come out clearly in his writings.'

This was an allegation with serious possible consequences at this time. The Japanese chief of police was making inquiries about Miao-Chi from Japanese monks. They spoke well of him, so he was not arrested. But a group of monks took him away to a lonely temple, for safety and seclusion, and he remained incommunicado. When Reichelt was in Formosa in the summer of 1929 he inquired, and found that Miao-Chi was alive; but Reichelt was urged not to come and see him, since secret police were all around. In the autumn his case came up and he was acquitted on all points. The Council of Elders begged him to return to his previous position. But in spite of the fact that the monks had cared for him during the six months of semi-captivity, he now was clear that he could not continue as a Buddhist abbot. He even gave up the editorship of his beloved *Asia's Light*, and went to stay with his family. Fortunately they too had moved nearer to Christianity by now, so he was well received. He planned to do a course at the Normal College at Taipeh, and then start a college himself in the New Year. But symptoms of tuberculosis now began to show, and he was advised to go to a high altitude with nourishing food. He went for a while to his old monastery, Fa Yün Ssu, where he gave lectures on Christianity, and was venerated by the younger monks.

In the New Year (1930) he came back to Taipeh, hoping to start his school; but his tuberculosis was more advanced. He went into the mission hospital, and from there wrote to many friends and disciples in China and Formosa, saying, 'Alas, I have never reached the point where I could lead each one of you to Christ, but now, from my sick bed—which may possibly become my death-bed—I beg you to seek him, the great Saviour, through prayer and faith, so that you may have happiness for time and eternity.'

One development at this moment was significant: a fear of death. For the Buddhist this is irrelevant—reincarnation removes its sting. But for the Christian this life has to be taken seriously and its accountability cannot be postponed. He began to worry about his own unworthiness, his pride, his misleading of those who came for help but to whom he had nothing to give. In his anxiety he sent for two missionary friends, and they spent the whole night with him, in prayer and conversation; by the morning he had found peace of soul and liberty. Next day he sent out a public announcement that he had become a Christian. The orthodox Buddhists were shocked and there was a paragraph in a Buddhist paper, a few days later, that Lo Miao-Chi should now be reckoned dead since he had renounced Buddhism.

He was able, in spite of his illness, to give testimony at meetings in the hospital, and to see many Buddhist friends, though he was not well enough to go to the church for baptism. (He seems to have been privately baptized in the hospital.) He died on 20 April, and was given Christian burial. The Buddhists also arranged a memorial service, which several Christians attended: so his death softened the antagonism. At his funeral it was his eldest brother who best expressed what the family felt: after thanking the Christian Church for giving him a home, he said 'Miao-Chi always showed us the way. We always felt secure in following him for he was always "of the truth", and so we shall continue to follow him.'

CHAPTER 13 | ## GEORGE I ('Siosi') TUPOU
(1797–1893)

The most colourful figure in the 'motorcade' for the Coronation of Queen Elizabeth II in 1953 was one of whom most of the British public had never heard till that day: the late Queen Salote of Tonga. Few of those who watched her large, gay person braving the rain in an open carriage probably knew even where Tonga was; fewer still will have known that her grandfather was the first Christian King of the United Kingdom of Tonga, one in whose lifetime there had been cases of reversion to cannibalism in the islands.

But King George (as we shall call him throughout, though the name only came to him on his baptism in 1831) belongs, not as might seem appropriate in the category of 'absolute beginners', but in this Part III: and this for three reasons. Firstly, because he is one of the early examples of one who became a Christian, not directly through the agency of the white missionaries but through the influence of some of his own people. Secondly, because even before the Europeans appeared from the ocean's edge, there had been a move away from one of the most powerful elements in Polynesian paganism—the sacred Kingship. And thirdly, because in his own reign we can see the new religion, Christianity, beginning to shape the political structures of the Kingship. Indeed, his reign might be taken as a classic instance of socio-cultural evolution under the impact of a changed *weltanschauung*.

*   *   *

Taufa'ahau Tupou was, experts have calculated, born some time in 1797. He was a young man of fine physique.

His great natural powers were enhanced by the most careful athletic training. As he surpassed his fellows in stature and length of limb, so was he superior in all sports that demand skill. None was so fleet of foot, none could meet him in a wrestling- or a boxing-match, none could endure against him in swimming in the surface, nor handle a *tafaanga** laden with fish in a seaway as he; none was his match in a fight to the death.[1]

Once, armed only with a Fijian 'throwing-club' he was attacked by five enemies with spears. Being swifter than any of them, he ran into some rocks, knocked down the leading man with his club, took his spear and attacked the next two so effectively that they, and their other two companions, fled. All Tongans, indeed, took athletics of all sorts seriously. Basil Thomson says of them:

All Tongans are a race of athletes . . . but their real passion is cricket. Soon after its introduction the game became a national danger. The plantations were neglected; the cocoa-nuts lay rotting on the ground: for the whole population played cricket from dawn till dusk all over the island, with a bat if they could get it, but otherwise with a cocoa-nut branch and an unripe orange. They played matches, one village against another, and all the men of each village took an innings. With perhaps seventy-three on one side and fifty-two on the other a match lasted for days; and party feeling sometimes ran so high that at the end the losers fell upon the victors with the bats and stumps to avenge their disgrace.[2]

But this was half a century later. In his youth George Taufa'ahau witnessed violence almost continuously. When he was only two the murder of his grandfather set off a civil war which continued off and on for many years. Boys of his own age were taught to torture wounded prisoners. He was present when in 1806 an English privateer, the *Port-au-Prince*, called in at

* A type of catamaran.

Ha'apai for repairs, and the hereditary chief, Finau Ulukalala, having welcomed the crew on shore then attacked the ship and murdered half of them. He remembered the night when his father plotted with the same chief, Finau, to avenge the murder of his grandfather. One of the English survivors of the *Port-au-Prince*, William Mariner, who had been befriended and adopted by Finau, was a witness of this cold-blooded return murder.[3] It is perhaps understandable that, before any Christian influence reached George Tupou directly he had had enough of feuds and bloodshed. His father died in 1820, and he found himself now ruler of the Ha'apai Islands, which were by now the political centre of the kingdom—sensibly so, since they are geographically central.

But for some generations there had been a political development in the islands which was of far greater moment for their future than anyone at the time could have guessed. Traditionally—that is, until towards the end of the fifteenth century—the supreme ruler, known as the Tu'i Tonga, was a Priest-King of divine origin. Since he was the intermediary between the gods and the people the annual first-fruits of the harvest were offered to him in solemn ritual. But about 1500 the Priest-King began to be bored with the civil, kingly aspects of his office; so he, the Tu'i Tonga, instituted a new line of temporal rulers, through his brother and the latter's lineage—an office now known as the Tu'i Ha'atakalaua. This secular ruler became so important, and the Tu'i Tonga with his now merely priestly role became so secondary, that a curious lineal development followed. The Chief Priest (Tu'i Tonga) was expected to take as his principal wife the eldest daughter of the secular ruler (Tu'i Ha'atakalaua): and, even stranger, their eldest daughter became higher in rank than either her own father or her brother; and if she, in turn, had a daughter this last was regarded as the most exalted being on earth, as 'the sacred child' (Tamahá). The last known 'sacred child' died in 1852—Amelia: 'This Polynesian great lady, who had made herself the repository of the family traditions and had compiled a valuable record of the early kings, was a prolongation into the second half of the nineteenth century of an almost legendary past.'[4]

But there was even a further development in the direction of 'secularization' of power. For in about 1600—a hundred years later—the sixth of the secular rulers (the Tu'i Ha'atakalaua) himself got tired of ruling the troublesome Tongans, and so created yet a third office, by making his son a sort of prime minister (Tu'i Kanokupolu) with his own dynasty. So by the time George Tupou took on the reins of office—he was the nineteenth Tu'i Kanokupolu—his kingship was even further removed from the original Sacred Monarchy. The last reigning Tu'i Ha'atakalaua was killed when he, George, was only two— this was in the civil war mentioned above—and though the last Sacred Monarch (Tu'i Tonga) lingered on till 1865, he was largely ignored, for George was made King of united Tonga in 1845. Of the last Sacred Monarch, whose name was Laufili-tonga, Sir Harry Luke says:

> The spread of Christianity, by displacing the worship of the ancient gods and of their representative among the living, had reduced what little remained of his dignities to next to nothing. Indeed, Laufili-tonga himself died a devout Roman Catholic, a paradoxical end for the vicar on earth of a Polynesian Olympus.[5]

There was another paradox that needs to be appreciated to see the special role of Christianity in Tonga. As one student of the Pacific Islands, Dr. Aarne Koskinen, has pointed out, Christianity was better suited to Polynesian peoples like the Tongans than to Melanesian: for 'the divine hierarchy of Christian religion could more easily be reproduced in a society [like the Polynesian] which was conscious of a rank structure within itself, and the organization of the unseen world was more easily comprehended.'[6] Yet the connection between the civil hierarchy and the traditional animistic religion was, as we have seen, already much weakened. In other islands where it was still strong, as in Tahiti, it was an obstacle to Christianity: chiefs, like Pomare I of Tahiti, remained heathen, for they knew that 'without their sacred powers the chiefs would decline to the level of ordinary people. In fact, converted rulers were equal to all other islanders before God.'[7] But this kind of resistance was already weakened in Tonga by the decline in the sacred kingship, which made many of the rulers there sceptical of the divine powers of their local deities. Finau Ukalala had already attempted to abolish the great festival of *Inaji*;* and when this blood-thirsty and unreliable king began to see that the invasion of Christianity was well-nigh irresistible, he put

---

* The harvest ritual of first-fruits, mentioned above.

his own gods to a scientific test. (One wonders whether the snippets of Bible teaching that had infiltrated his domain included the story of Elijah challenging the *baalim*.) Finau was told that he could have a missionary of his own in a few months if he would 'renounce the lying spirits and turn to the true God'. Many of his doubts were resolved, and at last he said to the native Christians, 'Well, I will; and I will spend the next Lord's day with you in worshipping your God.' Two of his wives, many servants, another chief, and his sister joined the Christians in worship on the Sunday; and on the Monday, in the charming ingenuous account by Sarah Farmer,

the King gave orders, that seven of the principal idols should be placed in a row. He then addressed them in language like this: 'I have brought you here to prove you; and I tell you beforehand what I am about to do that you may be without excuse.' Then, commencing with the first, he said, 'If you are a god, run away, or you shall be burned in the fire which I have prepared!' The god made no attempt to escape. He then spoke to the next in the same way, and so on till he came to the last. As none of them ran, the king gave orders that the sacred houses should be set on fire. His commands were promptly obeyed. Eighteen temples, with their gods, were burned down. . . . Though many joined with their whole heart, yet hundreds were grievously troubled at their king's impious conduct, and sat trembling and silent to watch the result, looking for no less than some awful calamity. As no harm happened to the doers of the daring deed, they came to the conclusion, that their gods must be liars after all, and they too joined the praying people.[8]

It was, as a matter of fact, George Tupou who had been the intermediary in persuading this Finau (King of Vava'u, the most northerly of the island groups) in April 1831, when on a political visit to Vava'u, that the Christian missionaries were worth inviting. So it is evident that George's enthusiasm for spreading the Christian faith was already aroused; although he himself was not baptized till 7 August of that year.

*   *   *

We shall see that this evangelistic zeal remained with King George all his life. And perhaps it was due to the fact that he himself was the product of a similar zeal among some of his own kind. This was indeed (and to some extent has remained) a characteristic of the South Sea Islanders. Pagan visitors to islands where Christianity had taken a foothold could not help noticing the change that had taken place: and they would take back to their own islands the first knowledge of Christianity.[9] Sometimes the islanders would anticipate the coming of missionaries: 'Although the meaning of the new religion was still not understood, the natives resolved to build places of worship, while the old heathen sanctuaries were destroyed and idols burnt. . . . Worship of the unknown God of the white man was begun as well as it could be.'[10] So the missionary calling at an island unvisited by white men would be surprised, according to John Williams, to find that the natives already called themselves Christians. The inhabitants of one Fiji island 'were told that the Christians prayed, but did not know what a prayer was. A heathen priest was asked. He advised the natives to hold their breath while he spoke to the white man's god.'[11]

It is interesting that the first Samoan Christian was converted when on a visit to Nuku'alofa, Tonga, in 1828, and he spread the knowledge of Christianity so effectively in Samoa that the Chief was converted, and after that a great many others. As a result, they sent for a Wesleyan missionary, and when he arrived in 1835 he found two thousand Samoans professing Christian faith. Of course, once a chief has taken the step, it is difficult for his subjects not to follow him. Finau, already mentioned, wrote to the white missionary, 'My island, sir, will turn to the Great God, because I am the only chief on the island; I have no one to control me. When I turn, they all turn!'[12]

But it was not so easy at first with George Tupou. It was early in 1829 that he visited Nuku'alofa, the capital of Tonga Island (Tongatapu) itself in the South, and expressly asked the Methodists to send him a missionary to his own capital, Lifuka, of the Ha'apai Islands. There was no white missionary to spare, so he was offered a native teacher, Peter Vi.[13] George was furious at first: 'Only a Tongan man!' he exclaimed. 'How should the people of Ha'apai pay any attention to him?' However, on the voyage home the royal convoy of canoes encountered a vicious storm, and we are told that George at once interpreted this as a rebuke for his choosiness, returned, apologized, and gratefully accepted the second-class offer. Peter Vi proved a good choice; the King made good friends with him; and indeed, Vi tells us, from that moment

George showed himself 'very mischievous to the gods'. The pagan priests of Ha'apai were alarmed at the risks he was taking, and there were plots against the King; so the latter came out openly and proclaimed himself a Christian. He started at once to urge his faith on other rulers—such as Finau, as we have seen—even though his own baptism did not come till nearly two years later. Before this he was married: and this was itself something of a test.

The king was to be married as a Christian to the single wife of his choice. Finau of Vava'u was invited to the wedding, and brought a retinue. . . . It was a national occasion. The heathen chiefs of Ha'apai pressed round their sovereign. Suddenly a great sickness fell upon him. The heathen were for conveying him perforce to . . . the sacred island containing the sepulchres of the kings, whither it was customary to carry them at the approach of death. [George] Taufa'ahau stoutly refused to be moved. . . . Peter Vi [who tells the story] was keeping watch at the king's chamber door, all the while 'secretly and earnestly praying to the Lord' against the enemies' machinations. With some difficulty he found Mr. Thomas*, and informed him of the hostile design. The missionary and he entered the royal apartments together, and found that a potion had been administered in Vi's absence to the sufferer by a heathen official whom they had reason to suspect. [They] . . . countered the perilous drug with an emetic, followed by other medicine. But the patient was now reduced to extreme weakness; for hours his life hung by a thread. 'No Christian slept that night,' says Vi. . . . At dawn a woman's cry sounded, which the hearers at first took to be the death-wail—the king's sister was weeping for joy; he had awakened, with the fever gone!

'Thus', concluded Peter Vi, 'the Lord heard our prayer, and blessed the medicine. Our king lived, and . . . from that time the *lotu*† spread and increased in strength, and the devil's kingdom grew weaker and weaker.'[14]

It is not surprising that the missionaries found George ready for baptism, which was administered on 7 August 1831.

I preached [wrote Thomas] on Acts ii. 32–41. . . . After the sermon the chief stood, and in a very humble and becoming manner made confession of his faith and his purpose to give himself and his children

* John Thomas, pioneer Methodist missionary of Tonga.

† The preaching, teaching, prayer: the usual word for Christianity there. ('*Lotoo*—Adoration, invocation, to invoke, to pray' according to W. Mariner (J. Martin *Account of the Natives of Tonga Islands* (1827) II, App. lxxvi).)

to Christ. . . . He had chosen for his name *George*—or (as we write it) *Joaji* (*Siosi*)—out of respect to our good old king [George III] whose memory is cherished in these islands. The three children are baptized as Charlotte (*Salote*), David (*Tefita*), and Josiah (*Josaia*).[15]

Very soon after this we find the king functioning as a local preacher.

He did not presume upon his high civil dignity; but conducted himself in the Church of God with becoming humility. He took his turn as a local preacher in common with the others. . . . Mr. Tucker heard him preach one of his first sermons. The great court house . . . would not contain the people who thronged to hear their King. . . . He preached with great plainness and simplicity, and in strict accordance with the teaching of God's word.[16]

And already he began to show an initiative which characterizes his whole reign. The missionary went into the chapel one day— a new one which George had built in 1835—

to consult with the King about the size and arrangement of the communion place, when he found that George had a scheme of his own. He brought out several handsomely-carved spears . . . that had often been used in war, and that had come to him as an heir-loom from his ancestors. These he converted into rails for the communion- place; while two clubs of beautiful manufacture, formerly wor- shipped as gods, were fixed at the bottom of the pulpit-stairs.[17]

Three years after George's baptism there was a remarkable 'Revival', a minor Pentecostal movement, within the mission churches. It started up in the north, in Vava'u, and was marked, as such phenomena are, by open confession, much weeping and shouting, and a great deal of spiritual emotion. Such was the enthusiasm that 'it was found necessary to give up the schools for a week or two, and to hold six prayer-meetings every day.'[18] It happened that George and his wife were on a visit to Vava'u at the time; they too were affected by this rush of the Holy Spirit, and 'the faith which in their case . . . had been comparatively notional, now reached the depths of the heart, and they entered unmistakably into the knowledge of salvation. . . .' Indeed, this had practical results: the King took the news back to Lifuka with him, and with it a new notion of how to order the interior of the church there.

When the building was under construction he had been grieved to find the pulpit made the highest position within the walls; it was etiquette in all Tongan assemblies that the king should sit above his subjects. To guard his dignity, therefore, he had a platform raised for himself at the opposite end of the church, from which he could overlook the Minister. On his return from Vava'u after the revival, *down came the* royal platform; henceforth His Majesty sat in God's house on the same floor with the common man.[19]

In 1841 the General Superintendant of the South Sea Mission (Wesleyan Methodist) visited Tonga, and happened to be there when King George preached at Nuku'alofa. He was much impressed when he met the King and Queen first.

He was sitting with the skeleton of a sermon in his hand, preparing for his Sabbath duties. I was greatly delighted at seeing this Christian King. He is a tall, fine-looking, well-made man; with a remarkably penetrating eye, and of dignified carriage. Christian benignity beamed from his countenance. His words were few, but well chosen. He does not think aloud; but deliberates and then speaks.

On the following Sunday he heard the King preach.

The King looked remarkably well in his snow-white cravat and black coat. There are several English ministers whose skin is much darker than his. He has not much action; but is deliberate and impressive; combining in his appearance the dignity of a King, the simplicity of a Christian, and the benignity of one called to preach the Gospel of the blessed God.[20]

*   *   *

Unfortunately it was almost impossible for the King to keep religion and politics separate. As Koskinen says, he had to oppose heathenism for political reasons. With the disappearance of the power of the Tu'i Tonga, who had provided the unity of the realm, George found that threats to his own supremacy were inevitably connected with attempts to revive a threatened paganism.[21] There was a further misfortune: that the arrival of a Roman Catholic mission happened to coincide with the challenges to George's authority. In 1837 a party of Roman Catholic priests, with their bishop, called at Vava'u, where George was staying at the time, and asked permission to start a mission. George demurred, saying, 'I and my people have all turned to God,' and referred the matter to Mr. Thomas. The latter, when approached by the Bishop, said that it was the King's business—he, not the missionaries, ruled the island. The

Bishop said he only wanted to leave priests on the island for two or three months to learn the language. The King thought it unlikely they could learn much in that time, and refused permission.[22] Between that date and a further attempt by the Roman Catholics, war broke out. It had not wholly died down when Bishop Pompallier of New Zealand returned, in 1841, to try once more. Failing to enter Vava'u, they established a mission, first in an island two hundred miles north, and, two years later, in Tongatapu itself, not far from the central capital. When war again broke out, the pagan chiefs, supported by some chiefs who had become Roman Catholics—the chiefs of Bea and Mua, and later the Tu'i Tonga himself (Laufilitonga)—formed the opposition to King George. Thus the war took on at least the aspect of a religious crusade.

It is difficult at this date to give an impartial assessment of blame in this matter: but there is no doubt that the Methodist missionaries were at least as culpable as the Roman Catholics in their controversial methods. Sarah Farmer gives us a dialogue between some 'loyalist' (i.e. Methodist) chiefs and the priests, which show how well the former had been drilled in Protestant controversial divinity. The same, after all, happened in other parts of the South Seas—Tahiti being the most notorious. In Fiji Protestants had quoted Luther's description of the Pope as Antichrist; and a French Catholic historian says that the Wesleyans once claimed that the Pope had become a Wesleyan when he realized that his own beliefs were heretical![23] And in Hawaii the (Protestant) Government sentenced certain natives who professed themselves Catholics to compulsory labour: and the authority for this enforced labour was the law against idolatry![24] Nor is this so far-fetched as it might seem, for Sarah Farmer says, of the chiefs who became Roman Catholics:

The chiefs of Bea and Mua embraced Popery, and so, after a few years, did the Tui-tonga. They made an agreement, however, with their teachers, that they should not be required to put away their wives, nor to give up their dances and other heathen customs. The Christian natives said that they could see very little difference between Popery and heathenism.[25]

In New Zealand, too, Mgr. Pompallier found that a tribe which welcomed Catholicism most enthusiastically proved to be one that had been a mortal enemy of the Protestant tribes.[26] And this kind of intermixture of political with religious rivalry was true of Tonga at this period. Since George was by 1845 the Tu'i Kanokupolu (secular ruler) of the whole of Tonga, the Roman Catholics claimed that their convert, the Tu'i Tonga, was the legitimate ruler, and George an ambitious usurper. When George heard of the plots he publicly accused the priests of responsibility for them. The Tu'i Tonga himself, being better acquainted than the priests with the political changes of the past, denied that he had any ambition for secular power, and said that indeed he had no right to it. But the priests still backed him, and referred to him as 'l'ancien roi détrôné'. (Perhaps French history, with its associations between Catholicism and monarchist legitimism, had an influence here.) At any rate, the priests went on to claim that the Catholic chiefs at Tongatapu were justified in ignoring the laws of George Tupou —based, they felt, on Protestant principles—and finally civil war again broke out in 1852. The missionaries stayed in the camps of their candidates and marched with (or behind) their troops. George showed his usual military skill; the war was won; and his victory meant the final unification of Tonga.[27] The Roman Catholics continued to minister to their minority on Tongatapu, preserving their aloofness. There is a faintly comic echo of these old religious wars in 1891, when the Lords and Commons met in Council in the capital, Nuku'alofa, to accept the new Civil Code, drawn up under the advice of Basil Thomson.

Mataka, the chief clerk . . . calls the roll. The new members are now to take the oath. The ceremony is imposing until the turn of the two Roman Catholic members arrives. They object to be sworn upon the Protestant Bible, and a clerk runs in haste for a version of the Bible translated into Tongan by the Roman Catholics. He returns with a thick shiny-covered book, which the two members kiss cheerfully. I examined it afterwards, and found it to be a French and English dictionary.

There is a further reason, which has to be frankly faced, why religion and politics could not easily be kept apart in these islands: and that is the strategic and economic supremacy of Tonga in the area. As the anthropologist, Ruth Benedict, has said, Fiji 'experienced its first European influence not at first hand from white men, but through the natives of the Polynesian island of Tonga who, stimulated by the promise of wealth from trade with Europeans and equipped with European fire-arms, effected in the first half of the 19th century a military, religious and cultural conquest of this area of Fiji.'[28] But they were able to do this partly because there were already large Tongan colonies in Fiji. The Fijians themselves were less enthusiastic in their reception of the Tongans. The latter preached everywhere, but also 'attempted at the same time to imbue their converts with a reverence for Tonga and its King George, which was hotly resented in some quarters. . . . [They] would be heard saying] "England, France and America are great countries, but Tonga is greater."[29]

All this lies behind King George's famous letter to the heathen king of Fiji, Thakombau, in 1854. He had already visited Thakombau the year before, on his way to Australia to inspect 'civilized society'. On his return he wrote to the Fijian king. A tactless and imperial consul, John B. Williams, referring to the cannibalism and savagery of Fiji (and Thakombau was a cannibal), had written that his island

ought to be destroyed and the people swept from the face of the earth. Then, and not till then, will commerce move uninterruptedly in this archipelago where the merchants can carry on so lucrative a business, and where they can find exports so numerous.

It is time the respectable nations were aroused from their slumber, and visited this group of islands, and punished the knowing and wilful cannibals. . . .

A ship of war could lay off Bau, knock down and destroy that town, while one is smoking a cigar.

George sympathized with Thakombau, and wrote,

I write to make known my love to you and the Bauan friends. When I arrived in Sydney, I received a letter which concerns you and the people of Bau. This letter is the writing of the consul at Rewa [John Williams] . . . and I am not certain whether Fiji will be in danger, or whether it will escape; for the consul's letter is a bad one. He says that you commanded the property of the white people to be burnt.

I expect to visit you . . . to bring away my canoe;* and when we have finished planting, we shall come to you. It is good, Thakombau,

---

* Tongan canoes had almost all been built in Fiji since the end of the eighteenth century, and made a good excuse to visit that island. Maafu, son of George's predecessor, was sent to Fiji for canoe-building, and by 1853 had organized Tongan forces throughout the Lau archipelago and battled his way to power.

that you should consider the thing which concerns the white people; and when the Fijian friends wish to do their minds, do not be guided by them. It is good you should be humble; it will be well for you and your land. I wish, Thakombau, that you would *lotu*. When I visit you, we will talk about it, for I desire that Bau and the Fiji friends may stand well. But it will be well for you, Thakombau, to think wisely in these days. This is the end of my writing. I, George Tubou.[30]

Thakombau did, in fact, after some resistance, become a Christian that year. In a war that followed George won a battle which rescued Thakombau, and this established George (who has been called a 'somewhat questionable heir to the kingship'[31]) all the more firmly in his position.

Later troubles were also semi-political, in the guise of ecclesiastical jurisdiction. For some time the Tongans had been jealous that the surplus of their church contributions had been going, via the Australian Methodist Conference, to help needy missions in other lands. George asked several times for leave to spend the surplus on their own missionary work—we have seen that the Tongans were evangelizing Fiji and other islands. Refusal led to a desire for self-government. Fiji continued to have internal disputes and had finally been ceded to the British Government in 1874. George was afraid that the same might happen to Tonga. And he was supported in this by an eccentric 'missionary', the Rev. Shirley Waldemar Baker. Baker had come to Tonga in 1860, but had gradually worked his way into politics, and by 1880 was Prime Minister. Indeed, not only was he Premier, but by 1890 he was also 'Minister of Foreign Affairs, President of the Court of Appeal, Auditor-General, Minister of Lands, Judge of the Land Court, Minister of Education, Agent-General, and Medical Attendant to the king'![32] Baker not only warded off annexation by Great Britain by persuading King George to accept a treaty with a German Consul-General—Tonga being thus recognized by one of the Great Powers; he also urged on the King that the Wesleyans of Tonga should have a church of their own. This was partly because Baker himself was under criticism from the Australian Conference. But it met George's own desires for independence. And so was set up the Wesleyan Free Church of Tonga, which was very much a State church. Worse, when many loyal Wesleyans objected to this, and tried to continue in their church, Baker saw fit to accuse them of supporting plots against his life (there was one such, for Baker was, not unnaturally, very unpopular), and to persecute them.

On the pretence that there was an insurrection against the king's authority on Tongatapu, he (Baker) summoned the men of Ha'apai and Vava'u to come and restore order. They came with all the savage ruffianism in them aroused by the remembrance that Tonga-tapu was their ancient enemy. . . . They spread over the country, plundering the houses of the Wesleyans, flogging and insulting all who refused to join the Free Church. The remnant of those who still held out, some two hundred souls, were huddled on board two small schooners and shipped off to Fiji.[33]

It is a measure of Baker's power that among the captives was George's own daughter.

By now, of course, the King was an old man. And fortunately for him the persecution did not last long: for Baker went too far, and the High Commissioner stepped in and ordered him off the island in 1890. It was this ejection which led to Basil Thomson arriving at Tonga to take over for some months as Assistant Prime Minister—an appointment which led not only to the recovery of order in the islands but the writing of the best, and most amusing book we possess on Tonga's history.

*   *   *

There is one matter on which even the most critical writers about Tonga agree: the effect of Christian teaching, and especially the teaching of George Tupou himself, upon the conduct of war. Reactions to some aspects of Tongan Method-ism may be various. Mr. Thomas, the missionary, tells us with some satisfaction of the effect of the Pentecostal revival at Lifuka in 1834 on one Englishman. This sailor was temporarily marooned on the island, and found himself

alone among a people speaking a strange language. There was no Missionary there; the only teacher being a native. The Englishman wished to make himself friendly; but he soon thought the people as strange as their tongue. Let him move where he might, he found nothing going on but singing and praying. . . . He could not understand a single word, but he knew well what they were doing. . . . Forgotten words came back to his memory—words learned in a Sunday school, or at a mother's knee. . . . His hard heart was melted. The English sailor knelt down among the Islanders of the Pacific.[34]

Sir Basil Thomson was less impressed with the similar phenomenon which he witnessed sixty years later, the *bolotu* or night-
service, a Tongan speciality. He found it an orgy of open confession and self-accusation—usually of a safely general kind,
but not always:

Tradition has it that the unregenerate Mary Bukato . . . showed
leanings towards repentance, and there was dire consternation
among the men of Sawana. . . . A night came when the enthusiasm
passed the bounds. The acclamations were mingled with the sobs of
the penitents . . . and in the midst Mary was seen standing, weeping
aloud. The dreadful day had come, and one after another the men
of the place slunk out to spread the dire news. . . . A terrible and
damning history fell from the lips of this penitent Phryne of the
South Seas. When she had finished there was scarcely a man in the
church, but the women sat and drank it all in, and many a household
in Sawana dates its domestic troubles from that terrible *bolotu* when
Mary 'told her soul'.[35]

The King took over the strict sabbatarianism of the missionaries, too, and some of the Tongan inhabitants of Fiji were in
fact younger and wilder men who had gone there to 'escape
home-restraints and the strict rule of King George'.[36] But
George was not peculiar in this: puritanism and the most rigid
sabbatarianism were characteristic of most of the Protestant
islands. 'When in 1826 an American man-of-war arrived in the
port of Honolulu, Hawaii, on a Sunday, its salute was only
answered on Monday'![37] More questionable was George's
somewhat nationalistic zeal for Tongan Methodism. We have
seen that he sent Tongan missionaries to Fiji, and converted
the chief there; he also sent teachers to Samoa in 1841, in spite
of the agreement (to which, admittedly, he had not been a
party) that Samoa should be the preserve of the London
Missionary Society which had been sending in teachers from
Tahiti. This had the effect of hardening the divisions between
what the Samoans called the *lotu* Tahiti and the *lotu* Tonga).
For years the dwindling Methodists in Samoa refused to use the
Scripture versions of the L.M.S. and stuck to the fragmentary
and crude translations by their Wesleyan missionary.[38] However, it is to Tonga's credit that indigenous missionaries went
out from its little islands so early and in such numbers: 'few
Christian nations, in proportion to their size, have produced so
many Missionaries as the Tongans.'[39]

And the effect of all this spread of Christianity can be seen, concretely, in the disappearance of the wilder, more savage and vindictive aspects of war. It was in the areas of Fiji populated by emigrant Tongans that cannibalism first started to disappear.[40] Both in the Tongan war of 1837, in which George took part, and in that of 1840, there was more reluctance to start fighting, more attempts at reconciliation first, and more mercy to prisoners and the vanquished than had been traditional on the islands. And in the 'religious' war of 1852 George was explicit that the women and children must be spared, that none of the enemy chiefs were to be killed, and that the goods of the Roman Catholic priests should be respected, even though they had sided with the enemy.[41] Tributes to King George, as a result of this, are impartial and unambiguous. Even a French Captain, Belland, who was sent to inquire into the complaints of the priests concerning the 1852 war, reported favourably to the King on the causes of the war, and sent a cordial message to George afterwards:

Tell the King I have seen and conversed with many chiefs of the South Sea Islands; but I never knew one so wise as he. The French have acknowledged his authority, by directing me to him as supreme chief of Tonga, and he must employ his authority in protecting all foreigners from insult, and must allow his subjects to choose what religion they please.[42]

Other tributes to the King's dignity, wisdom, and impartiality were made by a Capt. John Elphinstone Erskine in 1849, and Sir J. Everard Home, Captain of H.M.S. *Calliope* in 1852, both official visitors to Tonga.

There is one tribute from Sir Basil Thomson which is perhaps something of a back-hander. He is very critical of Tonga's Constitution-making, and its attempt at imitating Western democracy. The missionaries, he says, were to blame: 'brought up in Australia to believe that universal suffrage and representative government is the nearest approach to Utopia attainable by mortal man, they persuaded the king and chiefs against their better judgment to exchange the ancient communal system for a brand-new constitution on the English plan.'[43] As a result, in 1862,

a system evolved from centuries of experiment to suit the needs of Anglo-Saxons was forced in a single day upon a handful of ignorant

Orientals. . . . The *Consitutone* [*sic*] became henceforth the fetish oi the Tongan people. Most of them did not know what it was, but it had been introduced by the missionaries, and was intimately connected, they believed, with its outlandish fellow *Konisiensi* (Conscience), and in some mysterious way it elevated their country to the level of one of the Great Powers.[44]

But, says Thomson, King George's first written code of law, promulgated in Vava'u in 1839, though minimal and crude, was probably more suited to the people than 'the elaborate but often incoherent effusions of the missionary lawyers' which replaced it. And George himself, 'to his credit be it said', long resisted this attempt to impose a Western-type constitution, saying his people weren't ready for it.[45] Sir Basil should know, for he was largely responsible for the Constitution which replaced Baker's, after the latter's ignominious departure. But one cannot help feeling some element of British nineteenth-century condescension in his attitude: and Sir Harry Luke's later assessment is more favourable. He says (writing in 1962) that few features of Tonga are more remarkable than 'the genius of its inhabitants for grafting the best elements oi European civilization on to the best elements of their own.'[46] And there is no doubt that King George was, as much as any-one, responsible for this balance.

He was, as we have said, a very old man (93) when Baker left and Basil Thomson arrived. But when the latter had to have audience with George on official business, he found him remarkably on the spot. On one occasion he even admits that the old King scored off him.[47] Thomson's farewell interview with the King—who had not been enthusiastic about his arrival, and had had to meet (unfounded) criticisms that Thomson was being sent to herald a take-over of Tonga by the British Government—was moving. 'I was spared any speech-making. The old man said a few words full of quiet dignity and regret that pleased me more than any elaborate and effusive thanks would have done.'[48] And he admits that George's deliberate and spartan simplicity was impressive. By now (he says) the old King is less interested in politics: the Prime Minister goes in to ask for a meeting of the Privy Council, and George spends most of the time talking about a church he is building.[49] And the contrast between official luxury and George's asceticism is marked: 'In the king's palace there is a throne room furnished like an Australian parlour, with Kidderminster carpet, ormolu ornaments under glass shades, and crewel-work mats on the tables . . . while in a bare room on the ground-floor the king sleeps on his mat spread on the boards, and eats his yams from a single plate.'[50] And this is not just primitive disorder and slovenliness. For

his house was very meanly furnished: a green iron bedstead in the inner room covered with mats was the only bedroom furniture, and besides the table and office chairs in the middle room, there was only a shelf of the commonest crockery. . . . It was characteristic of the king that while he had a well-found house in Nuku'alofa, he lived from choice on the barest necessities, and spent a large portion of his income on building churches.[51]

Note. The following, by an anthropologist who studied Tongan religion and society thoroughly, will perhaps elucidate the 'secularization' of the sacred kingship, and also illustrate the passage from 'pagan' to Christian:

Taliai Tubou is the god of the Tui Kanokupolu, whose title is now assumed by the constitutional ruler of Tonga. Even before the advent of Christianity real power was passing out of the hands of the Tui Tonga into those of more active lords, notably the Tui Kanokupolu, who was in any case a very high chief. . . .
    Before his conversion to Christianity Tubou I [= George] worshipped Toki-i-Moana, whose sacred animal is, as the name implies, the sea-eel. A temple was built for him (Toki-i-Moana) in Uiha. . . . There was some question as to whether the king himself should not [sc. as two of his sons had been] be buried there [in the terraced native vaults in Uiha] . . . as doubtless he would have been if old native custom had been observed, but one of the outward symbols of recent Europeanization is a royal burial ground in Nuku'alofa

though, unfortunately, (as the writer, Mr. E. E. V. Collocot says), with concrete replacing the traditional and beautiful coral slabs.[52]

PART FOUR | IN OPEN SEA

We come to what might be called the 'post-missionary' period, though this term (as we shall see) can only be a relative one, and cannot be exactly defined chronologically. The meaning we are giving to the term will best be defined by the figures chosen to illustrate it. And here the choice is so wide as to be even more arbitrary than that by which the biographies were selected for the previous three parts.

The two sections into which this part naturally falls I have entitled 'Reproductions' and 'Transpositions'. Neither of these descriptions—least of all the first—is to be taken in a pejorative sense. To 'reproduce' in their own terms, and largely by their own efforts with comparatively little prompting from the white missionaries, the pattern of religious devotion, worship, and conduct handed down to them from the first teaching, is in itself no mean achievement. But it has to be distinguished from the other section because its influence is likely to decrease rapidly as time goes on. The second section explains itself. It will be obvious, however, that there is considerable overlap between the two; and some may feel that one or two of the biographies could have been located in a different section from that in which they are here given. If the characters themselves are outraged by their bedfellows, I apologize to their shades.

Section A. REPRODUCTIONS

CHAPTER 14 | VARIOUS

It would be easy to fill a book with brief biographies of African, Asian, etc., Christian men and women who have strikingly lived out their Christian convictions in a pattern closely copied from the Europeans who brought them their Christian faith. The majority of these would probably be Roman

Catholics, if only for the simple reason that they are the ones who have been most enthusiastically recorded. When the blessed Martin de Porrès was raised to the altar a few years ago it was clear that, apart from the merit of his case (which was high and deserved), one motive for the beatification was a desire to redress the balance: saints with white skins so out-number the rest that the more non-whites we can recognize as official intercessors in heaven the better. In the days of Race war it is good to have someone like this half-caste Dominican lay-brother from Lima on the Christian side.[1] It would no doubt also be salutary to be assured of the prayers of an Arab girl, Mary Baouardi (1846–78), born in a village near Nazareth of parents of the Greek Catholic rite, who became 'Sister Mary of Jesus Crucified'. She was admitted to the Carmelite order in Pau in 1867, was sent by them to Mangalore (India) in 1870, returned to Pau in 1872 after two years of spiritual suffering, received the stigmata there, and again in Bethlehem, to which she was sent in 1875, and died three years later. But her spirituality was wholly Western.[2] Fr. Cyriac Elias Chavara, (1805–71), the Founder and Prior-General of the Syrian Carmelite Congregation of Malabar, Founder too of the Religious Life for Women in Malabar, and Vicar General for the Syrian Churches, might seem to provide useful material for an area, and a tradition, not generally covered in mission history; but unfortunately, though evidently a worthy and holy man, Fr. Chavara does not seem to have achieved anything distinctive. It is true that he felt, as did other Syrian Christians, the falsity of the imposition by the Portuguese of Latin rites, vestments, and other Western customs upon his people; and he tried to urge a return to Syrian ways. But conservative opposition was too much for him, and the Latin rite remained in force during his lifetime.[3] Another Indian Catholic was Sister Alphonsa Muttathupadathu of Kudamaloor, Travancore (1910–46). Her baptismal name was Anna—and she was known by her friends as Annakutty. She joined the Poor Clares of Bharananganam, and was professed in 1936. She suffered from painful ailments (unspecified) which she is said to have borne with courage and dedication and, when she died at the age of thirty-six, she had gained such a reputation locally for sanctity that various cures were claimed to have been due to her intercession, and the usual hopes for her beatification and canonization have been expressed.[4] Moving to another continent, we have sister Josephine Bakhita of the Sudan (c. 1869–1947). She was born in the Sudanese province of Darfur, and was of the Daju negroid group, for long the most powerful tribal dynasty in that part of Africa—about six hundred miles West of Khartoum. She was abducted by Arabs when she was still a girl and later sold to a Turkish officer in El Obeid. A year later he had to sell all his slaves, and allowed Bakhita to be taken into service by the Italian vice-consul in Khartoum. In 1883, when she was about fourteen he was transferred to Italy, and took her with him. She was entrusted to the Canossian Daughters of Charity for her education. When her Italian mistress insisted on taking her back to Africa, maintaining that she was still of 'slave' status, the Sisters stepped in and brought a legal action to prove that as soon as she had landed on Italian soil she was automatically free. So she stayed with the Sisters, was baptized, and later joined the Order, being professed in 1896. The next year she was sent to Schio, in the foot-hills of the Alps. And there she died in 1947, having never returned to her country though she constantly prayed for the conversion of Africa, and had been much used by the missionary Fathers to give discourses at meetings up and down Italy. Again, having been taken early from her original environment she became, apart from skin-colour, an ordinary, Italian religious, though one of exemplary piety.[5]

If there were space, it would be tempting to give full biographies of three 'reproducers' who would be a vividly contrasting trio, and who also exhibited considerable independence of thought and action. But in the first two cases, their lives have been written and are easily accessible; the third, though very little known over here, differs little from countless other ex-slaves, adopted by their rescuers, and then sent back to work in their country of origin. So we must be content with bare sketches of their significance.

(i)

The first is 'Father Six' (1825–99)—Pierre Huu Triem, of Vietnam. He was born at, and lived through, a time of much persecution of Christians: he was accustomed as a student to take refuge with others from time to time in the hills. He was ordained deacon in 1858, and almost at once captured and tortured, and after six months in gaol was exiled. The worst persecution was under the King, Tu-Duc, from 1860 to 1862. But in 1860 Pierre, just ordained priest, was faced with a dilemma. A usurper led a rebellion against Tu-Duc; some Christians were tempted to join the rebel, to overthrow their persecutor. But Pierre ('Père Six', as he was known to the Europeans*), remembering his old bishop's teaching that 'rebellion is sin', told them to support the King. This was decisive, for four thousand Christians supporting the rebel might have led to the King's overthrow. After 1862 there was a peaceful period—enforced by France. But fortunately Père Six had won a good reputation with the emperor, and did not share the unpopularity of the French. He was parish priest of Phat Diem (1865–99), and built the Cathedral there—draining marshes and reclaiming land to do so—in the style of a Chinese pagoda. When Tu-Duc died in 1883 anarchy was threatened, and Père Six was consulted by the court: how could a trustworthy successor be chosen? He replied, quoting a Vietnamese tradition, and his advice was taken. In 1899 he was given almost the highest mandarin dignity, 'Honorary Minister of the Rites'. He was only an assistant priest, for the idea of an indigenous dean even was inconceivable then. But he was free to experiment with native adaptations: a passion play; the use of local wood and stone, local patterns and craftsmanship; prayers in 'Annamese' sung in the mode of Annamite rhythmic chants. He even introduced frequent communion (though Pius X's decree commending this practice did not come till 1905). In 1896 the French Governor-General of Indo-China said 'Phat Diem *is* Père Six'. And Lord Curzon[6] (later Viceroy of India) passed through in 1893, and wrote of him that his position was

almost exactly analogous to many a European prototype in the Middle Ages . . . the union of spiritual and temporal powers in the same hands. . . . (This phenomenon) may still be observed in the person of an Annamite Mandarin of the Second rank, who is also a priest of the Catholic Church. . . . Over seventy years of age, he has spent nearly half a century in Phat Diem. . . . Unlike his countrymen, who wear their hair twisted in a chignon at the back of the head, his own hair is cut short, but he adheres to the national sober-coloured turban.

* From the Annamite custom of naming their children by number.

Curzon goes on to describe his attempts at adaptation. His own name is an example. But more:

> In the body of the Church was an immense processional Sedan Chair, closed with curtains, and surrounded by poles and lanterns; a curious sort of castellated . . . catafalque employed in chanting the requiem for the dead. . . . [His] countrymen are familiar with such chairs, carried in religious processions and supposed to contain the spirits of the departed.

Further, when Père Six moves abroad 'he is attended by the green umbrellas and the roofed hammock of the Annamite Mandarin.' Curzon concludes: 'In bidding farewell to Phat Diem I felt that rarely in my travels had I encountered a more remarkable figure than this little pope in Annam. May his shadow not soon grow less!'

(ii)

The second provides a complete contrast: a twentieth century, American-educated, evangelical pastor, Ju-Ju (John) Sung (1901–44). Perhaps their only point of contact is that Sung also preached in Vietnam. His father was a pastor in Hinghwa, Fukien Province (South-East China), of the American Methodist Episcopal Church. Sung, thought unsuitable for the ministry, went to America and graduated well, in physics and chemistry, in 1923; he obtained his M.Sc.—coming top of the list—followed by an assistantship to the professor, and by his doctorate in 1926. He went to the Union Theological Seminary, but was unsatisfied by its 'liberal protestantism'. He nearly had a nervous breakdown, but saw a vision which he took to be a call to abandon his academic career. On his return to China he threw his diploma, medals, and so forth overboard. In Shanghai he adopted Chinese dress, and from this date (1928) until his death he worked as an itinerant, unattached evangelist. He became a sort of minor Billy Graham (better, a Billy Sunday) of the Far East. 'He would race back and forth on the platform or leap over the Communion rail and stand in the aisles. Or he would walk down the aisles and point his finger in the face of someone in the audience, then rush back to the front of the church and perhaps stand on the Communion rail to finish his sermon.'[7] He was uncompromising about his brand of evangelical Christianity, and refused to co-operate with 'liberals'—'The teaching of Confucius is better than theirs. What the Chinese need is Jesus Christ and His Cross.' His most spectacular work was in South-East Asia, mostly among the 'Chinese dispersion' of the Philippines, Singapore, Indonesia, and Malaya, Borneo and Sarawak, Thailand, Indo-China.

His work especially in Malaysia and Thailand led to the founding of seventy 'evangelistic bands' which were still active in 1954. He urged strongly that his fellow-Christians should cease their dependence on foreign missionary support. 'You should look to the Lord of all things, and realise that the time has come for the church to be self-propagating, self-governing and self-supporting—truly independent.' These three 'selves' became, of course, the slogan of the 'Three-Self Movement' which the Churches had to adopt under the Chinese People's Republic some quarter of a century later: but with a difference. Perhaps neither Sung nor the Chinese Communists knew that the terms go back to the nineteenth century—Henry Venn, Secretary General of the C.M.S., wrote, 'The breath of life in a native church' depends on 'self-government, self-support, self-extension.'[8] Sung lived that out.

(iii)

Finally we have Adrian Atiman (c. 1866–1956). He is worth a brief sketch, not only because he has scarcely been heard of in this country, but because so few celebrated African Christians of his period have been Roman Catholics. He was born near Timbuktu, but captured as a child in 1875 by Touaregs, while playing on the banks of the Niger. He was carried, in a sack, by camel to the North, towards the oases of Southern Algeria. He remembered little but the thirst—on occasion they had to drink not only camel's milk, but camel's urine. At Metlili he was seen, up for sale, by some White Fathers, and bought—for about £6. He was sent to St. Ugène, near Algiers, then for more education to Carthage, Tunis, and Malta. Here from 1861 he studied medicine, to become a 'medical catechist'. In 1888 he went with a group of White Fathers to Equatorial Africa. At Zanzibar he studied tropical medicine, and then the party set off for Lake Tanganyika, to the White Fathers' mission at Karema. Atiman opened a small dispensary and clinic and did his best with his limited equipment. At first he was stared at, and, finding that he spoke French, the children shouted 'Bwana Mwezi! Bwana Mwezi!' ('Mister Black-man').

The Fathers wanted to reach the Wabenda tribe, who had been hostile; so suggested to Atiman that he take a wife from this tribe. They chose a daughter of a Wabenda chief; and it certainly was not a love-match. The girl, Wansabira, was un-educated and heathen; she twice ran away from him, and at first was totally uninterested in his religion. His patience won in the end, and not only was she the means by which he obtained access to a number of non-Christian tribes in the area, but she bore him a son who entered the seminary in 1913 and later was ordained priest. In his youth Atiman had learned French and Italian; now he learned several of the local African languages. (His last words, on his death-bed, were a mixture of French and Swahili.) He became so trusted in the area that, apart from his medical work, he was consulted on family and social matters, even becoming a 'marriage broker'. He taught himself surgery from text-books, and performed amputations. He became known as the Grand Old Man of Karema. He received three Pontifical decorations, and three decorations from the Belgian Government for his work with colonial troops in the 1916–18 campaign. Finally, the highest honour of all, he was presented with the Welcome Medal of the Royal Society (for those who have done notable service in Africa): an honour he shared with such world-famous figures as Marshal Lyautey, Lord Lugard, Lord Hailey, and Albert Schweitzer. He died in 1956, after nearly seventy years given to Africa, a man of prayer and great simplicity. He was neither a black European nor a 'white man's nigger' but a universal citizen.[9]

CHAPTER 15

I have reserved for a separate chapter two outstanding person-alities who, though they belong in the realm of 'Reproductions', deserve slightly fuller treatment. The first is very little known over here—nothing has been published about him in English, and even the French material is not easily come by. The second had some publicity, soon after his death, but has since been largely forgotten; and, again, not all the facts about him are available in English publications. The fact that both were Roman Catholics is more or less accidental, though what was said at the beginning of the last chapter applies no doubt here.

i. 'PAUL' MEHMET-ALI MULLA-ZADÉ (1881–1959)

So far, among the various characters who have appeared before us not one comes from an Islamic background. This is not surprising, for—except in Indonesia, where the largest percentage of Christianized Muslims in the world could be found by the middle of this century—it is well known that the difficulties put in the way of conversion to Christianity by Islam are so formidable that the numbers have always remained very small.[1] And most of them have, for various reasons—of which perhaps the Muslim law against iconographic representation may be psychologically one of the strongest—become Protestants.

Paul Mulla, however, was not only a Roman Catholic but became a priest and a Monsignor in the Pontifical Institute in Rome. What is more, his movement of thought was very precise, and has been given to us in some detail.

He came from an honoured Turkish family which played an important role in the history of the island of Crete. In the sixteenth century one of his ancestors, who was the equivalent of the Chancellor of the Exchequer for Crete, recently then conquered by the Turks, married a Christian of Greek origin. They then added the title 'Zadé' to their name, which brought an added touch of nobility to it. Paul Mulla's maternal great-grandfather was Albanian and a nephew of the Viceroy of Egypt, Mehmet-Ali, who gave him the post of Governor-General of Crete. This Saïd Bey also married a Greek Christian. But in Paul's own family Christianity was never mentioned.

Paul was born in the palace of the former Governor-General (6 September 1881), the eldest of six children. His father was a doctor, and had studied in French at the military academy in Constantinople. He was a very pious Muslim, and took his family every Friday to the mosque. He was also both well-to-do and a man of culture: he founded a public library and a local newspaper. The children were taught privately—Turkish, Greek, Arabic, and Persian. An Imam came regularly to instruct them in the Koran. The doctor was a great Francophil: the family meal was always preceded by Islamic prayers, but after it the children came round the table, kissed their parents, and then all sang the 'Marseillaise'. So it is not surprising that Dr. Mulla decided to send his sons to France to complete their education.

So Mehmet-Ali (Paul) went to the Lycée at Aix-en-Provence in 1895. He was to study law, and he did extremely well; he obtained his baccalaureate, with honours, in Latin and Greek in 1899. The year before, he was joined by his younger brother, who had managed, in spite of the international blockade of Crete in 1898, to get on to a boat—thanks to the intervention of a French admiral. The brothers spent Sundays with a M. Edouard Jourdan, a lecturer in the Law Faculty, who acted as their ward.

Up till now (Paul wrote later) he had had his intelligence stretched; but none of this had nourished his spiritual needs. Looking back he attributed his spiritual awakening to the fact (unknown to him at the time, of course) that the Pope (Leo XIII) had that year (1899) consecrated the human race to the Sacred Heart. It was at this point that Paul started to study philosophy.

At first it was largely a matter of being introduced to the great names in Western thought—Plato, Aristotle, St. Anselm, St. Thomas, Descartes, Leibniz, and Maine de Biran. He was put in charge of the class library, and he plunged into Spencer, Kant, and—with delight—Leibniz. He began to think that his heart had been frozen up for fifteen years, but that now he was beginning to recapture the enthusiasm and idealism he had had when (he says) he was six.

It was at this point that a decisive meeting took place: in 1900 Maurice Blondel (1862–1949) was one of his examiners in his oral for the second part of his baccalaureate. Paul thought he saw something in the mind of this man which might meet his needs. He signed on in the Faculty of Letters to attend Blondel's lectures, while (to satisfy his father) continuing his studies in the Faculty of Law. In spite of winning the first prize in International Law in 1902, his real interests were becoming increasingly philosophical. Unfortunately Blondel was on sick leave till 1906, so Paul attended only a few of his lectures. But he read his writings carefully, especially his great work *L'Action*, and so was ready to discuss his problems with the great man when he, Blondel, was able to see him early in 1905.

To understand the nature of Blondel's influence on the young Turk, we need to say a little more, first about the latter's background, and second about Blondel's own approach. Paul was a young Muslim intellectual at a time when the Islamic thought of Westernized Turks was extremely fluid. On one side there was a self-conscious emphasis on Islam as the religious substratum to renascent Turkish nationalism; on the other side there was the development of a secular national philosophy which found its culmination in the abolition of the Caliphate in 1924 by the atheist, Kemal Attatürk. Things had not gone so far as that in 1900, when Paul was a student; but Kemal's predecessor, Ziya Gökalp, was no doubt representative of Turkish attitudes then. Gökalp said that Islam is a purely ethical religion; that the Islamic customary law was a divine revelation; but that religion and the State should be separated so that the three necessities for an Islamic state in the modern world, 'Turkification, Islamization, Modernization', could proceed together.[2]

This might not have been so if Paul had had any contact with the *sufi*, mystical tradition of Islam. (See, for instance, the autobiography of J. A. Subhan.)[3] But there were no influences of this form of mystic Muslim teaching and devotion in the background to the life of a young Turk like Paul. His description of what the Muslim world-outlook was to him shows this. In a lecture on his spiritual journey, Paul says

The egalitarian conception, in the Koran, of a revelation of the divine unity, repeated in a discontinuous series of messages to the peoples and generations of men, with its rhapsody of episodic tales with no local colour in them, and no third-dimensional existence in time; with, too, its blurred gallery of prophets with no living personality, among whom Christ takes his place inevitably as one among many, results in what is in effect practically a historical unreality. And this renders it very ill-equipped to defend itself against the no less levelling, relativistic, conception of a religious consciousness in which the feeling for the divine results in the all-too-human diversity of beliefs and modes of worship, mediated through the initiatives of great inspired individuals and the collaboration of the mass of the faithful. Among these the most that can be conceded is that Christianity is the most ideal expression of such a cult.[4]

This, evidently, was not a notion of Islam which could give a sensitive and searching intellect like Paul's much nourishment. And added to this, he says, was the other influence, breathed in in the very atmosphere around, of 'rationalism', 'immanentism'—all the secular movements of thought which, as we have said, culminated in Turkey becoming a secular state.

Few affirmations could have been more appropriate, at this stage in his development, than those of Maurice Blondel. For Blondel's approach was initially empirical, and only secondly 'rational'. He did not start with the analysis of ideas, of thought, as the scholastic rationalists might have done; but with the analysis of *action*. (Hence the title of his most famous thesis, which Paul read.) For, he argued, man, whether he likes it or not, is 'already embarked' on action; he can't avoid it, for even choosing to avoid an action is itself an active choice. Previously philosophers have not known what to make of action. Either, like Aristotle, they have subordinated practice to thought; or, like Kant, they have divided man up into two selves, a thinking self and an acting, choosing, moral self (the 'noumenal' and the 'phenomenal', with no real links between them), so that in effect the 'practical reason' takes precedence. Blondel quotes Pascal's famous phrase, 'nous sommes embarqués'—we are already embarked on the journey of life before we can begin to speculate on what it is all about—but adds, 'the trouble is that Pascal did not try to find out why we are embarked.' And Blondel's work is all concerned with this: with showing what it means to 'will' an action; and ultimately showing that man wills what he cannot in his own strength achieve.[5]

This was just the note to strike for a young man of great integrity, who knew he had to make moral choices, to act, but could not find the explanation for this necessity, nor his real destination. Blondel wrote afterward of his pupil that his final acceptance of Christianity came from a

convergence, in its own terms, between two series of phenomena and acts:–

First, acts of kindness, generosity, purity, a desire for the good, a need for direction and moral purification, an immense aspiration towards a kind of sanctity. And these all resulted in a growing humility in him, a sense of his own weakness, an urgent yearning of soul. And all these dispositions, heroic as they were, implied a work of grace to which he responded faithfully—though without knowing, or indeed needing to know, that it was grace.

And secondly, philosophical study, objective research, apologetic information, which helped to dissipate his prejudices, to uncover the insufficiency and inferiority of Islam, which showed him what one can only call the grand permanent miracle of the supernatural life in Christianity. All this little by little illuminated the meaning of the confused drawing, of the moral practices which seemed to him both fine and powerful, and brought him practically to a conviction.

That is why he felt at one and the same time a complete freedom to go where his generous instincts led him, and a feeling of rigorous obligation which he could only meet by risking his eternity on it.[6]

Paul himself described how he came to see that the Muslim denial of Christ's real death on the cross was arbitrary; and that, far from the idea of a 'Man-God', of a 'finite-Infinite', being absurd—as it must be if you have immanentist and Islamic presuppositions:

rationally no impossibility can be alleged against the hypothesis of a real presence of the Absolute, taking its place freely in the series of beings and of contingent facts, and dwelling substantially in the midst of its creation, so as to raise it, like leaven—and all this deliberately from compassion, aiming at assuming creation to itself. Given this perspective (I could see that) it is no longer Christianity which is relative to religion, but religion which is relative to Christianity.

And so Mehmet-Ali Mulla-Zadé was baptized on 25 January 1905, with Maurice Blondel as godfather. After completing his studies he went back and stayed briefly with his family in Crete. We only have indirect evidence of how his father received the news of his son's becoming a Christian: some years later his daughter, Paul's sister, died, and when Paul himself was ordained priest, old Dr. Mulla gave a cry of despair: 'I lost my daughter. Now I have lost my eldest son.'

Paul Mulla returned to France; was ordained priest in 1911; served as a nursing orderly in the 1914–18 war; and in 1919 was made lecturer in philosophy at the Catholic College at Aix. In 1924 he was promoted still higher. The Pontifical Institute for Oriental Studies in Rome was being reorganized, and the head of the Institute approached Maurice Blondel: did he know any among his old pupils who would be suitable to teach there? Blondel of course suggested Paul Mulla, who was appointed to teach about Muslim institutions—to which he added Arabic and Turkish studies and translations. He was consulted by the Secretariat of State and the Congregation of the Eastern Church. Pope Pius XI made special mention of him in his encyclical, *Rerum orientalium* (8 September 1928), in which he referred to the providential appearance of this Turkish Catholic priest who could help to bring together Byzantine and Islamic studies in one Institute, and help students who were going to exercise their ministry in Muslim lands.

He worked here from his appointment until his death on St. Matthias' day, 24 February, 1959. He fainted at the altar just after reading the words of the Gospel (which were his own last words): 'Come unto me, all ye that labour and are heavy laden. . . . For my yoke is easy, and my burden is light.' (Matt. 11:28–30.)

ii. PAUL TAKAHASHI NAGAÏ (1908–51)

When the American air-arm dropped the A-bomb on Nagasaki on 9 August 1945, one of the effects (still, perhaps, not much appreciated in Great Britain) was to wipe out 80 per cent of the strongest single Christian centre in Japan. Eight thousand Roman Catholics died, either immediately or within the next few months. Nagasaki had been the holy place for Roman Catholic Japanese, since it was the place where 26 Christians were crucified in 1597, and close on 37,000 massacred during the persecutions of 1637–8.* So when Japan was again open to the West in 1865 a chapel was built at Nagasaki—and to the astonishment of the French missionary a number of Japanese gathered round and showed by their behaviour that, though they had had no priest, and Christianity had been forbidden, for nearly two hundred years, they still kept some of their ancient faith, if only some of its outward signs. So this became the stronghold of the Catholic Mission, and when the cathedral of Urakami was built there it held a congregation of 6,000 (the largest Christian Cathedral in the Far East). Although to this day Christians represent about 0·5 per cent of the population of Japan, in the Nagasaki area out of a population of 250,000 no less than 10,000 were Roman Catholics. The bomb destroyed the Cathedral, and all but about 2,000 of its members. Among those members was a Dr. Nagaï.

* See chapter 2, above, pp. 13, 15.

He was born in 1908, of non-Christian parents. His father was a doctor, who had thrown his family idol into the river as a boy. Takahashi himself was brought up with the minimum of conventional religion, and as a young medical student became very self-consciously 'materialist'.

We were shown [he says], in dissection, the material elements which, they told us, constituted the human being. The marvellous structure of the body, taken as a whole, the complex system of its details, seemed to us wonderful. . . . Going on to physiology, I studied the complex and co-ordinated functions of the organism, expounded as physico-chemical phenomena of excitation and reaction. . . . The lessons we received seemed to leave no place for the pretended existence of souls and spirits.[7]

But when his mother died he had a strange experience: as her eyes fixed on him while he stood by her death-bed, he felt that there was 'something more' there, looking out at him through those eyes, than a merely physiological explanation could account for. At this time a friend lent him Pascal's *Pensées* (he had lodged earlier on with a Roman Catholic family in Nagasaki), and he now started to attend the Cathedral. After his return from military service in Manchuria, he was baptized (1933) and married a Christian girl, Midori (whose ancestors had been among the early Japanese Christians). He then took the name of Paul.

He became a lecturer in the medical school, at the teaching hospital of Nagasaki, specializing in radiology. In 1946 he was made a professor, but even before the bomb fell in 1945 he had contracted leukaemia through his subjection to X-rays. He was doing research in radio-physics, but he admits that neither he nor their professor of physics had any idea, even when the bomb fell, that the West had so far advanced as to be able to produce nuclear explosives. None of them recognized the bomb for what it was.

In his autobiography[8] he gives a detailed account of the day the bomb fell. And in an earlier book[9] he collected together the descriptions of eight survivors (five adults and three children), with concluding comments of his own. There have been several books giving similar stories of individuals involved in the explosion, but what is new here is the account of Dr. Nagaï's own part in the events, his general comments, and his subsequent experiences.

When the bomb fell Dr. Nagaï was at the hospital, in the Medical School. Parts of the hospital were destroyed in a moment, but the concrete sections remained standing as it was some distance from the centre of the explosion. However, the violent winds caused by the explosion threw everything—beds, desks, files, instruments—into complete chaos. Dr. Nagaï himself was buried under rubble, and one artery in his temple was severed. After some time he was able to extricate himself, and by then a small group of survivors—nurses, medical students, and lecturers—had formed. He took charge and they turned what was left into a casualty station. He was losing a lot of blood from the severed artery, as he could not spare one hand to keep pressure on it all the time. Taking his own pulse, he calculated that he could keep going for about three hours. Some five hours later he passed out, and one of the staff applied a ligature. He recovered enough to continue work until the fire which spread from the centre of Nagasaki reached the hospital. At last he had to give orders to evacuate the hospital (leaving some patients still alive in the burning wards) before the fire reached the X-ray department, which then blew up. They reformed the casualty station under the trees (it was now raining, a strange, oily kind of rain) up the hill above the hospital, and here they continued working almost without a pause for two days, improvising as best they could (since most of the drugs, syringes, dressings, and injections had been destroyed).

It was not until the third day that Nagaï had time to slip home and discover whether his wife was still alive—he suspected that she was not, for their house was near the centre of the explosion, and she had not come to the casualty station. When he got to his house he found, as he feared, that everything was flat—as if a steam-roller had passed over the area. Grubbing among the ruins he found some charred bones; they were, of course, unrecognizable, but near them was a rosary which he knew to be hers.

Fortunately his two children (a boy of ten and a girl of four) had been sent some miles away to relatives in the country when the heavy bombing had started a few weeks before. Their accounts of what happened when the bomb fell in the distance, and of the arrival of survivors later to their village, are among the stories he collected for his first book.

So far, there seems to be nothing outstanding in this little history—merely one of many thousands of personal tragedies. But what is really significant is what followed.

First, Dr. Nagaï himself, a few weeks after his rescue work, began to feel the effects of severe radiation sickness. The leukaemia which he had already contracted was seriously stimulated by overwork and by the increased radio-activity after the explosion. He took to his bed, from which he never got up again. Three years later, in 1948, he was critically ill and received the last sacraments; but he made a temporary recovery, and was able to continue with his work. For already he was making a clinical study *of his own illness*; he kept a microscope by his bed, and observed the signs of decay in his own body. These he noted, as he worked on his thesis, *An Introduction to Atomic Diseases*. He finally died in 1951. In 1949 he was made honorary Mayor of Nagasaki (though he was entirely confined to his bed). He was visited in person by the Emperor. The Pope sent him a special blessing. Mme Péron, wife of the President of Argentina, sent him a plaque of our Lady of Lujan, and the Catholic Doctors' Association of Italy sent him a statue of the Madonna. At his death, the City of Nagasaki sponsored a public funeral, which was celebrated by Paul Taguchi, Bishop of Nagasaki, and attended by the leading dignatories of the Church and of the Japanese Government.[10] How had he obtained all this fame?

On his sick-bed, besides his thesis on atomic diseases, he managed to write several small books, some of which were translated into a number of European languages. The only one that has appeared in English is the one already mentioned, *We of Nagasaki*,[11] the collection of stories of individuals on the day the bomb dropped. The important section of this is Dr. Nagaï's own concluding reflections, entitled—'Cracks and Fissures' (chapter X). He describes how the impact of an atomic bomb always leaves geographical fissures on the surface of the earth. But these heal over in time. However

the fissures which then appeared throughout the blast centre had not yet disappeared, four years after. . . . I am talking about the invisible chasms which appeared in the personal relationships of the survivors of that atomic wasteland. The rents in the ties of friendship and love have not closed up with the passage of time.[12]

And he illustrates this from some of the stories earlier in the book. For in the experience of everyone, to be a survivor meant to survive at the expense of someone else:

There was a time when Mr. Tanaka found Satoru's brother, Masaru, in need of succour, and made no move to help him. Of course, in the circumstances Tanaka was not to blame—what else could he have done? . . . Nevertheless, whenever Satoru runs into Tanaka on the street he is reminded for a brief second of his brother. . . . And what of Satoru himself? Did he not stay down in the air-raid shelter and forget all about his mother and sisters and brothers? To this day the memory pricks his conscience. Of course, he was just a schoolboy, and he had sustained an injury to his head* . . . so surely it was perfectly natural that it should not occur to him to try and save them. Nonetheless, Satoru has lost faith in himself.[13]

And indeed, Dr. Nagaï found himself in a similar dilemma:

The young students and nurses . . . kept going back into the danger zone with the one thought of rescuing their patients and their friends and colleagues who had been injured or succumbed to the smoke. . . . Finally the flames ate into the internal diseases wards. There was one last patient trapped in Ward One, and some of the doctors started to dash in to save her. I held them back. 'Doctor, there's somebody in that ward! Listen! She's calling! Let us go, please!'

But Dr. Nagaï had to say, 'It's too late. There's nothing to be done. I'll take the responsibility!'—and they abandoned the hospital. This dilemma was inescapable. Even of his own heroic rescue-work Dr. Nagaï is self-critical.

With the members of the first-aid squad around me, I stayed at the hospital and directed the rescue of the patients. It appeared as if I were perfectly oblivious of myself. I was rendering unselfish service to others. . . . Afterwards I was praised for it by everybody. But inside me, very different feelings were operating. I wanted to run home to my wife. In fact, as I carried one unconscious woman to safety, out of reach of the fire, my thoughts flew to my wife and I became utterly distraught. But I was out to win praise from every-body—I wanted to be called a hero for saving people from the very thick of the blaze without showing my private feelings; *that* was why I kept at it. . . . Actually, I took no more risks than such recognition would require.[14]

But it is Dr. Nagaï's autobiography, *Les Cloches de Nagasaki*,[15]

* In fact, he was pinned down with a five-inch nail from a beam sticking into his head so that he could not move!

which I find most impressive. In it we read of his days as a
student, and of his early married life, when as a young doctor
in the University Hospital he and his wife had no money even
to buy new clothes (she made them all), let alone to go to
theatres, etc., though they had friends whom they could visit to
listen to Mozart on gramophone records, and discuss the novels
of Bourget.[16] When he starts getting interested in research he
lives for it so intensely that he hardly notices his wife and
children—she even tells him twice that he has cut her in the
street. Their only moment of family life together is when all
four climb the hill to mass at the Cathedral on Sundays. And
there is the usual chat and gossip of medicos.

I had few friends; they were all like me, penniless scholars. One day
when I was with colleague Nakamura in our garden, he told me
he'd just achieved the parthenogenesis of frogs. Midori [Mrs. Nagai],
during this time was listening to us as she ironed my shirts. Nakamura
said to me, jokingly, 'Who knows, Dr. Nagai, perhaps one day we
shan't need wives to get children.' . . . And Midori retorted, 'Well,
suppose it is so. But do you think the sole end of marriage is to
bring children into the world?'[17]

And then comes the bomb, and the shattering of his happy
family, and soon the realization that his own life is threatened.
He manages to construct a shed, over the ruins of their old
house, with one room in which he lives—or rather in which his
bed on the floor is housed, and to which he is confined. Though
the rain comes in, and it is cold, and the fire is constantly
going out, for some time he keeps his two children with him:
'One of the motives which decided me to subject Makoto [his
son] to this life in the middle of skeletons and débris was the
desire to instil into him a profound hatred for war. A sojourn
in the atomic desert is enough to convert the most ardent
chauvinist into a convinced pacifist.'[18] But later he sends the
children to stay with relatives, and allows them only to come
and see him once a week; and this is because, though it leaves
him terribly lonely—lying solitary on his sick-bed in the one-
roomed shack—he knows that they must soon get used to doing
without a father, as, during the last five years, they had to get
used to doing without a mother.

Two of his old students come back to see him. They have been
away fighting, but now the war is over. Dr. Nagaï was as
distressed as any of them when the Emperor announced the

capitulation of Japan, a few days after the bomb. Though a Catholic, he was also a patriot. But he saw the war in a different light from those who had not been through the atomic experience.

The returned soldiers said:

'. . . Terrible, isn't it? But we won't forget. We'll get even with them. They'll pay for it; of course it'll take time, but that doesn't matter.'

'. . . Is that really what you think?' I asked them.

'. . . Certainly. . . . Japan wasn't so weak that we had to give in. We've still got plenty of strength left.'

Dr. Nagaï then talks of the experience of Nagasaki, and when they refer to the 'God of War', he expostulates:

'The god of war?—A sheer creation of man, like the god of hiccups. . . . We have fabricated gods, and then we have asked them to conform to what we want. That's how we came to believe in the invincibility of our country, and in legends like the "divine wind".* . . . Your way of looking at things comes from a primitive nationalistic faith, which came under judgement 2,000 years ago. . . . The battles of Yoshitsune are picturesque, and there is beauty in the portrait of General Nogi. But in the atom bomb?'

And he draws the obvious conclusions, showing them that at least the University can be proud that, though its buildings are in ruins, the majority of its staff and students dead, many of the survivors invalids (like him) and all bereaved of some if not of the whole of their families, yet the work of rescue did go on.

But it is harder to comfort a man who finds all reasons for living gone, than to rebuke young hot-headed militarists. Ichitaro-san, for instance, when demobbed, returned to find his wife and all five children dead at Nagasaki. 'I've got nothing to live for now,' he said to Dr. Nagaï. The latter gave him, for response, the text of his address which was to be read in two days' time at a service of remembrance for the victims. Dr. Nagaï was the lay representative at this service, and the address gives us an impressive picture of the man. Here is a part of it:

On the 9th August, 1945, at 10.30 a.m., a meeting of the Supreme War Council was held at the Imperial H.Q., to decide whether to

* A story of an early invasion of Japan, when the wind changed and blew the invader out of the harbour.

15

capitulate or continue the war. At this moment an atom bomb exploded, precisely at 11.02 a.m., over the Urakami district of Nagasaki.

Eight thousand catholic souls were dispatched in a moment to be judged by their Creator, and a devastating fire reduced this Christian city in a few hours to ashes. That same day at midnight the cathedral caught fire and was destroyed. At this hour, too, His Majesty the Emperor announced his decision to end the war.

On the 15th August the Imperial Rescript, which put an end to hostilities, was formally promulgated, and peace came to the whole world. That day was the Feast of the Assumption of the blessed Virgin, to which, you remember, the Cathedral of Urakami was dedicated.

Can all these coincidences be pure chance? Or mustn't we rather see here the delicate work of the divine will?

I've been told that the second atom bomb . . . was first meant for another town. But the sky over the latter was found to be covered with clouds; the project was clearly impossible; a change of plan had to take place at the last moment. That was how Nagasaki, up till then a 'reserve target', was finally chosen. More than that, I've learned that when the bomb was launched, the wind made it veer to the north of the munition works which were the objective, so that it exploded above the cathedral. So Urakami had at no moment been designated by the American pilots. It was Providence that steered the missile.

Can't one see a profound connection . . . between the cessation of the war and the destruction of Urakami? Urakami, the only catholic and consecrated segment of all Japan, was it not chosen as a suitable victim, to be sacrificed and burned on the altar of expiation, for the crimes committed by humanity in this world war? . . .

Before this moment, many occasions had been offered of ending the war; whole towns had been destroyed . . . God had not accepted these worthless offerings. But when Urakami was destroyed, he accepted this sacrifice at last, forgave men, and inspired the Emperor to end the war.

Our Church of Urakami has kept its faith intact during 400 years in a Japan that proscribed it, it has bled under all forms of persecution, and during this war it hasn't ceased to pray for peace. . . .

Eight thousand catholics, including priests and the cathedral, have been sacrificed. . . . How happy they are to have departed this life without experiencing defeat! . . . Compared with theirs, our lot is a truly miserable one. Our country conquered, our city destroyed. . . .

Why are we not dead too . . . ? Why must we continue this miserable existence? It is because we have sinned. . . . Those who have been left behind are those who alone were too embedded in sins to be a worthy offering. . . .

Blessed are those who mourn, for they shall be comforted. We must continue our sad journey faithfully to the end . . . aided by Him who carried His cross to the top of Calvary: Jesus Christ.

God gives, and God takes away; may his Name be praised. Let us thank Him that . . . through this sacrifice peace has been given to the world, and freedom of belief to Japan. And may the souls of the faithful departed through the mercy of God rest in peace.[19]*

It is not only Protestants who will demur at the theology implied in some of those phrases, and some in the Reformed tradition may be tempted to suggest that pagan notions of expiation imported into the Catholic doctrine of the sacrifice of the mass can easily lead to a failure to stress the unique sacrifice of Christ. But this is, after all, a layman speaking—speaking not very long after he had lost wife, home, friends. It is surely magnificent in that context, that a positive meaning could be found in this hideous tragedy. And Ichitaro-san, to whom he lent it, went away after reading it, his face lit up.

From his death-bed Dr. Nagaï directed that the profits on royalties from his books should go towards the rebuilding of the Cathedral, and those on the English and American editions to a library and sports equipment for the children of Nagasaki. His own thesis on atomic diseases was never, so far as I can discover, published. But his other books have sold extremely well, and one was the basis of a film which made a great impression in Japan. His little girl, Kayamo, was four when the bomb fell. She contributed her story to the collection he edited four years later; and what she said provides a charming, graphic tail-piece to her father's life:

Every day lots of people died everywhere. . . . That was four years ago. Daddy has been sick in bed ever since. He's lost a lot of weight and he's so thin now. But me, I'm getting very big and tall. Cousin Fujie says I'm getting to look the way my mother used to. I'm always looking in the mirror to see.

My mother's grave doesn't get any bigger or any smaller.[20]

* See Appendix 11, p. 320.

Section B TRANSPOSITIONS

In this section we shall look at some representative figures who have taken the Christian faith, in some cases directly from the visitors (i.e. the missionaries), in others at second or third remove, through the family or the local community, but then have transformed it into something recognizably different, individual, home-grown. As a result, their long-term influence has been and is likely to continue to be important out of proportion to their number or their prominence.

Three obvious candidates are missing, for (I hope) good reasons. One is the Indian poet, Narayan Vama Tilak ('The Christian Poet of Maharashtra'). Although there are several good short lives of him,[1] and a fascinating book by his wife, Lakshmibai Tilak (*I Follow After*),[2] Tilak himself expressed the view that a nation's soul is most truly revealed in its poetry. But Tilak wrote his poetry in Marathi (outstanding poetry, we are told); and even though he made a few English translations himself, and though much of his poetry has been translated by others—skilled linguists like Dr. Macnicol—it is next to impossible truly to appreciate a creative writer thus at second hand; and his mere biography, without precisely the 'transpositions' that his poetry achieved, would be misleadingly commonplace.

The second is Toyohiko Kagawa, whose influence as a translator of Christian conviction into social action in Japan was enormous at the same time. There should be plenty of material for a biography of him—and indeed several biographies have been written. But it appears that much of his own work is still in Japanese, and those who know that language say that when they are ultimately translated into English it will be seen that the usual picture of Kagawa as a 'liberal protestant' exponent of the 'social gospel' must be modified.[3] So it seems better to await the appearance of this material.

Finally, Sadhu Sundar Singh would seem to demand a place. But, apart from the unsolved mystery of his death, his work and his unique personality are so well known and have been so thoroughly documented,[4] that I have preferred to use another Indian whose life is less familiar to the general reader.

CHAPTER 16 | **UPADHYAY BRAHMABANDHAV** (1861–1907)

Bhawani Charan Banerji was born in 1861 at Khanyan, thirty-five miles from Calcutta. His father was a high-caste Brahman, a Police Inspector. At thirteen the boy entered Hooghly Collegiate School, and five years later the Metropolitan College, Calcutta. He was a great swimmer and athlete, and very strong. After College he taught for a year in the Free Church Institution, and then took private pupils. Soon after this he met two of the great leaders of the Hindu Renaissance: first, the great Ramakrishna, for Upadhyay (see p. 213) attended a temple on the banks of the Hooghly where Ramakrishna taught. Later (1897) he wrote of him: 'We knew Ramakrishna in the last days of his life. . . . We loved and admired him, and it is no exaggeration to say that we were loved in return. The sense of sin was very acute in him.' The other leader was Keshub Chunder Sen, of the Brahmo Samaj ('Society of God'). By this time Keshub had developed his own branch of this intellectual movement for the rebirth of Hinduism, a branch in which he tried to make a synthesis of world religions, with yogic methods from Hinduism and elements of Christianity. Upadhyay attended his 'Bible Class'. After Keshub's death in 1884, five of his disciples rented a house in Calcutta and published a hand-written journal from there, *The Journal*.

Another close friend of Upadhyay's was Narain Dutta, better known in the West as Swami Vivekananda. Together they studied Vedantism. Both had sat at the feet of the grand old man, Ramakrishna; but Vivekananda was more faithful to Ramakrishna's mystical, essentially Hindu approach, whereas Upadhyay kept closer to Keshub's syncretistic, and practical line. It is interesting, however, that (as we shall see) when Upadhyay was lecturing in England it was mostly Vivekananda's Vedantism that he expounded.

From 1886 to 1887 the friends started the 'Concord Club', and published a magazine, the *Young Man* (later called *Concord*), and out of it developed two classes, one to study the Bible (this time under a missionary, Fr. Townsend of the Oxford Mission to Calcutta), the other to study Shakespeare. In 1888 the

'Union Academy' was founded in Hyderabad, and Upadhyay went there to teach Sanskrit. He then started attending a Bible Class run by a C.M.S. missionary, and to everybody's surprise, and the distress of the Hindus, in 1890 he announced his intention of becoming a Christian. Surprise, because he was known to be anti-European—at the age of seventeen he had run away from school to 'learn the art of fighting and drive out the English'. He met some opposition and had now to do his own sweeping and cleaning. However, he was baptized by an Anglican clergyman on 26 February 1891.

But his position was already unusual. A few days after his baptism he was talking to a devout Roman Catholic priest, who 'started, grew pale, and said "What have you done, young man?"' when he heard of his baptism. Upadhyay replied that he believed in the Divinity of Christ and in the necessity of baptism, and so had obeyed the light he saw: but as to the question of the Church of Christ he had not made up his mind: 'he could not satisfy himself with any church.' Indeed, he refused to attend church services of the C.M.S., when asked, saying that he did not belong to the Church of England. However, he had some time before picked up a stray book, Bruno's *Catholic Belief*, and now read it. And in September—seven months after his baptism by the C.M.S. clergyman—he was conditionally baptized by a Jesuit priest.

He was clear, however—more clear than any other Christian of his time—that this step was in no sense away from India's heritage: rather, he considered that it brought him into closer relationship with the Hindu *Samaj*, and he took the step because he wanted to be 'the first Indian to sing the praises of the same Triune *Sachchidanandan* in the sacred tongue of the Rishis'.[5]*

There were several other Hindus who followed Upadhyay, and the alarm went forth. Lectures against Christianity were organized; and 'sceptical literature of Europe and America was pressed into service against the religion of Christ. Young men read *Free Thought*, and studied the works of Bradlaugh and Ingersoll. Some of them turned open sceptics and spoke with no unmeasured contempt of religion—whether Christianity or Hinduism.'[6] To counter this Upadhyay brought out a short treatise on the existence of God. But the Sindh became a centre

* 'Being-Thought-Beatitude': roughly equivalent to 'infinitude'. But see further Appendix 12, p. 321.

of religious ferment, and Brahmo Samaj missionaries came from
Bengal, Arya Samaj* missionaries from the Punjab, and
Theosophists from England, all to oppose Upadhyay and 'the
Catholic movement'.

Upadhyay replied to this in still more decisive—and Indian—
fashion by becoming a *bhikshi sannyasi* (travelling holy man). He
explained that his Indian name was Bhawani Charan Banerji,
but that

> I have adopted a new name. My family surname is *Vandya* [praised]
> Upadhyay [teacher, lit., sub-teacher], and my baptismal name is
> *Brahmabandhav* [Theophilus]. I have abandoned the first portion of
> my family surname, because I am a disciple of Jesus Christ, the Man
> of Sorrows, the despised man. So my new name is Upadhyay
> Brahmabandhav. I hereby declare that henceforward I shall be
> known and addressed as Upadhyay Brahmabandhav or, in short,
> Upadhyayji; and not Banerji, which is an English corruption of the
> first portion of my family name, Vandyaji.

This meant adopting the *garic*—the dress of a Hindu mendicant
—and living on alms. But he was, of course, still a practising
Catholic, and he started turning up in Church in his Hindu
dress. The parish priest (Fr. Salinger) objected, so Upadhyay
appealed to the Archbishop of Bombay. The latter was not too
keen to allow it—in spite of the fact that a number of Catholic
missionaries supported it—but Upadhyay was very importun-
ate and won his point. Indeed, many, including Fr. Salinger
himself, came to see the the importance of his innovation.[7]

At this time Upadhyay had his headquarters in Hyderabad,
was conducting a monthly philosophical journal, *Sophia*, which
had a high reputation, and had opened a library and reading
room with Catholic literature and secular magazines and
papers. He also travelled much, lecturing: in 1894 he gave
lectures, on the Nature of God and the End of Man, in the
capital of Punjab, which was a stronghold of the Arya Samaj;
and in 1895 he wrote to Annie Besant—an open letter—
challenging her to a public discussion on the nature of God (for
he believed that she understood neither Hinduism nor Christianity!). But she refused, so he started to lecture against her
Theosophy.

* 'Society of the Aryas' ('noble men'), started 1875: strongly nationalist;
distinct from the Brahmo Samaj ('Society of God') founded by Rammohun
Roy, *c.* 1820.

All this makes him sound very contentious. But we are told that he was gentle and understanding toward the Christian converts he made: a Christian husband was urged to love his Hindu wife, the Christian son to obey his Hindu father, all the more devotedly; the convert would be instructed to follow his local social customs, e.g. shaving head and beard at the death of his father. In 1898 Upadhyay was joined by another *sannyasi*, and 'the two with cymbals in hand went about singing hymns in Bengali and Sanskrit and receiving alms. To the public of Calcutta this looked peculiar and strange'—and many of the Catholics thought he had apostatized.

He now had the idea—extraordinarily prescient for its time— of starting a Christian monastery along Hindu lines. As he wrote,

Monastic life is exceedingly congenial to the soil of India. In this age of materialism, when contemplative life is despised, India is still dotted over with monasteries. On mountain tops, in forest glades, on the banks of rivers, in the heart of ancient cities are to be found *asrams* [hermitages] presided over by famous *sannyasis* whose disciples range the country . . . keeping alive the religious fervour of the Hindu race. . . .

We need, he says a place where Hindu Catholics can be trained in the monastic life:

There should be two classes of *sannyasis*, the one contemplative, the other itinerant. The contemplative monks will give the lie to the prevalent notion that meditative life is idleness, shew by their steady contemplation of the Infinite Goodness that it is possible to live the life of God on earth, and repair, by their self-immolation, the injury done to human nature by the ravages of sin. The itinerant monks will issue forth . . . to carry the torch of Catholic faith to the darkest . . . corners of India. . . .

[This *matha*—monastery—] should be conducted on strictly Hindu lines. There should not be the least trace of Europeanism in the mode of life . . . of the Hindu Catholic monks. The *Parivrajakas* [itinerants] should be well versed in the Vedanta philosophy as well as in the philosophy of St. Thomas.[8]

Unfortunately this courageous and original idea did not win the approval of the Church authorities, who were worried by Upadhyay's restlessness, and felt that much cautious preparation was necessary for so adventurous a step. It has been suggested that with more patience Upadhyay might have brought them round[9] but he was determined to go ahead. So in 1899 three of them started off in Jabalpur, assisted by two Catholic Brahman youths.

They slept on the bare floor without any pillow and with but one blanket. . . . One *chadar* and one *dhotee* made up their dress. They were not allowed to use another till this had been quite worn out. They got up at 4.0 a.m., and retired at 10.0 p.m., passing the day in study, prayer and meditation. Each novice, after completing his course of studies, was to make a retreat and then had to roam about in the cities of India, all by himself, for 6 months, begging his way from place to place, and if he returned alive to the central *matha* he was to get the *garic* garb.

Incidentally, they observed the rules of the caste system (this at least was ordered by the Bishop of Nagpur—following the lines laid down two hundred and fifty years before by the Jesuit Robert de Nobili), and the Brahman boys wore the sacred thread, and their hair in a bunch on the crown.

Upadhyay wrote later that this time of asceticism was also a time of great joy for him; and one of his companions in the enterprise was Mr. B. Animananda, who later wrote his life, and spoke admiringly of this period. But it did not last long. For the Apostolic Delegate (Mgr. Zaleski) wrote to the Bishop of Nagpur (who had become favourable to the project), opposing it; and finally the Bishop said he would have to apply to Rome for authorization. Upadhyay obeyed, and planned to go himself to Rome to present the case; but fell ill, and having postponed the trip, changed his mind.

Now he went to Karachi and then to Calcutta, where he renewed his literary work. He turned *Sophia* into a weekly, part political, part religio-philosophical. Here he began to reappraise the Vedanta, which formerly he had attacked. He said that he, like most European scholars, had misinterpreted the Vedanta; that it could be interpreted theistically—a loftier theism than Aristotle's; that Christianity in India should be expounded in terms of the Vedanta, not in terms of Aristotelian scholasticism; and that far from forsaking Hinduism to become a Christian, 'he grew more of a Hindu the more he clung to the cross.' But all this was much too risky for the ecclesiastical authorities, and the Apostolic Delegate stopped *Sophia* circulating with its 'dangerous doctrine', and warned the faithful against it. Upadhyay had already asked for a Censor to pass all his articles before publication (a reasonable request), but Mgr. Zaleski refused—perhaps, suggests Mr. Kemchand (himself a Catholic), because Zaleski was afraid that Upadhyay's 'profound and acute philosophical acumen' would carry the censors with him. In any case, it was clearly a mistake, and was a big step towards alienating Upadhyay.

Upadhyay tried again, with a Hindu journalist, by starting the *Twentieth Century*, a magazine in which he continued his theistic interpretation of the Vedanta, writing under the pen-name *Nar Haridâs* ('Servant of the God-Man'). But once again the Delegate stepped in, warning the faithful against it; and it soon collapsed. But not before a young Brahman, reading these anonymous articles, wrote to Upadhyay, said he was deserting the religion of his ancestors, and urged him to read the articles of 'Nar Haridâs' in the *Twentieth Century* to persuade him to return to Hinduism!

In 1901 he worked with the famous Debindranath Tagore ('the modern Sankar of India', as he has been called) in a school which Upadhyay started in Calcutta, and which when successful was transferred to Bolepur (about 100 miles away). They worked happily with their thirty boys, till it was rumoured that 'the poet was under the thumb of the philosopher'—that Christianity was beginning, under Upadhyay's influence, to penetrate the school. So Tagore withdrew. Upadhyay now started a refuge for the old and sick (as earlier, in 1897, he had gone to nurse the plague-stricken in Karachi, sweeping out their houses, cooking for them, and bringing medical aid). He also had plans for a National College, with stress on study of Hindu culture; but this came to nothing.

In 1902 his long-planned trip to Europe at last came off. He stayed briefly in Rome—hearing mass in St. Peter's, and making his confession to an English priest there. Then to London and Oxford. At Oxford he lectured on Hindu Thought (at the invitation of the Professor of Sanskrit in Oxford who had read his articles in *Twentieth Century*), Hindu Theism, Ethics, and Sociology. Dr. Edward Caird, the Master of Balliol was in the chair for the last two. He visited Littlemore, and said there, 'Here lived Newman, of blessed memory, a religious hero of the 19th century, who turned the tide of rationalism and brought back faith in England.' He also gave three speeches in Cambridge, at Trinity College. Then he lectured in characteristic vein to the North London Theosophical Society, on 'Eastern and Western Thought'. Here is a digest of what he said:

He said that England was very ignorant of Indian thought: her Missionaries and politicians came to India and never thought of learning anything from the Hindus. . . . When the English intellect has learned to appreciate the Indian intellect, then would they be in a position to federate humanity, but not before, and such federation must come through mutal respect, and not through domination. . . . India had reared up a wonderful philosophy . . . that had stood for centuries. Where was the thought of Europe? It was in chaos. One philosophy arose, but was soon to be chased away by another . . . there was no stability in European thought. The peculiarity of Indian culture was conquest of nature. The English conquered nature by sending gun-boats to bombard towns on the shores of distant seas, but the Indians conquered nature by disregarding and defying nature. . . .

Afterwards a leading writer (W. T. Stead) wrote an article[10] about his visit.

Last year a penniless Brahmin, Swami Upadhyay by name, conceived the idea that our ancient Universities would be improved by the institution of chairs of Indian Philosophy. So he set off like the disciples of old, without staff or scrip, without money in his wallet,* to convert the Dons of Oxford and of Cambridge to a sense of their need. Strange to say, he met with a very favourable reception at Oxford. At Cambridge he succeeded in forming an influential committee which has undertaken to see to it that a three years' course of lectures in Hindu Philosophy shall be delivered . . . provided a competent Hindu lecturer were forthcoming. . . .

The Cambridge Committee had, indeed, some most distinguished names on it,† and Upadhyay was to be the liaison in Calcutta. But the scheme fell through, partly for financial reasons, but mainly because of failure to agree on the candidate for the chair.

While in England he had also pursued his Christian apologetic purpose. He wrote two articles, which were published in the Roman Catholic weekly, *The Tablet* (3 and 31 January 1903), in which he pleads for an Indian presentation of the Gospel to India. 'Christianity . . . is too much mixed up with

* He was indeed short of money at times.
† Hastings Rashdall, John McTaggart, W. R. Sorley, G. F. Stout, G. Lowes Dickinson, T. Piele, W. H. D. Rouse.

beef and pork, spoon and fork, too tightly pantalooned and petticoated to manifest its universality.' Hindu thought, he says, has 'reared up a magnificent theism which in its essential conclusions agrees wonderfully with the philosophy of S. Thomas.' He complains of wrong, Western conceptions of what Vedantism really means by *māya*. '*Māya* is less than being but more than nothing.' Māya does not mean 'nothing' in the sense in which 'a barren woman's son' is nothing—i.e. pure contradiction in logic. But the world is 'unreal'—not in Berkeley or Hume's sense, but, 'inasmuch as it can be made to continue or be blotted out without causing any disturbance in the volume of being.' In other words, God is not dependent for his being on his creatures, though creativity is part of the nature of God. Hence, on a true understanding of the Vedanta, 'Hindu thought may be made to serve the cause of Christianity in the same way in India as Greek thought was made to do in Europe.'[11] In his second article he pleaded for a more sympathetic under-standing of caste: 'Hinduism is not at all a dogmatic religious system like Christianity. Christianity tolerates the widest divergencies in social ways and manners but insists on uni-formity in matters of faith. On the contrary, Hinduism allows endless variations in religious beliefs but checks the slightest rebellion against its social constitution.'[12] So Christians must not be too socially revolutionary in their approach to Indian traditionalism.

It is not surprising that, at this date, his articles were met with surprise and some hostility from his fellow-Catholics. A Jesuit professor of Sanskrit wrote the next month that Upadhyay's project was hopeless: 'the Vedantic system . . . is one of the saddest, if not absolutely the saddest, aberration ever perpetrated by the human mind.'[13] So an attempt to use it as a philosophical foundation for Christianity was vain.

Upadhyay was back in Calcutta in September 1903, and continued with his educational work. He took a more and more active part in Hindu religious festivals, and people were in-creasingly convinced that he had left Christianity and returned to Hinduism; but 'he smiles at their simplicity and comforts himself with the thought that "time will set all things right".'[14] And his reported lectures show that he was still within Christian orthodoxy. For instance in a lecture given in English in 1904, though he defends the greatness of Krishna against Europeans, he stresses quite clearly the difference between Hindu and Christian theology:

According to Hinduism all things, visible and invisible, are appearances of God. . . . Whenever man sinks low in irreligion . . . the Lord creates himself from age to age as a human person by way of reflection. . . . This descent as a human person is called *Avatara* . . . [which is] supernatural and not subject to the painful bondage of karma.

The doctrine of the Christian incarnation is altogether different and is wholly a matter of faith. The theory that an incarnate saviour, understood in the Christian sense, is as necessary as the sunlight is to the eye, is erroneous. All Christian theologians hold that human nature cries for redemption but cannot instinctively conceive of the scheme of redemption. . . . [This redemption] is a pure condescension, and is not a necessity of nature, though nature too is of God. [So] the sectarian missionary device to oust Krishna from the *Gita* and bring in Christ instead, is an historical error, and also a theological blunder whether considered from the Hindu or Christian point of view.

Up till now he had been obedient to the ecclesiastical authorities, even though deeply disappointed at their unwillingness to support or even try to understand his aims. When Catholics were, in 1901, forbidden to read the *Twentieth Century* he submitted, 'as a loyal child of the Church', to the head of the hierarchy. He wrote:

It [the hierarchy] has wrongly accused me of disobedience. The first interdict against *Sophia* was issued on the ground of my having had nothing to do with it. But as soon as I resumed its editorship the faithful were allowed to read it though not without episcopal permission. And now be it known that since the interdict against the *Twentieth Century*, which is plainly directed against my writings, I have not penned a single line on theological questions, nor shall I pen any until the interdict be removed.

When in England he had an interview with Cardinal Vaughan, who let him ventilate his views in the *Tablet*, as we have seen; and his article opened with a letter of recommendation from the Archbishop of Calcutta—'We declare that Brahmabandhav (Theophilus) Upadhyay, a Brahmin of Calcutta, is a true Catholic of good character, burning with zeal for the conversion of his countrymen. . . .' And in the article he said plainly, 'Since my conversion to the Catholic faith my mind has been occupied with the sole object only of winning over India to the Catholic Church' (January 1903). In 1904 a letter was circulated that he had become an apostate. He replied,

Rest assured that for me it is impossible to go against the Holy Church. Never, for a moment, since my baptism have I been even tempted (I am not boasting) to doubt the divine authority of the Pope of Rome over my faith and morals. Moreover, I have never failed to submit to lawful ecclesiastical authorities. To protest or appeal against a particular magistrate, after due submission, in order to test whether that particular magistrate is in agreement with central authority, is not disloyalty.

He celebrated the Nativity on Christmas Day, 1904; received ashes on Ash Wednesday 1905 in the Cathedral Church; was seen, some months after that, in St. Xavier's Church on a Sunday morning; and the same year, talking to an Indian Baptist minister, protested his Christian faith. He again observed Christmas in 1905.

In 1906 he did become irregular in Christian worship—he was very much caught up with the nationalist 'Swadeshi' movement, and indeed from 1905 to 1907 his weekly paper, *Sandhya* (Twilight), became a sort of headquarters for the agitation against partition. He said of this time that 'pressure of work' prevented him from going to church, and that if one had really important work to do one was exempted from church-attendance. But on Good Friday 1907 he wrote to a friend in a way that implied he was observing the day in abstinence.

All this must be taken into account when considering the last few months and weeks of his life. In February he was known to have made a solemn act of self-dedication, which included the Lord's Prayer in Sanskrit, a canticle in praise of the Trinity, and a hymn on Jesus Christ the Incarnate Logos. Yet he had some time before that undergone the Hindu ceremony of *prayaschitta* (purification) because his contacts with Europeans had rendered him impure. This caused some eyebrows to be raised (both Christian and Hindu), but he hastened to explain, 'I am not sorry for being a Christian, I do not want to make *prayaschitta* on that account, but because I have mixed with the Europeans.'

His articles in *Sandhya* were, however, regarded by the civil authorities as so anti-imperial and seditious that he was arrested. He knew he would be likely to be convicted; so he took the opportunity before going to prison to present himself at the Campbell Hospital, Calcutta, for an operation for a hernia which had been troubling him since he had dysentery in 1900. The operation was successful, but he developed tetanus after it and died quite suddenly on 27 October (1907). On his admission ticket to the hospital he was merely registered as a Brahman: the section headings, 'Caste', 'Religion', 'Nationality' were not filled in. So he did not receive Christian burial—a Jesuit arrived at the hospital while the bier was being carried away, but could do nothing. As a result of this, and his behaviour in the previous year or two, many thought that he had ceased to be a Christian. But his closest Hindu friends were clear that it was a Christian they were dealing with. And the Rev. B. A. Nag, a Baptist minister who knew him intimately, wrote in 1908 that it was

absolutely groundless that he had ceased to be Christian and become Hindu again. Upadhyay was a great friend of mine, though he was a Roman Catholic and I a Protestant. Yet we often had spiritual fellowship together. [Though he often gave grounds for misunderstanding . . .] after a personal close and frank conversation with him, I always found him loyal and devoted to Jesus as his Lord and Saviour.

It seems clear that, though an impulsive man, and one of changing moods, and though his life seems littered with rather grandiose plans that never quite came off, perhaps to some extent because of a lack of steady application, he had both a fine philosophical mind and a very profound conviction of the centrality of the Incarnation and the possibility of combining Hindu cultural history with the Christian faith. Fr. Joseph Rickaby, the Jesuit Thomist philosopher, who met him when he visited Oxford, wrote in 1908:

I have heard him much spoken against, but he made a good impression on me. . . . I heard him once lecture at Manchester College [Oxford]. He argued earnestly that *not all* Hindu Philosophy is pantheistic. I was particularly struck with the thorough understanding that he showed of the philosophies current in Oxford. He told me he saw no hope of the conversion of India as a country but he thought more might be done for the conversion of high caste natives. In Oxford he suffered from insufficient clothing and poverty.

It is possible that if the Church authorities had been more sensitive to the real needs, and appreciative of the positive contribution, of India in his time he might have made a greater impact. Certainly it took fifty years before his hopes for a truly Indian form of the religious life began to be realized by Roman Catholics in indigenous *ashrams*. And his basic Christian convictions could never really have been doubted by anyone who read what he wrote, only three years before his death, in 1904: 'There is only one other fact similar to [the Incarnation] in greatness, and that is the formation of the Catholic Church in the Upper Chamber at Jerusalem.'

CHAPTER 17

The remaining examples of 'transpositions' can be given in a more summary form, if only because the material for the lives is fairly accessible.

i. LU CHENG-HSIANG (DOM PIERRE-CÉLESTIN LOU, O.S.B.) (1871–1949)

In 1897 Hsü Ching-ch'eng, then Chinese Minister to St. Petersburg and later a martyr in the Boxer uprising, asserted that over-Westernization was quite impossible for a Chinese; hence he advised Lu Cheng-hsiang, a future prime minister, to become a Christian in order to Westernize himself thoroughly. Lu not only accepted this advice but subsequently married a Belgian lady, spent a great many years abroad, and finally after his wife died, became a priest in Belgium.[1]

This potted biography of one of the most distinguished and unusual Chinese of this century is perhaps over-simplified, but is not far from the truth. There is no doubt that 'Fr. Lou' (as we shall call him, though he did not become that till 1933) was influenced in his study of Roman Catholicism by the desire to understand Europe. Lou was working in the Chinese embassy in Russia when his first chief, Hsü Ching-ch'eng (not a Christian),[2] urged the young man to 'Europeanise himself for love of China.' And he went on:

The strength of Europe is not to be found in her armaments; it is not to be found in her science; it is to be found in her religion. . . . Take the most ancient branch of that religion, that which goes back most nearly to its origins. . . . If you can do so, enter into it. . . . Make yourself its follower, and study the interior life which must be the secret of it. When you have . . . grasped the heart and the strength of the religion of Christ, bring them back and give them to China.[3]

He was not urging Lou to become a Christian, for he was already that, but to study the Roman Catholic Church, and, if he could, to become a Catholic.

Lou was born in Shanghai of a well-to-do family; his father was a catechist of the L.M.S. At about thirteen the boy entered the Foreign Language School and specialized in French, first in Shanghai and later in Peking. He had no ambition for a diplomatic career, and his father was afraid at the corruption of many officials of the Imperial Dynasty; but he was sent as an interpreter to the Chinese Legation in St. Petersburg in 1892, and this led inevitably to a commitment to the Foreign Service. He was in Russia when the secret treaty was drawn up between Russia and China, authorizing the Trans-Manchurian railway and giving advantages to Russia at China's expense. His chief, Hsü Ching-ch'eng (the one who had advised him to Westernize at all costs) was recalled to Peking in 1897, and in 1900 was made a scapegoat for the internal disturbances of the Boxer Rising, and was executed—though he was wholly innocent. Lou remained at St. Petersburg in the Legation till 1906, eleven years of interesting, but anxious diplomatic service. While there he met Mlle Berthe Bovy, and they were married in the Roman Catholic Church, though Lou was still then a Protestant. His wife used no influence to persuade him, but in 1911 he joined her church.

In 1907 he became head of a newly-founded Legation at the Hague, and so was there to represent China at the Second International Peace Conference; but returned in 1911 to St. Petersburg as Special Commissioner to revise the treaty with Russia. At this point, however, occurred the Chinese National Revolution, and Lou, having seen the humiliation of China in Russia, and experienced the loss of his chief by arbitrary execution (which he took to be typical of the Manchu regime), strongly supported Dr. Sun Yat-sen. Lou revisited China in

1912, as Premier under Yüan Shih-kai in the newly formed Cabinet. In 1915 he had to return again, reluctantly, to take on, not only Foreign Affairs (which he retained) but the post of Premier again, as Yüan's own chief supporter, who was Prime Minister, had resigned. Lou's reluctance was not only because he wanted to stick to Foreign Affairs but because Yüan's personal ambitions were becoming evident. His fears became all the clearer when he found himself having to sign, in 1915, the secret treaty incorporating Yüan's surrender to Japan's 'Twenty-One Demands'. This was an even greater humiliation than the Russian treaty; and it later became clear that Yüan had agreed to it, not merely because he needed money (which the Treaty would give him), and because the Japanese were a formidable military threat, but because they had offered to back him in his own personal ambitions to be Emperor.

But Lou's most important assignment was after the First World War. China had supported the Allies, and had hoped for reasonable treatment—the return of territory occupied by the Germans (Shantung)—afterwards. So he represented the Chinese Government at the Peace Conference in Paris (1919). Lloyd George was impervious to China's requests (and, apparently, somewhat ignorant of their history), and Lou was deeply distressed at the humiliations of his country. In the middle of the Conference the Cabinet in Peking resigned (12 June), and the Chinese delegation in Paris was left without instructions. When the Treaty of Versailles was ready for signature, on 28 June, Lou was in a quandary; his previous instructions from Tuan Ch'i-jui's regime were to sign, but Tuan had fallen, and Lou decided to disobey and absent himself with the rest. To his delight, when new instructions finally came on 10 July they indicated that the Chinese should not sign.

Back in China after the Versailles Conference he gave up his post of Foreign Secretary, and took on the Vice-Directorship of the Office for Famine Relief, which gave him an insight into the needs of ordinary people. But in 1922 he left China. His wife's health was poor, and as they had a small property in Switzerland they went there. He did not want to return to public life, but after a while found he needed to earn his living, so he took over the Chinese Legation in Switzerland. In 1926, after several years of serious illness, his wife died. In 1927, having for some time thought of the Religious Life (he and his wife were childless), he went to the Abbey of Saint-André at Bruges. He had originally thought of becoming a mere Benedictine Oblate, but the Abbot suggested he become a monk, he took the habit in 1928, and was ordained priest in 1933. He spent the rest of his life writing and speaking on behalf of the Christianization of Chinese culture and civilization.

He was a Confucianist, and remained one as a Catholic. He was anxious to defend Confucianism against those who regarded it as an obsolete, hieratic philosophy of conservatism; indeed, he wished to show that it was compatible with the Chinese Nationalist revolution which overthrew the Manchu régime. But still more he wanted to show that it was compatible with Christianity.

The intellectual and spiritual tradition of Confucianism, the cult of the Most High (Ch'ang t'i), the practice of filial piety, the eagerness to give proof of virtue, in order to . . . understand man better . . . all that makes up the spirit of the Chinese race since the time of Yao, Choen and of Yu, the contemporaries of Abraham, in submission to the master of ten thousand generations, Confucius, and to that other great philosopher, Mencius—by all this I have ceaselessly desired to be moulded and nourished.[4]

And he felt this particularly as a statesman, for he came to see that the only safeguard for the conduct of international affairs lay in the Natural Law, and that is something held in common between Christians and Confucians. (Another Chinese Roman Catholic John C. Wu, a distinguished professor of Law, has written powerfully to the same effect.[5]) This Natural Law is 'the first principle of all social life and the foundation of public happiness'. Far from instituting a petrified monarchy and a static, inflexible hierarchical tyranny,

the religious basis of political power has been the corrective principle of all the abuses to which . . . the successive dynasties which ruled the Chinese people allowed themselves to succumb. In consequence of our classical books, our political tradition never ceases to tell the Emperor that 'no one, in the whole world, is noble by his birth'.* This mentality provoked many political revolutions. But it banished for all time from the Chinese heart the myth of an imperial divinity, of an Emperor or a dynasty which could pretend to substitute itself for Heaven.[6]

And finally, he points to the importance of the other element in

* Li Chi, *Book of Rites*, Book IX, Part III, Chap. v.

Chinese religion—Buddhism. It was the Buddhist monk, Hsüang Tsang, in the seventh century A.D., who gave monasticism to China, and it was monasticism which was the instrument of Buddhism's penetration: 'thanks to this monastic constitution, which responds to one of the most profound aspirations of the Chinese soul, it overran the whole of China, winning the Court and the people, erecting its temples . . . in all the towns and villages . . . giving spiritual sustenance to a number of souls. . . .'[7] But Buddhist monasticism had its profound defects and superstitions. Perhaps (he prays) a new Chinese Benedictinism will save the country.*

ii. SAMUEL ADJAYI CROWTHER (c. 1806–91)

The first African Bishop of the Anglican Church has had a good deal written about him, but, since the first life of him written in 1908[8] there have been several reassessments, especially from the African point of view, which present him in a new light, and show him to be a man of more considerable stature than was at first thought.

He was born a Yoruba, but when he was about fifteen, in 1821, he was taken as a slave, during a local war between the Yoruba and the Eyo Muslims. He was separated from his mother, whom he never expected to see again, though by chance they met twenty-five years later, in 1846. After changing hands several times, he was embarked, with many others, on a Portuguese ship. This however was captured by two British men-of-war, and he and other slaves were taken on board H.M.S. *Myrmidon*, in April 1822. In June they reached Freetown, Sierra Leone, and he was put to school. He was baptized in 1825, and taken to England the next year. Back in Sierra Leone in 1827, he became the first pupil in the later famous Fourah Bay College. In 1841 being now a catechist, he was chosen by the linguist, the Rev. F. J. Schön, to accompany an expedition up the Niger, to find out ways of stopping the slave-trade, and of bringing the Gospel to the people there. He made such a good impression on Schön that the latter wrote to the C.M.S. in England, and he was brought to London to study at their Islington Church College in 1842. He had started Greek at Fourah Bay, and now he did so well that the Professor of Greek at Cambridge, brought in as external examiner, said

* See also Appendix 17, p. 324.

I should like, with your permission, to take young Crowther's answers to those Paley questions [i.e. questions on Paley's *Evidences*] back with me to Cambridge, and there read a few of them in the Combination Room to certain of my old Trinity friends. If . . . they still contend that he does not possess a logical faculty, they will tempt us to question whether they do not lack . . . common fairness of judgement and Christian candour.[9]

Samuel was ordained by Bishop Blomfield of London in 1843, and returned to Freetown. After some time working there, especially among Muslim Africans, he was moved to Abeokuta, Nigeria. It was there that, in 1846, he heard that his mother was still alive, and they were reunited. He baptized her himself in 1848, and she lived to be over a hundred.

In 1853 Crowther was invited to join a second expedition up the Niger, which was successful at least in that for the first time there had been no loss of life. (The expedition of 1841 had been particularly disastrous.)* Out of this arose in 1857 the 'Niger Mission' with which Crowther was to be associated for the rest of his life. In 1864 Crowther, after a great deal of persuasion and the utmost diffidence on his part, was consecrated 'Bishop of the Niger'—as the old books called it, though strictly it was bishop of an immense diocese described in the royal licence as 'The countries of Western Africa beyond our dominions', which meant in effect from the Equator to Senegal, except for Lagos, the Gold Coast, and Sierra Leone.[10] He came almost straight back from England after his consecration, and set to work, ordaining African priests and opening new work. He has been called, 'a little man with nerves of steel, upon whose constitution neither lagoon nor mosquito could leave any deadly germ, whom incessant work did not seem to wear. Intellectually alert, spiritually optimistic and full of faith, he was always on the tiptoe of new achievements, and yet no man had more native dignity or common sense.'[11] During his time there was persecution of Christians both at Abeokuta (1867) and (later) at Bonny. There was also much criticism from Europeans, including some of the white missionaries; and the usual problems of the loose morals and anti-black feelings of European traders. There were also problems arising from irregular

* Other expeditions were: Mungo Park (1805); Brothers Lander (1830); Macgregor Laird (1832–3); Beecroft (1836, 1840); Vovernment (1841) and Beecroft (1845).

behaviour among some of the converts (much exaggerated, of course, by the whites), and at one point Crowther offered to resign. But his resignation was not accepted; instead there was a redivision of the work. But Crowther had obviously been distressed, and his tough health affected, by dissension and the need to make disciplinary decisions. He had paid a final visit to England to appeal for more missionaries at a great Exeter Hall meeting (20 January 1890). But two years later he died, on the last day of 1891.

Even his critics allow that Crowther was man of great dignity and dependability. It has sometimes been suggested that, as a bishop had in those days to have a Doctorate of Divinity, the authorities were nonplussed how to grant Crowther one, but finally agreed to regard his Travel Journals (which were published as of geographical interest), and his Yoruba Grammar as sufficient qualification. But in fact he took a great deal of trouble over his linguistic work, never travelling without a note-book, and 'watching the mouth' of the elders; 'in tracing out words and their various uses, I am . . . led to search at length into some of the traditions . . . of the Yorubas.'[12] And indeed, apart from his work on language, he was so much trusted by the British Government that between 1871 and 1876 'he was in effect "undesignated consul" on the river'—being used as the intermediary for presenting gifts to chiefs, etc.[13]

He has been regarded as very much a 'black Englishman'; and indeed he was at home with Victorian ways of life. But he was for his time more aware than most of the importance of preserving traditional customs, so far as possible. He commended the use of 'native airs' or 'songs of suitable Scriptural compositions' adapted to them;[14] and in a charge to his clergy in the Niger Delta Pastorate, given at Lokoja in 1869, he said:

Christianity has come into the world to abolish . . . all false religions. . . . But it should be borne in mind that Christianity does not undertake to destroy national assimilation. . . . Their [the Africans'] mutual-aid clubs should not be despised, but where there is any connexion with superstitions, they should be corrected and improved after the Christian model. Amusements . . . tend to relieve the mind and sharpen the intellect. If any such is not immoral or indecent . . . it should not be checked because of its being native and of heathen origin. . . . [These may be] fables, story-telling, proverbs and songs, which may be regarded as stores of their national education. . . .[15]

It is true that Crowther did not reside in his diocese, but in Lagos, two hundred miles away from the nearest mission station, for nine months of the year. And he was unsympathetic to complaints by heathen chiefs in the Niger Delta about the insubordination of Christian slaves. The Bishop defended them and tells how he met the chiefs' complaints that these Christian slaves were reluctant to go to the market on Sunday.

I told them that . . . though they own the slaves who must obey them, yet they own and enslave the body only, but that God claims both body and soul; that it was His will that they enslave their bodies, and demand their services during six days in the week, but God demands the service of their souls on the seventh. . . . I put the question to them individually whether when God does send His messenger Death to take away the soul of any of their slaves, could the owner prevent that soul from obeying the summons by the hand of death? They unanimously replied, "No." I then said, "well, in that case God has taken away the most important part of that slave which belongs to him, and left the body to them . . . which they had purchased with their money; that they were perfectly at liberty to employ it whenever they pleased, Sunday or not:" they remained puzzled. I said if the dead body did not obey their orders, it should be compelled to do so by being beaten; they were silent: I said, "you must make it obey your orders—put it into the canoe, lash it to its seat, and lash the paddles into his hands and compel it to the paddle;" —here they saw the impossibility.[16]

This exercise in primitive Christian apologetics is both amusing and characteristic of Crowther.

The chief criticism of the Bishop has been that, however well-intentioned, he failed to handle the disciplinary problems of his pastorate. Even one of his African defenders has admitted that he was

too fatherly and too tender in his dealings with his agents. . . . Straightforward and transparently guileless, he believed everything that his African agents reported to him, and . . . he always stood by his agents unless the charges preferred against them were proven to the hilt. . . . No one can dispute that the Bishop made many unfortunate appointments, but even in Yorubaland the European missionaries made such appointments.[17]

But this criticism of Crowther is taken by some white missionary historians to show that Henry Venn's (of C.M.S.) revolutionary step in insisting on having an African bishop was premature.

This view has been repeated in various forms.[18] But more recent studies have suggested a very different interpretation. It is clear that the opposition to Crowther's appointment as bishop was much stronger in Nigeria than Henry Venn realized. Henry Townsend, in particular, though an intrepid missionary himself, was against black advancement: 'I have a great doubt [he wrote] of young black clergymen. They want years of experience to give stability to their characters; we would rather have them as schoolmasters and catechists.' And there was a letter of protest from four European missionaries in 1851:

Native teachers of whatever grade have been received and respected by the chiefs and people only as being the agents or servants of white men. . . . Our esteemed brother Mr. Crowther was often treated as the white man's inferior, and more frequently called so, notwithstanding our frequent assertions to the contrary. . . . The superiority of the white man over the black man, the negro has been forward to acknowledge. The correctness of this belief no white man can deny.[19]

A standard history of missions by Bishop Stephen Neill presents the traditional view thus:

When the old bishop [Crowther] died things were found to be in a state of utter confusion, and grave irregularities in the conduct of many of his helpers came to light. At last the [C.M.S.] did what it ought to have done in the beginning and reconstituted the mission as a joint Africa-European venture. There was strong feeling in Lagos, because Crowther's successor as bishop was not an African; but undoubtedly the right action was taken. The labours of three successive European bishops over fifty years were needed before things were really set to rights. . . .[20]

Of the resentment there can be no doubt: when the new European Diocesan with his two African assistant bishops arrived (1893) 'There was no public welcome in Lagos. . . . The boycott was total. Lagos was in mourning.'[21] And now that missionary history is beginning to be written, at last, by other than Europeans it is becoming clearer that Venn's 'doctrinaire principles' were probably more far-seeing than anyone, except possibly Crowther himself, knew. Before he died Crowther had investigated some of the charges against his people, and found that many of them were simply false; and yet the decisions of the Finance Committee, made on the basis of the charges, simply overrode Crowther—in the presence of the Bishop the Secretary suspended pastors whom the Bishop had ordained (1890). As the African historian puts it, a deadlock had been reached: 'There was no bridge between the two opinions [Venn's and the younger missionaries'] on the parent Committee, or between Africans brought up under Venn and Europeans going out in the new age when Britain was acquiring political power in Africa.'[22]

What Bishop Stephen Neill calls 'undoubtedly the right action' taken by the C.M.S. ignored this major political fact: that the Europeans now arriving in West Africa would be less and less willing to accept direction from a black superior. Indeed, two of Venn's English followers protested, against the decision of 1894, that 'the racial arrogance of the English was responsible for the decisions taken on the Niger Mission. This was why the mission among five generations of Christians had not yet evolved into churches; why an English curate of little ability was preferred for bishop to godly and outstanding Negroes. . . .'[23] And this decision, by securing English control of the high positions in the Church for the next half century, kept the Church well in the rear of general advance. 'Sixty years later the Church discovered that while the senior political and administrative posts in the Government were passing into African hands, the church lagged behind with an English episcopate.'[24]

Similar decisions were being taken in other denominations: a Methodist missionary wrote home in 1884 that there was trouble in Lagos, that 'race feeling' was the cause, and that therefore 'our authority and status as Europeans must be clearly laid down'; another accused the African minister, James Johnson, in 1877 of 'antagonism against members of the ruling race.'[25] And the results of all these decisions were quite simply: schisms. A schism in the Presbyterian Mission in Calabar (1882); one barely averted in the Methodist Church in Lagos (1884); a secession from the Baptist Church in Lagos (1888); and a number of new independent African churches—one of them tried to persuade the Anglican bishop, James Johnson, to join and lead them—from about 1891 onwards. It is good that old Samuel Crowther was spared the sight of all this disunity. For he had always held to a simple central conviction: that the

Africans were 'tailor-made' for Christianity, and left to themselves would hold to it and be shaped by it. In about 1870 he was on one of his journeys, and had to stay the night at a village near Ilorin. Ten years earlier the Baptists had started a mission there, but had had to abandon it. The station was in ruins, but in a corner he noticed a hut, screened off with mats; and a group of men with books holding a meeting. Every Sunday they met for prayers, and were teaching some younger Africans to read the Bible. They had been persecuted for this, but had persisted. There were (wrote Crowther), 'fifteen males and seven females. Of all, only three females had been baptized; but all determined to adhere to the religion which they found to be the truth, which they would not change for any other. . . . Twenty native Christians among a large population of about 50,000 maintain their stand in the very ruins of their missionaries' station.' And he asks possible objectors to Christian missions:

what could have been the worldly inducements held out to these converts, since left by their missionaries for a period of ten years, which made them stand steadfast to the doctrine which they had been taught? . . . [They had] no missionaries to comfort, encourage, or support them in those trying hours [of persecution]; no superior buildings to boast of, but instead of which they struggle to maintain their new faith in a humble shed among the very ruins.[26]

iii. INI KOPURIA (?1901–195?)

Some of the fiercest fighting, and heaviest casualties in the Second World War occurred on Guadalcanal (or Guadalcanar, as it used to be spelt). Being one of the key islands in the Solomons, it was on the outer edge of Japanese advance. Most of Melanesia did not suffer so severely from the war as New Guinea, the Gilbert Islands, and others. One middle-aged but vigorous Melanesian, an ex-police sergeant, joined the Americans, and was found to have such power among his own people that he was made head of the local corps, and was called 'Chief Ini'.

He was born near Maravovo, on Guadalcanal Island, early in the century, and educated, first at St. Michael's School, Pamua, and then at St. Barnabas School, Norfolk Island. He was small, very dark for a Melanesian, and thickset. He was obstinate, firm-willed, and a natural leader. When still at school he made a vow to maintain silence throughout Lent and wrote a note to the teacher (who had urged them to adopt a Lenten rule) saying that this was his rule, and would she please not ask him any questions in class till Easter. It required the Bishop's intervention to assure him that his vow could be dispensed—and even then he did not give in for three days.

He was expected to become a teacher, but—again, perhaps, to be different—chose the police force. At first he found the discipline in it irksome; but he came to see the point of it, and ended up as a Sergeant. He was thought so well of that after he had left the force, in 1927, when there had been a number of murders on Mala Island, Ini was asked by the Commissioner to return to the force and go to the island to sort matters out. He replied that he was now not his own boss, and must consult the Bishop; but he wrote characteristically to the Warden of the College at Siota: 'I could not refuse outright, but it would be bad for me to go to Mala with a rifle. I shall probably want to go later with the Gospel.'[27]

In 1924, while still in the police, he had a serious illness. While he was ill he had a vision in which he believed Christ was telling him that he was not doing the work he was meant to do. He had no clearer guidance than this, so he retired for some months of quiet to Maravovo, and then consulted his old schoolmaster from there, now Bishop John Mainwaring Steward, and asked whether he might not found an Anglican 'Brotherhood' of young men who would go and preach the gospel in every village from which he had taken prisoners to gaol.[28] The Bishop welcomed the idea, and together they drew up a simple rule: the brother should make annual promises, and during the year he should remain unmarried, receive no pay—only board and lodging wherever he went—and be at the direction of the Brotherhood.

In 1925 Ini therefore left the police force, and went for some months of study to the College at Siota, where the Bishop lived; then back to his own home village, Maravovo, to prepare the site for the Brotherhood.

On 28 October 1925, he took his vows—in his case, they were for life, and included the words (of his own composition):

Trinity most Holy, from this day till the day of my death I vow in the Name of Father, Son and Holy Ghost, before Archangels and Angels, spirits and the Saints, before Bishop John Steward, Bishop

Frederick Molyneux, the Rev. Arthur Hopkins, representing the
Church of Melanesia, I vow a three-fold vow:
    Myself and my land; my portion with Thy servants.
    I will receive no pay from the Mission for work to which Thou
shalt send me, or which I shall do for Thee.
    I will remain Thy celibate all my days till I die.
    Strengthen me to remain steadfast, quiet, faithful in this all the
days of my life. . . .

Tabalia, where Ini gave his own land to the Brotherhood,
became the centre, and its annual meeting was always there, on
the anniversary of 28 October. The Brotherhood grew considerably—in 1960–1, when Dr. Howard A. Johnson was on the
Solomon Uslands there were 74 brothers, and many others in
training.[29] The Brotherhood is organized in 'households' of
eight; and from these they go out in pairs to evangelize the
other islands. By 1956 they had covered not only from Santa
Cruz to New Britain but had extended their work to the untouched areas of New Guinea. On their annual meeting, where
vows are renewed, there are reports from the *Moemera* (Head) of
each household, and criticisms of each other:

There was a rule that no Brother must criticize another Brother,
but at the Annual Meeting Ini asked each in turn, beginning with
the youngest, if he had anything against any other Brother, and then
he must speak. Then the Brother accused replied and discussed it,
and it soon was evident who was at fault and he apologized. Later
such a meeting was held each week in each Household. No one ever
questioned Ini's decisions, all followed him loyally for he was a man
of strong personality, short, thick set, very dark, always merry, and
very wise.[30]

When the Japanese invaded the Solomon Islands some of the
Brothers were shot, and others wounded. The Japanese destroyed their church and houses at their headquarters in Tam-
balia, and carried off the gold chalice and paten which Bishop
Steward had presented to them, and which they had hidden in
a clump of bamboos. The households there were dispersed, and
it was then that Ini joined up with the Americans, who, seeing
his power over the others, made him head of the labour corps
of Melanesians working for them—calling him Chief Ini. He
had been ordained deacon some years before, but never
became a priest. Indeed, his own end was sad: for he broke his
vows, and had an affair with a girl. He asked to be released

from his life-vow, and was re-admitted into Church communion.[31] He died not long after—largely, it seems, of a broken heart. But the Brotherhood (*Retatasiu* was its indigenous name) more than survived the founder's temporary defection. And from the first it has had a fine independence of spirit—indeed, Ini himself had been somewhat anti-European in spite of his enormous affection and respect for his mentor, Bishop Steward.

This independence had been encouraged from the days of Bishops Selwyn and Patterson, who had never wanted Christianity in Melanesia to be a mere copy of English religion. And it is significant that anthropologists have been able, without *parti pris*, to confirm the rightness of their instincts from the results. It is true that one such anthropologist, Miss Margaret Mead, studying similar material (the Manus people on an island off New Guinea), made a surprising discovery. From her earliest experience with this people, in 1928–9, she and others would, she says, have predicted that the coming of Western ways of life would only slowly affect the local traditions. But in fact when she revisited the island in 1953–4 she found that Westernization had been speedy and wholesale. And, unexpectedly, the very rapidity was found to be most effective:

Rapid change is not only possible, but may actually be very desirable—that instead of advocating slow partial changes, we should advocate that a people who choose to practise a new technology or enter into drastically new kinds of economic relationships will do this more easily if they live in different houses, wear different clothes, and eat different, or differently cooked, food. . . . [Whereas] partial change can be seen not as a bridge between old and new, but rather as the condition within which discordant and discrepant institutions and practices develop and proliferate. . . .[32]

But another ethnologist, Professor Raymond Firth, examining a less developed island in Melanesia—closer to the kinds in which the *Retatasiu* have worked—found that in some respects change, though rapid, was effected through a kind of acceptance of the position abandoned; that, in fact, a truly indigenous Christian sacramentalism has been successful in neutralizing the powers of 'magic' and 'possession' not by denying their existence but by acknowledging them and exorcizing them. He visited the island of Tikopia (in the British Solomon Islands Protectorate, 120 miles south-east from Vanikoro: Polynesian in culture, but visited by the Melanesian steam yacht, the *Southern Cross*, about twice a year). He went first in 1928–9, then again in 1952 and 1966. In 1966 he noted that

a most spectular change, involving complete cessation of ritual practices, was the ending of spirit mediumship. In 1928–9 and in 1952 spirit mediums flourished, in the Christian sector of the community as in the pagan sector. By 1966 no one was practising the cult . . . I could not find the slightest evidence of any private or secret practices.

The reasons given him were that 'formerly the gods were many, and now they are only one, the God of the Gospel'; and this had happened because the Melanesian mission priest, himself a Tikopia familiar with the cult, had forbidden it. He baptized one woman medium, ordering the spirits to refrain from coming to her any more—and they had not come. Another medium, a man who used to enter mild trance states, 'gave a farewell feast to his spirits and ceased to practise'.[33] A little earlier, about 1955,

Father Ellison, the Melanesian priest, went with the Ariki [chief] Tafua through the district and buried the oil bottles dedicated to the spirits. . . . The Ariki Tafua came to Pa Rarosingano's house, (a popular medium) where an oven was prepared. Breadfruit was cooked, and the oil bottle and ceremonial bark-cloth offering to the spirit laid out. The medium, his wife and children and the chief then partook of a farewell meal, the medium having gone into a trance state. He was allegedly possessed by his familiar spirit . . . the chief's own dead brother. The Ariki then told his brother's spirit to cease coming to men and to go and stay in limbo. Then he put his hand on the medium's head and 'blocked the path of the spirit', at the same time making the sign of the Cross on the medium's forehead. . . . The spirit is reported to have said, 'You are right, brother. You have told me to go into limbo, and this is fine. But had you come just to make me go while continuing to perform your own *kava* [ritual dance], it would have been very bad.'[34]

In others words, the fact that the chief was now a Christian, and prepared to affect a sweeping reform was acceptable to the 'spirit'.

No encounters quite so dramatic with spirits are recorded in Ini Kopuria's career. But he had an evident flair for using local material and modes. In addition to the obvious matter of a 'habit' for his Brothers (which is simple and truly 'contemporary Melanesian' in style), he introduced such experiments as dramatic presentation of Christian teaching: very necessary when, in their travels, the Brothers may find a different language in every island. And the *raison d'être* of the *Retatasiu* was missionary. What was said above (in chapter 13) about Polynesians being outstanding for 'self-propagating' their faith applies to this movement in Melanesia too. As one observer has said, Melanesia, 'operating on a shoestring has—in proportion to its numerical strength—more "foreign" missionaries than has the entire Episcopal Church in the United States of America.'[35]

PART FIVE | IMPROVISATIONS

Christians have always made the claim that their faith is 'revolutionary'. And so, historically, I think it can be shown to be: but not always by design, and not always in the way intended by its purveyors.

Some of the people looked at in this section would be described by Christian orthodoxy as Christian 'deviants'. In a work of this sort such a term would be loaded. I have therefore called them 'improvisators'. In most cases they were living in disturbed social and political situations, and their Christian faith (however marginal, tenuous, or distorted it may seem to the cool onlooker from a secure mainland of Christian tradition) acted as a booster—or sometimes a fuse—to the explosive forces already building up. In view of the importance of the social conditions in these lives it is convenient to move from one continent to another, if only to show the remarkable similarity of development, uninfluenced by each other.

CHAPTER 18

a. LATIN AMERICA

i. DONA MARÍA ANGEL (?1690–1715?)

In Western Guatemala an Indian tribe, the Tzendales in Chiapas, began in the early eighteenth century to form an alliance with other tribes, and to develop a new cult which was a mixture of Indian paganism and Christian rites. The first sign of its growth was when in Diasolo a priest was beaten, nearly to death, while trying to remove some ornaments from the church to a near-by town. And then in mid 1712 the priest of Cancuc was told that an Indian girl had had a remarkable revelation. He summoned her, and 'standing in their midst she calmly told how the Virgin had appeared to her, and commanded that a chapel to her glory should be built on the spot where she had made her presence visible'. Actually this chapel already existed, erected by the Indians themselves: but the Bishop had ordered that it was not to be used for religious rites. Supported by María's vision, they now defied the parish priest, and in August sent messages to all the Tzendales in her name telling them to bring all their silver, ornaments, and money to Cancuc, since 'there is now neither God nor king of the Spaniards'. There was a great festival of the Virgin in the chapel, and a council of war for the extermination of the Spaniards led to a successful attack on three local towns, the fiscal and others being beaten or tortured to death by the 'soldiers of the Virgin'. And now María became extremely powerful: 'In the chapel at Cancuc she issued her mandates. Before the spurious altar of the Virgin hung a screen of Indian matting, behind which the priestess would retire; thence issuing forth she pronounced the commands of holy Mary.' Her Secretary-of-State was a Tzendale who called himself Sebastian Gomez de la Gloria, and claimed that St. Peter had taken him to heaven and appointed him his Vicar on earth. So he now 'ordained' priests (by sprinkling holy water over them), and the movement spread fast. La Gloria celebrated mass, and so did María (now called Dona María Angel), and after the first mass there was a feast, with bull-fights, games, and dances in the church.

Unfortunately for the movement, dissensions developed within it, and La Gloria had to issue an edict in the name of St. Peter: 'God is angry with the world because He is not venerated as He should be, because old customs are abandoned. . . . But for the masses celebrated by your priests, the world would come to an end; through them only will God's anger be removed . . .' and stricter church discipline was ordered on pain of death. There was also a challenge to the movement from María's aunt, who claimed a rival revelation, and an Indian supporter who claimed to be Christ. These were both executed.

The Government finally decided to suppress the movement; but even with the President's own intervention, after the failure of two invading forces, it was not till the end of the year that Cancuc was finally captured. And even then the rebellion was not over, for it had spread to Ciudad Real. La Gloria and María escaped into the woods early in 1713, and were never heard of again. But the long-term effects of this religio-politico movement were severe, and can be traced as late as 1785 or even 1800.[1]

17

ii. ANTONIO CONSELHEIRO (*c.* 1842–97)

From this fantastic, short-lived but ong-echoing aberration among syncretistic Indians in Guatemala, we move to a more credible but tragic story from nineteenth-century Brazil. Conselheiro, born in the Maciel family in the wild country of the Sertão (between Bahia and Pernambuco), was part-Indian. His full name was Antoni Vicente Mendes Maciel; and he was fairly well educated for his time. His father employed him as accountant at his store, and he became its manager when his father died in 1855. In 1858 he married, but he found his wife regularly unfaithful—'la cabra tira el monte', he would say ('the she-goat will be off into the mountains'). In 1859 he went down to live in a larger town, and became a lawyer's clerk, and then entered politics. But when his wife ran off with a police officer he became distraught. He tracked his rival down to another town, but then dared not attack him—instead he assaulted a relative who had sheltered him. For this he was imprisoned (though the victim took his side and defended an injured husband's right to revenge). He soon escaped from prison, and then was not seen for ten years.

He had always been extremely devout; and now he appeared, in 1874, as a hermit, with long hair and a pilgrim's staff, living on alms. He preached the coming of the Kingdom, and soon had a following of women. He became known as the *Conselheiro* (Counsellor), and for the next thirteen years travelled widely, holding religious services, preaching wild apocalyptic, and giving spiritual advice. In 1887 the Government of Bahia made the mistake of arresting him and bringing him to the capital. He offered no resistance, and would not let his followers defend him, in spite of rough treatment. He was accused of murdering his wife and mother—but when he demonstrated that they were still alive, he was released.

Now his following doubled, and he began to demand to preach in churches—when the demand was refused he pronounced a curse upon the priests—and his disciples claimed that he worked miracles. The Archbishop prohibited him, but he ignored this.

In 1893 a Republic was set up. Conselheiro denounced it, and started to defy tax-paying. He withdrew with his followers to a remote part of Sertão, and set up a New Zion in Canudos, in 1893. They built a huge church, and he proclaimed a Reign of the Saints. In 1895 two friars and a priest bravely came to Canudos, which was now a fortified city, to persuade Conselheiro to return to the Church. He let them preach and confess some of his followers, and regularize their marriages, but the task was too great, and they withdrew.

In 1896 the Government suspected that the movement was secretly political, to restore the Monarchy. Between January and June 1897 four expeditions were beaten off by Conselheiro's followers. But finally a new general, with five thousand men, reinforced in July with others, beseiged the town. The demand for surrender was ignored, but as famine grew worse more of the women sneaked out and gave themselves up. Finally, with artillery battering down the walls, his people starving, and the statue of Jesus in his church blown to pieces, Conselheiro fell into despair.

Wrapping himself in silence, he refused all food, passed all the day in prayer in an angle of the ruined church before an image of a saint, and stalked about the streets occasionally, a living skeleton shrouded in mutism.

One day, after he had been missed for several hours . . . his inseparable friend found him face downwards on the ground, dead and already cold, clasping a silver crucifix against his breast, within the ruined church. His face was calm, his body almost mere skin and bones, worn out with fasting and with the death of his illusions, but his soul unconquerable.

In a sense he had preached a return of the Monarchy: but it was a mystic Monarch—a King, Don Sebastian, who would come and rule in glory, blot out injustice, cast down the mighty, and exalt the poor to their inheritance. One of the hymns his followers sang was:

Visita nos bena fazer	Our King, Don Sebastian
Nosso rei Don Sebastiao	will come to visit us,
Coitado daquelle pobre	and free us from the reign
Que estiver na lei do cão.	of the dog.[2]

iii. HIDALGO Y COSTILLA (1753–1811)
    JOSÉ MARÍA MORELOS Y PAVAN (1765–1816)

From these marginal 'improvisations' we move to one which is much more historically central. In most of Latin America the movement for independence came from the *criollos* (American-born Spaniards) in the cities, who reacted against Napoleon's invasion of Spain and occupation of Madrid by forming groups loyal to the Spanish crown, but groups which gradually wanted permanent independence and so became revolutionary without fully realizing which way they were going. But Mexico was the exception. Here revolution started in a rural village, and among Indians. It was led by two priests, a *criollo* and a *mestizo* (half-caste).

Hidalgo was the son of a poor farmer, but educated well at Valladolid, a college (San Nicolás) of which he became rector.

Rather above . . . medium height, of somewhat stout proportions, large limbs and ruddy-brown complexion, he presented altogether a robust constitution. . . . His heart was kind and sympathetic; his voice sonorous, vibrating and most pleasing to the ear. . . . He had the true scholarly stoop; and in all his features, air and attitude a most profoundly meditative expression. . . . Yet the clear, black, brilliant eyes betrayed the activity of the mind, and through them shone the light from the burning fires within it.[3]

By 1800 he began to have a reputation for dangerous thinking —studying the French revolution and the works of Rousseau. He was also accused of heresy and immorality to the Inquisition —though these accusations were ignored (some say because the Bishop was somewhat involved in them himself) until they became useful against him later. He was sent to the remote village of Dolores the same year, as parish priest. And there he took the side of the Indians and *mestizos*. He learned several Indian dialects, taught husbandry, organized a pottery, tannery, brickery, and a silk-worm industry; built up an orchestra for the Indians, and taught that the Church has a mission of social redemption for the poor.[4]

In the near-by city a revolutionary society had been started, and Hidalgo sympathized. Early in September 1810 he learned that the authorities were investigating the society, and on Sunday 16 September, hearing that arrests were about to be made, he announced to the congregation that there would be no mass; instead he distributed weapons, opened the gaol, and armed the prisoners, and then summoned all the villagers to the church by ringing the bells. He preached to them: 'My children, this day a new dispensation comes to us. Are you ready to receive it? Will you be free? Will you make the effort to recover from the hated Spaniards the lands stolen from your forefathers three hundred years ago?' The crowds shouted, Yes—'Viva

Nuestra Señora de Guadalupe, muera el mal gobierno, mueran los gachupines!'* This was the famous 'Grito de Dolores'— cry of Dolores, ever after regarded as the battle-cry of the Mexican revolution.

He led the rather motley 'army' of ragged, barefooted Indians, which grew to over 50,000 in a short time. Several towns fell before them, and Hidalgo led them, pistol in hand, trying to moderate their wildness, and prevent massacre and pillage. He issued a proclamation that there was to be no more plunder and rapine, but it was ignored—all he could do was to save a few individual lives. He ordered the emancipation of slaves, released all Indians, and all castes, from the payment of tributes. For a time he was so successful that in several cities there were masses for thanksgiving, and in the Cathedral of Guadalajara he was welcomed by the chapter with holy water, and—since he was regarded as the leader of a Royalist revolution—a solemn Te Deum was sung. But he saw that he was being welcomed for the wrong reason. When offered a pardon for himself and all the rebels on condition that he declared his loyalty to the deposed King Ferdinand, in exile, he refused:

We will not lay aside our arms till we have wrested the jewel of liberty from the hand of the oppressor. We are resolved to enter into no arrangement which has not for its basis the liberty of the nation, and the enjoyment of those rights which the God of nature has granted to all men—inalienable rights. . . . Pardon, your excellencies, is for criminals, not for defenders of their country.

But, though his army still swelled (80,000 by the beginning of the year 1811), he began to suffer set-backs. One battle was lost through pure mischance—the blowing up of an ammunition wagon by a stray bomb. In March he was captured—largely by trickery. He was taken, shackled to others, through the streets of Chihuahua for trial. He had proclaimed that his regime would guarantee the establishment of the Roman Catholic religion; and he was supported by many of the ordinary clergy, especially those who had the Indians' interests at heart—'More than 100 parish priests . . . and some 50 members of religious brotherhoods took the field' with him.[5] Yet he was condemned by the Church. Before handing him over to the

* 'Long live our Lady of Guadalupe, death to the government, death to the *gachupines*!'

secular arm the Bishop-elect of Michoacán said: 'Hidalgo, a pastor of souls, a priest of Jesus Christ, a minister of the God of Peace, has raised a standard of rebellion and seduced a number of innocent people.' And the Holy Office called him 'a partisan of French liberty, a libertine, a formal heretic, a Judaiser, a Lutheran, a Calvinist, a rebel, a schismatic, and a suspected atheist.' He was excommunicated, and then executed on 31 July—his head, with others', displayed on the corner of the local granary in Guanajuato.

However, his cause was not wholly lost, for his lieutenant was carrying on the battle. This was José Morelos. He was a *mestizo*, of poor education but great ability, and was Hidalgo's curate. He was only forty-five (Hidalgo was nearer fifty-eight) when the revolution broke out. He had been a farm-hand till twenty-five, was squat, and strong, a good judge of men and fine leader.

A rigid catholic, he always confessed himself before going into action; and his religious scruples were such that after his first engagement he never personally celebrated mass, but delegated the performance of that ceremony to an army chaplain. . . . No personal motive influenced him in his valiant struggle for liberty. . . . To decorations and titles . . . he was wholly indifferent; he preferred the simple appelation of 'Servant of the Nation.'[6]

After Hidalgo's capture he rallied the forces, and by 1813 controlled most of Southern Mexico. He convened a congress declaring Mexico independent, and promulgated a Constitution in 1814. An historian has called him 'the most extraordinary man produced by the war of independence.'[7]

But the Spanish forces were too strong in the end. In 1815 he lost a crucial battle near the river Zacatula and was captured. He was taken to the Inquisition of Mexico, condemned as a heretic, unfrocked—though the bishop of Oajaca who performed the ceremony burst into tears while doing it. He was then handed over as Hidalgo had been to the secular arm and imprisoned in shackles. 'The inquisition jailer is said to have been so moved by his fame and elevation of character, as well as by sympathy for his priestly office, that he offered to let him escape, but Morelos declined, saying: "God forbid that I should imperil you and your innocent family to prolong my own life." '[8] He was condemned to be shot on 20 December (1815): 'The last prayer over, Morelos himself bandaged his eyes and was led forth with arms tied, slowly dragging the heavy shackles. He complied, calm as ever, murmuring: "Lord, thou knowest if I have done well; if ill, I implore thy infinite mercy." '

For the moment the revolution was a failure. Hidalgo and Morelos had miscalculated. They were never joined by the majority of the *criollos*, whose support could have been decisive: they were all for independence, but not by a revolution—still less by one led by a body of wild and uneducated Indians. But in the long run their social-agrarian revolution came, a hundred years later: 16 September is still regarded as Mexico's Independence Day, and Morelos' bones lie beneath the Monument of the Revolution in the capital.*

b. THE PHILIPPINES

iv. JOSÉ RIZAL (1861–96)

It is an interesting coincidence that, just as two Mexican priests were at the origins of the Mexican revolution, so three Filipino priests were 'martyred' for the cause of Philippine Independence. Fr. José Burgos was a *criollo* (i.e. of Spanish blood, born in the Philippines), Fr. Jacinto Zamora was a *mestizo* (of mixed Spanish and Filipino blood), and Fr. Mariano Gomez was an 'indigenous native'.[10] On 20 January 1872,

---

* The same tradition—of priests moved by their Christian concern to support, even lead, movements of social radicalism—is not dead in Latin America. Fr. Camilo Torres, of Colombia, studied at the University of Minnesota and Louvain; then taught sociology at the University of Bogotá back in Colombia. For supporting movements of social reform he was unfrocked by the extreme conservative Luis Cardinal Concha Cordoba (who voted against the schema on Religious Liberty at Vatican II). Camilo was undeterred: he said that 'I consider the work of a priest is to take a person to God, to work toward the love of one's brother'. If circumstances make such a love impossible, then those circumstances must be changed: and that means political action. For a time he tried to work on a mass movement, hoping to start a newspaper. But in the end, frustrated in this, he joined the guerrillas. On 15 February 1966 the Government announced that he had been killed in an encounter with Colombian troops. His name has become a legend among the young: a Christian Democrat youth conference kept a moment of silence in his memory; and a fellow Colombian priest, Fr. German Guzman, has said that 'generations which fight for authentic democracy will realize his sacrifice . . . every day he grows closer to the conscience of people who want to be free'.

pay-day, the labourers at the arsenal at Cavite found that their wages were not forthcoming. From time immemorial labourers at this government institution had been exempt from tribute and forced labour. But a new Governor (short of cash) had reversed this; so in 1872 their tax was deducted from their pay envelopes. The soldiers mutinied, killed the Spanish commandant and took possession of the fortress. But the next day reinforcements arrived, the rebels surrendered, and the revolt was hastily put down. However, it was clear that behind it there had been popular feeling smouldering, and these three priests, who had been associated with opposition to the 'friars', were made examples of. 'Their trial was behind locked doors; they were given no opportunity to face and cross-examine witnesses. The prosecution brought no concrete evidence against them; they bribed . . . one of the co-accused to testify against them. . . .'[11] Burgos and his friends had been campaigning for the 'secularization' of the parishes, i.e. taking them out of the hands of the 'regulars' (Dominicans especially, but also Franciscans, Jesuits, and others) and promoting Filipinos from mere curacies to be parish priests. The campaign was regarded by the Spaniards—and by the hierarchy—as subversive; the three were accused of being master-minds behind the revolt; and they were executed. It is to the credit of the Archbishop of Manila (Martinez) that he refused to obey the behest of the Government and unfrock them first: theirs was a political, not a canonical, offence. From the moment of their death, however, they became the heroes of Independence.

Staying at the house of Fr. Burgos at the time was a young man, Rizal, whose more famous brother, José, was the future leader. José himself was staying with Fr. Burgos's own nephew, at the same time. José Rizal was of Malay extraction (with some strains of Chinese as well as Spanish blood). His parents were fairly well off; and he studied at the Jesuit college— originally with a view to ordination. But the execution of the three priests brought his own restiveness to a head. Already his family had been involved in trouble with the religious administrators of the *hacienda* (farm-estate) of which they were tenants, and this had given them fellow-feeling with the Filipino clergy who were protesting against the stranglehold of the Spanish orders. José knew that the priests had had nothing to do with the military revolt and that their execution was a total miscarriage of justice. And so from this time José was devoted to the cause of reform.

Reform—not yet Filipino independence, still less revolution. He was already something of a poet, writing some of the first poems ever to be written in the (native) Tagalog dialect; and now he went to Europe in 1882 to further his education. He travelled much—Spain first, then Paris, and Germany. He graduated in 1885 as a Doctor of Philosophy and Letters, and then took an additional course in medicine. While in Spain he cultivated the friendship of Filipinos and helped to develop a patriotic Filipino movement. It was probably in Paris that he became a freemason—though in fact he only reached the third degree.

But his most influential work abroad was his writing. Not only did he found, and frequently contribute articles and poems to, a Filipino periodical, *La Solidaridad*, but he wrote two novels, *Noli me Tangere* (1886)—called, in its first English translation, *The Social Cancer*—and *El Filibusterismo* (1891),[12] which had an enormous influence. The second is dedicated to the memory of the three priests (Burgos, he tells us, was 30 at the time of his execution; Gomez, 85; and Zamora, 35),[13] put to death 'by garotting in Bagumbayan Field, 28th February, 1872'. The novels are long, rambling, repetitious, and rather solemn; but they do present vigorously the religious and social abuses from which the Philippines were suffering. He did not advocate rebellion (*filibusterismo*), but he warned that it might come if nothing were done.

Rizal returned to the Philippines in 1887, and opened an eye clinic. Copies of his first novel (*Noli*) had arrived, and the Governor-General sent for him. Rizal defended the novel, and the Governor appeared satisfied, but sent the book to the Committee of the University Faculty of Santo Tomas to judge it. The Committee condemned it as 'heretical, impious, and scandalous to the religious order, and unpatriotic and subversive to public order, libellous to the Government of Spain.'[14] A Censorship Commission of friars and laymen, also consulted, advised that 'the importation, reproduction and circulation of this pernicious book in the Islands be absolutely prohibited.' So it was banned, though for the moment Rizal was left in peace.

However, later in the year the Government asked for a review of farm-holdings in Calemba. The Dominicans tried to get the tenants to say that they (the owners) charged a low rent and received small returns. But Rizal helped to draw up a detailed report, which he translated into Tagalog and got the people to sign. The Dominicans first threatened all who signed; then offered to reduce their rents if the people would refuse to sign. But Rizal insisted, and the document went in to the Government. It was pigeon-holed. The people petitioned again; no notice was taken. So Rizal started a campaign against the friars. He was accused of being 'a German spy, an agent of Bismarck, a Protestant, and a freemason.' So he decided to leave— still on friendly terms with the Jesuits, one of whom said of *Noli* that it told nothing but the truth.

He travelled to London, via Hong Kong and New York, and studied in the British Museum; from there he moved on to Switzerland, and in 1891 wrote his second novel. He wanted to return to Manila, but was warned against this, so stayed in Hong Kong, setting up a medical and optician's practice. His father, mother, brother, and four sisters joined him there. His mother, 'so devout and religious, no longer wished to believe in the priests; she said everything was a fraud; she wished only to believe in God and in the Virgin Mary. And his sisters were like their mother'. He finally returned to the Philippines in 1892, and received a pardon for himself and his family. But after a short stay he was deported to Dapitan. He was watched there by priests and the police. When accused of having become a Protestant he laughed:

If your Reverence knew what I have lost for not declaring myself in accord with the Protestant ideas, your Reverence would not say such a thing. . . . If only your Reverence heard my discussions with a Protestant minister in the long summer twilights in Odenwald. . . . Almost every month a Catholic priest from a little town on the banks of the Rhine came there to visit [me]; and this priest, an intimate friend of the Protestant, gave me an example of Christian fraternity. They considered themselves as two servants of the same God, and instead of passing the time quarrelling . . . each one fulfilled his duty, leaving it to his Master to judge later as to who has interpreted His will better.

He had, in 1892, told the organizers of the Filipino League, recently formed, that he did not agree with their plea for rebellion; and when this League developed into the even more extreme organization, the 'Katipunan', he rejected it even more strongly. Meanwhile he was living with a girl he had met in Hong Kong. He wanted to marry her; the Church said he must renounce his Masonic affiliations (he had never gone far with them, and had been inactive in Masonry for some years), and he agreed, and applied for a dispensation—which never arrived.

Then in 1896 he was surprised to receive a letter from the Governor-General offering him a safe permit to come back, if he would join the Cuban army. He agreed and returned. He sailed to Singapore, but the captain of his ship received a telegram after they had left Port Said ordering him to detain Rizal. He was imprisoned in Barcelona, and then shipped back to Manila. When he was landed, on 3 November, he was tried for treason—on a trumped-up charge that he was connected with a recent uprising and with the Katipunan. He was sentenced to death, and executed on 30 December at Balintawak, outside the city.

There has been much controversy about his last few hours in prison. The Jesuits maintained that he had recanted his 'heresies', had made his confession (five times in twenty-four hours!), been hastily married to the girl he had been living with, and had died in full communion with the Catholic Church. This has been disputed, and there certainly seems to have been some mystery about what happened to the original of his 'Recantation' or of his marriage certificate. The evidence is probably in favour of his having returned to his childhood faith. But the report given by the Jesuits themselves of how his retractation was obtained certainly gives the impression of considerable moral blackmail.[15]

In any case, whether the retractation was true or false, his death was, even more than that of the three priests, later regarded as the turning-point of the revolution. Not only did the Philippines become independent in six years' time, but the Philippine Independent Church was born, more or less directly, from his ashes. It is true, he seems to have had no direct contact with the founder of that Church (the 'P.I.C.'—now in communion with the Protestant Episcopal Church of the United States), Gregorio Aglipayi (1860–1960). But the P.I.C. officially canonized Rizal (along with the three priests, Burgos, Gomez, and Zamora) in 1904, so it clearly recognized Rizal as one of its heroes. Indeed, critics would say that there was a direct connection between the curious theology (semi-unitarian) that developed in the P.I.C. later, and Rizal's own at one time rather tenuous association with orthodox Christianity. At the height of his power his characteristic expression of semi-adherence to the Christian faith was phrased thus:

I have distinguished true religion from false, from superstition, from that which traffics with the holy word to extract money. . . . I have had the opportunity of studying the religions of Europe. I have found Christianity splendid, and Catholicism attractive as well as poetic. It is Christianity made poetic and beautiful, much finer than insipid Protestantism—but these are unknown in my country, especially by our peasants. . . . The education, eminently and solidly Catholic, which [I] received from my most tender childhood has moulded my customs in the same way as a vessel that preserves the perfume of the substance it formerly contained.[16]

Even two Jesuit authors who are critical of Rizal, and more strongly still critical of Aglipayi and the P.I.C., admit that the execution of the three priests was a crime: 'The circumstances of their arrest and of their trial, the promptness with which Governor Izuierdo signed the death sentence, and the refusal of the Archbishop of Manila to unfrock the priests . . . cast a strong suspicion, as Rizal remarked, upon the government's good faith.'[17] José Rizal, besides being a leader and inspirer, was 'an eye-specialist, a practical horticulturalist and farmer, naturalist, anthropologist (he wrote about the skulls and ethnology of the Far East), a folk-lorist, cartographer, archaeologist and sanitarian'. On the anniversary of his death, Manuel Roxas, the President of the Philippines, said of him in 1946:

In the half century since his death, Rizal has dominated our national consciousness more completely than any other figure of our history.

With equal fervor he embraced the great ethical concepts of Liberalism, Humanity, and the concept of Mankind's greatest Martyr, Jesus Christ. . . .

The proposition of racial superiority Rizal abhorred and confounded. . . . Rizal thundered, 'Law knows no color of skin, nor does reason differentiate between nostrils . . .'.

José Rizal was not an advocate of revolution nor of violence. . . . But when men were refused the right to worship God in a manner of their own choosing . . . when official injustice and cruelty went unchecked and unpunished . . . he issued clear and certain warning . . . that liberty would prevail in the end against tyranny.[18]

c. AFRICA

V. JOHN CHILEMBWE (?1871–1915)

The choice of illustrative biographies from Africa is endless; and the pattern varies so starkly from place to place and from generation to generation that even a dozen would not be really representative. In some parts the rising Independent Christian movements have been connected with a primitivism which is only revolutionary in the sense that it tries to reverse the development of history. The Ethiopian Church of Nyasaland (*Calici ca Makolo*—'Church of the ancestors'), for instance, founded in 1942, tries to combine traditional African magico-religious beliefs with elements of Protestantism. One of its members, a widow,

when invited by the preacher to speak during a service, told how the younger generation only wanted to become like the Whites and were forgetting the ways of their ancestors. She said, for instance, that their ancestors would not have intercourse with their wives during menstruation, and that the present ignorance of this rule was responsible for much of the disease in the country.[19]

Thus the opposition to the Government in Nyasaland (Malawi) in 1958–9 came not from the Independent Sects, but from the political (Congress) Party, and from the Church of Scotland.[20] John Chilembwe is an exception, and is probably one of the best known Independent Church leaders, in spite of the fact that the uprising which his movement led to was short-lived, and not very costly in human life. His case has been exceptionally well documented, and he was a man of considerable education, initiative, and character far more balanced and self-aware than many leaders of similar movements.

His life, however, is so easily available in English that only a brief summary is really necessary.[21] In 1892, in the Shire Highlands, Nyasaland, he worked for the strange, vigorous, radical evangelist, Joseph Booth, who had come from Australia sponsored by the Zambesi Industrial Mission. Booth sympathized with African grievances against the white man, and published a book in 1897, *Africa for the Africans*. This was the year he took Chilembwe to America to graduate and to be ordained. Chilembwe returned in 1900, inspired by Booth's ideas, and with American money started the 'Ajawa Providence Industrial Mission' (P.I.M.) at Chiradzulu. Unfortunately this was near the 'Bruce Estates' whose superintendent was W. J. Livingstone—a relative of the great David, but very different: he was a land-grabber, and had earlier been fined £5 (it should have been imprisonment) for assaulting an African prisoner.

In mid 1900 the Ashanti war started in the Gold Coast, and 300 Nyasaland troops were sent; and similarly, in 1904, Africans were used in the campaign against the Mad Mullah. Chilembwe protested: Africans who lost relatives in the war were not compensated—their widows were taxed as usual, and not even informed of their husband's deaths. In 1902–3 the hut-tax was doubled, which led to unrest. His Providence Mission developed, and caused jealousy among the white farmers. The *Central African Times* of 1906 complained that too many Africans were seeking education which 'makes the native aspire to something better and hence must be discouraged, because cheap labour is the main desideratum at the present time'.

Yet so far Chilembwe was a 'gradualist', not a revolutionary, and did not join others who were preaching rebellion against the whites. He taught and preached and his wife (an American negress) gave sewing lessons. By 1913 he had built the most imposing brick church in the region, and most Europeans thought him highly respectable. But tension grew, as Europeans burned grass-hut churches to prove that 'the natives were only squatters' and could be used for forced labour. Booth was expelled the country, but continued his pro-African petitions from abroad. As late as 1913 Chilembwe was still writing like an old-fashioned pastor: 'Last Sunday . . . a hundred souls were added to the church by baptism; out of those there was an old lady almost . . . seventy years old. . . . She walked every Sunday the distance of twenty miles . . . to her baptism class.'

But Chilembwe was bound to be influenced by events, and in 1914 he secretly advised his followers not to pay taxes. World War I led to more demands for African troops, and this was the last straw for Chilembwe. He even sent a secret letter to the Germans, soliciting help for a rising against the English. Nothing came of this, but on Saturday night, 23 January 1915, the rebellion began.

It was successful for only a few hours. Three Europeans were killed, among them the chief target, Livingstone; a few whites were wounded. But the revolt was put down within a day or two; Chilembwe's church was demolished, and he was tracked down on 3 February, and shot. The whole episode was so small scale that it is chiefly famous for Chilembwe's notorious Sunday morning service on 24 January, when Livingstone's head was exhibited on a pole before the Africans while the usual form of devotions proceeded. (Accounts differ: the Europeans said that Chilembwe preached a fanatical anti-British sermon, and one said that Livingstone's head 'was a subject of certain hideous rites performed by the officiating high priest'. The African account is that Chilembwe preached, advocating 'resignation and courage in face of the retribution which would surely fall on them'. This is certainly more consonant with the speech, recorded by an African witness, on the morning of the rebellion:

You are all patriots as you sit. Patriots mean [*sic*] to die for Amor Patria. This very night you are to go and strike the blow and then die. I do not say that you are going to win the war at all. You have no weapons with you and you are not at all trained military men even. One great thing you must remember is that Omnia Vincit Amor so for love your own country and country men. . . .

This is the only way to show the white man that the treatment they are treating our men and women was most bad. . . .

You must not think that with that blow, you are going to defeat white men and then become Kings of your own country, no. If one of you has such an idea in his head, 'God forbid', he must throw such idea now. . . . I am also warning strongly against seizing property from anybody, does not matter what or where. If among you there is a lecher, such a man must not go with you. You are Patriots not Lechers. . . .

God's speed. Deus vobiscum.*[22]

The rebellion led to an official Commission of Inquiry which annoyed all sides: the Europeans, because it admitted that some of them, especially Livingstone, were to blame for conditions which led to the revolt; the Church of Scotland, because it said that 'there is a certain danger that in the absence of adequate supervision religious instruction may possibly be made a vehicle for undesirable political propaganda by natives. . . . [But] in the Roman Catholic and Anglican Missions this danger does not exist to the same extent.' The Presbyterians,

---

* Mwase's account, as given to him by a witness. No doubt this is Mwase's Latin. It seems unlikely that Chilembwe would have used it to his congregation!

who were not in any case responsible for Chilembwe, retorted 'That Protestant methods open a door to disloyalty which is closed to Romanism and Anglicanism is a doctrine new to us, and, we think, to those . . . who know anything of Church History.' But the Commission failed to note two lessons which the rebellion teaches. First, that there is an element of 'subversion' in Christian teaching as such, once it is taken seriously. And second, that there was nothing atavistic about Chilembwe's religio-political outlook—his followers came from different tribal traditions; therefore the future of this kind of challenge to white domination would not be old chiefdoms writ large. And those who knew the man spoke warmly of his humanity. Joseph Booth as an old man in 1919 wrote of

Poor kindhearted Chilembwe who wept with and for the writer's fever-stricken and apparently dying child; nursed and fed the father with a woman's kindness during ten months of utter prostration; . . . and (in 1894, the writer being away) soothed the dying hours of my sweet son John Edward (eighteen years old).[23]

And Mwase, who did not know him but probably had a firsthand account of him from one of Chilembwe's followers whom he met in prison in 1931, said that

John [Chilembwe] was very popular man all round. . . . He always visited the sick in their death beds—does not matter a Christian of his Church or any other people around the villages near him. . . . He helped making Coffin for the dead if timbers were available and even support [supply?] cloths for the dead person. Old men and women he helped them by clothing them out of his own expenses. . . . Had no idea of sending away uneducated people and those poor in dressing before him. . . . Never talked ostentatiously to anybody, nor to deliver a vaunting speech to his audience.[24]

vi. SIMON KIMBANGU (1889–1951)

The contrast between John Chilembwe and Simon Kimbangu is striking. Kimbangu, though evidently literate, had none of Chilembwe's education; he never intended to start a movement; his political interests and vision were almost nil, in spite of the development of a section of his followers; and yet, unlike Chilembwe, a religious movement grew out of his activities which in numbers and maturity now deserves to be taken seriously by other Christians.

He was born in Nkamba (Central Congo) in 1889, and his

early contacts and education were with the Baptist mission. The Roman Catholics of the time regarded the area of his upbringing as marked by a 'protestantisme farouche' (as one of them put it[25]), and they had kept away from it. He was probably employed as a catechist at the mission; he certainly had been for a time a 'boy' in the service of a white pastor. He heard a 'call' from God when still young, but ignored it. The call came again later, several times, usually in the form 'Go home to your village, for I wish to enrol you among my labourers.' To escape it he fled to Kinshasa (Leopoldville); but still it came. When he tried to evade it he fell ill. Finally the voice said imperiously; 'If you will not go you will die here in Kinshasa'. So he went back to his village.

Here he had other dreams and visions, at least once falling into a fit and lying unconscious. Finally a stranger (neither black, white, nor mulatto) whom he had seen once before in a vision, came to him and showed him a Bible, saying: 'This is a good book. You must study it and preach.' Kimbangu protested that he was not fit. The voice told him to give it to his mother and let her preach; and then to go and visit a sick child in a near-by village. He refused both commands. Then the voice said sharply: 'There is a sick child in a certain village. You must go there, pray, lay your hands on the child and heal it. If you do not go I shall require your soul of you.' He went, laid his hands on the child; the child had a convulsion, but recovered. There were now many of these incidents: the best-known was on 6 April 1921 when, on his way to market, he suddenly felt urged to visit a woman's house; he found her sick, and in agony, laid his hands on her, and she was healed.

His reputation began to spread, and people began to visit his house. He built an enclosure in front of his house where his visitors could gather. Everyone, patients as well as followers, joined first in a service—singing, prayer, Bible-reading and a sermon. Simon himself would be worked up by this:

When the sermon found its way into the prophet's heart, it awakened his power [lit. 'longing', 'yearning'] and he began to shake in the manner of the *bangunza* ['prophet'; lit. 'one who speaks on behalf of a chief', a herald or preacher]. He went quickly into his house and there awaited those who sought his help.[26]

His reputation—in spite of some failures in healing—became such that the mission hospitals nearby were deserted, and (more serious to the Administration) men started leaving their work to attend his services. Healing was only a part of his work: his central message was a simple evangelical call: 'Change your mind. Believe in Jesus Christ and he will save you. Abolish and abjure all *minkisi* [fetishes], practise monogamy, and worship the true God.'

His followers believed (and believe to this day[27]) that this time was a genuine Pentecost—they speak of 'the Holy Spirit who spoke to us through the prophet, Simon Kimbangu'. Nkamba began to be called 'Jerusalem'. A nearby stream in which Simon told blind people to wash, was believed to have supernatural powers—and continued to be a source of pilgrimage after his arrest and to this day. So great were the crowds that came that Simon had to appoint assistants: he laid his hands on 'apostles' or 'second-hand prophets' and sent them out to various other centres. Like him, their spirit-possession was accompanied by violent bodily movements, dancing, and shaking. At first the effect of this revival was to strengthen the Protestant churches around—Simon claimed not to rival but to supplement. But then, dissatisfied, his followers began to leave their churches and join him. Some traditional churches accused him of attracting them by the retention of pagan elements: but this was not true of his version. Indeed, when one of his disciples asked Simon to free him from his first wife because she was ill-natured, so that he could keep a second whom he loved, Simon replied: 'We must obey the Word of God; I have but one Bible and one Lord, whose words I cannot alter. If you wish to be a true child of God, leave your second wife.' The man was by no means satisfied.

No doubt part of his enthusiastic reception was due to the feeling that at last 'one of our number' had become a prophet—that 'not only white people' could be famous. And this led to the accusation by the Belgians of 'anti-whiteism'. But this was certainly false. Simon himself retained good will towards the white churches, and said explicitly that it was 'evil thoughts' that had prompted one congregation (at Mambi) to suggest a secession and the forming of a black church: he was alarmed at the idea, and urged them to go to the mission station and join in the Lord's Supper there. When some were still dissatisfied he said: 'We are like wives to our Whites . . . for they have come here, and given us the Gospel; they suffered many hardships in order to come to us; they have bought us for a great price and so they are wedded to us. If we leave them, they will be sore afflicted.' And when asked whether they should pay taxes he said: 'Give the rulers of the country all they ask of you, but give your heart to God.'

However, reports of large numbers of workers leaving the railway, the plantations, the cement factory, chalk-pits and oil company to go to Nkamba raised serious doubts about the movement. And when some converts left the Roman Catholic missions the church authorities urged the Administration to intervene. Morel, the Administrator of Thysville, hearing that there were groups claiming that 'We have found the God of the Blacks', and urging others not pay taxes, went to investigate Kimbangu's activities at Nkamba; but all he met was religious services of an ecstatic nature. But complaints still came in, and the movement was by now said to number ten thousand followers. Finally a warrant for Kimbangu's arrest was issued on 21 June 1921. Simon himself had told his people that they must not resist. He stepped forward and let himself be taken; when soldiers started to beat him with their rifles, and his people sprang to his rescue, he repeated: 'No violence'. However, soon after he escaped and hid for a time; meanwhile his village was destroyed and many of his folk arrested. Finally on 10 September he returned and gave himself up. He seems to have been basing his behaviour on the arrest of Jesus; at any rate, his followers used biblical language to describe it:

When he came to his village, many people came joyfully forth to meet him, but he said to them: 'I have only a little time to be with you, for my enemies are nigh unto me'. He taught them, saying that they must now believe in God only and not in him. He prayed for a long time and gave his soul into the hands of God, whereafter he asked the others to pray for him. He then read the twenty-third psalm.

He was arrested on 14 September, and taken for trial to Thysville. The trial lasted eighteen days—15 September–3 October. The Colony's newspaper, *L'Avenir colonial belge*, representing commerce and industry, demanded blood: 'We believe that the best way—and we are not alone in this—would be to *hang* the principal culprits. Let us make a few examples of them then we can sleep in peace.' It was, in effect, not a court of law, but a court-martial: the judge, sole president, was Commandant de

Rossi; accused had no counsel, either chosen by themselves or appointed by the Conseil de Guerre. In fact, it has been pointed out by M. Jules Chomé[28] that the whole procedure was of doubtful legality. An Order declaring the whole region subject to *régime militaire mitigé* (semi-martial law) was issued on 12 August; but by then Kimbangu had been forced into hiding, there was no preaching; most of his apostles were in chains, so could not have committed the crimes charged. And when another revolt had been suppressed a few weeks *earlier*, the procureur (Gorlier) had said that the rebels must be tried by ordinary law obtaining before the imposing of martial law. Yet no one at Kimbangu's trial questioned the competence of the military tribunal; and when the Ministère Publique (Attorney General), M. Dupuis, raised the matter fifteen days after judgment had been given, de Rossi curtly dismissed the doubt.

Kimbangu and his followers denied nothing. They even said: 'The State, and all the Whites, will go to hell if they don't believe our teaching'; and one of them dared to ask why Africans were forbidden to have their God, their Prophet, their Bible, since the Whites have theirs?

The charges themselves were curiously vague and tendentious:

That: the Administrator on June 6th, ordered to arrest the prophet-in-chief, Kibango [*sic*], (at Nkamba), was there violently attacked by the crowd and that two soldiers were wounded by stone-throwing and knives. . . .

That: the crowds gathered by the prophets were manifestly hostile to the state. . . .

That: the said-named Kibango, spreading and deliberately causing to be spread false rumours of healings and resurrections, and posing as a messenger of God, brought alarm into the spirits of the indigenous populace and by his actions and words seriously threatened public peace and tranquillity. . . .

That Kibango . . . by expounding the Bible, and having it expounded by his assistants, according to his own views, thus imposing his will on the peoples, and affirming his prestige. . . .

That: Kibango, though confirmed by the doctors as sound in body in mind and therefore responsible for all his acts, has nervous crises which are merely simulated, that certain cases of nervous illness may have been cured by suggestion, but that the afore-mentioned made use of this to deceive the good faith of the masses who should thus become instruments of his purpose, viz., the destruction of the State's authority. . . .

That: Kibango . . . made himself redeemer and saviour of the black race. . . .

That: Kibango . . . persuaded others to believe that a new God was to come, a God more powerful than the State itself, and that this God was represented by him. . . .

That: it is clear from official reports, . . . that the Whites are deeply hated by the followers of Kibango, that this hatred has infiltrated and spread with alarming rapidity among the natives, and that undeniably Kibango's teaching was responsible for a near-strike and for absenteeism from work among a great number of workers. . . .

On these charges, duly proved, the State Attorney (Dupuis) demanded a life sentence with hard labour for Kimbangu, and imprisonment of from two to ten years for his subordinates. But the judge went further: de Rossi announced the death penalty for Simon, life penal servitude for his apostles, and twenty years for chiefs who had sheltered him. M. Dupuis at once arose and announced that he would appeal for clemency—it was unthinkable that the death penalty should be imposed where there had been no proof of loss of life. *L'Avenir colonial belge* attacked him fiercely for this: 'M. Dupuis' native policy is woeful. . . . Commerce is rightly terrified to see someone placed in charge of the district who cares so little about its interests. . . . When a man feels that he is judging contrary to public opinion he should recuse himself . . .' (13 November 1921). But King Albert of Belgium finally issued an order commuting the sentence to life imprisonment. Simon was sent to Lubumbashi (Elizabethville), and was incarcerated for thirty years till his death in 1951. His conduct was exemplary, and there were two attempts to have him released and pardoned, but both seem to have been opposed by the Roman Catholic authorities and certainly came to nothing. At first he was in solitary confinement, but later he was put in charge of the prison kitchen, and in 1950 a visitor found him fat and well.

There is a story that on his death-bed in prison he became a Roman Catholic: a strange story, because just as in the case of Rizal* the evidence is conflicting and it seems difficult to get at the truth. It is claimed that a Congolese Benedictine priest, Fr. François Xavier Nsenkoto, visited him in prison in 1951; that Simon had been complaining of his chains ('Do they think

---

* See p. 249, above.

I'd run away?'), but later had 'offered up' his thirty years' imprisonment as a penance for all the harm he'd done by his teaching; that he abjured his teaching, and 'died in the arms of our Lady'.

This, however, is strenuously denied by his followers, and the most recent historian of the movement says that his son and successor, His Eminence Joseph Diangienda, visited the prison hospital at Simon's death and discovered without any doubt that no such baptism had taken place.[29]

What is important, however, is what happened to the movement after his removal to prison. There were splits from it, and certain sections did become both anti-White and syncretic. But the main body, 'The Church of Christ on Earth through the Prophet Simon Kimbangu', has become a very solid, responsibly organized, stable, and politically well-balanced church of Protestant 'pentecostalist' type. It has continued its original puritan, anti-'fetish', monogamous tradition. It is piquant that a movement which started with the reputation for anti-White, semi-anarchist radicalism (a reputation based on inadequate evidence and culpable confusion) should have both resisted the resort to violence during the struggles for Congo's Independence, and also have refused, after Independence, the offer from some quarters to become 'The National Church of the Congo'. The Church supports, of course, all attempts at nation-building: but in the words of its leader, it 'condemns any policies which tend to restore . . . political structures based on tribalism, regionalism or racialism because . . . [these] kill all efforts at bringing men together as Christ has commanded. . . . As all men are created in the image of God, all men are bound to treat one another as brethren.'[30] More recently it has achieved recognition by its affiliation to the World Council of Churches (August 1969).

d. MAORILAND

vii. t. w. ratana (1873–1939)

Almost every uprising, the world over, can be traced back to some question about land. In New Zealand the white rulers and the Maori chiefs thought they had settled for ever the vexed problem of landownership at the Treaty of Waitangi (1840).

But almost immediately after its acceptance the Europeans began to ignore the Treaty. Many of them said that the Maoris could not in any case have understood the Treaty they had signed. In January 1843 the Governor of New Zealand, Joseph Soames, wrote caustically:

We have always had serious doubts whether the Treaty of Waitangi, made with naked savages by a Consul invested with no plenipotentiary powers, without ratification by the Crown, could be treated by lawyers as anything but a praiseworthy device for amusing and pacifying savages for the moment.[31]

The settlers started again acquiring land, and the Maori Wars commenced. Resistance by the Maoris often took quasi-religious forms. One example was the wild, pagan 'Hau Hau' movement, led by one Te Ua Haumene, who had been priest of a native Maori cult, then a Wesleyan convert, and finally a prophet claiming miraculous powers. This movement was suppressed. More influential and respectable was the 'Ringatu' movement. Its founder was an impressive man, Te Kooti Rikirangi. Born about 1830, he had been arrested during the Maori War and deported to the Chatham Islands. In captivity he studied the Bible, and developed the 'Ringatu' movement. The word means 'upraised hand', used at the end of prayers; the Hau Hau people had used it as a magic sign for averting bullets; Te Kooti used it as an act of homage to God. In fact, he disowned Hau Hau, and converted two of its followers in gaol. In 1868 he and his men captured a schooner and forced the crew to take them back to New Zealand. Here he travelled round on a white horse, collecting followers. Several attempts were made to capture him, but he was a skilful soldier, and in 1872 he escaped into the 'King Country'. There was a general amnesty in 1883, and he was left in peace to propagate his religion. This had none of the fanatic nature of Hau Hauism—Te Kooti refused to allow his followers to practise cannibalism or the traditional mutilation of dead enemies. He died in 1893, but the movement went on—indeed, was fully constituted as the Ringatu Church in 1938.

Unfortunately, in spite of the sympathetic work of individual church leaders, the missionary clergy were widely suspected by the Maori of being agents of the government in a plot to subdue them. Any sect which preserved the power of the old *tohunga* (priests) by creating their equivalent was much more likely to hold the Maori than Anglicanism or Methodism. It is true that there were the beginnings of Maori advancement even in the nineteenth century: there were four Maori Members of Parliament as early as 1867. But the Maori were not at this stage interested in politics, and these educated Maori did not represent them.

Towards the turn of the century a woman *tohunga*, priestess of the 'Holy Ghost mission' at Parewanui, prophesied that her nephew would take on her work. He was Tahupoteki Wiremu Ratana, and as a boy he used to attend her services, though his parents were Anglican, and his grandfather had founded several Anglican churches. 'Bill' Ratana, as he came to be known, married a Methodist in 1900, and she turned his mind back to religion—till then he had worked on the land, looked after horses, played football, and been something of a drunkard.

About this time, as he ploughed . . . Ratana heard voices. Occasionally he became excited, threw himself about and raved widly. He seemed to be insane . . . but [his wife and others] said that it would be wrong to interfere for the spirit of the Lord was working in [him].

His 'call' came in 1918 when two whales were washed up on the shore at Whangaehu, where the Ratanas were camping. They dragged the whales up, stored their blubber, and this provided them with food, heat, and light for several hundred guests during the next twelve months. Soon after this he saw a vision— a small round cloud rising from the sea—and then heard a voice from the mist:

Fear not, I am the Holy Ghost. I have travelled around the world to find the people upon whom I can stand. I have come . . . to choose you, the Maori people. Repent! Cleanse yourself and your family as white as snow, as sinless as the wood-pigeon.

Ratana, I appoint you as the Mouthpiece of God. . . . Unite the Maori people, turning them to Jehovah of the Thousands.

It is said that after this and other visions Ratana went into his house, threw out all the beer in it, and smashed the telephone—through which he had acted as a local bookie! He now preached against drink, and spent much time in prayer and study of the Bible. He gave up his own tribal affiliations, united his followers across tribal divisions, and moderated their bitterness against the 'Pakeha' (white people). He became in fact a full-time religious leader.

In 1920 there was the biggest gathering of Maoris since the Treaty of Waitangi, at his home. He had a church building, four large marquees, 130 tents—and still many people had to sleep in the open. At this stage he was not regarded as having started a new denomination: a Methodist minister presided, a Roman Catholic priest said mass for the Roman Catholics and the Protestants had a united service. Archdeacon Williams of Waiapu referred favourably to Ratana's work that November, and the Synod of Nelson diocese passed a resolution thanking God for his inspiration.

Cures began to be reported—including some by post, for Ratana was by now travelling round the country, and had an enormous mail to which his assistants typed replies, signed by him. One European lady was said to have been cured after receiving a letter from him; and there were about two thousand Maoris who claimed to have been cured by him. Ratana himself was modest in his own claims, and certainly never advised people to avoid doctors. 'During a healing session when Ratana was seated on the verandah with a queue of patients, a European visitor called out: "Is it true that you advise people not to use medicine?" Ratana smiled and pulled out of his waistcoat pocket a small jar of ointment. He then rolled up his sleeve displaying a rash on his skin. "I'm using this for them", he said, "and it's very good stuff".' In 1921 at a big Christmas meeting various denominations were again catered for—Canon W. Williams celebrating Holy Communion for about three hundred communicants. It was only between 1921 and 1924 that, with increased anti-European talk, the idea of a separate Ratana Church began to be formulated. There was a specific attempt in 1922 to get the Ratana Movement affiliated with, and recognized by, the orthodox churches—especially Anglican and Methodist. There was much discussion about Ratana's doctrine of 'Angels', to whom he seemed to be attributing semi-divine status. But the crucial theological discussion was mismanaged, and Ratana decided that he must go his own way—afterwards he prayed: 'Lord God our Father, prevent us in all our doings and certainly protect us from intellectuals.'

By 1925 the Anglican Church felt itself obliged to state that the Ratana Church was now 'a schismatic sect'. The Methodists remained more friendly, though even they found the Ratana language strange, and complained that the name of Christ was not sufficiently prominent.

One reason for the popularity of the new Church was Ratana's own pro-Maori engagement. He used to say that the two whales—washed up on the shore, were the spiritual and the material-political elements. 'In one of my hands is the Bible; in the other is the Treaty of Waitangi.' He decided to visit England and plead that the terms of the Treaty be properly carried out. His party visited England in 1924, but instructions from the New Zealand Cabinet prevented them from seeing the King or Prince of Wales, and they were politely treated as mere holiday visitors. Back in New Zealand, and disappointed, he turned to practical work for the Maori: founding a school, and a Ratana Bank. He built a large temple in 1926, and in that year there were probably eleven and a half thousand Maori members of his church—eighteen per cent of the Maori race. (The 1956 census gave the numbers: 18,776 members—about 13·7 per cent of the total population. So the movement had declined by then, but was still strong.)

From 1922 the New Zealand Labour Party had its seats increased from nine to seventeen, and by 1928 Labour actually held the balance of power—between the Liberal (United) Opposition and the Reform Government. In 1922 Ratana supported his son as a candidate for Western Maori; but it was not till 1931 that the first Ratana candidate was successful. In 1935 the Labour Party took office, and since the Ratana movement identified itself with Labour Party politics (which backed the trades unions, and tried to appeal beyond the industrial working class to the rural strongholds, through advocating cheaper credit and guaranteed prices) it was the Ratana movement which largely controlled the four Maori seats in Parliament. Ratana himself visited the Prime Minister in 1935, and, characteristically, placed four objects on his table—a potato, a gold watch, a greenstone *tiki*, and a *huia* feather. He explained that a potato cannot grow without soil (i.e. Maori need land); that the watch had belonged to his ancestor, and now was broken (i.e. the law relating to Maori land was broken, and only new machinery—laws—could mend it); that the *tiki* represented the spirit and tradition of the Maori people; and that if the Prime

Minister would save them, he would earn the *huia* feather of the ariki (Paramount Chief of the Maori).

The New Zealand anthropologist Dr. Joan Metge, an expert on Maori culture, has suggested that there are four possible ways of 'indigenising': *first*, to retain the form in which a word, idea, action, or institution is received, making only minor adjustments to render it pronounceable or feasible in the new situation; *second*, to take over a form already present in the (receiving) culture, and give it a specifically Christian meaning; *third*, to create a new form, drawing on the historically established resources of the existing cult; and *fourth*, to create a radically new form, drawing on recent developments or on a prophetic experience. She gives ample illustrations of the first three, but says that the fourth is comparatively rare. Indeed, in New Zealand none of the orthodox Christian denominations attempted this,

but Ratana rejected old Maori symbols, and developed original symbols, e.g. concentric circles representing the Eye of God; himself with two whales on the shore [*sc.*, referring to the visionary experience in his life]; an aeroplane and a car joined by a rope ladder, symbolizing his [Ratana's] 'descent' from spiritual to secular, political work; and a combined star and crescent moon (*whetumarama*)—referring to the occultations of Venus and Mars with the new moon before his first faith-healing tour, and interpreted as the 'shining light' of his mission.[32]

Ratana died in 1939. He was a strange amalgam of the ill-educated enthusiastic prophet and the leader full of horse sense. 'Sometimes he was the Mangui, inspired by God . . . and at other times he was just Bill Ratana who wanted everyone to have a drink and be happy.'[33] And sometimes both at once. 'Once he drank a bottle of whisky in front of the assembled people. He said as he tossed aside the empty bottle: "No, that's the devil. And I, your Mangui, have taken him inside myself so that you, the Morehu, will not be harmed. Don't touch the stuff!" ' His contribution was that he arrived on the scene at a time, just after the war, when there was much economic uncertainty and the Maori people were in need of some moral leadership. He provided a combination of the traditional and the progressive in his programme by which their frustrations could be directed towards a creative and united development.

e. CHINA

viii. HUNG HSIU-CH'ÜAN (1814–64) AND THE TAIPING REBELLION

British foreign policy has not often been discussed in theological terms. But on 12 March 1861 Lord John Russell attacked the 'Taiping' Movement in Parliament, saying of the leaders, and especially of its originator, Hung Hsiu-ch'üan, that 'their doctrine is really a blasphemous parody of Christianity. Some of them claim to be the sons and brothers of Christ'.[34] What was the real nature of this 'Christian improvisation'?

Hung Hsiu-ch'üan was born in 1814 about thirty miles from Canton; his father was a farmer, and in youth Hung had no contact with Western civilization. He showed sufficient promise at school for his family to envisage further education for him, though he was the fourth child out of five. The usual goal of such further education was the civil service examination, leading to an administrative post. Hung started well, but failed after three attempts at the 'prefectural' level, earning his living in the meanwhile as a country schoolmaster. As he was thirty-one at his third attempt, it was clear that his ambitions were to be denied. The result was a deeply frustrated young man, ready to step into the long line of revolutionaries, with some of the same grievances that the later Boxers* built their movement on, but without their anti-foreign, anti-white virulence.

At the time he failed his first attempt, in 1833 or 1834, Hung was in Canton, and happened to hear a Chinese Christian evangelist preach. The latter gave him a set of tracts in Chinese; but Hung did not then study them. However, after his second failure he had something of a breakdown—he was said to have been laid up for forty days—and during this he saw a vision, which became central to his life and the movement he started. He was, he claimed, carried up to heaven; there he saw a venerable old man, who was the Creator and the 'Heavenly Father'. This old man gave him a message that man had neglected heavenly truth, was worshipping demons, and that even Confucius—whom Hung saw summoned before him—had failed in passing on the true doctrine. Another vision showed him a middle-aged man, known as 'the Elder Brother', and Hung later realized that this was Jesus. Finally, after his third failure,

* See chapter 2, above, pp. 35 ff.

in 1843, a cousin came and borrowed the set of Christian tracts which Hung had not read. This cousin, Li Chung-fang, returned them and commended them. Hung now read them himself and was immediately struck by them. They showed him, he thought, that this 'Elder Brother' he had seen was indeed Jesus 'Saviour of the World'; and that he, Hung, had been designated in the visions the prophet of a new (or revived old) religion, and as a second Son of God.

He started to preach to his immediate entourage, and soon had a number of converts, especially two who became prominent later, Hung Jen-kan and Feng Yün-shan. Their first overt acts were iconoclastic: believing they were commanded to destroy 'the idols' they abjured Buddhist rites, destroyed memorial tablets to the ancestors, and went into temples to smash the images. Hung was sacked from his school for this, and soon they decided that his home area was the wrong place for the movement, so they left in 1844 and started preaching in Kwangsi province. They claimed to have made thousands of converts in the next two years. It has been plausibly suggested that the particular appeal of Hung's teaching was that it helped to fill a gap between the sophisticated and essentially aristocratic nature of Confucianism and the unco-ordinated occasionalism of popular superstition.

There is indeed throughout Chinese thought and literature a lack of dramatic tension, and it was this lack that the Christian message, alien though it was, supplied with a terrible urgency. . . . Similarly, although agrarian rebellion encouraged by popular superstitions was endemic throughout Chinese history, and much of Hung Hsiuch'üan's economic programme—'land, food, clothing and money must be held and used in common, so that there is no inequality anywhere and no one wants for food or warmth'—may be traced to the speculation of ancient Chinese philosophers, yet the notion that all men are the children of a Heavenly Father, much more strongly personified than any of the deities in the native pantheon, soon showed it had a unique power to gather followers.[35]

Certainly the economic conditions were becoming serious and that combined with a metaphysical hunger explains his following.

In February 1847, having heard that a foreigner was preaching doctrine similar to his in Canton, he went there to seek him out. It was the Rev. Issachar J. Roberts, a Southern Baptist missionary from America. Hung told him about his vision and, with some hesitation, Roberts agreed to accept him as a catechumen. After two months of Christian teaching Hung, short of money, had to return home—he was thus never baptized; he appears to have asked for baptism but Roberts judged it premature. In June he was off to Kwangsi again, where he found that Feng had been gathering even more followers. For a time he and Feng were in prison, suspected because of their anti-traditionalist teachings of being in league with revolutionary secret societies. This only united their work the more. And they were consistent: when Hung's father died in 1848 none of the customary funeral rites were observed.

Their movement was still non-political. But famines of 1847 and 1849 added to current unrest, and led to widespread banditry. The movement of Hung and Feng, by now known as the *Pai Shang-ti Hui* ('God Worshippers'), was well enough organized to be able to protect its members against bandits; and since the local governments were too weak to do this, protection became an added incentive to join Hung. It is true that Hung may have believed even in 1844 that the religion of the Heavenly Father could only prosper ultimately if the Ch'ing dynasty were overthrown. But this remained below the surface as yet. So far, and until 1850, the 'God Worshippers' only assumed a military aspect as a defence against bandits. But in July 1850 the Manchu government, worried at the failure of the local officials of Kwangsi, sent additional aid to quell lawlessness. Inevitably there were clashes between the Manchu troops and Hung's 'God Worshippers', until in December a full-scale assault was launched against them. Hung's forces won a notable victory, and as a result, in January 1851 at a celebration to mark the victory, Hung declared himself *the T'ien-wang* (i.e. Heavenly King), and the new state he and his followers set up was called *T'ai-p'ing t'ien-kuo* ('Heavenly Kingdom of Great Peace'). From then on they were popularly known as 'the Taipings'.

It must be remembered that in two hundred years, from 1650–1850, the population of China had increased from about 100 million to more than 300 million. Furthermore, in the South the Manchu regime had always been associated with Tartars, northern foreigners, powers of darkness. Hung shared this view, and his revelation was easily linked up with a command to overthrow the evil one.

So a disciplined force of some 10,000 set off from Kwangsi to bring heavenly peace to China. Secret anti-Manchu societies, like the 'Triad Society', who had the same political aims, asked to join. Hung decided that they could not be more than military allies, since they would not accept his revelation or his discipline. The alliance continued to be an uneasy one. However, from 1851 the Taipings made rapid advances: through Hunan, to the north, and then from the Yangtze river eastward. True, this was not without loss: in 1852 Feng, Hung's first disciple, one of his generals and probably the most level-headed of the leaders, was killed in battle. But city after city fell to them, and in 1853 they took Nanking. This was now made the Taiping capital. Later history shows that this was probably a mistake. By January of that year they had surrounded and taken the Wuhang conurbation, on the Yangtze. They could now have either consolidated their grip on central China, or advanced straight on Peking. But they found the rich Yangtze valley too tempting, hence the capture of Nanking. True, they did send an expedition up towards Peking, and by October 1853 were as near as the suburbs of Tientsin. But their lines of communication from Nanking were too long, they had no horsemen to deal with the northern cavalry, and, coming from the south, they found the winter too severe. Meanwhile in the area west of Nanking they were having only temporary successes. Opposition to them developed in Hunan, which they had never occupied, and gradually they were confined to the Lower Yangtze Valley. Added to this, dissension had broken out within the Taiping hierarchy. In 1856 rivalry for power led to Hung's ordering of the assassination of two of his former right-hand men, and the advancement of less capable relatives, elder brothers and cousins of his own. Hung's original preaching included a strongly disciplined ascetic element; but by now Hung himself made no attempt to observe what he had preached. Indeed, he had long ceased to be the administrative head (he had never been the military leader) of the movement, and was content with spiritual leadership plus luxurious—and libidinous—living. There was a time when the Western powers (British and American—the French were more reserved) thought that the Taipings were worth supporting in their

opposition to the Manchu regime, especially when they discovered after 1853 (the capture of Nanking) that the movement
had Christian connections, or at least used Christian terminology. But their approaches were not made use of by Hung,
who insisted on a protocol to which America and Britain were
unused, and as time went on the European authorities could
see that the Taipings were a spent force. In fact in 1860
Western representatives assisted the national troops to resist the
Taipings at Shanghai; and in 1863 'Chinese Gordon' was in
command of an imperial army. Finally the Taiping forces still
holding Nanking were starved out in 1864, and Hung himself
committed suicide. The final pockets of resistance were wiped
out in 1866. It has been calculated that during the thirteen
years of the rebellion some twenty million people lost their
lives.

*   *   *

In 1861 a missionary of the London Missionary Society, the
Rev. Joseph Edkins, paid a visit to the Taiping capital, Nanking. There were still hopes then that the apparently Christian
origins of the movement would prevail; but like others he was
aware that Hung and his followers' knowledge of Christianity
was very limited, and he visited the capital in the hopes that he
might do something to improve that knowledge. On the way he
noted that one prominent Buddhist temple, in Sucheu, was in
semi-ruins, the noses of the images chopped off, the priests'
books scattered on the ground: this confirmed the iconoclasm
of the Taiping. When Edkins got to Nanking (with a special
permit from the Taipings) he went to see the Rev. I. J. Roberts,
the very man from whom Hung had received two months'
instruction. Roberts had accepted an invitation from Hung to
Nanking, with the same hopes that Edkins had of bringing the
movement closer to traditional Christianity. He (Roberts) was
much respected, and had been pressed to become Foreign
Minister, but refused. Edkins also had a contact which,
independently of Roberts, had taken him to Nanking: he hoped
to meet the Taiping Prime Minister who was 'an old acquaintance of my own at Shanghai, a baptised convert at Hongkong,
in good standing for several years in the community of native
Christians there gathered, a catechist of the L.M.S., and as

such trusted and respected in a high degree.'³⁶ Edkins, accompanied by Roberts, was able to get a fair idea of what Taiping life at the top was like. Edkins was impressed with the discipline; the condemnation of opium-smoking; the puritan-type morals; the public prayer and worship on all official occasions as well as in the family circle; and the absence of any anti-Western bias. But he was also able to confirm what he had heard about the 'unsoundness', from the orthodox Christian point of view, of Taiping theology. Roberts told him of the difficulty he had had in arranging an official meeting with Hung himself who, though extremely friendly, insisted that Roberts, like all other visitors, kneel to him as the *T'ien-wang* ('Heavenly King'). He refused, for, he said, there is only one 'Heavenly King'—God, Yahweh. He was then told that all would kneel to worship, not Hung, but the 'Heavenly Father'. But Roberts was dubious about this too, as it might be misunderstood.

On entering the hall of audience, [Roberts] stood at the end of one of the long rows of high officials who were ranged to the number of about twenty on the east and west sides of the hall. All, including the missionary, appeared in their court robes. When the time of worship came, 'the Kan-wang',* the ci-devant preacher in the London Mission at Hongkong, called out in a loud voice from where he stood, near the principal chief [i.e. Hung]; 'Lo-hiau-tsieuen pai Tien fu' ('Mr. Roberts, worship the Heavenly Father'). Taken by surprise, the missionary, after a moment's hesitation, knelt, with his face turned away from Hung Hsiu-ch'üan, while the Kan-wang offered an extemporaneous prayer. Then all rose, and made many genuflexions to Hung, the missionary excepted. A long conversation ensued between the old acquaintances.³⁷

Edkins with Roberts was able to meet two or three Taiping officials whose grasp and knowledge of Christian teaching was fairly thorough. They were even able to defend customs which seemed dubious to the Protestant missionaries.

On Sunday, 31 March, Roberts and Joseph Edkins had worship at the house of Hwang at twelve noon. Roberts offered prayer. 'On the table were displayed, as offerings to the Trinity, three cups of tea and nine bowls of food. On objecting to this

* lit. 'Shield King': Hung Jen-kan, Hung's cousin and one of the earliest converts; the man Edkins had known and was hoping to meet; promoted to power after Hung's assassination of 1856; the best educated of the 'wangs' (princes: titles given to military leaders from 1851).

custom of offerings we were told that it was appointed by the Tien-wang (Hung) as a visible act of homage to God, suitable for those who had lately embraced Christianity.'[38] But their conclusion was that these officials, and even the Prime Minister, had little influence on popular belief; and that 'the task of converting the Taiping chief to correct scriptural opinions was a hopeless one'.[39] Roberts and Edkins had done their best at this: Edkins brought with him a number of treatises he had written on the divinity of Christ which he asked should be forwarded to Hung. They received Hung's replies while still there. The replies were very polite: 'I praise the disciples from the Western ocean. They are indeed faithful and true in showing gratitude to the Heavenly Father and Brother [i.e., Jesus]. The heavenly kingdom of the Father and Brother is eternal and unending . . .' etc. But he is clear that his own revelation, when he went up to Heaven, must be accepted, and was very 'grieved that his old American friend should doubt his claims'. Cannot the missionaries have a bit more faith? God showed himself to Joshua, why not to him, Hung? As to the missionaries' teachings about Jesus: well, he, Hung, had read an article by this very Joseph Edkins in the Chinese Monthly Magazine for 1857 on the 'Festal Letters' of Athanasius; and Edkins had quoted Arius' view that Christ is inferior to the Father; Athanasius and the Council had condemned Arius—but, assuredly, Arius was right!

To recognise the Brother without the Father is to lose sight of the distinction of rank. The Father is greater than the Son—the Elder Brother than the Younger. All the world should together recognise the Elder Brother and the Ruler. . . . Christ ought to be revered as God. To regard the Son as the Father agrees with the Father's will. . . . Let all the disciples combine with brave heart, to elevate the Father, the Brother and myself, and the young prince.*

Not having seen God, do not say that He has not been seen. The Elder Brother and I have seen the Father, plainly and certainly so. . . .

The Father gave forth the Scriptures, and whatever faults there are in them, he has commanded me to correct them, and publish them to the world in their amended form.

Hung acceded to Edkins' request to stay on in Nanking and

* His young son of thirteen, acting as regent while Hung concerned himself with religious affairs.

start a mission station there; but Edkins, after hesitation, decided that the political future was too uncertain, and Hung's views too heterodox, for its utility to be guaranteed, and withdrew his request before leaving. From the historical point of view it is clear now that he and Roberts could have done little to alter the tragic course of events.

*   *   *

One sinologist has suggested that the missionaries were unnecessarily finnicky about Hung Hsiu-ch'üan's heterodoxy:

> This Taiping movement would appear to be exactly what is meant by indigenisation; namely, a wholly spontaneous response coming from the depths of a man's soul, and containing native elements of thought which the man has instinctively incorporated with the new message. . . .
>
> A main theological scandal was that the Taiping Emperor (Hung) spoke of Jesus Christ as his elder brother, who gave him, the younger brother, help and direction. . . . [The missionaries failed] to realize the very marked distinction there is between the elder and the younger brother in the traditional Chinese ethical code. The elder brother practically occupies the position of the father in the West, whilst the Chinese father occupies a higher, almost a divine position.[40]

This certainly points to the tragedy of the Taiping's frustrated relationship to Christianity; but the most recent research on the movement seems to show that the earlier judgement was in its doctrinal aspects not so wide of the mark.[41] Dr. Boardman (admittedly limiting himself to the first three years of the Rebellion, 1851–4) has studied all the Taiping writings, and compared them with what Christian literature could have been available to Hung and his early followers; he has also assessed the relationship of the Taiping creed to traditional Chinese modes of thought. He specifically asks the question; 'Are the Biblical elements [in the Taiping teaching] sufficiently expressive of the genius of Christianity to qualify the Taiping religion as a form of Christianity?'[42] His cautious conclusion is on the whole negative.* The Taipings took from the Old Testament those elements in the character and activity of Yahweh which could be seen as a call to Chinese revolutionary strategy. The title 'New Testament' was in their translation altered to *Ch'in-ting ch'ien-i chao-sheng-shu* (roughly 'Scripture that has been

* See Appendix 15, p. 323.

previously authorized, transmitted, and proclaimed') : implying, probably, that Hung's own revelations were the 'newer' testament.[43] Some orthodox notions, like 'atonement', the cross of Christ, resurrection, even the Trinity, appear, but as undigested lumps, and unrelated to the rest. There is no suggestion that Christians should love one another; and Hung's cousin says of the leader that he 'used often to praise the doctrines of Christianity, "but", added he, "too much patience and humility do not suit our present times, for therewith it would be impossible to manage this perverted generation." '[44] Though there seem to have been 'Pentecostal' elements in the movement, the Taiping notion of the Holy Spirit was somewhat eccentric: because his follower, Yang Hsiu-ch'ing, known as 'the Eastern King', had received a visit from God, Hung says that: 'The Eastern King is the beloved Son of God, and he, with [my] Great Elder Brother and me, were all born of the one venerable mother. Before the existence of heaven and earth all three of us were as close as sons of one father. . . . That which descended to the Eastern King was the Holy Spirit . . . [and his] function then is to be the wind or the Comforter.'[45] There is no Eucharist; but Baptism is retained, and practised in a curious way—self-baptizing, in a basin of water, based on Hung's own exerience: 'On a certain night he was on his knees performing with a basin of water the rite of self-baptism. This was outdoors near the gate of his courtyard. As soon as the sprinkling was finished, "Heaven suddenly sent down a great rain" which drenched him to the skin. The T'ien-wang (Hung) took this as a sign that the Heavenly Father himself had performed the ceremony.'[46]

On the other hand, there is no doubt that, at least in the early days, the social and patriotic aims of the movement were admirable. The Manchu régime against which they were in revolt was certainly corrupt, nepotistic, and static; it is for this reason that contemporary Maoist historians regard the Taiping favourably as an early revolutionary experiment.* The promise that death in battle would guarantee a place in heaven inspired the ordinary troops with great heroism. The fact of later corruption and luxury among the leaders does not detract from the sincerity of the cause in the early stages when it could appeal to uneducated farmers. The brotherhood of man is expounded by

---

* We are indebted to their favourable regard for some of the scholarship which present-day students like Dr. Boardman are able to use.

referring to Christ's brotherly concern for his earthly associates: '[God] repeatedly sent his own son down into this world. He swept away and destroyed the fiends . . . he saved all [his] brothers and sisters. [Therefore] sincerity and filial feeling should be displayed.'[47] And Dr. Boardman reaches the modest conclusion that since the Taiping army possessed a discipline and zeal quite unlike their opponents, at least 'the Biblical component was an effective instrument of mass control and an important factor in Taiping military success'.[48]

ix. GENERAL FENG YÜ-HSIANG (c. 1880–1948)

If the Taiping present only a marginal case for the assimilation of the new 'Western religion', 'the Christian General', as he was called by the missionaries who welcomed him, presents in an acute form the problem of the Christianization of power. Whatever may be thought of his increasing disillusionment with the Church as an organization, it seems certain that he continued to regard himself as a Christian until his curious and unhappy death.

Feng was born of humble parents, about 1880, in central China.* Their home in Anhwei was destroyed by fire and they migrated north, to Chihli province. He joined the army—by then an increasingly respectable profession, which it had not always been—at about eighteen. He had heard discouraging stories about missionaries, but never met any who impressed him until the Boxer Rising (1900) when he was present at the sacking by the Boxers of a mission. He was sorry for the Christians, in a detached way. In the army he began to advance in rank and authority, and also to educate himself. He began to read, and, up till then a loyal supporter of the Emperor, in 1908 he read of the treatment of Chinese women by the Manchus in the seventeenth century, and became anti-Manchu on the spot. Later he was a member of a study group, some of whom joined in the revolution of 1911, and Feng became involved with them. When Yüan Shih-kai became President of China in 1912, Feng was appointed a battalion commander.

It was at this point that he became a Christian. Dr. John R. Mott, the American Christian leader, conducted a series of missions in Asia, and at Peking in early 1913 Feng attended one of his meetings and was converted. He was baptized in 1914 by

* Besides the Notes, see Appendix 16, p. 323.

a Chinese pastor of the Methodist Episcopal Church. There is no doubt that his conversion was genuine, even if it was largely the moral, disciplinary element in Christianity which appealed to him. He was a man of strong emotions and fierce temper; he and others observed that his Christian faith helped him to bring this under control.

Yüan Shih-kai soon deserted the republicanism of Sun Yat-sen, father of the Revolution, and had himself declared Emperor of China on 1 January 1916. This was so unpopular that he renounced the throne in March and died three months later. There was a brief attempt to bring back the old Emperor's son, P'u-Yi, but the boy Emperor lasted only twelve days on the throne. It is generally thought that Feng supported Sun Yat-sen throughout, though perhaps looking back in later life he exaggerated the extent of his republican loyalty. But his troops —he was by now in command of the '16th Mixed Brigade'— were certainly among the first in the field in the decisive battles that ended the brief restoration of the monarchy.

It was during the years that followed that Feng gained his highest reputation as a commander and trainer of troops. Even his critics admitted that he was unusual in his care for his men— their intellectual and moral as well as their physical training. He had been made Defence Commissioner of Ch'angte in 1918, and he used his years there to propagate a spartan and puritanical régime. There were daily services, and men were encouraged to read their Bibles and pray. Many were converted to Christianity, though there was no compulsion and no favouritism shown towards converts. (One estimate says that 2,000 of his men were baptized in 1919, and that at one time eight out of ten were 'sincere Christians'.) He took a personal interest in them, knew all the officers by name (in 1913, in command of a regiment of about 1,600 men, he knew the names of about 1,400). Brothels were closed, drinking and smoking forbidden, and a religious form of patriotism inculcated. The men were devoted to him.

But it was a small army—an expanded brigade. In 1920 he left Hunan, after his peaceful and successful two years at Ch'angte. He became military governor of Shensi in 1921. Here his problems really began: especially financial. He did his best to bring order, but the area was vast, and he was there for only about six months. A local war broke out in 1922, and he was

rewarded at the end of it by being made Governor of Hunan—
an even more exacting task. Here again, though he was in the
post for under six months, he made a start with reforms. It was
here too that Feng impressed his men as a rain-maker: there
had been severe drought, and Feng appointed three days of
fasting and prayer for rain, which he led—and the prayer was
swiftly answered!

In 1922 he was made Inspecting Commissioner for the Army
in Peking. At this stage he was still extremely popular; indeed
a newspaper ballot put him second only to Sun Yat-sen among
'the twelve greatest Chinese'. Once again, at his training
station at Nanyüan, he encouraged evangelistic campaigns. He
was also concerned to raise more money for his unpaid men, and
this involved him in what some have described as intrigues.
(Earlier than that, in 1916, he had been directly responsible for
the execution—some would say murder—of an opponent who
had blocked a unified military administration, and who also—
this, too, must have been a motive—had murdered Feng's own
father-in-law.) In 1923 his first wife died, and he married an
educated Christian Chinese girl, who had a great influence on
him for the next decade and more. In November 1924 he
became famous for a 'coup' by which the young deposed
Emperor P'u-Yi, who was still presiding over a shadow court in
Peking, was politely told he must leave the palace; he took
refuge in his father's house, where Feng's troops kept him under
guard. Later P'u-Yi fled to Japan. And so the monarchy finally
came to an end.

Sun Yat-sen was invited back to China in that same year,
1924, to try to reconcile the warring northern and southern
factions. He agreed, and sent his proposals for a truly representative National Assembly—with delegates from industrial
and rural areas, educational and university establishments,
chambers of commerce, and armies—other than those governed
by the war-lords in the north. The Peking Government did not
accept these proposals, but he came all the same to China in
December. Unfortunately Sun's cancer of the liver worsened,
and he died in March 1925.

From 1925 Feng took up an appointment as Governor of the
North-West. By now he can be described as a 'war-lord', an
appelation which sounds more sinister to us than perhaps it was
in reality. True, the 'war-lord era' was a devasting one for

China, and prolonged a tradition of powerful regionalism and independence which rendered Sun Yat-sen's republican hopes impossibly premature. But given the system, and until it could be effectively suppressed, war-lords were sometimes the only providers of some form of social control, discipline, and education—though more often, of course, they battened on the land, oppressed the peasants with taxes, and ministered only to their personal ambitions.

At any rate, Feng as a highly skilful tactician and an efficient and usually just military organizer was inevitably involved in the fighting between rival armies—much too complicated to summarize. One of the most famous of his exploits was in 1924, during the 'Second Chihli-Fengtien war'. General Wu P'ei-fu had recently made Feng Commander of the 'Third Route Army' in the north. This General Wu was the man whom Feng had described back in 1918 as 'my friend', and for whom (according to one of the missionaries) Feng held out hopes of conversion to Christianity. Wu, he said, was 'on the way'—and the evidence he adduced was that Wu had just published a military catechism, based on one which Feng himself had published a little earlier, and there had referred to Cromwell's godly soldiers and how he and his Ironsides used to kneel in prayer before battle.[49] But since then they had had differences of opinion, and in October 1924, when General Wu had ordered Feng to march with his army and invade Jehol in the north, Feng plotted behind his back, and, in a lightning counter-move, turned against his superior, marched back towards Peking and occupied the capital, all in two days. One historian has said of this enterprise: 'In an era when betrayals were the order of the day, Feng's coup against Wu P'ei-fu . . . would be remembered as one of the most outstanding.'[50] Feng himself, however, claimed that his act, which certainly ended Wu's military pre-eminence, was necessary for the sake of the nation. 'Today,' he is reported to have said to his conspirator, 'Wu and Ts'ao K'un are dictating to the Government, the nation is in chaos and the people are troubled. For a long time I have been determined to act on behalf of the nation to eliminate these evils.'[51] And later he claimed, probably with unjustified hindsight, that he was acting on behalf of Sun Yat-sen and the Kuomintang principles. But whatever the truth about his motives, the result was that he became for the time being a pivotal figure. In 1927, for instance, when the Kuomintang was divided into right and left wings, Feng intervened at a crucial moment of the war and both sides had to come and negotiate with him about a truce. This year he became Commander-in-Chief of the Second Army Group; the next year, Minister of War and vice-chairman of the 'Executive Yüan'; in 1930 a member of the State Council; in 1932 Minister of Home Affairs—though he did not take up this post, since he knew he would only be a rubber stamp to the Kuomintang. But from 1930 on, no longer having an army behind him, he was of less political importance; it was not till the Japanese encroachment in the North in 1935 that Feng came back into his own—he was made Vice-Chairman of the Military Affairs Commission in early 1936. When the Sino-Japanese war broke out, the next year, Feng was his old self again, and fully occupied until the end of the war in 1945.

But for some years now he had increasingly opposed Chiang Kai-shek. He had visited Russia in 1926, with Borodin, and had been deeply interested in the practical results of Communism. Indeed, until he turned against Russian interventionist policy in 1927, he was thought by the Russians to be one of their great hopes against Chiang Kai-shek and the Kuomintang. He had, temporarily at least, to side with the Kuomintang from 1927, but his opposition to Russia at that stage was probably more xenophobic than anti-communist. At any rate by 1945 he was sufficiently opposed to Chiang to decide that he could not co-operate or keep silent: so he withdrew to America. Here he rallied American support for an anti-Chiang policy—in favour of the 'Democratic League' and of the anti-Chiang factions within the Kuomintang. He claimed that the Chinese Communists were not 'communist' in the sense condemned by Americans, but continued Sun Yat-sen's republicanism. At this stage the Chinese Communists themselves did not regard Feng as an ally—for he appeared to be in favour of a 'third force', neither pro-Chiang nor pro-communist. But they later claimed him as one of their heroes.

For in 1948 he decided to return to China. The Chiang cause was clearly lost, the Communists were unbeatable, and he no doubt hoped to support the revolutionary element in the Kuomintang to break out and finally turn against Chiang. He was sailing via Russia, and had reached the Black Sea, when in September it was announced that he and one of his daughters had died on board, as a result of a fire. There is still speculation whether or not his death was accidental—and if not, whether it was on Chiang's orders. But though not impossible, this seems unlikely.* At any rate by the time his body reached China the People's Republic was in existence. And in 1953 his ashes were given honourable burial, and Chairman Mao sent a funeral scroll. In 1954 the Communists brought out an edition of Feng's poems; and his widow to this day has an official position in the People's Government.

*   *   *

It has been suggested that Feng's admiration for Sun Yat-sen was an after-thought, an attempt at vindicating his own opportunist career or a mere climbing on to a bandwagon. This seems to suggest that Feng was a more subtle, devious man than perhaps he really was. Indeed, the contrast between him and Sun, both as men and as 'Christians', is instructive.

Sun Yat-sen has been described as 'a Christian most of the time and a man of ideals always'; and he himself once said 'I do not belong to the Christianity of the Churches but to the Christianity of Jesus who was a revolutionary'. Formally, he was a Congregationalist (like Lu Cheng-hsiang—'Dom Célestin Lou'†). In the famous episode of his kidnapping by the Manchu Government, in London on 11 October 1896, Sun was actually on his way to Dr. and Mrs. Cantlie, his friends, who were taking him to St. Martin-in-the-Fields that Sunday morning when he was waylaid. And in prison he afterwards testified to having prayed much and been upheld by the grace of God. It is true that when the Revolution was successful Sun rather embarrassed his missionary friends by making a formal pilgrimage, on 15 February 1912, to the mausoleum of the first Ming Emperor near Nanking and there paying tribute to the 'ancestors', with a prayer which included such words as: 'I have heard that in the past many would-be deliverers of their country have ascended this lofty mound wherein is your sepulchre. It has served then as a holy inspiration. . . . Your people have come here today to inform Your Majesty of the final victory. . . . May your example inspire your descendants in the times which are to come. Spirit! Accept this offering.'[52]

And after Sun's death the Party made a cult of him, with

* See Appendix 18, p. 324.   † See chapter 17, above, pp. 223 ff.

veneration at his tomb, and the solemn weekly reading of his will in all schools. But there was also a Christian funeral service for him; and so orthodox a Christian as the Roman Catholic Dom Célestin Lou,* having asserted the 'discreet influence' of Christianity in China, said of Sun:

According to his explicit declarations, Dr. Sun Yat-sen, founder of the Republic, borrowed from Christian teaching the social and political principles of justice, of liberty and equilibrium (*sic*) which inspired his public life. . . . Dr. Sun Yat-sen belonged, as I also used to belong, to the London Missionary Society.[53]

By contrast Feng would, I suspect, have been less tolerant of other religious systems than Sun, though the General insisted on the value of Confucius and Mencius. When in 1925 people began to say of him that 'the Christian General' had become 'the Red General', he dismissed the accusation by an appeal to the wisdom of the Chinese sages. He was critical of Roman Catholics, though he admired the work of the Jesuits in the seventeenth century and their influence in the Chinese court. He also became (understandably) strongly anti-British, especially after the 'May 30th Incident',* and was disappointed that the missionaries did not more strongly and openly disown their countrymen's brutality as shown there. It is perhaps significant of the kind of Christian influences which he met (and he met no other) that one of his missionary biographers, Dr. Marshall Broomhall, deplores the 'anti-foreign' element in his patriotism, without showing any profound understanding of the reasons for it.[54] It is sad that towards the end he was on bad terms with his second wife—who had always been further to the left than he—and that he was rumoured to have been unfaithful to her.

But when all qualifications have been made it is remarkable that one of the most colourful and powerful military figures of the period was, like the founder of Chinese Nationalism, profoundly stamped with the Christian faith he had freely accepted in early days. One cannot help wondering how Feng would have developed had his Christian experience been wider. For there is no doubt that the Christians with whom he had most to do in the formative stages were somewhat gullible and apt to

---

* On 30th May 1925 the police in Shanghai, under a British officer, fired on a crowd of angry Chinese demonstrators, 'like cattle', and twelve Chinese students were killed. This sparked off violent anti-British feeling.

make over-simplified judgements. One of them, revealing a somewhat Old Testament conception of righteousness, says in praise of Feng that:

Some years ago the General thrashed one of his Colonels for going to a house of ill fame. The Colonel has got splendidly converted since. It is said that some time ago the General had a man shot who would go to vile resorts after repeated warnings. Eternal shame upon our Canadian and British leaders because they did not shield our boys.[55]

Little wonder that Feng believed so simply and literally that the Lord was (militarily) on his side. His was, in fact, an honest-to-God, uncomplicated soldier's view of a fundamentalist version of Christianity—familiar in armies other than Chinese. The Christians he quoted were General Gordon and Oliver Cromwell. Yet there is no reason to doubt the genuine nature of his original 'conversion', so far as it went; nor the sincerity of his somewhat emotional prayers, aspirations, and tears of penitence (during a missionary meeting 'a missionary on the platform said there was a pool of tears where the General's head was bowed'[56]); nor, indeed, the evidence of many who knew him that after he became a Christian his once ungovernable temper was much more under control. The fact that the People's Republic of China later honoured him (as they also did Sun Yat-sen) may be taken by some as proof of his betrayal of Christianity. I prefer to take it as proof of the genuineness of Feng's continuous and often compassionate concern for the welfare of the *lao-pai-hsing*.*[57]

CONCLUSION

CHAPTER 19 | THE WIDENING LENS

Looking back over this parade of variegated characters, some prominent, some insignificant, some colourful, some rather pedestrian, it might be tempting to dismiss the whole collection as merely part of past history—with a grudging exception, perhaps, for the 'improvisators' of Part V, who are in any case out of the 'main stream'. Those who are interested in, and

* 'the common people'

write about, 'the Third World' today barely mention the sort of people who fill the previous pages of this book. And in the predictions for the future both those from 'Euramerica' who are busy telling the inhabitants of the Third World what to do, and those inhabitants themselves, are not often found discussing the role of 'non-western' Christianity in this context. Our interest in the 'patterns of acceptance' we have tried broadly to sketch would perhaps be regarded as an archaeological interest only. Archaeology is, no doubt, a popular subject these days; but often at best a dilettante, at worst an escapist, one.

And this dismissal is understandable for a number of reasons, most of which have been (I hope) frankly faced in the course of this book. But it will be convenient to summarize them.

i. 'CHRISTIANITY GOES WITH IMPERIALISM'

This charge is so familiar, and on the whole so just, that little space need be devoted to it. China provides so clear a case, and subsequent developments in China show so cogently what follows from the case, that a summary of the accusations against the churches here will do for many other parts of the Third World. It was made in 1901 by a highly educated Chinese, Dr. Wên Ch'ing, who trained as a doctor in Scotland and later became Principal of Amoy University. He made the elementary accusations that the European Christians did nothing to protest against the 'most favoured nation' clause of the treaties forced upon China, and that the churches used the privileges won for them by power politics; further, that they refused to respect Chinese traditions, e.g. by building their churches without regard to *fêng-shui* (geomancy, considered important by Chinese in choosing building-sites). But, more important, he said that 'Chinese Christians in the missionaries' employ were in practice outside Chinese law'; and that 'converts (especially Roman Catholics) refused to *kow-tow* to the magistrate or any official', thus insulting the latter, and setting the Christians socially above the converts' non-Christian relatives; and, finally, that the missionaries 'have kept their converts at the intellectual level of the middle ages', protecting them against 'the discoveries of modern science and exegesis' for fear they might be led into infidelity.[1]

These accusations could be applied to many other areas; and

they cannot be easily dismissed since they explain many of the weaknesses of Christians in the Third World.

ii. 'CHRISTIANITY HAS BEEN A DIVISIVE INFLUENCE'

Not content with bringing different versions of the Christian faith to the Third World, the Christians once there proceeded to abuse each other, to teach their converts to abuse each other, and even to lead them into battle against each other. Catholics and Protestants have fought each other not only in Uganda* but also in West Africa (Nigeria), in the South Seas, and in Madagascar. In Polynesia, the war of 1840 between George Tupou of Tonga (a Wesleyan) and some Fijians was called by the Wesleyans a war against 'pagans' in spite of the fact that many on the latter side were in fact Roman Catholics;[2] and a little later in Hawaii the (again Wesleyan) government sentenced to compulsory labour natives that called themselves 'papists', and did so according to a law against idolatry![3] In Madagascar there was perhaps nothing that can be called an outright, full-scale 'Catholic-Protestant War'; but the period of martyrdoms† was succeeded fairly swiftly by rivalry and opposition between the first arrivals (Protestant) and the Jesuits. Indeed a life has been written of a Malagasy Roman Catholic, Victoire Rasoamanarivo (1848–94), to show her heroism in the face of attacks by—not Pagans but Protestants.

From 1886 the Catholics were more and more menaced. Rainimaharavo, Victoire's paternal uncle, tried to persuade her to desert Catholicism, and threatened that if she did not do so he would take away all her belongings and servants, throw her out of the family and refuse her burial in the family tomb. . . . From the first day of the persecution she was dragged by force to the Protestant school. Rosalie, a slave of her household who was a catechumen, encouraged her: 'Let us recite the rosary together and take courage: Mary, who bruised the serpent's head, will deliver us'. After three days the mistress sent her home: 'Take your girl back, we can't teach her anything: she does nothing but cry'.[4]

The compliment was returned when after the French invasion of 1895 there was a reaction against the Hova people (Protestant), and the Jesuits were supported by the new government in blocking Protestant missionary work.[5]

* See chapter 2, above, p. 22 ff. (and the corrections to this statement).
† See chapter 2, above, pp. 18–21.

And (the accusation continues) as if warring between Christian churches were not enough, there has been warring *within* one Christian church—even one so monolithic as the Roman Catholic Church. We have seen, in the life of Fr. Vaz,* how the Portuguese claims to patronage (*padroado*) set Roman Catholics against their fellows and threw the validity of their mutual sacraments into dispute. What can the non-Christians of Bombay have thought when in 1853 the Bishop of Bombay, Hartman, (appointed by Propaganda in Rome) went to visit the church of St. Michael, Upper Mahim, which the 'Padroists' (Portuguese) believed to be rightfully theirs? The luckless bishop was locked up in the church for fourteen days, and nearly starved while not only legal but physical battles raged outside.[6]

iii. 'CHRISTIANITY MAKES WAY FOR SECULARISM'

The third charge against the missionaries is that they kept their converts at the infantile stage of religion and concealed from them the fact that in Euramerica secular notions were rapidly replacing the traditional religious assumptions. It is interesting that one instance of 'secularism' creeping into a traditional faith can be discerned in the Taiping movement of the 1850s.† As we have seen, the Taiping was in many ways a highly 'supernaturalist' faith; but when the Taipings took over the biblical command to shun idols, they gave it, in the main, a rationalist rather than a supernaturalist interpretation.

Though the Taipings sometimes allude to God's command from Mount Sinai (against idolatry), the main appeal is to reason. Why, they argue, abandon reason and worship material objects? '[When you] bow down to lumps of clay, to wood and stone, [I] ask when did you lose [your] mind?' Intelligent creatures should not worship mere matter.[7]

iv. 'CHRISTIANITY HAS OBSTRUCTED THE WAY TO SOCIAL PROGRESS'

The rationalist element we have just alluded to in the Taiping movement is perhaps a further reason why Chinese Marxists have regarded that movement as one of its precursors. A recent pro-Maoist study by an Asian Christian has described the

---

* See chapter 10, above, pp. 131 ff.   † See chapter 18, above, pp. 267 ff.

Taiping as 'this strongly Christian mass movement'[8]; and no doubt the term refers to the Taiping social policy. But in general the attitude of Marxists, especially those of the Third World, towards Christianity is well-known: the missionaries have only made significant numbers of converts, and in a lasting way, in countries still dominated by Euramerican capitalism It is no accident that the Philippines have the largest proportion of Christians of any country in South-East Asia; and the proportion has increased since they came within the American sphere of influence. The Communist therefore must remove all traces of this religion, which cannot dissociate itself from the rule of the oppressors.

*   *   *

The case for the prosecution is formidable. If true, the bulk of this book is at best a piece of academic history, irrelevant to present and future problems. What can we reply?

(a)

The first thing that may be said is that if the prediction of one demographer is fulfilled (though it has been dismissed by some as extremely improbable) then the subject of this book will by no means belong to archaeology. For Dr. David B. Barrett calculates, working on present statistics, that by A.D. 2000 there may well be 350 million Christians in Africa.[9] If this is so (and his argument, which may seem fantastic, is carefully based) Africa may well 'tip the balance and transform Christianity permanently into a primarily non-Western religion'.

This speculation is bound to be controversial. But even if it is accepted, the Marxist objection (no. iv above) will still stand: that 'non-Western' will still mean 'capitalist'. And this, of course, is not the same as the 'secularist' objection (no. iii above), that all religions are being replaced by modern positivism. The difference between the two objections is well illustrated in one important Chinese figure, Ch'en Tu-hsiu of Anhwei. He started as a 'secularist'. He founded the influential journal *Ch'ing Nien* (Youth); and in 1919 he was writing: 'In order to foster Democracy, we must oppose Confucianism, chastity, and old ethics and old politics. In order to foster

Science we must oppose the old arts and religion. In order to foster both Democracy and Science, we must oppose our natural heritage and our old literature.' He even published an article in his journal urging the Chinese to study Christianity and to incorporate 'the loftiness and greatness of Jesus Christ' into their blood. At this stage he was commending and using John Dewey, the American pragmatist philosopher, who was lecturing to the students in Peking in 1919. But in a surprisingly short time he abandoned democratic liberalism, and became one of the pioneers of Chinese Marxism. He saw that Dewey's hopes of evolving democracy, and with it industrialism, on a Western pattern were unrealistic; no doubt he sensed that whereas Confucianism 'had grown into a very concrete pattern of life, science . . . could hardly govern all human relationships. Nor could democracy, which results from an essentially evolutionary process, be imposed from above. Hence neither the one nor the other fitted the frame vacated by Confucianism.'[10] It has been suggested that, though Sun Yat-sen is still lauded by Maoists as the father of the Chinese revolution, it was Ch'en Tu-hsiu who was the real genius of it: for Sun's patriotism led him to a romantic glorification of the Chinese tradition which mixed with his Christian-ethical idealism to produce a somewhat effervescent broth; his nickname was *Sun Wu K'ung* ('Wu K'ung' means 'aware of vacuity', i.e. a person who boasts much but achieves little).[11] But in the long run it was the Marxists who were able to bring a hope which could be as real for the peasants as for the intellectuals; and could do so because Marxism provided something in the nature of a religious faith which Dewey (and Bertrand Russell, who also visited China in the 'twenties) could not provide. If Marxism can be validly described as an off-shoot of Judaic-Christian eschatology, Maoism might be pictured as an egalitarian off-shoot of ethical Confucianism with Christian-personalist tinges. 'Of all the things in the world, people are the most precious', said Mao; and his eulogy of Norman Bethune, the Canadian doctor who worked in Yenan and died in 1939 of the disease he was treating, sounds like any orthodox 'lives of the saints':

We must all learn the spirit of absolute selflessness from him. . . . A man's ability may be great or small, but if he has this spirit, he is already noble-minded and pure, a man of moral integrity and above vulgar interests, a man who is of value to the people.[12]

20

(b)

Thus the main reply to the charge (iii) that secularism is steadily replacing traditional religions in the Third World, as it has already done in Euramerica, is that the case is non-proven. True, there is a popular Christian reply to this: namely that secularism is the grandchild of Christianity: that it was biblical faith that 'de-sacralized' the world and so made it open to secular-scientific understanding.[13] Curiously, this seems to be a new and subtler version of 'Christian imperialism': to claim everything, even what will result in Christianity's demise, for Christian teaching. In any case, even if the argument is plausible for some of the developments in the West, it is demonstrably untrue for many parts of the Third World, since 'de-sacralization' was already occurring in areas untouched by Christianity: Tonga, we saw,* was one example; Uganda is probably another; and the Far East can show many. In any case secularism as a total philosophy of life is being challenged by others than Christians. We are told that two Indian politicians deserted the Socialist Party of India a few years ago, and moved, one to Theosophy, the other to strict 'advaita' Hinduism. The latter said:

For many years, I have worshipped at the shrine of the goddess, Dialectical Materialism. . . . But while the main quest of philosophy remains unsatisfied, it has become patent to me that materialism of any sort robs man of the means to become truly human. In a material civilization, man has no rational incentive to be good. . . . I feel further that the task of social reconstruction cannot succeed under the inspiration of a materialist philosophy.[14]

For secular man is often intensely lonely: and there is a vertical as well as a historical loneliness—not only no living companions, but to have no dead ones either, no roots in history. Hence the search for an identity with a respectable historical pedigree. This is one of the impulses behind the search for *négritude*, the cult of the African personality in Africa. On the surface, and for the time being, this is associated with a rejection of Christianity; but as African history is studied more by Africans they will discover the extent to which pride in their own African past was in fact often recaptured and then commended by African Christians as Christians. We have seen that

* See chapter 13, above, pp. 173 ff.

even the conservative Bishop Crowther* went some way in the direction of retaining African *moeurs*. James Johnson, later assistant bishop, went further: he had no difficulty in persuading the C.M.S., for instance, to pass a minute in 1883 urging the retention of African names at the baptism of Africans. Some went further still. The most extreme was Dr. Mojola Agbebi, leader of the Native Baptist Church in the Niger Delta. He was the first pastor to doff European clothes and wear the voluminous *agbada*. In 1911 he was invited to read a paper at the 'First Universal Races Congress' in London University. In his lecture, 'The West African Problem', he accuses the white missionaries of having disturbed traditional African society and ethics; and then defends African customs, including human sacrifices and cannibalism! On the latter he says:

Cannibalism is not general in Africa. What led some communities to institute a sacrifice of human victims led other communities to go a step further and turn the sacrifice into what they consider profitable use, by solemnly partaking of it as a sacrament. In some cases victims of human sacrifice consider it more honourable to be eaten by men to whom they are supposed to be imparting some virtue or for whom they are fufilling some indispensable and important function, than to be devoured by senseless and ignominious worms. The eating of human or non-human flesh differs only in kind, and human flesh is said to be the most delicious of all viands. . . . Christianity is a superstructure [*sic*] of cannibalism. . . . In administering the Lord's Supper to converts from cannibalism I have often felt some uneasiness in repeating the formula 'Take, eat, this is my body. . . . This is my blood'.[15]

His uneasiness, however, is not logically compatible with his defence of cannibalism and of a theology of adaptation of African ways to Christian preaching: it evidently betrays the survival of a 'post-African' consciousness.

But it is not only in the Third World that a nostalgia for lost meanings and values stands in contrast with a developing secularism. In the United States (we are told) there is a new search for historical roots among the white Americans; and this takes the paradoxical form of glorifying the Amerindian whom the Whites virtually exterminated (physically to begin with, socially and culturally later). The glorifying may take the form of experimenting with *peyote* (the mushroom-like plant with

* See chapter 17, above, pp. 228 ff.

hallucinogenic effects which plays a part in some Amerindian religious cults); or it may assume the dimensions of a group confessional for the sins of predatory America. A literary critic who has studied this phenomenon, Mr. Leslie Fiedler, quotes a characteristic letter from a young white American 'dropout', who had been attending a meeting of the Native American Church, 'an Indian peyote cult with fundamentalist Christian trimmings'; as a result of this he had decided to join the Cheyenne. For 'while we have been playing checkers they (the Amerindians) have been playing give away. As a result they have nothing but poverty, anonymity, happiness, lack of neuroses, wonderful children and a way of life that is free, democratic and in complete fulfilment of the American dream.'[16] And one of the most extraordinary, lyrical celebrations of this 'vanishing American' comes in a strange, erotic, beautiful novel by a Canadian poet, Leonard Cohen, in which he constantly invokes the shade of an Iroquois girl— none other than the Catherine Tekakwitha whose life we told in Part II.* As a modern Western intellectual Mr. Cohen, of course, does not approve of her Christianity: 'Catherine Tekakwitha', he apostrophizes, 'I have come to rescue you from the Jesuits'; he resents her virginity and her austerities; he comments savagely on the recorded information that when Catherine died her face miraculously turned white, which the Jesuits regarded as 'un argument nouveau de crédibilité, dont Dieu favorisait les sauvages pour leur faire goûter la foi'.[17] And yet he is strangely captivated by her simplicity and natural innocence:

Catherine Tekakwitha, who are you? . . . Are you the Iroquois Virgin? Are you the Lily of the Shores of the Mohawk River? Can I love you in my own way? . . . I fell in love with a religious picture of you. You were standing among birch trees, my favourite trees. . . . Do I have any right to come after you with my dusty mind full of the junk of maybe five thousand books?[18]

No doubt this search for roots, in Africa or in pre-European America, has elements of the merely nostalgic, the dilettante, the sentimental and unreal: sooner or later after the mystic experiments comes the bill for the drug which launched them. And in their present form they are certainly not a recovering of

* See chapter 7, above, p. 91 ff.

Christian memories: in some cases they are quite self-consciously neo-Pagan. But Christians will claim that what is negatively Pagan in these yearnings will ultimately be discarded, what positively Pagan be fulfilled, in a total Christian vision. And the evidence for this lies—in spite of the huge mistakes and disastrous failures—in the material this book has tried to survey. Where, for instance, the 'pattern of acceptance' has been a natural one, spontaneously following the magnetic fields that caused it, there has been genuine self-realization: as in the case of the Batak Christians, of whom a skilled observer has noted that on becoming Christians they 'not only remain Bataks, but . . . *become* Batak'. And he quotes a young Batak editor as saying: 'Christianity's message of the equality of all men before God—you notice that I emphasise "before God"—has freed us from an oppressive inferiority complex, and given us the power as a nation of rising to higher things.'[19]

(c)

And fortunately for the Christian churches the reaction against the 'nothing but' type of materialist secularism ('man is nothing but his genes/behaviour/motor impulses') is coming at a time when the older 'theologies of exclusion' are fast disappearing. By 'theologies of exclusion' I mean any type of dogmatism, Catholic or Protestant, which says that outside the Church (or Bible) is no salvation. We saw earlier* the discomfort of a Japanese convert when he found it natural to join in the family veneration of the ancestors. A Japanese bishop, some years later, had no hesitations:

I . . . was born in a Buddhist home. My father and mother both died without the knowledge of God in Christ. I have, however, been home six times since their death to hold memorial services. When I was baptised the ancestral tablets were all burnt, so that there are no special tokens of remembrance which I can use. We sing a hymn together, after which I read from the Scripture (Romans ii) and we have some prayer. I believe that inasmuch as the soul is immortal and they died without the knowledge of God, He will, because He is love, save them in some way that I know not.[20]

It is for this very reason that the daring, sometimes dubious, experimentalists whom we looked at in Part V take on such

* See chapter 11, above, esp. p. 150.   See also Appendix 17, p. 324.

importance. And yet departures from 'exclusionist theology' can be noted even in profoundly conservative traditions. There is a curious and significant incident in the life of a Chinese pastor, Ren (1852–1929), who was converted, and later ordained, by the China Inland Mission—which has the reputation for the most unbendingly exclusionist Protestant theology. But there is a passage in his quaint and improving autobiography which is startling if one ponders its implications. A friend of his was working as a servant in the Christian mission at Soochow in 1868, and Ren, while visiting him there, met the C.I.M. pastor, the Rev. H. Cordon. Cordon asked Ren to teach him Chinese. Ren was discouraged by his relatives who warned him that Christians gouged out their pupils' eyes. He did not know what to do.

Suddenly I remembered that the Goddess of Mercy [Kwannon] was very powerful and that formerly I had worshipped her. . . . Why should I not seek guidance from her? I arose at dawn and having washed I . . . set off for the temple. Lighting both incense and candles, I prostrated myself before the Goddess of Mercy, and said in all sincerity: 'If it will be good for me to go to the home of the Westerner, graciously grant me the Upper Lot; but if not give me the Lower one'. Seizing the bamboo container I shook it, and lo! out fell the Upper Lot. When the Buddhist priest handed me the verse which corresponded with the Lot, I gave him a handful of money, and laughing for very joy returned home.[21]

Thus, guided by the 'merciful *bodhisattva*', he came to the mission as a teacher of Chinese; later he was converted and finally ordained in a denomination that would (surely) strenuously deny a grace of God operating through a *bodhisattva*.

And this has come about, this waning of 'exclusionism', as the Christians of the Third World have taken over from their Euramerican mentors (or sometimes just taken over, not from anyone) the task of interpreting the patterns. We are seeing Nigerian historians repainting the picture of West Africa; reassessments of traditional African religious concepts by African philosophers and anthropologists;[22] a plea for 'African Socialism' by a Nigerian Roman Catholic priest;[23] reinterpretations of Indian philosophy in Christian terms by an Indian Roman Catholic priest;[24] an account of Chinese attitudes to the West by a Chinese Roman Catholic priest;[25] interpretations of Western monasticism in terms of Asian philosophy and practice;[26] and so forth. The spontaneity and vigour of this kind of work is significant and not so well known as it should be.

And always, apart from the theoretical work, there is the living, daily witness of non-intellectuals—people who have received something which they count too valuable to keep to themselves. It seems fitting to conclude with one such.

It is the story of Rachel ('Lakeri') Sebulimba of Uganda. Sleeping sickness had been diagnosed there in 1901. Rachel, an African teacher, was in a Christian class at Ngogwe. She was reading for the much prized teacher's certificate, when she heard that sleeping sickness[27] had broken out on an island in Lake Victoria, and that people were dying there, without having had the Christian faith brought to them. She asked permission to go and teach them before it was too late. She was warned of the near certainty that she would contract the disease if she did, but she was determined to go. 'I know all this,' she said, but 'these people are dying and know nothing of Christ, the Saviour of the world; I know and love Him, and must go and tell them of Him.' She worked effectively on the island for some time, then returned. Some months later she was diagnosed: infected. She was in Mengo hospital, and continued evangelistic work there so long as she could move. Bishop Tucker describes how he was celebrating Holy Communion in Mengo cathedral one day when, at the end of the row of communicants, a woman came up, 'with slowly dragging footsteps'. The African assistant priest whispered to the bishop: 'It is Lakeri!' She had sat by herself in a corner of the cathedral as she knew that people would 'shrink away from her as they would from death itself'. Almost her last words were (in Luganda): 'If He takes me it will be well, or if He leaves me a while longer, it will be well also.'[28]

NOTES

PREFACE

Page	Note	
xii	1	A. Choi, *L'Érection du premier Vicariat apostolique et les Origines du Catholicisme en Korée, 1592–1837* (Swisse-Schoënbeck-Beckenried, 1961), 126, n. 1.
xiii	2	See chapter 17, pp. 226 ff. and refs.
	3	See chapter 18, pp. 266 ff. and refs.
	4	ibid., pp. 254 ff. and refs.
	5	G. S. Mwase, *Strike a Blow and Die* (Harvard, 1967). See chapter 18, p. 251, n. 21.
xv	6	J. B. Coulbeaux, *Vers la Lumière* (Paris, 1926).

CHAPTER I

Page	Note	
1	1	Ku Hing-ming, *Spirit of the Chinese People* (Peking, 1915); cited in A. Chih, *L'Occident 'Chrétien' vu par les Chinois vers la fin du XIXe Siècle, 1870–1900* (Paris, 1962), 227.
	2	Sun Yat-sen, *The Triple Demism (San Minchui)*, trans. Paschale d'Elia (Wuchang, 1931), 511–12 and see Appendix 1, p. 315.
	3	E. E. Wallis, *The Daiyuma Story* (London, 1961), 178, 199, 210 ff. 'All of them were angry at Daiyuma . . . for bringing in the sickness from outside.'

In the early nineteenth century the same thing happened to the American Indians of the north-west. In about 1840 'The white man's diseases were spreading recurrently through the tribes, taking a toll more terrible than any Black Death known to Europe's history. Over two-thirds of the Indians of the Pacific north-west simply disappeared.' (R. I. Burns, *The Jesuits and the Indian Wars of the North-West* (Yale, 1966), 13.)

	4	See e.g. Alan Moorehead, *The Fatal Impact* (London, 1966), 55–6. I have plagiarized the title of Mr. Moorehead's book for this chapter, with a difference. I am concerned in these pages to suggest that the impact was not wholly fatal: fatal sometimes, fruitful sometimes, fateful always.
2	5	Douglas L. Oliver, *The Pacific Islands* (Harvard, 1951), 176 f.
	6	R. H. Pearce, *The Savages of America* (Baltimore, 1953), 19.
3	7	Colin Rae, *Malaboch* (Cape Town & London, 1898), 104–6.
	8	Sarah S. Farmer, *Tonga and the Friendly Islands* (London, 1855) 382.
	9	ibid., 410.
4	10	ibid., 365 f.
	11	R. Pierce Beaver, *Pioneers in Mission* (Grand Rapids, Michigan, 1966), 207.

5   12   Francis Parkman, *Count Frontenac* (Toronto, 1898), V., 393–5.

     13   R. I. Burns, loc. cit., 34.

     14   William Ellis, *A Vindication of the South Sea Missions* (London, 1831), 18 f.

6   15   ibid., 31 f.

     16   M. Jarrett-Kerr, *Christ and the New Nations* (London, 1966), chapter 1.

     17   Ku Hing-ming, in *North China Herald*, 1 July 1891 (cited in A. Chih, loc. cit., 157).

     18   Y. C. Wang, *Chinese Intellectuals in the West, 1879–1949* (North Carolina, 1966), 42, n. 5.

7   19   J. F. A. Ajayi, *Christian Missions in Nigeria, 1841–1891* (London, 1965), 262.

     20   Anne Luck, *African Saint—Apolo Kivebalayu* (London, 1963).

8   21   Basil Thomson, *Diversions of a Prime Minister* (London, 1894), 378 f.

9   22   W. M. Hinton, *Fanshen* (New York and London, 1966), 492.

CHAPTER 2
Page   Note
10   1   K. S. Latourette, *A History of the Expansion of Christianity* (London, 1943), V, 259.

11   2   *Histoire de la glorieuse Mort de neuf Chrestiens Iaponais* (Anon) (Douai, 1612), 187.

      3   ibid., 91–2.

12   4   ibid., 130–1.

13   5   C. R. Boxer, *The Christian Century in Japan* (California, 1951), 187.

      6   ibid., 166.

      7   ibid., 167.

14   8   ibid., 473, n.

      9   ibid., 235.

     10   ibid., 204.

     11   ibid., 235–6.

15   12   ibid., 339.

     13   ibid., 333.

     14   ibid., 343.

     15   ibid., 395–6.

16   16   ibid., 361, 358.

     17   *Annales de la Propaganda de la Foi*, vol. 40, 117 (cited in A. Launay, *Histoire Générale de la Société des Missions Étrangères* (Paris, 1894), III, 457 ff).

     18   W. Ellis, *The Martyr Church of Madagascar* (London, 1870), 48.

17   19   ibid., 90.

18   20   ibid., 110.

     21   Boxer, loc. cit., 340 f.

19   22   Ellis, loc. cit., 116.

     23   ibid., 120–3.

20	24	ibid., 162.
21	25	ibid., 170 ff.
	26	ibid., 107–8.
	27	Figures given in Charles W. Forman, 'A Study in the Self-Propagating Church', in Wilbur C. Harr, *Frontiers of the Christian World Mission since 1938* (New York, 1962), 116.
	28	Ellis, loc. cit., Conclusion.
22	29	J. F. Faupel, *African Holocaust* (London, 1962), *passim*. Soeur Marie-Andrée du Sacré-Coeur's more recent *Uganda, Terre des Martyrs* (Paris, 1957) does not add much. The pioneer study was J. P. Thoonen, *Black Martyrs* (London, 1941), which is still valuable.
	30	Colin Macinnes, article in *The Spectator*, 1 February 1963, p. 126.
	31	Faupel, loc. cit., 47.
23	32	*Mackay of Uganda*, by his sister (London, 1890), 120–1.
	33	ibid., 136.
24	34	Faupel, loc. cit., 34.
	35	ibid., 41–2.
26	36	ibid., 98. Mackay, loc. cit., 267. Also see Dawson, *James Hannington, Bishop and Martyr* (London, 1889), 371.
27	37	Faupel, loc. cit., 30–1.
	38	ibid., 75.
	39	ibid., 117–18.
28	40	ibid., 136–7 (citing James Miti, unpubl. MS in Luganda).
	41	Thoonen, loc. cit., 290–1.
	42	Faupel, 207 and n.
29	43	J. A. Rowe, and 'The Purge of Christians at Mwanga's Court', in *Journal of African History* (London), V, i (1964), 57.
	44	ibid., 68.
	45	ibid., *passim*, esp. 70–1.
30	46	D. A. Low, 'Converts and Martyrs in Buganda', in C. G. Baëta (Ed.), *Christianity in Tropical Africa* (London, 1968), 158.
	47	ibid., 161–2.
31	48	K. S. Latourette, *A History of Christian Missions in China* (London, 1929), 512, 517.
	49	E. Smirnov, *A Short History of the historical Development and present Positions of Russian Orthodox Missions* (London, 1903), 76.
32	50	Bryson (Mrs.) of Tientsin, *Cross and Crown, Stories of the Chinese Martyrs* (London, 1904), 17–19.
	51	ibid., 95–6.
	52	ibid., 53.
	53	V. Purcell, *The Boxer Uprising—a background Study* (London, 1963), 184 f.
33	54	ibid., 122–3.
	55	ibid., 222 (quoting Jerome Ch'ên).
	56	ibid., 239.
34	57	ibid., 220–1.

34   58   E. R. Hughes, *The Invasion of China by the Western World* (London, 1937), 79.
     59   Purcell, loc. cit., 322–3.
     60   J. Leclercq, *La Vie du Père Lebbe* (Paris, 1961), 74.
35   61   ibid., 81–2.

CHAPTER 3
Page   Note
38   1   For this, and the whole account of Grace (Gracia) Hosakawa, I am indebted to C. R. Boxer, 'Hosakawa Tadaoki and the Jesuits, 1587–1645', in *Japan Soc. Transactions and Proceedings* (1934–5), vol. XXXII, 79–119.
42   2   Fernão Guerreiro's account, in *Relaçam Annual* (Lisbon, 1603), 195–6 (cited in Boxer, loc. cit., 93–5).
43   3   Boxer, loc. cit. 102.
44   4   ibid., 112–13, cited also in J. Murdoch and I. Yamagata, *A History of Japan, 1542–1651* (Kobe, 3 vols, 1903), II, 608.
45   5   C. R. Boxer, *Christian Century in Japan*, 153.
     6   ibid., 337–8.
     7   ibid., 141 f.
     8   Of the five Christian *daimyo* of Kyūshū, three were in one camp and one in the other over the dispute on the succession to Hideyoshi. Murdoch and Yamagata, loc. cit., II, 392.
     9   G. Sansom, *A History of Japan* (London, 3 vols, 1961), II, 395.
     10   Murdoch and Yamagata, loc. cit. 257.
     11   ibid., 401.
46   12   ibid., 409, 595–7.
     13   ibid., 607.
     14   For this, and the whole account of Gotô, I am indebted to H. Cieslik, SJ, *Gotô Juan* ('Ein Beitrag zur Missions-Geschichte Word-Japans', no. xii in the *Schriftenreihe der Neuen Zeitschrift für Missionswissenschaft*) (1954). (I am also indebted to Mrs. R. J. N. Tod for translating this for me.)
49   15   K. Wittfogel, *Oriental Despotism* (Yale, 1957), 200. In Wittfogel's terminology, Japan never developed a fully 'hydraulic despotism'.

CHAPTER 4
Page   Note
50   1   A. H. Rowbotham, *Missionary and Mandarin* (California, 1942), 64.
51   2   V. Cronin, *The Wise Man from the West* (London, 1955), 211–13.
52   3   Abbé Huc, *Christianity in China*, English trans. (London, 1857, 2 vols.), II, 172–3. (Cronin differs from Huc in this as in other matters. But Cronin used the scholarly work of Paschale d'Elia, *Fonti Ricciani* (Rome, 1942–1949, 3 vols.), and his account is to be preferred.)
     4   Huc, loc. cit. K. M. Pannikar, in his *Asia and Western Dominance* (London, 1953), 135, says that Hsü 'was said to be a Christian'. This suggests some doubt, but in fact there is none.

53	5	Cronin, loc. cit., 219.

6 ibid., 229. Dr. Joseph Needham, in *Science and Civilization in China* (London, vol. I, 1954), 149, agrees that this was a remarkable achievement, in view of the lost tradition of early Chinese mathematics. He tells us further that Hsü Kuang-ch'i wrote a learned book on agriculture. Dr. Needham writes generally in somewhat unsympathetic terms of the Jesuits' Chinese converts, so his appreciation here is the more noteworthy.

7 Huc, loc. cit., 211.

54 8 ibid., 212.

9 Cronin, loc. cit., 266.

10 Huc, loc. cit., 246–7.

11 Rowbotham, loc. cit., 67. cf. Cronin, loc. cit., 276. And consult the useful book by Rachel Attwater, *Adam Schall* (London, 1963).

55 12 Rowbotham, loc. cit., 73.

13 Pannikar, loc. cit., 396.

14 P. Couplet, *Histoire d'une dame Chrétienne de la Chine* (etc.) (for full title, see Bibl.) (Paris, 1688). Père Couplet was 'Procureur-Général' of the Jesuits in China at the time.

15 Couplet, loc. cit., 7. (Many authorities have mistakenly referred to this lady as 'daughter' of Paul Hsü—e.g. Rowbotham, loc. cit., 310; Latourette (1929), 91. But it seems clear that she was his granddaughter. See the section on Hsü Kuang-ch'i by J. C. Yang in A. W. Hummel (Ed.), *Eminent Chinese of the Ch'in Period, 1644–1912* (2 vols, U.S. Govt. Printing Office, 1943), I, 316–19. Also P. d'Elia, loc. cit., II, 252–3.)

56 16 Couplet, loc. cit., 73.

17 ibid., 23.

18 Huc uses the phrase *Co-lao*, which he translates 'Prime Minister'. This is the French missionaries' way of rendering the fact that Hsü was made Grand Secretary of the Tung-ko in 1632, and in 1633 Grand Secretary of the Wên-yûan ko (Hummel, loc. cit.). Hsü died a few months after this.

19 Couplet, loc. cit., 23.

57 20 Huc was writing in about 1850; his generalizations about Chinese characteristics are typical of European writers of that time. Ricci would never have written such a sentence.

21 Huc, loc. cit., 309–10.

22 ibid., 212.

58 23 ibid., 310–11. Hsü was posthumously awarded the honorary title of 'Junior Guardian' (changed in 1643 to 'Grand Guardian') of the Heir Apparent, and 'canonized' as Wên-ting. (The relationship between his titles is as follows: the highest government body in China was the *Nei Yuan*, or *Nei Ko*, i.e. Imperial Chancery or Grand Secretariat. Its members were called *Ta Hsüeh Shih* (Grand Secretaries) or more popularly *Ko-lao* (see n. 18, above). But when Paul became

Grand Secretary of the *Wên-yûan-ko*, this made him, in effect, the first man in China after the monarch himself. See G. H. Dunne, *Generation of Giants* (London, 1962), 58, 220.

58	24	See n. 15 on p. 55, above.
	25	See Appendix 2, below, p. 315.
	26	Couplet, loc. cit., 8–9.
59	27	ibid., 25–6.
60	28	cf. the accusation against the Jesuits, referred to on p. 60, above.
61	29	Couplet, loc. cit., 42–3; and see Appendix 3, below, p. 315.
62	30	ibid., 65 ff.
	31	ibid., 67.
63	32	ibid., 71–2.
	33	Couplet, loc. cit., 117.
64	34	ibid., 114. A fine illustration of the lady in this dress forms the frontispiece of Couplet's book.
	35	ibid., 35–6.
	36	P. d'Elia, *Catholic Native Episcopacy in China* (Shanghai, 1927), 31–2.
	37	Couplet, loc. cit., 146.

CHAPTER 5

Page	Note	
65	1	Boxer (1951, loc. cit.), 79.
	2	ibid., 81.
	3	ibid., 84.
66	4	ibid., 85.
67	5	Léon Besse, *La Mission au Maduré* (Trichinopoly, 1916), 680–1.
	6	ibid., 682.
	7	ibid., 724.
68	8	L. M. Zaleski, *The Martyrs of India* (Mangalore, 1913), 233.
70	9	Pierre Dahmen, *Devasagayam, un Martyr de Travancore* (Xaveriana, 9e séries, no. 100, April, 1932, Louvain), 129.
71	10	L. Besse, loc. cit., 724 f.
	11	L. Besse, *Fr. Breschi, his Life and his Works* (Trichinopoly, 1918), 250.
	12	ibid., 96.
	13	R. Caldwell, *Records of the Early History of the Tinnevelly Mission* (London, 1881), 32.
	14	ibid., 47.
	15	ibid., 151.
72	16	R. D. Paul, *Chosen Vessels* (Madras, 1961), 30 (quoting C. F. Schwartz, *Remains* (London, 1826)).
	17	ibid., 31.
73	18	ibid., 28.
	19	*S.P.C.K. Report* (London, 1792), 110–11.
74	20	Sattianaden, *Sermon* (London, 1792), 9.

75	21	ibid., 13.
	22	Caldwell, loc. cit., 69.
	23	ibid., 101.
76	24	ibid., 121 f.
	25	ibid., 34 f.
	26	J. Hough, *A History of Christianity in India* (London, 1845), III, 678–9. (But Hough rejects the criticism. He points out that the main reason for the success of Christianity here was 'the general prevalence of the same *caste* in the parts where the Gospel was chiefly preached.')
	27	Caldwell, loc. cit., 76 f.
77	28	Cited in Caldwell, 42.
	29	ibid., 82.

CHAPTER 6

Page	Note	
78	1	C. P. Groves, *The Planting of Christianity in Africa* (4 vols, London, 1948), I, 128 f. Also T. Ohm, *Les principaux Faits de l'Histoire des Missions* (Paris, 1961), 78.
	2	F. Coillard, *On the Threshold of Central Africa* (English trans., London, 1902), 44.
79	3	See the photograph of Queen Mokwaë, with slaves bringing food, in Coillard, loc. cit., opp. 212.
80	4	ibid., 214.
	5	ibid., 215.
	6	ibid., 216.
81	7	ibid., 311–12.
	8	ibid., 334.
	9	ibid., 360.
	10	ibid., 350.
82	11	ibid., 397.
	12	ibid., 421–3, and footnote.
	13	ibid., 433.
	14	ibid., 337.
83	15	ibid., 563.
	16	Cited in R. Allier, *La Psychologie de la Conversion chez les Peuples non-civilisés* (2 vols, Paris, 1925), I, 407. (I am grateful to Bishop Stephen Neill for drawing my attention to this book. Coillard's *Threshold* ends with his farewell to Africa in 1896. We are fortunate in having Allier's book to continue the account from there. Allier draws on the archives of the *Journal des Missions évangéliques* of the Paris Evangelical Missionary Society.)
84	17	Allier, loc. cit., I. 409.
	18	L. H. Gann, *A History of Northern Rhodesia* (London, 1964), 72.
	19	ibid., 82.
85	20	Allier, loc. cit., 410–11.
	21	ibid., 413.
86	22	ibid., II, 201–2.

CHAPTER 7

Page   Note
87   1   F. Parkman, *The Conspiracy of Pontiac* (Toronto, 1898), *Works* Vol. X, part I, 77.

        2   F. Parkman, *Count Frontenac*, *Works* Vol. V, 396.

        3   Experience Mayhew, *Indian Christians* (London, 1727), 221.

        4   ibid., xiv.

88   5   David Brainerd, *Journal*, 20 September 1744 and 9 May 1745, (given in Jonathan Edwards, *The Life of David Brainerd* (Extracts, edited John Wesley (Dublin, 1812), 131–2, 178–182).

89   6   Mayhew, loc. cit., 45–6.

90   7   ibid., 49.

        8   R. H. Pearce, loc. cit., 31 (quoting *Maine Historical Soc. Coll*, 1889, Series 2, IV, 294).

        9   Mayhew, loc. cit., Introduction.

        10   ibid., 50–1.

91   11   ibid., 50.

        12   ibid., 52.

        13   R. I. Burns, loc. cit., 74.

92   14   F. Parkman, *Count Frontenac*, *Works* Vol. V, 396–7 and n.

        15   F. Parkman, *The Jesuits in North America*, *Works* Vol. II, 450 (quoting Ragueneau, *Relation des Hurons*, 1646, 58).

        16   ibid., 417–18.

        17   T. J. Campbell, *The Jesuits* (London, 1921), 337 f.

        18   Thomas Hughes, *History of the Society of Jesus in North America* (London, 3 vols, 1917), II (1645–1773), 337–9.

93   19   We find 'Kateri Tekakwitha', 'Cateri Tegakwitha', 'Catherine Tegakouita'. 'Kateri Tegaquitha' is the name given in a recent scholarly work by an anthropologist of the University of California, W. H. Oswalt, *This Land was Theirs* (New York, 1966), 399.

        20   Oswalt, loc. cit., 401.

        21   Parkman, *Works* Vol. II, 73–4, and notes.

        22   Daniel Sargent, *Catherine Tekakwitha* (London, 1937), chap. III.

95   23   Oswalt, loc. cit., 443.

        24   ibid., 417.

        25   Sargent, loc. cit., chap. VIII.

99   26   F. Parkman, *The Discovery of the West* (1869; new edition, London, 1962), 196.

The Decree declaring Kateri Tegaquitha 'venerable' was of 13 October 1961.

In addition to the sources given above, I have used: the letters of P. Cholenec, S.J., in *Lettres édifiantes et curieuses*, VI (Paris, 1781), 40–100.

P. Edouard Lecompte, S.J., *Catherine Tekakwitha, Une Vierge Iroquoise* (Montreal, 1927).

Maurice Vaussard (Ed.), *The Golden Legend Overseas* (1931), 53–60.

CHAPTER 8
Page *Note*
101 1 Anon, *The Catholic Church in Korea* (Hong Kong, 1924), 17.
102 2 ibid., 18.
3 A. Choi, *L'Érection du premier Vicariat . . . en Korée* (see above p. xii, note 1), 9, (citing Yi Neung-hoa, *Histoire du Christianisme et de la Diplomatie coréenne* (Seoul, 1927), 51). (I am indebted to Bishop Richard Rutt, of Taëjon, for the reference to Choi's book.)
4 Choi, loc. cit., 22 ff.
103 5 ibid., Appendix, 97–9, (citing original in *Propaganda Fide*, S.O.R. f. 457, which Choi was the first to consult).
6 ibid., Appendix, 106–8.
108 7 Charles Dallet, *Histoire de l'Église de Corée* (2 vols, Paris, 1874), II, 266–79.
111 8 ibid., 287–9. (Kim wrote this account in Latin.)
114 9 M. Trollope, *The Church in Korea* (London, 1915), 122.
10 *The Catholic Church in Korea* (Anon), 101.

CHAPTER 9
Page *Note*
116 1 A. Olichon, *Aux Origines du Clergé Chinois: le Prêtre André Ly* (Paris, 1933). Y. C. Wang, loc. cit., 33, quotes a Chinese authority, Hao Fang, in 1932, for the following figures, which are not likely to be slanted favourably towards the Church: 100 in 1596; 2,000 in 1608; 150,000 in 1650.
2 Fr. Launay says that in Szechwan there were said to be 4,000 Christians in 1756; 25,000 in 1792; and 40,000 in 1801. (Launay, *Histoire générale de la Société des Mission Étrangères* (Paris, 1894), II, 393.)
3 Olichon, loc. cit., 82.
117 4 André Ly, *Diarium* (Journal), A. Launay (Ed.) (Paris, 1906), 299. This is the famous diary kept in Latin, 1746–63, and communicated seriatim to his superiors in the *Missions Étrangères;* it was preserved in their archives, and edited for publication, in the original Latin, by Adrien Launay.
118 5 ibid., 399–40.
6 ibid., 221. ('The Chinese are proud, inconstant, ungrateful, and so are not worthy of Holy Orders.')
7 Olichon, loc. cit., 128 (quoting a letter of Mgr. Le Blanc, Vicar Apostolic of the Province).
119 8 *Diarium,* 505.
120 9 Olichon, loc. cit., 172 ff.
10 ibid., 224.
121 11 ibid., 228. (citing Launay, *Histoire de la Mission de Se-Tchouan* (Paris, 1903), 238 f.).
12 *Diarium,* 326.
13 Olichon, loc. cit., 236 (and see Appendix 4, below, p. 316).
122 14 Both of these in *Diarium,* 29.
21—(24pp.)

122	15	ibid., 265–6.
123	16	Olichon, loc. cit., 311.
	17	*Diarium*, 3 August 1748.
	18	ibid., 325.
124	19	ibid., 280.
	20	ibid., 34.
	21	ibid., 58.
	22	ibid., 204.
125	23	ibid., 97–8.
	24	ibid., 97–8.
126	25	ibid., 181.
127	26	ibid., 297.
	27	ibid., 522.
128	28	Olichon, loc. cit., 394 (from a letter to M. de Lalande in the Archives of the *Missions Étrangères*).
129	29	*Diarium*, 677.
	30	ibid., 59.
130	31	Launay, in Introduction to *Diarium*, ii, iv–v.
	32	Olichon, loc. cit., 406.

The two main sources for chapter 9 are those given above: Ly's *Diarium* and the book by Olichon, who was Apostolic Protonotary, and Director of the *Union Missionnaire du Clergé Français*. Launay's 3 vol. *History of the Société des Missions Étrangères* is always valuable. Olichon also refers to Launay's *Histoire de la Mission de Se-Tchouan* (1903); to Servière's *Les anciens Missions de la Compagnie de Jésus en Chine* (1924); to Degert, *Histoire des Seminaires français jusqu'à la Révolution* (Paris, 1912); and to Otto Maas, *Las Misiones franciscanas en Chine* (1933). I have not found any of these in English libraries.

CHAPTER 10

Page	Note	
136	1	J. E. Tennant, *Christianity in Ceylon* (London, 1850), 72.
	2	S. G. Perera, *The Life of the Ven. Father Joseph Vaz* (Colombo, 1942, 2nd ed., 1953), 69.
137	3	Perera, loc. cit., 78.
	4	ibid., 78 (quoting Robert Knox, *An Historical Relation of the Island of Ceylon* (London, 1681).
138	5	ibid., 152.
139	6	ibid., 142–3 (quoting the 'Neville Collection'—*Vijitavelle Rajavalia* MS in the British Museum).
140	7	ibid., 195.
	8	Tennant, loc. cit., 96 f.
141	9	Perera, loc. cit., 223–4.
	10	ibid., 255.

For sources for chapter 10 I have drawn extensively on Fr. Perera's *Life of Vaz*. Tennant is also useful. For the problem of the *padroado*, E. R. Hull's *Bombay Mission History* (2 vols, Bombay, 1930) contains much out-of-the-way information.

Charles Gasbarri, *A Saint for the New India* (Bombay, 1960), says that 'the veneration in which Fr. Vaz is held and the graces received from him fill 1,300 pages which constitute the process for his beatification. . . . A petition with 2,000 signatures was handed to Pius XII, with a test of the Process' (199). I am indebted to the Jesuit Library in Farm St. for this book.

CHAPTER 11

Page	Note	
151	1	I owe this curious piece of information to H. McAleavy, *Black Flags in Vietnam* (London, 1968), 56.
152	2	Fr. Paul Sato, who instructed Seodzi and later baptized him, must have been a priest well before 1892, when this autobiography of Seodzi was published. Bishop Stephen Neill states that the two first Japanese converts to Orthodoxy, Paul Sawabe and John Sakai, 'were ordained at the first Synod in 1895', (*A History of Christian Missions* (London, 1964), 446). Thomas Ohm, however (loc. cit., 1961), gives 1875 as the date of the ordination of the first Japanese Orthodox priest; so clearly Paul Sato was earlier than those mentioned by Bishop Neill, and if Ohm's dates are correct Sawabe and Sakai cannot have been the first.
	3	Numbers given in S. Neill, loc. cit., 446.
	4	Walter Kolarz, *Religion in the Soviet Union* (London, 1961), 47.
	5	*Japanese Christian Year Book*, 1962.
153	6	Sergei Seodzi, *How I became a Christian* (St. Petersburg, 1892), on which this chapter is based. I am deeply grateful to Dr. N. Zernov for telling me about, and loaning me, this rare book, and I am no less grateful to the Rev. Eric Rowland for translating it from the Russian. There is no English edition.

CHAPTER 12

Page	Note	
154	1	See note, Appendix 5, below, p. 316, concerning Reichelt, *The transformed Abbot, Miao-Chi* (London, 1954).
155	2	A. C. Moule, *Christians in China before the Year 1550* (London, 1930), 28–9, also John Foster, *Christianity in China under the T'ang Dynasty* (London, 1939), 35, 134–51, etc.
167	3	It is fair to say that the Christian notion of 'reserve in communicating religious truth' might be taken by some as similarly dishonest. The matter must be judged in its context.
168	4	For instance, the notion of a sort of trinity, developed by Hun Yen Ching in the *Avatamska Sutra*, by which the fundamental plan of the universe has three essential aspects: the *ti*—body, or model; the *hsiang*—image made manifest through revelation; and the *yung*—realization or activity (Reichelt, loc. cit., 128).

CHAPTER 13

Page	Note	
172	1	Basil Thomson, *The Diversions of a Prime Minister* (London, 1894), 342–3.
	2	ibid., 150–1.
173	3	John Martin, *An Account of the Natives of Tonga Islands, etc.* (London, 1827, 2 vols.). This fascinating book by a castaway has been used by all subsequent writers on Tongan history, language and ethnology.
	4	H. Luke, *Islands of the South Pacific* (London, 1962), 177–8.
174	5	ibid., 178.
	6	A. A. Koskinen, *Missionary Influence as a Political Factor in the Pacific Islands* (Helsinki, 1953), 38 n. (This important study is difficult to come by in England. I am indebted to the excellent library of the Selly Oak Colleges, Birmingham, for the loan of it.)
	7	ibid., 41.
175	8	Sarah S. Farmer, loc. cit., 210–11. (This charming book, though written for children, and from a totally uncritical point of view, does provide a valuable summary of contemporary records.)
176	9	Koskinen, loc. cit., 28–30 (quoting the report of two L. M. S. Missionaries at Raitea, 18 October 1821, in *Quarterly Chron. of Transactions of L.M.S.* II, 242).
	10	ibid., 30, (quoting L.M.S. *Qu. Chron.*, ibid., I. 231).
	11	G. C. Henderson, *Fiji and the Fijians* (London, 1931), 169.
	12	G. C. Findlay and W. W. Holdsworth, *History of the Wesleyan Methodist Missionary Society* (London, 1921, 5 vols.), III, 289.
	13	See Appendix 7, below, p. 317.
177	14	Findlay and Holdsworth, loc. cit., 298–9.
178	15	ibid., 300.
	16	Farmer, loc. cit., 253.
	17	ibid., 254.
	18	ibid., 243.
179	19	Findlay and Holdsworth, loc. cit., 306 n.
	20	Farmer, loc. cit., 334–5.
	21	Koskinen, loc. cit., 22–4.
180	22	Farmer, loc. cit., 262–3.
	23	Koskinen, loc. cit., 116.
	24	H. Bingham, *A Residence of twenty-one Years in the Sandwich Islands* (Hartford, Conn., 1849), 421.
	25	Farmer, loc. cit., 262–3.
	26	Koskinen, loc. cit., 120.
181	27	Thomas West, *Ten Years in South Central Polynesia* (London, 1863), 54 f, 58, 291 ff, 306, 325, 334 f.
182	28	Ruth Benedict, Introduction to B. Quain, *Fijian Village* (Chicago, 1948), ix–x.
	29	Quain, loc. cit., 23 (citing H. Pritchard, *Polynesian Reminiscences* (London, 1866), 294–6).

183	30	J. Waterhouse, *The King and People of Fiji* (London, 1866), 243–7.
	31	Quain, loc. cit., 22–3.
	32	Thomson, loc. cit., 16.
184	33	ibid., 7.
	34	Farmer, loc. cit., 249.
185	35	Thomson, loc. cit., 79–80.
	36	Findlay and Holdsworth, loc. cit., 411.
	37	H. Bingham, loc. cit., 284 (and Koskinen, loc. cit., 38).
	38	Findlay and Holdsworth, loc. cit., 352, 353 n.
	39	ibid., 346 n.
186	40	ibid., 411.
	41	Farmer, loc. cit., 412, 410.
	42	ibid., 412.
	43	Thomson, loc. cit., 205.
187	44	ibid., 365.
	45	ibid., 222.
	46	H. Luke, loc. cit., 189.
	47	Thomson, loc. cit., 250. (Thomson had prepared a draft of the 'Speech from the Throne' with tactful references to the stormy past—viz. to Baker's Premiership. The King demurred, and finally Thomson said: 'But why allude to the past?' 'And was it I who did so?' said the King, with a gently triumphant laugh; and they agreed to cut out the reference altogether.)
	48	ibid., 282.
	49	ibid., 63.
188	50	ibid., 249.
	51	ibid., 66. (and see Appendix 8, below, p. 317).
	52	E. E. V. Collocot, 'Notes on the Tongan Religion', in *Journal of the Polynesian Society*, (Wellington, N.Z.) XXX, ii. 235 (i. 159–61, and ii. 227–36, are also relevant).

CHAPTER 14

Page   Note

190	1	There is no scholarly life of St. Martin de Porrès (1579–1639) that I have come across.
	2	Fr. Buzy, *Life of the Servant of God, Sister Mary of Jesus Crucified*, English trans. (London, 1925). I have not seen the 2 vol. life of her by the Carmelite Fr. Lazarus, which is summarized by Réné Schwab in M. Vaussard, loc. cit., 176–205.
	3	Fr. Valerian, *The Servant of God, Fr. Cyriac Elias Chavara*, trans. from a biography published in the Malayalam language (Travancore, 1953), (and see Appendix 9, below, p. 318.).
191	4	K. C. Chacko, *Sister Alphonsa* (Trivandrum, 4th ed., 1956). (I am grateful to Fr. Bede Griffiths, OSB, for this and the previous biography.)
	5	A. Roche, *Bakhita, Pearl of the Sudan* (Langley, Bucks, 1964). (I am grateful to the Verona Fathers of Mirfield, Yorks, for this biography.)

192   6   A. Olichon, *Father Six*, English trans. (London, 1954). This is the main source for this life.

Olichon tells also that when a Coadjutor Bishop of West Tongking was consecrated in 1895 the cathedral was full, and the congregation became unruly at a delay in the Bishop's arrival. The Vicar-General, famous for his size and oratory, went into the pulpit to quieten them, but they ignored him. Père Six mounted the pulpit and raised his hand. At once all shouted 'The Kham-Sai! The Kham-Sai!' (Viceroy). He spoke in a soft voice, but there was complete silence.

George N. Curzon's account occurs in an article 'A Little Pope in Annam', in *The National Observer* (London and Edinburgh, 11 February 1893), pp. 313–14. The files of this rare magazine are only contained in six libraries in England; it had a chequered history, starting as the *Scots Observer* in 1888, changing its name four times, and ending, absorbed into the *British Review*, in 1897. I am grateful to the Manchester Public Library for access to it.

It is interesting that in *Informations Catholiques Internationales*, No. 153, 15 March 1963, there are two photographs juxtaposed, one of the new-style 'church of the Blessed Martyrs' at Hai Dang, Saigon; the other of Father Six's cathedral, Phat Diem, in the north. The contrast is striking: Fr. Six's is married to the locality, the other is an intruder.

The Bishop of Phat Diem, Le Huu Tu, was named adviser to the Ho Chi Minh Government in 1946, and the Viet Minh was studiously deferential to the indigenous and patriotic Catholic elements of the north at this time. (See E. J. Hammer, *The Struggle for Indo-China* (Stanford, 1954), 275–6.

193   7   Leslie T. Lyall, *John Sung* (London, 1954), 49. See also D. Bentley-Taylor, *The Weathercock's Reward* (London, 1967), 133 ff.

194   8   W. Knight, *The Missionary Secretariat of Henry Venn* (London, 1882), 416.

195   9   There is no full-scale life of Atiman, so far as I know. My source is a long article in *Grands Lacs* ('Revue Général des Missions d'Afrique') No. 188 (December 1956—January 1957). There is a children's biography of him (G. Nicoleau, *Atiman, le petit Esclave du Niger* (Paris, n.d.), but this seems to be based, word for word, on the above article. I am indebted to the White Fathers, Namur, for both of these sources. There is slight material on Atiman in G. D. Kittler, *The White Fathers* (London, 1957), 204–7.

CHAPTER 15

Page	Note	
196	1	See Appendix 10, below, p. 318.
198	2	A. van Leeuwen, *Christianity in World History* (London, 1964), 388.

198	3	J. A. Subhan, *How a Sufi Found his Lord* (Lucknow, n.d. [1942]); and see Appendix 10, below, p. 318.
	4	Mulla, 'Cheminements Spirituels', originally read at a philosophical symposium at Gallarate, Italy, then published in French under this title in the Jesuit monthly, *Études* (Paris), October 1959, 69–79.
	5	M. Blondel, *Letter on Apologetics*, English trans. (London, 1965), *passim*. (See also my article 'The Importance of Maurice Blondel' in *Prism* (London) September 1965.)
	6	Blondel, unpublished note, c. 1906–7. (This, and much other biographical material, is contained in the Bulletin of the Archbishopric of Aix, after Mgr. Mulla's death. I owe this copy to the kindness of M. l'Abbé G. Bry, of Aix-en-Provence; and for other material I am indebted to M. Jean Guitton of the Académie Française, and to Mme Charles Flory, daughter of the late Maurice Blondel.)
202	7	Paul Nagaï, *Les Cloches de Nagasaki* (Paris, 1962), 16 f.
	8	ibid., chaps. II and III.
	9	Paul Nagaï, *We of Nagasaki* (London, 1951), *passim*.
204	10	I am indebted for some of these details, not included in the two books listed above, to an article by Fr. Patrick Drummond in *The Far East*—the journal of the Maynooth Mission in China—September 1951. Fr. Michael O'Neill, of St. Columban's, Eire, kindly lent me this article and gave me information about Dr. Nagaï.
	11	Nagaï, loc. cit. (1951).
	12	ibid., 183.
	13	ibid., 190–2.
205	14	ibid., 200.
	15	Nagaï, loc. cit. (1962).
206	16	ibid., 23.
	17	ibid., 101.
	18	ibid., 168.
209	19	ibid., 152–6.
	20	(The above section appeared, at greater length, as an article in *Prism* (London) August 1963, No. 76. I am indebted to the Editor for permission to reprint this. (See also Appendix 11, below, p. 320.)

CHAPTER 16

Page	Note	
210	1	J. C. Winslow, *Narayan Vaman Tilak* (Calcutta, 1923).
	2	Lakshmibai Tilak, *I Follow After* (Madras, 1950).
	3	H. Ruedi-Weber, *Asia and the Ecumenical Movement* (London, 1966), 192.
	4	A. J. Appasamy, *Sundar Singh* (London, 1958) and refs. there.
212	5	B. Animananda, *Swami Upadhyay Brahmabandhav* (Calcutta, 1908), Part I, 15, and cf. Appendix 12, below, p. 321.

212   6   Animananda, loc. cit., 15–16.
213   7   E. R. Hull, loc. cit., II, 517–21 (citing Kemchand, bio-graphical note on Upadhyay).
214   8   Animananda, loc. cit., 25.
        9   E. R. Hull, loc. cit., (citing Kemchand).
217   10   In *Review of Reviews* (London, 15 July 1903).
218   11   *The Tablet* (London, 3 January 1903), 7–9.
       12   ibid. (31 January 1903), 164–5.
       13   ibid. (14 February 1903), 258–9.
       14   Animananda, loc. cit., 52 (and see Appendix 13, below, p. 321).

CHAPTER 17
Page   Note
222   1   Y. C. Wang, loc. cit., 93.
        2   Called 'Shu King-Shen' in Dom Pierre-Célestin Lou, *Ways of Confucius and of Christ* (London, 1948; English trans. of *Souvenirs et Pensées*, 1945).
223   3   ibid., 12.
225   4   ibid., 51.
        5   John C. Wu, *Fountain of Justice* (London, 1959).
        6   Lou, loc. cit., 120.
226   7   ibid., 121.
        8   Jesse Page, *The Black Bishop* (London, 1908).
227   9   ibid., 71.
       10   J. F. A. Ajayi, *Christian Missions in Nigeria, 1841–1891* (London, 1965), 208.
       11   F. D. Walker, *The Romance of the Black River* (London, 1933), 130.
228   12   Ajayi, loc. cit., 127–8.
       13   ibid., 214.
       14   ibid., 225.
       15   D. A. C. Crowther, *Charge*, cited in Harry Sawyer, 'Christian Evangelistic Strategy in West Africa', in *Internat. Rev. of Missions*, IV, 215, July 1965.
229   16   E. A. Ayendale, *The Missionary Impact on Modern Nigeria, 1842–1914* (London, 1966), 88.
       17   ibid., 212–13.
230   18   e.g. Eugene Stock, *History of the Church Missionary Society* (London, 1899), III, 394–6; Latourette, loc. cit. (1943), V, 436–7; S. Neill, loc. cit. (1964), 377–8.
       19   Ajayi, loc. cit., 180–1.
       20   Neill, loc. cit., 377–8.
       21   J. B. Webster, *The African Churches among the Yoruba* (London, 1964), 39–40.
231   22   Ajayi, loc. cit., 247–8.
       23   Webster, loc. cit., 29.
       24   ibid., 41.
       25   Ajayi, loc. cit., 259–60.
232   26   J. Page, loc. cit., 236–7.

233	27	M. Lycet, *Brothers* (London, 1935), 14.
	28	C. E. Fox, *Lord of the Southern Isles* (London, 1958), 193.
234	29	H. A. Johnson, *Global Odyssey* (London, 1963), 308–9.
	30	Fox, loc. cit., 194.
235	31	Personal communication from Canon C. E. Fox, 21 December 1963; he worked for eleven years under Ini, as a member of the Brotherhood.
	32	M. Mead, *New Lives for Old* (London, 1956), 450 ff.
236	33	R. Firth, *Tikopia Ritual and Belief* (London, 1967), 356.
	34	ibid., 357–8.
237	35	H. A. Johnson, loc. cit., 310.

CHAPTER 18

Page	Note	
239	1	For the whole movement, cf. H. H. Bancroft, *History of Central America* (San Francisco, 1882–7), II, 697–705 (Works, Vol. VII). For an even more syncretistic, though respectable, Indian mixture of Christianity and paganism, see O. La Farge, *Santa Eulalia* (Chicago, 1947). The cult is proudly national and xenophobic, and combines Catholic external practices with Mayan ritual and legend (see esp. pp. 69 ff.).
241	2	R. B. Cunninghame Graham, *A Brazilian Mystic* (London, 1920), based on a Portuguese biography of Euclydes da Cunha (English trans. 1943), which I have also consulted.
242	3	Bancroft, *History of Mexico* (San Francisco, 1883–8), (Works, Vol. XII) 103–4.
	4	H. Herring, *History of Latin America* (London, 1954), 254 ff.
243	5	J. Lloyd Mecham, *Church and State in Latin America* (North Carolina, 1934), 60. (The same was true of the Independence Movement in the Argentine: in La Plata many priests and religious assisted the revolution, and after mass used to read to the people articles declaring the principles of the Revolution (ibid., 59).
244	6	Bancroft, loc. cit. (1883–8), 295 f.
	7	Herring, loc. cit., 257.
	8	Bancroft, ibid., 622.
245	9	cf. *Camilo Torres, Priest and Revolutionary*, ed. Garcia and Calle (London, 1969).
	10	J. M. Cavanna Y Manso, *Rizal and the Philippines of his Day* (Manila, 1957), 122.
246	11	G. F. Fabella, *Rizal the Historian and other Historical Essays* (Quezon, 1960), 73.
247	12	José Rizal, *The Social Cancer* (New York, 1912), and *Noli Me Tangere* (Manila, 1957).
	13	It may seem strange that an old priest (Gomez) of eighty-five should have been executed with the two young men. But his age has been checked with Philippine historians. (Personal communication.)

247 14 This, and much else, comes from R. Palma, *José Rizal, the Pride of the Malay Race* (New York, 1947), 94, etc.

249 15 Palma, loc. cit. Also C. Derbyshire, Introduction to Rizal, *The Social Cancer* (1912), for the view that the whole story was an invention of the Jesuits. Cavanna, loc. cit., maintains, on the other hand, that the evidence for its genuineness is incontestable (222).

250 16 Cavanna, loc. cit., 100–1.

     17 Achutegui and Bernard, *Religious Revolution in the Philippines* (Manila, 1960), I, 25–6.

     18 Palma, loc. cit., 371–4.

251 19 R. L. Wishlade, *Sectarianism in Southern Nyasaland* (London, 1965), 47–8.

     20 ibid., 135–6.

     21 Shepperson and Price, *Independent African* (Edinburgh, 1958); G. S. Mwase, *Strike a Blow and Die!* (Harvard, 1967).

253 22 Mwase, loc. cit., 48–50.

254 23 Shepperson and Price, loc. cit., 358.

     24 Mwase, loc. cit., 25–6.

255 25 Efraim Andersson, *Messianic Popular Movements in the Lower Congo* (Uppsala, 1958), 50.

     26 ibid., 54–5 (quoting an African witness).

256 27 M-L. Martin, *Prophetic Christianity in the Congo* (Johannesburg, 1969), 4.

258 28 J. Chomé, *La Passion de Simon Kimbangu* (Paris, 2nd ed., 1960), 58–9.

260 29 M-L. Martin, loc. cit., 37. (And see Appendix 14, below, p. 322.)

     30 ibid., 19.

261 31 E. Holt, *The Strangest War* (New York, 1962), 61.

265 32 Joan Metge, 'Christ and Culture', in *South East Asia Journal of Theology* (Singapore), vol. 8, no. 3, 1967, pp. 25, 31.

     33 J. Henderson, *Ratana, the Man, the Church, the Political Movement* (Wellington, N.Z., 1963), 104. I have used this book widely; and also the appropriate sections of *An Encyclopaedia of New Zealand* (Wellington, 1966).

     34 Cited in Flavia Anderson, *The Rebel Emperor* (London, 1958), 278.

267 35 H. McAleavy, loc. cit., 64.

271 36 Jane R. Edkins, *Chinese Scenes and People* (London, 1863), 264. (This narrative of her husband's visit to Nanking is the source for all this section.)

     37 ibid., 275.

272 38 ibid., 287.

     39 ibid., 299.

273 40 E. R. Hughes, loc. cit., 66–8.

     41 E. P. Boardman, *Christian Influence upon the Ideology of the Taiping Rebellion* (Wisconsin, 1952), and see Appendix 15, below, p. 323).

     42 ibid., 107.

274	43	ibid., 117.
	44	ibid., 113.
	45	ibid., 95, n. 101.
	46	ibid., 77.
275	47	ibid., cited p. 38, fn. 6.
	48	ibid., 121.
278	49	J. Goforth, *A Chinese Christian General* (London, [1919]), 11.
	50	E. E. Chubb, *Twentieth Century China* (Columbia, 1964), 127–8.
	51	J. E. Sheridan, *Chinese Warlord* (Stanford, 1966), 115.
280	52	B. Martin, *Strange Vigour* (London, 1944), 225–6.
281	53	Dom Celestin-Lou, loc. cit.
	54	M. Broomhall, *General Feng—a good Soldier of Christ Jesus* (London, 1923), 51.
282	55	Goforth, loc. cit., 4.
	56	ibid., 7.
	57	Sheridan, loc. cit., 285–93. (and see Appendix 16, below, p. 323).

CHAPTER 19

Page Note

283	1	V. Purcell, *The Boxer Uprising* (London, 1963), 131–4 (quoting Wên Ch'ing (this is the Mandarin form of his name; the Hokkien form is 'Dr. Lim Boon-ken'); work of 1901).
284	2	B. Quain, loc. cit., 22–3.
	3	Koskinen, loc. cit., 118.
	4	E. Fourcadier, *La Vie Héroïque de Victoire Rasoamanarivo* (Paris, 1937; 2nd ed., 1948), 46 ff.
	5	C. W. Forman, art. in W. C. Harr, *Frontiers of the Christian World Mission since 1938* (New York, 1962), 138–9.
285	6	E. R. Hull, loc. cit., II, 427–9.
	7	Boardman, loc. cit., 66. Dr. Boardman points out that the Gutzlaff translation (1847) of Leviticus xix, 4 translates 'idols' by $p'u$-s-a, which is also the Chinese abbreviation for Bodhisattva. The Biblical use of the word $p'u$-s-a was, he suggests, helpful as it could justify the destruction of Bodhisattvas in temples.
286	8	C. R. Hensman, *China—Yellow Peril?—Red Hope?* (London, 1968), 55.
	9	David B. Barrett, 'A.D. 2,000: 350 million Christians in Africa', in *International Review of Missions*, Vol. LIX, No. 233, January 1970.
287	10	Y. C. Wang, *Chinese Intellectuals in the West*, North Carolina, 1966), 314.
	11	ibid., 335–6.
	12	Mao Tse-Tung, *Selected Works* (London, 1954), II, 337–8. Also *Thoughts of Chairman Mao* (Peking, 1967), Sect. 17, 171–2, 21 December 1939. Bethune was in the Eighth Army, a Canadian Communist.

288 13 e.g. A. van Leeuwen, loc. cit.; Harvey Cox, *The Secular City* (London, 1966); C. F. von Weizsäcker, *The Relevance of Science* (London, 1964).

14 M. M. Thomas, *The Christian Response to the Asian Revolution* (London, 1966), 122 (citing Jayaprakash Narain, *Socialism, Sarvodaya, and Democracy* (Bombay, 1964).

289 15 G. Spiller, *Inter-racial Problems* (London, 1911), 346. (There were also papers, at this 'Universal Races Congress', by other eminent non-white scholars, such as Dr. J. Tengo Jabavu, or Dr. W. E. B. Du Bois of New York, as well as Africanists such as Sir Harry Johnston.)

290 16 Leslie A. Fiedler, *The Return of the Vanishing American* (London, 1968), 174.

17 Leonard Cohen, *Beautiful Losers* (Toronto/Montreal, 1966), 211.

18 ibid., 3–4.

291 19 W. Freytag, *Spiritual Revolution in the East* (London, 1946), 85–6. See also Dr. Debrunner's study of Christian Missions in Togoland, in which he shows, with detailed evidence, that it was through the Ewe Evangelical Church that the Ewe became conscious of 'nationhood'. (H. Debrunner, *A Church between Colonial Powers* (London, 1965), 120–2.)

20 Cited in Murao and Murray Walton, *Japan and Christ, a Study in Religious Issues* (London, 1928), 42.

292 21 Ren, *A tamarisk Garden, blessed with Rain* (autobiography of Pastor Ren, trans. Taylor and Broomhall (London, 1930), 34).

22 F. M. Lufuluabo, *Vers une Théodicée Bantoue*, (Louvain, 1961), and *La Notion Luba-Bantoue de l'Être* (ibid., 1964); Anon, *Des Prêtres noirs s'interrogent*, (Paris, 1957).

23 B. Onuoha, *The Elements of African Socialism* (London, 1965).

24 R. Pannikar, *The Unknown Christ of Hinduism* (London, 1964).

25 A. Chih, *L'Occident 'Chrétien' vu par les Chinois vers la fin du XIXe Siècle, 1870–1900* (Paris, 1962).

293 26 See transcriptions of conference in Bangkok, 'Bangkok, Rencontre Monastique', *Rythmes du Monde* (Bruges, 1969), vol. XVII, nos. 1–2.

27 A. R. Cook, *Uganda Memoirs, 1897–1940* (Kamapala, 1945), 164.

28 A. R. Tucker, *Eighteen Years in Uganda and East Africa* (London, 1911), 309–11.
(I owe the reference to Rachel—'Lakeri'—and, indeed, much else) to Canon John V. Taylor of the C.M.S. See also his *The Growth of the Church in Uganda* (London, 1956).

APPENDIXES

(1) *page 1, note, 2.*
Sun Yat-sen, *The Triple Demism*, §945–6, pp. 511–12:
'The more civilization progresses the more complex does the question of clothing become. . . . The men of primitive times . . . had an abundant growth of hair upon their body; that hair was the "natural clothing" of mankind. . . . With garments of animal skin as clothing, the hair of the body gradually lost its function and disappeared. . . . Savages and men whose civilization is still young still have much hair upon the body. Compare the Chinese with the Europeans; the body of the Europeans has much more hair than that of the Chinese; the reason is that the Europeans have not yet attained the degree of natural evolution reached by the Chinese.'
The Editor suggests that these remarks (made in 1924) were perhaps 'to amuse his audience', since Sun Yat-sen, as a Bachelor of Medicine, must have known them to be unscientific. But there are no signs of humour in the passage.

(2) *page 58, note 25*
There is a curious example of confession through a third party in one of the *Lettres Édifiantes*, written not by the Jesuits but by the French *Missions Étrangères* priests. It was written in 1703 by Père de Chavagnac about the mission in China:
'Je me souviens d'un expédient que trouve la femme d'un mandarin peu de jours après mon arrivé dans cette ville [Foun-tcheou-fou]. Comme elle ne pouvoit être entendue du missionnaire à qui elle vouloit se confesser, elle fit venir son fils aîné, et elle lui découvrit ses péchés, afin qu'il en fît le détail au confesseur et qu'il lui redît ensuite les avis et les instructions qu'elle en auroit reçus. Trouveroit-on en Europe ces exemples de simplicité et de ferveur?' (*Choix de Lettres Édifiantes* (Bruxelles, 1838), II, 260–1.) The Sacrament of Penance administered through the intermediary of one's own son is certainly an edifying, if desperate, expedient.

(3) *page 61, note 29*
The Abbé Huc says blandly on the subject of Chinese Rites:
'One day they invited Fr. Ricci to a sort of solemn sacrifice that they were about to celebrate in the temple of Confucius, and he had made no objection to be present, imagining that the honours rendered to the great philosopher of China were of a purely civil character. Doubtless, however, he was mistaken, for Rome subsequently came

to a contrary decision, and condemned these practices.' (Huc, *Christianity in China* (London, 1857), II, 137.)

The abbé was not to know that Rome would reverse the decision in 1939 and vindicate Ricci.

(4) page 121, note 13

In an article of the *Revue Historique des Missions* we are told that when Gregory Lô, the first Chinese bishop, ordained three Chinese priests, the bishop made use of the Pope's permission and said Mass in Chinese; but the three priests insisted on saying Mass in Latin— without understanding a word of what they were saying. A European priest said: 'I have assisted at Mass said by one of these. He sweated, was in an agony of mind, and those present were equally put out and irritated. God knows how many faults and mistakes he made, all hot and bothered as he was, reciting parrot-like what he could not understand' (9 October 1688). They apparently always said a Requiem Mass—presumably one was as much as they could manage to learn—even on Easter Day! During Paschal time the alleluias would be liberally sprinkled throughout. It was axiomatic, of course, in those days that a Mass would not be valid unless every consonant of the Canon were correctly pronounced. (Article cited in Columba Carey-Elwes, *China and the Cross* (London, 1957).)

(5) page 154,　The transformed Abbot

The account of Miao-Chi's life comes entirely from Karl Reichelt's book. This English translation, which is also an abridgement, is made from Reichelt's *Fromhetstyper og Helligdommer i Ost-Asia* (Oslo). One of the translators, H. F. Wickings, has this note on Dr. Reichelt:

'Shortly after he wrote the Preface to the English edition, in 1952, Dr. Reichelt passed away in the Brotherhood he had established at Tao Feng Shan, Shatin, Hong Kong. He possessed great insight into Buddhism and its practices.' In fact, the 'Christian Study Centre on Chinese Religion and Culture', of which Dr. Reichelt was the inspiration, still functions at Shatin, and publishes Quarterly Notes, entitled *Ching Feng*.

Dr. Reichelt's book on Miao-Chi was, he says, based on notes made by him in their talks together; on Miao-Chi's own diaries, which he left to Reichelt when they met; on materials gathered from his fellow-monks in Formosa and China; on letters; on articles in the periodical he edited, *Ta-Kuang* ('Asia's Light'); and on talks with Dr. McClure of Formosa and other missionaries who knew and helped Miao-Chi. So this life cannot be described as the kind of 'one-source work' criticized in our introductory chapter.

(6) *page 157*
Canon M. A. C. Warren, who visited the remarkable community of *It-to-en* some years ago, at its centre a few miles outside Kyoto, tells me that it has rules as strict as those of a religious order; and that among their work the brothers clear out the night-soil from the houses in the neighbourhood, a task usually given by the Japanese to the most depressed members of society. And when the city of Nagoya was devastated some years ago by a hurricane it was the members of the *It-to-en* who were first on the scene.

(7) *page 176, note 13*
There is a charming account of Basil Thomson's meeting with this same Peter Vi in 1890:
'. . . the oldest native minister, and a contemporary of the king. He paid us a visit in a hand-cart . . . with a black coat over his *vala*, and a tall hat, carefully brushed the wrong way, upon his reverend head. The poor old gentleman had lost the use of his lower limbs and of part of his intellect; but he said a prayer over us, and went his way, leaving a vapour of respectability behind him which doubtless served to rehabilitate such disreputable politicians as we were believed to be.'
(B. Thomson, *The Diversions of a Prime Minister* (London, 1894), 58.)

(8) *page 188, note 51*
There seems to be no life of King George I Tupou, though there is plenty of material in the sources given in the notes, and elsewhere. The tributes to him, mentioned on p. 186, are perhaps worth giving, since they are not easily available. Sir Everard Home (Captain of H.M.S. *Calliope*) visited Tonga on 8 August 1852. Afterwards he wrote to King George:
'Sir, it gave me sincere pleasure yesterday, to see you in full and peaceable possession of your fort of Bea. . . . Glory as a Christian Prince attends your clemency to those who have fallen into your power. Grateful should they be to God that they are the subjects of so just and merciful a King. It gave me real pleasure to see the great and judicious exertions which you made for the welfare of your subjects, of all ages, when I was at Vavau, in 1844. These things I shall represent to the Government of the Queen of England, as well as the warm interest that was taken, under your immediate direction, and my own observation, for the safety of the Rev. M. Pieplu and the Rev. M. Nivelleau, priests of the Roman Catholic Religion, residing in the fort of Bea; for the security of the chapel and the ornaments it contained; as well as of the private property of those gentlemen, the total destruction of which by fire seemed to be inevitable, and must have followed without your exertions to prevent it.'

318 Patterns of Christian Acceptance

And John Elphinstone Erskine (Captain) who visited Tonga in August 1849, wrote afterwards, in his *Journal of a Cruise among the Islands of the West Pacific:*

'The King came on board in one of our boats. . . . No stipulation had been made with me . . . on the subject of honours to be paid to him; nor could the simple dignity of his manner have been excelled by the most powerful monarch, accustomed daily to such marks of respect . . . [referring to the salute of thirteen guns which the ship had given him]. George sat on a chair during dinner, and followed all our English customs. . . . [The King was shown round the ship] . . . and was much pleased when Mr. Miller, the gunner, exhibited the use of a diving-dress and helmet. . . . He [George] was easily made to understand the principle of the apparatus, and remarked, turning to his courtiers: "How useless is strength unaccompanied by wisdom!"'

(Farmer, *Tonga* (London, 1855), 411 f, 413 f.)

(9) *page 190, note 3*
The life of Fr. Cyriac Chavara, translated from a biography published in Malayalam language, has the note:

'With the approval of the Archbishop, he [Fr. Cyriac] wrote out clearly every minute detail of the Syrian rite as it is said today. He also laid down the exact procedure for High Mass, Solemn High Mass, Vespers, etc. He popularised the Syrian calendar for church services; the Office for the Dead was also codified by him. With the permission of the Holy See he translated the services for Holy Saturday from the Latin original and added it on to the Syrian Liturgy . . . incorporated in the Syrian missal.' (Valerian, *The Servant of God* (Travancore, 1953), Introduction p. vi.) In fact, however, they were not used in his time.

(10) *page 196, note 1*
Examples of prominent Muslims who became Christians, and whose lives are available are:

Henry Jessup. *Kamil* (Philadelphia, 1899).

Isaac Malek Yonan. *The Beloved Physician of Teheran* (Nashville, Tenn., 1934).

Marcus Abd-el-Masih, the Egyptian convert; baptized in Alexandria, 1907; ordained Pastor of the Evangelical Church of Egypt, 1922. *Moslem World*, vol. xxv, no. 3 (July 1945).

Hassan Dehqani-Tafti. *Design of My World* (London, 1959). Autobiography of the Persian (Iranian) convert, the first Persian to be consecrated Bishop of the Anglican Church, Iran, 1961.

J. A. Subhan. *How a Sufi found his Lord* (Lucknow, n.d.) [1942]. (See p. 198, above.) He was an Indian Muslim, of Mongol stock—his ancestors came to India with Ghengis Khan in the 13th–14th centuries. He was born in Calcutta, 1897, and destined to be a *maulvi*. He was strictly and legalistically Muslim, till he studied English. This led him back to the *Qu'ran*, and to dissatisfaction with mere Islamic ritual. He came across Muslim mysticism, *Sufi*, and this transformed him. He became a *Salik* (traveller) along the road towards Allah. Formerly he had cultivated the fear of God, the 'Night Avenger'; but now Allah became his Beloved. 'The practice of Dhikr (mental concentration in prayer) would often send me into a state of semi-unconsciousness. . . . It was a glorious privilege to desire nothing but Allah, to know nothing but Allah, to be aware of the existence of nothing but Allah.' Subhan moved on from there to Christianity; was baptized in 1912 in Calcutta; became a Roman Catholic in 1921, but left Roman Catholicism in 1925, for the Methodist Episcopal Church, Hyderabad—of which he became a bishop.

There is also a remarkable story of a Muslim in Northern Nigeria, told by Dr. Walter Miller of Zaria, adviser and friend of Lord Lugard.

Towards the end of the last century there was a Muslim *Malam* (teacher) in Kano, called Ibrahim. He functioned at court and was well-known to the Emir, Bello. As a student he knew the *Qu'ran* well. He made the pilgrimage to Mecca, but was disillusioned by what he found. He returned to Africa via Cairo and Medina, and on the way happened to hear a missionary preaching about Jesus at a street corner. He was intrigued, and began to study the *Tafsir* (exegesis of the *Qu'ran*) and meditate on it. He was struck by the contradiction between the lofty titles ('Word of God', 'Spirit—Breath—from God', etc.) given to *Isa* (Jesus) in the *Qu'ran*, and the hesitancy in the style of the passages referring to him. He began to ask 'Who is this of whom our own Prophet writes? Can this be a man like the others mentioned in the Sacred Book? Is not this a greater than all, greater even than Mahommed himself?'

He gathered a few round him. At first he was ignored by the orthodox in Kano, but as his movement grew the Emir sent for him. He defended himself: the Emir, knowing the *Qu'ran*, must have known of *Isa*, yet had kept the knowledge dark. Bello said it was unwise to discuss a matter which might harm Islam; but Ibrahim refused to keep silent, in spite of threats. He was finally impaled on a stake in the market place. He endured hours of agony before dying; and warned his disciples to flee to the boundaries of the three provinces (Zaria, Kano and Bauchi). He prophesied that God would one day reveal the true faith to them.

His followers fled, and many were killed; but one group held together under another leader who before his own death prophesied too that they would one day learn the truth about 'the prophet *Isa*', through strangers from the West. All this time they were loyal Muslims, and had never met a Christian.

But in 1913 Dr. Miller had been playing hockey with schoolboys at the mission when he noticed two strangers, young Hausa Muslims, watching and evidently wanting to speak. They were descendants of the group, living on the borders of Zaria, Bauchi and Kano, and had walked thirty-five miles. They had made inquiries, and then told their people: 'This is it: we have found it at last!'

They stayed a week, then disappeared. Dr. Miller thought they had gone for good. But soon two more arrived, and spoke of groups in villages ten, fifteen, twenty miles from each other, waiting for knowledge. The lay Christians in Kano undertook to visit these groups. So enthusiastic was their reception that a deputation asked whether land could be procured where all could live together as a community and receive instruction. Land was found, and a community of about 120 formed there. They started a sugar-cane industry; and (more remarkable) remained on good terms with their Muslim neighbours.

Alas, it was short-lived. In 1921–2 there was a severe outbreak of sleeping-sickness, and the village (Gimi) had to be abandoned, the greater part of its inhabitants having died. But the younger ones left and many received good education. Some of the descendants of this spontaneous Christian community were, and are, in responsible government posts.

See W. R. S. Miller, *Reflections of a Pioneer* (London, 1936), 106–19; Ayendale, *The Missionary Impact on Modern Nigeria* (London, 1966), p. 150—he calls it the '*ansa* movement'. For later information, see, *C.M.S. Report*, 1914–15, p. 51; 1915–16, p. 43; 1916–17, p. 30; 1917–18, p. 29; 1921–22, p. 20.

I owe the reference to Ibrahim's story to Canon J. V. Taylor, of C.M.S. It has been filled out for me by Canon M. A. C. Warren, as he heard it from Dr. Miller.

(11) *page 209, note 19*
There is a biography of Nagaï which I have not seen: J. Schilliger, *Saint of the Atom Bomb* (1955).

From correspondence with the Librarian of the Royal Society of Medicine in London, and Professor William C. Molony, Director of the Hematological Laboratory, Boston City Hospital, it appears that Dr. Nagaï's thesis was probably never published. There has been considerable research on atomic disease in Japan; but in the conditions immediately after the war, especially in Nagasaki where the medical school was largely destroyed, facilities were minimal for this type of work.

(12) *page 212, note 5*
Saccidânanda (or Sachchidanandan) has been described as:
'A classical formula from late Vedanta. It was preceded by the almost equivalent formula: *sat-cit-ananta* (infinity), attested from the time of the Upanishads (*Taittiriya Upan*). Shankara, in his commentary on the Aphorisms of the Brahman (*Brahma-Sutra*) of Bâdarâyana, established . . . that the *nirguna Brahman*, though it cannot be called *anandamaya* (the double sense of "abounding in happiness", and "constituted by happiness" is excluded), nevertheless really is in essence "happiness", as the Chandogya Upan. and the Taittirya Upan. have said.' So: 'For the *sannyâsi* who has received "illumination", the ultimate and indivisible (*akhanda*) simplicity of the Absolute can be named, by a reduplication, SAT (being), CIT (thought), ANANDA (blessedness). He knows that the Divinity does not *have*, but *is*, by essence, Existence, Intelligence, Happiness.' (Monchanin and Le Saux, *Ermites du Saccidânanda* (Paris, 1957), 176 and n.)

(13) *page 218, note 14*
The only material that I know of in English concerning Upadhyay is a section by S. N. Hay (Part 6, 'Modern India and Pakistan') in W. T. de Bary, Hay, Weiler, and Yarrow, *Sources of Indian Tradition* (Columbia, 1958) pp. 732–8. This gives a brief biography, and four very short extracts. There is also a brief quotation from *The Blade*, Swami Animananda's biography of Upadhyay, in Monchanin, loc. cit. It is surprising that this man who, whatever his faults, anticipated so much of the modern thinking about 'Hindu-Christian dialogue' should have remained in such obscurity. Since both Animananda's life of him, and Upadhyay's own work, *The Infinite and the Finite* (pub. by the Rev. Brother Joseph, S.J. (Trichinopoly, 1918) 3rd ed. revised) are so inaccessible, I shall give a few extracts here from the latter, which was a lecture given in Trichinopoly by Upadhyay in 1896.

He starts by saying that he will take the existence of God for granted, and not try to prove it; but try to expound His nature and relation to creatures. He will not appeal to scriptures—'the Vedas, the Puranas, the Bible or the Koran'—but 'only to reason, the common heritage of all'.

'Look at the myriad creatures: all are imperfect—we can predicate of all of them the particle "not". . . . By contrast, above the reign of negation we turn to that eternal abode where the Infinite Being reigns. . . . Here reigns the immutable "Is". "Is not" and "Cannot" can never approach there. . . . This Infinite Being is beyond the providence of "not"; He is full being.

'Sophists may say: but "God cannot forget Himself, cannot kill Himself, cannot create a space enclosed by a straight line". I answer:

"God cannot forget Himself" is equivalent to "God is not not-know-ledge", since forgetting means *no* knowledge. . . . What, again, is a space enclosed by two straight lines? It is impossible and cannot come under the category of being; it is nothing. If He creates, He must create beings: He cannot create non-beings. So all the nots of the sophists affirm the absolute positiveness of God in regard to His nature. . . .

'But how can He have consciousness, for that implies negation? I must go out of myself to know myself; the fact of my power being limited makes me conscious of some other power that limits it: to be conscious is to feel a negation. This philosophy has been propounded by Hamilton and Herbert Spencer. But Infinitude can have con-sciousness without being subject to limitation. By knowing Himself He knows all possible beings: the creature must go outside himself (to know), but God is not in need of going outside Himself.

'So, too, with love. It is a limitation in us: but God has no craving to satisfy: He Himself is love, and in loving Himself He loves all. . . .

'. . . [With regard to creation] Science has very little concern with efficient causality, which transfers from non-existence to exist-ence what was incapable of self-existence. Its chief concern is with changes and new appearances of things already existing. . . . The philosophy of existence is beyond the province of Science.'

Since this book was completed there has appeared *The Acknow-ledged Christ of the Indian Renaissance*, by M. M. Thomas (London, 1969). This has a short chapter on Upadhyay ('Brahmobandhav Upadhyay') which is both sympathetic and useful, drawing as it does on unpublished studies by Indian scholars. Mr. Thomas comes to the same conclusion as myself, that Upadhyay was a more orthodox Christian than he was thought to be at the time. Indeed he holds that Upadhyay was too anxious 'to press Indian thought into the Thomist mould' and that this was a limitation which prevented him from offering the required bridge between Indian thought and Christianity. He adds that Upadhyay's acceptance of the scholastic picture of nature and grace, with the latter as a supernatural 'extra', paved the way for his integration of the caste-system, unmodified, within the Christian scheme.

(14) *page 260, note 29*
Fr. Van Wing, S.J., wrote in 1954 that Kimbangu was visited by 'un prêtre catholique indigène' and was baptized by him (*Zaïre*, Revue Congolaise (Bruxelles, XII, 6, 1954), 581). In 1960 he cor-rected this: Kimbangu was not baptized by the priest, but by 'une autre personne qui, pour des raisons de sécurité, ne désire pas etre nommément désignée' (*Zaïre* (XIV, 1960), 234). Dr. M-L. Martin (see Bibliography) has more recently checked this story for the

second time, and it appears to be wholly legendary. Even the *soeurs religieuses* in charge of the hospital where Kimbangu died in 1951 said that 'il est resté méchant jusqu'à la fin'. (Personal communication, 26 May 1969.)

(15) *page 273*
Professor John Foster has argued, on the contrary, that his chief impression, on studying Hung's sources as well as his teaching, is 'how biblical it all is'. Of the collection of pamphlets (nine volumes) by Liang Fa which Hung studied, about a quarter were direct quotation from Holy Scripture; and there is no doubt that this study coloured much of Hung's thought. It is possible that if closer links could have been maintained between Christians and the rebels, the deterioration of the Taiping movement might have been halted. (See John Foster, 'The Christian Origins of the Taiping Rebellion', in *International Review of Missions*, vol. xi, no. 158 (April, 1951).) But Boardman (1952) seems to me right in concluding that the Biblical elements Hung assimilated were few, highly selective, and only tenuously Christian. Flavia Anderson (1958) makes out a good case —though she tells it in the rather too colourful terms of a heavenly drama—for the other Taiping leaders, especially Jen-Kan, the 'Shield Prince', and his continued closeness to central Christian teaching.

(16) *page 275*
James E. Sheridan's life of Feng Yü-hsiang, *Chinese Warlord* (Stanford, 1966), will now be the standard life. It is based on very wide reading, especially of original Chinese sources, and I have used it extensively. It is on the whole unsympathetic to Feng, especially to his moralistic Christianity, and on political matters seldom gives him the benefit of the doubt. Where it does appreciate his contribution, therefore, it is all the more to be heeded. It ought, however, to be added that those people I know who were acquainted with Feng speak of him warmly as a person of great integrity and courage.

In addition to the pamphlet by Dr. Goforth, and the small book by Broomhall (both uncritical, though useful factually), there is a life in English (1926) by Feng's one-time Chaplain-General, Marcus Ch'eng. I have not succeeded in finding this book in any English library; but it is said to be encomiastic without qualification, though, again, giving valuable historical evidence.

(17) *pages 226 and 291*
Dom Pierre-Célestin Lou was created titular Abbot of Blandin (Ghent, Belgium) before his death on 15 June, 1949. I am told that he continued to keep the memorial tablets of his Chinese

ancestors in his monastic cell at Saint-Andrée (Bruges) throughout
his time there, and to commemorate them with sticks of incense from
time to time. His collection of essays, published posthumously
under the title *La Rencontre des Humanités et la Découverte de l'Évangile*,
expresses the same attitude. In it he argues that the Chinese concept of filial devotion—and, indeed, the Chinese language and
script—provide an admirable basis for the Gospel.

(18) *page 280*
Professor Owen Lattimore, who knew Feng has just produced
evidence that Feng's death on board was certainly an accident and
in no way political. See the *Guardian* 21 October 1971, page 14,
col. 4.

BIBLIOGRAPHY

All the books referred to in the text and notes will be found here, together with a selection of others which I have consulted though not specifically cited. I have marked with one * or two ** stars those books which have been most extensively used or quoted.

ABD-EL-MASIH, 'Marcus' (the Egyptian Convert, baptized in Alexandria 1907, and ordained Pastor of the Evangelical Church of Egypt, 1922), *The Moslem World* (Hartford, Connecticut, July 1945).

ABRAHAM, W. E., *The Mind of Africa* (London, 1962).

ACHUTEGUI, PEDRO S. DE, and BERNARD, MIGUEL A., *Religious Revolution in the Philippines* (Life of Aglipayi) (2 vols., Manila, 1960).

AJAYI, J. F. A., *Christian Missions in Nigeria, 1841–1891* (London, 1965).

ALLIER, RAOUL, *La Psychologie de la Conversion chez les Peuples non-civilisés* (2 vols., Paris, 1925).

ANDERSON (née Giffard), FLAVIA, *The Rebel Emperor* (London, 1958).

ANDERSSON, EFRAIM, *Messianic Popular Movements in the Lower Congo* (Uppsala, Studia Ethnica Upsaliensia, XIV, 1958).

ANDERSSON, EFRAIM, *Churches at the Grass Roots* ('A Study in Congo-Brazzaville') (London, 1968).

ANIMANANDA, *Swami Upadhyay Brahmabandhav* (Calcutta, 1908).*

ANTONIO, W. V. D', and PIKE, F. B., *Religion, Revolution and Reform* (London, 1965).

APPASAMY, A. J., *Sundar Singh* (London, 1958).

APPASAMY, DEWADAN BAHADUR A. S., *Fifty Years' Pilgrimage of a Convert* (London, 1924).

ATIMAN, *see under* NICOLEAU.

ATTWATER, RACHEL, *Adam Schall* (London, 1963).

AYENDALE, E. A., *The Missionary Impact on Modern Nigeria, 1842–1914* (London, 1966).

BAËTA, C. G., *Prophetism in Ghana* (London, 1962).

BAËTA, C. G., (Ed.), *Christianity in Tropical Africa* (London, 1968).

BALANDIER, G, *Sociologie de l'Afrique Noire* (Paris, 1955).

BANCROFT, H. H., *History of Central America* (3 vols., San Francisco, 1882–7).

BANCROFT, H. H., *History of Mexico* (6 vols., San Francisco, 1883–8).

BARNETT, DONALD L., and NJAMA, KARARI, *Mau Mau from within* (London, 1966).

BARRETT, DAVID B., *Schism and Renewal in Africa* (London, 1969).

BARRETT, DAVID B., 'A.D. 2,000: 350 million Christians in Africa', (article in *International Review of Missions*, vol. LIX, No. 233, London, January 1970).

BARY, W. T. DE, HAY, S., WEILER, R, and YARROW, A., *Sources of Indian Tradition* (Columbia, 1958).

BEAVER, R. PIERCE, see under PIERCE.

BENTLEY-TAYLOR, DAVID, *The Weathercock's Reward* ('Christian Progress in Muslim Java'), (London, 1967).

BERNARD, MIGUEL A., *see under* ACHUTEGUI.

BESSE, LÉON, *La Mission au Maduré* (Trichinopoly, 1916).

BESSE, LÉON, *Fr. Breschi, his Life and his Works* (Trichinopoly, 1918).

BINGHAM, HIRAM, *A Residence of twenty-one Years in the Sandwich Islands* (Hartford, Conn., 1849).

BISHOP, JORDAN, *Latin America and Revolution* (London, 1965).

BISWAS, N. K., *see under* PEACEY, J. R.

BLONDEL, MAURICE, *Letter on Apologetics* (London, 1965).

BLYDEN, E. W., *Christianity, Islam and the Negro Race* (London, 1887).

BLYDEN, E. W., *West Africa Before Europe* (London, 1905).

BOARDMAN, EUGENE POWERS, *Christian Influence upon the Ideology of the Taiping Rebellion* (Wisconsin, 1952).*

BOLSHAKOFF, SERGE, *Foreign Missions of the Russian Orthodox Church* (London, 1943).

BOREHAM, F. W., *G. A. Selwyn* (London, n.d.).

BOUNIOL, J. *The White Fathers and their Missions* (London, 1929).

BOXER, C. R., 'Hosakawa Tadaoki and the Jesuits, 1587–1645', in *Japan Soc. Transactions and Proceedings*, (London, 1934–5), vol. XXXII.

BOXER, C. R., *The Christian Century in Japan* (California, 1951).**

BOXER, C. R., *Race Relations in the Portuguese Colonial Empire* (London, 1963).

BRAINERD, D., *see under* EDWARDS, J.

BRANDEL-SYRIER, MIA, *African Women in Search of God* (London, 1962).

BRODRICK, ALAN H., *Little China—the Annamese Lands* (London, 1942).

BROOMHALL, MARSHALL, *General Feng—a good Soldier of Christ Jesus* (London, 1923).

BROWN, C. CAMPBELL, *A Chinese St. Francis—the Life of Brother Mao* (Edinburgh, n.d.).

BRYSON, (Mrs.) of Tientsin, *Cross and Crown, Stories of the Chinese Martyrs* (London, 1904).

BUEHRLE, M. C., *Kateri of the Mohawks* (Milwaukee, 1954).

BURNS, ROBERT I, S.J. *The Jesuits and the Indian Wars of the North-west* (Yale, 1966).

BURTIN, F. *Vie de Cateri Tekakwitha* (Quebec, 1898).

BUZY, FR., *Life of the Servant of God, Sister Mary of Jesus Crucified,* (English trans., London, 1925).

CALDWELL, RT. REV. R., *Records of the Early History of the Tinnevelly Mission* (London, 1881).

CAMPBELL, T. J., S.J., *Pioneers of North America* (New York, 1908).

CAMPBELL, T. J., S.J., *The Jesuits* (London, 1921).

CARY-ELWES, COLUMBA, *China and the Cross* (London, 1957). *Catholic Church in Korea, see under* KOREA.

CAVANNA, JESUS M., Y. MANSO., *see under* MANSO.

CHACKO, K. C. *Sister Alphonsa* (Trivandrum, 4th ed., 1956).

CHALMERS, J. A., *Tiyo Soga* (London, 1878).

CHAUCHETIÈRE, P., S.J. *La Vie de la S. Catherine Tegakwitha,* 'dite à présent la saincte sauvage' (Paris, 17—?).

CHAVAGNAC, PÈRE DE, *Choix de Lettres édifiantes* (Brussels, 1838).

CH'ENG, MARCUS, *Marshal Feng, the Man and his Work* (Shanghai, 1926).

CHIH, ANDRÉ, *L'Occident 'Chrétien' vu par les Chinois vers la fin du XIXe Siècle, 1870–1900* (Paris, 1962).

CHOI, ANDREAS, *L'Érection du premier Vicariat apostolique et les Origines du Catholicisme en Korée, 1592–1837* (Swisse-Schoënbeck-Beckenried, 1961).

CHOLENEC, P., *Lettres edifiantes et curieuses* (Paris, 1781).

CHOMÉ, JULES, *La Passion de Simon Kimbangu* (Paris, 2nd ed., 1960).

CHUBB, E. EDMUND, *Twentieth Century China* (Columbia, 1964).

CIESLIK, HUBERT, S.J. *Gotô Juan* ('Ein Beitrag zur Missions-Geschichte Word-Japans', no. xii in the *Schriftenreihe der Neuen Zietschrift ür Missionswissenschaft*) (1954).

COHEN, LEONARD, *Beautiful Losers* (Toronto/Montreal, 1966).

COILLARD, FRANÇOIS, *On the Threshold of Central Africa* (London, 1902).*

COLLOCOT, E. E. V., 'Notes on the Tongan Religion', in *Journal of the Polynesian Soc.* (Wellington, N.Z.), vol. XXX.

CONSIDINE, J. J. (ed.), *The Church in the New Latin America* (Tenbury Wells, Worcs., 1964).

COOK, ALBERT R., *Uganda Memoirs, 1897–1940* (Kampala, 1945).

COPWAY, REV. G., *The Life Letters and Speeches of Kah-ge-ga-Bowh, or G. Copway, Chief, Ojibway Nation* (New York, 1850).

COULBEAUX, J. B., *Vers la Lumière—le bienheureux Abba Ghèbre-Michael* (Paris, 2nd ed., 1926).

COUPLET, PHILLIPUS, *Histoire d'une dame Chrétienne de la Chine* (Candide Hiu)—'où par occasion les usages de ces Peuples, l'établissement de la Religion, les Manières des Missionaires, et les Exercices de Piété des nouveaux Chrétiens sont expliqués' (Paris, 1688).**

COWAN, JAMES, *The New Zealand Wars and the Pioneering Period* (2 vols., Wellington, 1922).

COX, HARVEY, *The Secular City* (London, 1966).

CRONIN, VINCENT, *The Wise Man from the West* (Life of Ricci) (London, 1955).

CUNHA, EUCLYDES DA, *Rebellion in the Backlands* (*Os Sertoẽs*, trans. S. Putman) (Chicago, 1943).*

CUNNINGHAME GRAHAM, *see under* GRAHAM.

CYNN, HUGH HUENG-WO, *The Rebirth of Korea* (London, 1920).

DAIIMEN, PIERRE, S.J., *Devasagayam, un Martyr de Travancore* (Xaveriana, 9e séries, no. 100, April, 1932, Louvain).*

D'ANTONIO, *see under* ANTONIO.

DALLET, CHARLES, *Histoire de l'Église de Corée* (2 vols., Paris, 1874).**

DAVIS, J. D., *Joseph Neeisima* (New York, 1894).

DAWSON, E. C., *Bishop James Hannington, 1847–1885* (London, 1889).

DEBRUNNER, H., *A Church between Colonial Powers* (The Church in Togo) (London, 1965).

DEHQANI-TAFTI, HASSAN, *Design of My World* (London, 1959).

DUNNE, G. H., S.J., *Generation of Giants* (London, 1962).

EDKINS, JANE R., *Chinese Scenes and People* 'with a Narrative of a visit to Nanking by her husband, the Rev. Joseph Edkins' (London, 1863).

EDWARDS, JONATHAN, *Life of David Brainerd* (extracts, ed. J. Wesley) (Dublin, 1812).

ELIA, PASQUALE D', *Catholic Native Episcopacy in China* (Shanghai, 1927).

ELIA, PASQUALE D', *Fonti Ricciani*—Documenti Originali Concernenti Matteo Ricci e la Storia Delle Prime Relazioni tra l'Europa e la Cina (1579–1615). Editi e Commentati da Pasquale M. d'Elia, S.I. (3 vols., Rome, 1942–9).

ELLIS, WILLIAM, *A Vindication of the South Sea Missions* (London, 1831).

ELLIS, WILLIAM, *The Martyr Church of Madagascar* (London, 1870).*

ENCYCLOPAEDIA OF NEW ZEALAND (Wellington, N.Z., 1966).

ENNIS, THOMAS E., *French Policy and Development in Indo-China* (Chicago, 1936).

EVERY, E. F., *South American Memories of Thirty Years* (London, 1933).

FABELLA, GABRIEL F., *Rizal the Historian and other Historical Essays* (Quezon, 1960).

FAIRBANK, JOHN K., *see under* TENG, SU-YÜ.

FARB, PETER, *Man's Rise to Civilization as shown by the Indians of North America* (London, 1969).

FARGE, OLIVER LA, *Santa Eulalia* ('The Religion of a Cuchamatán Indian Town') (Chicago, 1947).

FARMER, SARAH S., *Tonga and the Friendly Islands* (London, 1855).**

FARRANT, JEAN, *Mashonaland Martyr—Bernard Mizeki* (London, 1966).

FAUPEL, J. F., *African Holocaust* (London, 1962).

FIEDLER, LESLIE A., *The Return of the Vanishing American* (London, 1968).

FINDLAY, G. C., and HOLDSWORTH, W. W., *The History of the Wesleyan Methodist Missionary Society* (5 vols., London, 1921).

FIRTH, R., *Tikopia Ritual and Belief* (London, 1967).

FORMAN, C. W., *Christianity in the non-Western World* (New York, 1967).

FOSTER, JOHN, *Christianity in China under the T'ang Dynasty* (London, 1939).

FOURCADIER, ÉTIENNE, *La Vie Héroïque de Victoire Rasoamanarivo* (Paris, 1937, 2nd ed., 1948).

FOX, C. E., *Lord of the Southern Isles* (History of Melanesian Mission, 1849–1949) (London, 1958).

FRASER, DONALD, *Winning an African People* (London, 1914).

FRASER, DONALD, *Daniel Mtusu, the Autobiography of an African* (London, 1925).

FREYTAG, WALTER, *Spiritual Revolution in the East* (London, 1946).

GANN, L. H., *A History of Northern Rhodesia* (London, 1964).

GARCIA and CALLE, *see under* TORRES, CAMILLO.

GASBARRI, CHARLES, S.J. *A Saint for the New India* (Bombay, 1960).

GATHERU, R. MUGO, *Child of Two Worlds* (A Kikuyu Story) (London, 1964).

GENSE, J. H. and CONTI, A., *In the Days of Gonzalo Garcia, 1557–1597* (Bombay, 1957).

GLUCKMAN, MAX, *The Judicial Process among the Barotse* (Manchester, 1955).

GOFORTH, J., *A Chinese Christian General* (Feng) (London, n.d.) (1919).

GRAHAM, AELRED, *Zen Catholicism* (London, 1964).

GRAHAM, AELRED, *Conversations, Christian and Buddhist* (London, 1969).

GRAHAM, R. B. CUNNINGHAME, *A Brazilian Mystic* (London, 1920).*

GROVES, C. P., *The Planting of Christianity in Africa* (4 vols., London, 1948–58).

HAIL, WILLIAM JAMES, *Tsëng Kuo-fan and the Taiping Rebellion* (Yale, 1927; 2nd rev. ed. New York, 1964).

HALDANE, CHARLOTTE, *Tempest over Tahiti* (London, 1964).

HAMMER, ELLEN J., *The Struggle for Indo-China* (Stanford, 1954).

HAMMER, RAYMOND, *Japan's Religious Ferment* (London, 1961).

HARR, WILBUR C. (Ed.), *Frontiers of the Christian World Mission since 1938* (New York, 1962).

HARRIS, W. WADÉ, *see under* PLATT, W. J.

HAYWARD, VICTOR E., *Church as Christian Community* ('Three Studies of North Indian Churches') (London, 1966).

HENDERSON, G. C., *Fiji and the Fijians, 1835–1856* (London, 1931).

HENDERSON, J., *Ratana, the Man, the Church, the Political Movement* (Wellington, N.Z., 1963).

HENSMAN, C. R. *China, Yellow Peril?—Red Hope?* (London, 1968).

HERRING, HUBERT, *History of Latin America* (London, 1954).

HING-MING, KU, *Spirit of the Chinese People* (Peking, 1915).

HINTON, W. M., *Fanshen* (New York and London, 1966).
Histoire de la glorieuse Mort de neuf Chrestiens Iaponais (Anon) (Douai, 1612).
HOLDSWORTH, W. W., *see under* FINDLAY.
HOLT, EDGAR, *The Strangest War* (New York, 1962).
HOSTEN, H., *Mīrzā Zū-L-Qarnain* ('An Armenian at the Court of Akbar') (Calcutta, 1916), Asiatic Society of Bengal, v. 4.
HOUGH, JAMES, *A History of Christianity in India* (London, 1845).
HUC, L'ABBÉ, *Christianity in China* (English trans., 2 vols., London, 1857).
HUGHES, E. R., *The Invasion of China by the Western World* (London, 1937).
HUGHES, THOMAS, *History of the Society of Jesus in North America* (3 vols., London, 1917).
HULL, E. R., *Bombay Mission History* (2 vols., Bombay, 1930).
HUMMEL, A. W. (Ed.), *Eminent Chinese of the Ch'in Period (1644–1912)* (2 vols., U.S. Govt. Printing Office, 1943).

IDOWU, BOLAJII, *Towards an indigenous Church* (Ibadan, 1965).
IGLEHART, CHARLES W., *Cross and Crisis in Japan* (New York, 1957).
ISHII, TOKICHI, *A Gentleman in Prison*, trans. C. Macdonald (London, 1923).

JARRETT-KERR, M. W. R., *see under* KERR.
JESSUP, HENRY, *Kamil* (Abdul Aistany Messiah—a Syrian Convert) (Philadelphia, 1899).
JOHNSON, HOWARD A, *Global Odyssey* (London, 1963).
JONES, FRANCIS PRICE, *The Church in Communist China* (New York, 1962).
Journal of African History (London)
Journal of the Polynesian Society (Wellington, N.Z.).

KERR, MARTIN W. R. JARRETT-, *Christ and the New Nations* (London, 1966).
KESTELOOT, LILYAN, *Les Écrivains noirs de la Langue Française* (Brussels, 1965).
KITTLER, GLEN D., *The White Fathers* (London, 1957).
KNIGHT, W. *The Missionary Secretariat of Henry Venn* (London, 1882).
KNOX, ROBERT, *An Historical Relation of the Island of Ceylon* (London, 1681).
KOLARZ, WALTER, *Religion in the Soviet Union* (London, 1961).
KOREA, *The Catholic Church in Korea* (Anon) (Hong Kong, 1924).
KOSKINEN, A. A. *Missionary Influence as a Political Factor in the Pacific Islands* (Helsinki, 1953).**
KRAEMER, HENDRIK, *From Missionfield to Independent Church* (London, 1958).
KU HING-MING, See Hing-Ming, Ku.

LA FARGE, *see under* FARGE.

LANTERNARI, VITTORIA, *The Religion of the Oppressed* (London, 1966).

LATOURETTE, K. S. *A History of Christian Missions in China* (London, 1929).

LATOURETTE, K. S. *A History of the Expansion of Christianity* (6 vols., London, 1943).

LAUNAY, ADRIEN, *Histoire générale de la Société des Missions Étrangères* (3 vols., Paris, 1894).

LAUNAY, ADRIEN, *Histoire de la Mission de Se-Tchouan* (Paris, 1903).

LECLERCQ, JEAN, *La Vie du Père Lebbe* (Paris and Brussels, 1961).

LECOMPTE, P. EDOUARD, S. J., *Catherine Tekakwitha, Une Vierge Iroquoise* (Montreal, 1927).

LEE, ROBERT, *Stranger in the Land* (The Church in Japan) (London, 1967).

LEEUWEN, AREND VAN, *Christianity in World History* (London, 1964).

Life of Christ by Chinese Artists, The (London, 1938).

LOU, DOM PIERRE-CÉLESTIN (LOU TSENG-TSIANG), *Ways of Confucius and of Christ* (London, 1948).

LOU, DOM PIERRE-CÉLESTIN, *La Rencontre des Humanités et la Dècouverte de l'Évangile* (Paris, 1949).

LOW, D. A., 'Converts and Martyrs in Buganda' in BAËTA (1968), see above.

LUCK, ANNE, *African Saint—Apolo Kivebalayu* (London, 1963).

LUFULUABO, FRANÇOIS M., *Vers une Théodicée Bantoue* (Louvain, 1961).

LUFULUABO, FRANÇOIS, M., *La Notion Luba-Bantoue de l'Être* (Louvain, 1964).

LUKE, SIR HARRY, *Islands of the South Pacific* (London, 1962).

LUTZ, JESSIE G. (Ed.), *Christian Missions in China* ('Evangelists of What?') (Boston, 1965).

LY, ANDRÉ, *Diarium (Journal)*, ed. A. Launay (Paris, 1906).**

LYALL, LESLIE T., *John Sung* (London, 1954).

LYCET, MARGARET, *Brothers* (London, 1935).

MACKAY, *Mackay of Uganda*, by his sister (London, 1890).

MACKAY, J. A., *The other Spanish Christ* (London, 1932).

MACKINTOSH, C. W., *Coillard of the Zambesi* (London, 1907).

MACNICOL, NICOL, *Pandita Ramabai* (London, 1926).

MANSO, JESUS M. CAVANNA Y., *Rizal and the Philippines of his Day* (Manila, 1957).

MAO TSE-TUNG, *Selected Works* (2 vols., London, 1954).

MAO TSE-TUNG, *Thoughts of Chairman Mao* (Peking, 1967).

MARCUS, *see under* ABD-EL-MASIH

MARIE (Soeur Marie-Andrée du Sacré-Coeur), *Uganda, Terre des Martyrs* (Paris, 1957).

MARTIN, BERNARD, *Strange Vigour* (Life of Sun Yat-sen) (London, 1944).

MARTIN, JOHN, *An Account of the Natives of Tonga Islands, etc.* (2 vols., London, 1827).

MARTIN, MARIE-LOUISE, *Prophetic Christianity in the Congo* (Kimbangu) (Johannesburg, 1969).**

MAYER, PHILIP, *Townsmen or Tribesmen* (Cape Town, 1961).

MAYHEW, EXPERIENCE, *Indian Christians* (or 'Some Account of the Lives and dying Speeches of a considerable number of Christian-ized Indians of Martha's Vineyard') (London, 1727).

MCALEAVY, HENRY, *Black Flags in Vietnam* (London, 1968).

MEAD, MARGARET, *New Lives for Old* (London, 1956).

MECHAM, J. LLOYD, *Church and State in Latin America* (N. Carolina, 1934).

METGE, JOAN, 'Christ and Culture', in *South East Asia Journal of Theology* (Singapore, 1967).

MICHAEL, FRANZ, and CHUNG-LI CHANG. *The Taiping Rebellion, History and Documents* (vol. I, History) (Seattle, 1966).

MICHALSON, CARL, *Japanese Contributions to Christian Theology* (West-minster, Pa., 1960).

MICHIHATA, REV. TAISEI, *From Buddha to the Christ* (Tokyo, 1937).

MILLER, W. R. S., *Reflections of a Pioneer* (London, 1936).

MONCHANIN, J., AND LE SAUX, H., *Ermites du Saccidânanda* (Paris, 1957).

MONSTERLEET, JEAN, *Martyrs in China* (London, 1953).

MOOREHEAD, ALAN, *The Fatal Impact* (London, 1966).

MOULE, A. C., *Christians in China before the Year 1550* (London, 1930).

MTUSU, DANIEL, *see under* FRASER, D.

MURAO, M. S. and WALTON, J. MURRAY, *Japan and Christ, a Study in Religious Issues* (London, 1928).

MURDOCH, JAMES, and YAMAGATA, ISOH, *A History of Japan, 1542–1651* (3 vols., Kobe, 1903).

MWASE, G. S., *Strike a Blow and Die!*, English trans., R. T. Rotberg (Harvard, 1967).

NAGAÏ, PAUL, *We of Nagasaki* (London, 1951).

NAGAÏ, PAUL, *Les Cloches de Nagasaki* (Paris, 1954, 2nd ed., 1962).

NARAIN, JAYAPRAKASH, *Socialism, Sarvodaya and Democracy* (Bombay, 1964).

NEEDHAM, JOSEPH, *Science and Civilization in China* (London, vol. I, 1954; vol. II, 1956; vol. III, 1959; vol. IV, 1969).

NEEISIMA, *see under* DAVIS, J. D.

NEILL, STEPHEN, *A History of Christian Missions* (London, 1964).

NEILL, STEPHEN, *Colonialism and Mission* (London, 1966).

NEUNG-HOA, YI, *Histoire du Christianisme et de la Diplomatie coréenne*, (Seoul, 1927).

NICOLEAU, G., *Atiman* ('le petit Esclave du Niger') (Paris, n.d.).

NJAMA, K., *see under* BARNETT, D. L.

OHM, T., *Asia looks at Western Christianity* (New York, 1959).

OHM, T., *Les principaux Faits de l'Histoire des Missions* (Paris, 1961).

OLICHON, ARMAND, *Aux Origines du Clergé Chinois: le Prêtre André Ly* (Paris, 1933).**

OLICHON, ARMAND, *Father Six*, English trans. (London, 1954).

OLIVER, DOUGLAS L., *The Pacific Islands* (Harvard, 1951).

ONUOHA, FR. BEDE, *The Elements of African Socialism* (London, 1965).

OOSTHUIZEN, G. C., *The Theology of a South African Messiah* (Leiden/Köln, 1967).

OOSTHUIZEN, G. C., *Post-Christianity in Africa* (London, 1968).

OSWALT, WENDELL H., *This Land was Theirs* (New York, 1966).

PAGE, JESSE, *The Black Bishop* (London, 1908).

PALMA, RAPHAEL, *José Rizal, the Pride of the Malay Race* (New York, 1947).

PANNIKAR, K. M., *Asia and Western Dominance* (London, 1953).

PANNIKAR, K. M., *The Foundations of New India* (London, 1953).

PANNIKAR, FR. RAYMOND, *The Unknown Christ of Hinduism* (London, 1964).

PAREKH, MANILAL C., *Keshub Chunder Sen* (Bombay, 1926).

PARKMAN, FRANCIS, *The Jesuits in North America*, *Works*, vol. II (Toronto, 1898).

PARKMAN, FRANCIS, *Count Frontenac*, *Works*, vol. V (Toronto, 1898).

PARKMAN, FRANCIS, *The Conspiracy of Pontiac*, *Works*, vol. X (Toronto, 1898).

PARKMAN, FRANCIS, *The Discovery of the West* (1869; new ed., London, 1962).

PAUL, RAJAIAH D., *Chosen Vessels* (Madras, 1961).

PEACEY, J. R., *The Flute of Jesus* (Life of Nirod Kumar Biswas) (London, 1949).

PEARCE, ROY HARVEY, *The Savages of America* (Baltimore, 1953).

PERHAM, MARGERY, *Ten Africans* (London, 1936).

PERERA, S. G., *The Life of the Ven. Father Joseph Vaz* (Colombo, 1942).

PIERCE BEAVER, R., *Pioneers in Mission* (Grand Rapids, Michigan, 1966).

PIKE, F. B. *see under* ANTONIO, W. V. D'.

PLATT, W. J., *An African Prophet* (W. Wadé Harris) (London, 1934).

POPLEY, H. A., *K. T. Paul, Christian Leader* (Calcutta, 1938).

PORTWAY, DONALD, *Korea, Land of Morning Calm* (New York, 1953).

PRASAD, BISHEWAR (Ed.), *Ideas in History*—proceedings of a Seminar on ideas motivating social and religious movements and political and economic policies during the 18th and 19th centuries in India (London and Delhi, 1968).

Prêtres noirs s'interrogent, Des (Anon) (Paris, 1957).

PRICE, T., *see under* SHEPPERSON

PRITCHARD, H. *Polynesian Reminiscences* (London, 1866).
PURCELL, VICTOR, *The Boxer Uprising—a background Study* (London, 1963).

QARNAIN, MIRZA ZU-L., *see under* HOSTEN, H.
QUAIN, V. BUELL, *Fijian Village* (Chicago, 1948).

RAE, COLIN, *Malaboch* (Cape Town and London, 1898).
REICHELT, KARL, *The transformed Abbot, Miao-Chi*, (English trans. London, 1954).**
REN, PASTOR, *A tamarisk Garden, blessed with Rain* (autobiography), trans. Taylor and Broomhall (London, 1930).
RIZAL, JOSÉ, *The Social Cancer*, trans. C. Derbyshire (New York, 1912).
RIZAL, JOSÉ, *Noli Me Tangere* and *El Filibusterismo*, English trans. Osias (Manila, 1957).
ROCHE, ALOYSIUS, *Bakhita, Pearl of the Sudan* (Langley, Bucks, 1964).
ROWBOTHAM, ARNOLD H., *Missionary and Mandarin* (California, 1942).
ROWE, J. A., 'The Purge of Christians at Mwanga's Court' in *Journal of African History* vol. V, i (London, 1964).
RUEDI-WEBER, HANS, *see under* WEBER.
Rythmes du Monde, 'Bangkok, Rencontre Monastique' (Bruges, 1969), vol. XVII, nos. 1–2.

SANSOM, GEORGE, *A History of Japan* (3 vols., London, 1961).
SARGENT, DANIEL, *Catherine Tekakwitha* (London, 1937).*
SATTHIANADHAN, S., *Sketches of Indian Christians* (Calcutta, 1896).
SATTIANADEN, *Sermon* (London, 1792).
SAUX, H., *see under* MONCHANIN
SCHURZ, W. L., *This New World* (Latin America) (London, 1956).
SCHWARTZ, C. F., *Remains* (London, 1826).
SEHOZA, SAMUEL, *A Year in Chains*, trans. G. Dale (London, 1919).
SENGHOR, L. S., *On African Socialism* (London, 1964).
SEODZI, SERGEI, *How I became a Christian* (St. Petersburg, 1892).**
SHEPPERSON, G., and PRICE, T., *Independent African* (J. Chilembwe) (Edinburgh, 1958).**
SHERIDAN, JAMES E., *Chinese Warlord* (Stanford, 1966).*
SIMON, GOTTFRIED, *The Progress and Arrest of Islam in Sumatra* (London, n.d. [1912]).
SMIRNOV, E., *A Short History of the historical Development and present Positions of Russian Orthodox Missions* (London, 1903).
SMITH, EDWIN, W., *Aggrey of Africa* (London, 1926).
SOGA, TIYO, *see under* CHALMERS
Son of Man, The, pictures and carvings by Indian, African and Chinese Artists (London, 1939).
SPAE, JOSEPH, *Catholicism in Japan* (Tokyo, 1964).
S.P.C.K. Report (London, 1792).

SPILLER, G., *Inter-racial Problems* (Report of the 'First Universal Races Congress') (London, 1911).

STOCK, EUGENE, *History of the Church Missionary Society* (London, 1899).

SUBHAN, J. A., *How a Sufi Found his Lord* (Lucknow, n.d. [1942]).

SUN YAT-SEN, *The Triple Demism* (*San Minchui*), trans. Paschale d'Elia (Wuchang, 1931).

SWARTZ, *Remains* (London, 1826).

TAYLOR, DAVID BENTLEY, *see under* BENTLEY-TAYLOR.

TAYLOR, JOHN V., *The Growth of the Church in Uganda* (London, 1956).

TAYLOR, JOHN V., *The primal Vision* (London, 1963).

TENG, SU-YÜ and FAIRBANK, JOHN K., *China's Response to the West* (Harvard, 1954).

TENNANT, J. E., *Christianity in Ceylon* (London, 1850).

THOMAS, M. M., *The Christian Response to the Asian Revolution* (London, 1966).

THOMAS, M. M., *The Acknowledged Christ of the Indian Renaissance* (London, 1969).

THOMSON, BASIL, *The Diversions of a Prime Minister* (London, 1894).

THOONEN, J. P., *Black Martyrs* (London, 1941).

TILAK, LAKSHMIBAI, *I Follow After* (Madras, 1950).

TILAK, LAKSHMIBAI, *From Brahma to Christ* (Life of N. V. Tilak) (London, 1956).

TIPPET, A. R., *Solomon Islands Christianity* (London, 1967).

TORRES, CAMILO, *Camilo Torres, Priest and Revolutionary* (ed. Garcia and Calle), (London, 1969).

TRIMINGHAM, J. SPENCER, *Islam in Ethiopia* (London, 1952).

TROLLOPE, M. NAPIER, *The Church in Korea* (London, 1915).

TUCKER, ALFRED R., *Eighteen Years in Uganda and East Africa* (London, 1911).

UPADHYAYA, BRAHMABANDHAV, *The Finite and the Infinite* (Trichinopoly, 1918).

VALERIAN, FR., *The Servant of God* (Fr. Cyriac Elias Chavara) (Travancore, 1953).

VAN LEEUWEN, *see under* LEEUWEN, A. VAN.

VAUSSARD, M. (Ed.), *The Golden Legend Overseas* (E.T., London, 1931).

WALKER, F. DEAVILLE, *The Romance of the Black River* (story of the C.M.S. Nigeria Mission) (London, 1933).

WALLIS, E. E., *The Daiyuma Story* (among the Auka Indians) (London, 1961).

WALWORTH, C., *Life and Times of Kateri Tekakwitha* (Buffalo, 1891).

WANG, Y. C., *Chinese Intellectuals in the West, 1879–1949* (North Carolina, 1966).

WARD, W. E. F., *Fraser of Trinity and Achimota* (Ghana, 1965).

WATERHOUSE, JOSEPH, *The King and People of Fiji* (London, 1866).

WEBER, HANS REUDI-, *Asia and the Ecumenical Movement* (London, 1966).

WEBSTER, J. BERTIN, *The African Churches among the Yoruba* (London, 1964).

WEIZSÄCKER, C. F. VON, *The Relevance of Science* (London, 1964).

WELBOURN, F. J., *East African Rebels* (London, 1961).

WELBOURN, F. J., and OGOT, B. A., *A Place to feel at Home* (London, 1966).

WEST, THOMAS, *Ten Years in South Central Polynesia* (London, 1863).

WHITTEMORE, LEWIS B., *Struggle for Freedom* (The Philippine Independent Church) (Seabury Press, U.S., 1961).

WINSLOW, J. C., *Narayan Vaman Tilak* (Calcutta, 1923).

WISHLADE, R. L., *Sectarianism in Southern Nyasaland* (London, 1965).

WITTFOGEL, KARL, *Oriental Despotism* (Yale, 1957).

WORSLEY, PETER, *The Third World* (2nd ed., London, 1967).

WU, CHAO-KWANG, *The international Aspect of the Missionary Movement in China* (Baltimore, 1930).

WU, JOHN C., *Fountain of Justice* (London, 1959).

YAMAGATA, ISOH, *see under* MURDOCH

YAT-SEN, SUN, *see under* SUN YAT-SEN

YIM, LOUISE, *My forty-year fight for Korea* (London, 1952).

YONAN, ISAAC MALEK, *The beloved Physician of Teheran* ('The Miracle of the Conversion of Dr. Sa'eed Khan, Kurdistan, Lokman-Il-Mulk') (Nashville, Tenn., 1934).

YOUNG, MIRIAM, *Seen and heard in a Punjab Village* (London, 1931).

ZALESKI, L. M., *The Martyrs of India* (Mangalore, 1913).*

ZWEMER, S. M., *The Law of Apostasy in Islam* (Cairo, n.d., [1924]).

Note

The bulk of this book was completed by 1968/9. Since then I have tried to keep track of subsequent publications relevant to the subject. In 1970 and 1971, however, the literature has so proliferated that the task has become impossible. This must be my excuse for obvious omissions. But these publications all confirm my main thesis, that the history can now be written from the 'receiving' rather than the 'giving' end. Further, they tend to confirm most of the interpretations given in this book. To give two examples: all the most recent literature on the Taipings, the Boxers, and Sun Yat-sen's leadership, stress the positive contribution of these movements, as against the missionaries' accounts of them; and further studies of Christianity in West Africa bring out the continuing force of African tradition, beneath the relatively superficial Western-Christian dressing. Thus a stop-press inclusion of all recent studies, even if it had been possible, would not have greatly altered the main stresses of my book.

INDEX

Abyssinia, xv
Africa, 2, 25, 77–86, 251–60, 292
Agbebi, Dr. Mojola, 289
Aglipaya, Gregorio, 249
Ajawa Providence Industrial Mission, 251–2
alcoholic drinks, 96n
Algonquins, 93
Ali, Haider, 72
A-lo-pên, 155
Amitabha, 158–9, 160, 163, 166, 167
Amlak, Ghebre Michael, xv
ancestors, veneration of, 105, 116–17, 150, 291, 315–16, 324
Angel, Dona Maria, 238–9
Anglican Church, xiii, 162, 167, 226–31, 232–7, 253, 262–4. *See also* Church Missionary Society, Society for Promoting Christian Knowledge, the United Society for the Propagation of the Gospel, and the Oxford Mission to Calcutta
Animananda, B., 215
Arya Samaj, 213
Asia's Light (periodical), 166, 169, 170
Atiman, Adrian, 194–5
atomic bomb, effects of, 201–9
Auca people, 1

Baker, Rev. Shirley Waldemar, 183–4, 187
Bakhita, Josephine, 191
Baldaeus, Philip, 135
Baluère, Fr. de la, 118
Banerji, Bhawani Charan, *see* Upadhyay Brahmabandhav
Baouardi, Mary, 190
Baptists, 221, 289
Barotse people, 79
Barrett, Dr. David B., 286
Bassett, Fr., 116, 125
Béguin, 83
Belland, Capt., 186
Bellarmine, Cardinal, 56
Benedict, Ruth, 181
Benedictines, 225, 226, 259

Besant, Annie, 213
Bethune, Norman, 287
Bigot, Fr., 4
Blomfield, Bishop, 227
Blondel, Maurice, 197–8, 199–200
Boardman, Dr., 273
Boiteux, 85–6
Booth, Joseph, 251, 254
Bowman, Joseph, 4
Boxer, Prof. C. R., 44
Boxer rising, 31–6, 151, 223, 275
Brahmo Samaj, 213
Brainerd, David, 87–8, 96n
Brazil, 240–1
Brébeuf, Fr., 98
Broomhall, Dr. Marshall, 31, 281
Brotherhood movement, 233–7
Brunière, de la, 107
Buchanan, Dr. Claudius, 75
Buddhism, 50, 52, 58, 138, 142, 154–70, 226
Buddhist Reform Association, 166
Buganda, 22–30
Burgos, Fr. José, 245–6, 247, 249–50
Buttery, Fr., 68

Cabral, Fr., 66
Caldwell, Bishop, 76
Cartier, Jacques, 95
Carvalho, Fr., 49
Castro, Matthias de, 132
Castro, Thomas de, 132, 133
Catholicism, *see* Roman Catholicism
Cattaneo, Fr., 50, 51, 53–4
Caughnawaga, 92, 95–6
Cécile, Captain, later Rear-Admiral, 107, 113
Cespedes, Fr. Gregorio de, 39–42, 101
Ceylon, 130–41
Chauchetière, Fr. P., 96, 98
Chauncy, Dr. Charles, 4
Chavara, Fr. Cyriac Elias, 190, 318
Ch'en (party leader), 9
Ch'en Tu-hsiu, 286–7
Chengtu, 123, 128
Chiang Kai-shek, 279
Chilembwe, John, 251–4

Chin Nieh Shê movement, 158
Chin Shan Ssu movement, 159
China, 6, 8–9, 30–6, 50–64, 115–30, 153–5, 158–71, 222–6, 266–82, 283, 292
China Inland Mission (C.I.M.), 31, 282, 292
Ching Feng Shan Brotherhood, 166
Chiu Hua Shan, 161
Cholenec, Fr. P., 96, 97–8
Church Missionary Society (C.M.S.), 22, 24, 25, 194, 212, 226, 229, 230–1, 289
Clement X, Pope, 115
Clement XI, Pope, 116
Cohen, Leonard, 290
Coillard, François, 78–84
Collocot, E. E. V., 188
Communism, 8–9, 279–80, 285–7
Confucianism, 50, 52, 56, 225, 267, 287
Congo, 254–60
Congregationalists, 10, 280. *See also* London Missionary Society
Conselheiro, Antonio, 240–1
Cordon, H., 292
Cossacks, 151
Costilla, Hidalgo y, *see* Hildalgo
Couplet, Fr. Phillipus, 55, 56, 58, 61, 63, 64
Crowther, Bishop Samuel Adjayi, 226–32
Curzon, Lord, 192–3

Dallet, Fr. C., 103–4
Danish Protestant Mission (in Madras), 71
Daté Masumané, 45–9
Dewey, John, 287
Dharmapala, Prince, 131
Diangienda, Joseph, 260
disease, introduction of, 1–2
Dominicans, 247–8
Druilletes, Fr., 92
Dupuis, 258, 259
Dutch (in Ceylon), 134–5, 138, 140
Dutch Reformed Church, 135–6, 138
Dutta, Narain, *see* Vivekananda, Swami

Ecuador, 1
Edkins, Rev. Joseph, 270–1
Edwards, Jonathan, 87
Eliot, John, 87
Ellis, William, 6, 21
Erskine, Capt. John Elphinstone, 186, 318
Ethiopian Church (in Nyasaland), 251

Farmer, Sarah S., 180
'Father Six', *see* Triem, Pierre Huu
Faupel, Fr. J. F., 24, 28
Feng Yü-hsiang, General, 275–82, 323
Feng Yün-shan, 267
Ficoyemon, Michael, 12
Fiedler, Leslie, 290
Fiji, 181–3, 185, 186
Filipino League, 248
Firth, Prof. Raymond, 235
Formosa Academy, 166
Foster, Prof. John, 323
Fourah Bay College, 226
Franciscans, 12–14, 46

George, King of Tonga, 171–88
Gericke, 77
German Lutheran pastors, 71
Goa, 65, 66, 130–4
Gomez, Fr. Mariano, 245, 247, 249–50
Gouvea, Mgr., 105, 106
Guadalcanal, 232
Guatemala, 238–9
Guerreiro, Fernão, 42

Hannington, Bishop, 25
Hannit, Japheth, 89–91
Hartman, Bishop, 285
Hau Hau movement, 261
Haumene, Te Ua, 261
Hidalgo y Costilla, 242–5
Home, Sir J. Everard, 186
Hosakawa, Grace, 37–44
Hosakawa, Okinoto, 44
Hosakawa, Tadaoki Sansai, 37–8, 41, 43
Houng-tchoung, 108–9
Hora people, 21–2
Hsü, Basil, 61–2

Hsü, Candida, 55, 58–64
Hsü, Ching-ch'eng, 222–3
Hsü, Kuang-ch'i (Paul), 50–8
Hsü, Yuan-tu, 58
Huc, Fr., 57
Hung Hsiu-Ch'üan, 266–75
Hung Jen-kan, 267–9

Ibrahim, 319–20
Imbert, Bishop, 107
India, 65–77, 211–22
Iroquois, 92–3, 96n, 98, 99
Islam, *see* Muslims
It-to-en community, 157

Jaenicke, 71
Jaffna, 134–6
Japan, 6, 12–16, 37–50, 142–53,
   201–9
Jesuits, xiv, 4–6, 12–15, 18, 37, 46,
   48, 50, 56, 57, 60, 61, 65, 86, 87,
   92, 95, 115, 126, 134, 136, 281,
   249–50, 284
Jogues, Fr., 98
Johnson, Dr. Howard A., 234
Johnson, James, 231, 289
Juan Canal, 47
Juan, Gotô, 44–50

Kagawa, Toyohiko, 157, 210
Kaggwa, Andrew, 25
Kalemba, Matthias, 24, 26–7
Kanara, 131–2, 134
Kandy, 137–40
K'ang-hsi, Emperor, 117
Karema, 194–5
Kasatkin, Ivan, *see* Nikolai, Fr.
'Katipunan', 248–9
Kemal Attaturk, 198
Khervé, Père, 128
Kiernander, John Zachariah, 71
Kim, André, 107–14, 150
Kimbangu, Simon, 254–60, 322–3
Kisula, Matthew, 28
Kivebalayu, Canon Apolo, 7
Kobodaishi, 155
Kohlkoff, 73, 74
Konishi, 45
Kopuria, Ini, 232–7
Korea, 41, 101–10, 150
Koskinen, Dr. Aarne, 174

Kotzebuc, Count Otto van, 5–6
Ku Hing-Ming, 1
Kuandu, Ishé, 85
Kuomintang, 278–9
Kuruman, 78
Kwannon Temple, 155

La Gloria, Sebastian Gomez de, 239
Lagos, 229, 230, 231
Lamberville, Fr., 95
Lannoy, General Benedict, 67–9
Latin, use of, 121, 123, 162, 316
Latin America, 238–45, 290
Latourette, Kenneth Scott, 10
Laufilitonga, 174, 180
Launay, Fr., 130
Lebbe, Père Vincent, 34–5
Lefebvre, Fr., 126
Lewanika, king, 79–84
Lhut, Daniel Greysolong du, 99
Li, Mrs., 32
Li Chih-tsao, 53
Litia, 82, 84
Livingstone, David, 78
Livingstone, W. J., 252–3
Livinhac, Père, 26–7
Lô, Gregory, 64, 115
Lobengula, King, 78–9
London   Missionary   Society
   (L.M.S.), 3, 5, 10, 16, 31, 78, 185,
   223, 270, 281
Lou, Dom Pierre-Célestin, 222–6,
   280–1
Lourdel, Père, 23, 26
Low, Prof. D. A., 29–30
Lu Cheng-hsiang, *see* Lou, Dom
   Pierre-Célestin
Luke, Sir Harry, 187
Ly, André, 115–30
Ly-Paul, *see* Hsü Kuang-chi

Maciel, Antoni Vicente Mendes, *see*
   Conselheiro, Antonio
Mackay, Alexander, 22–4, 27
Madagascar, 16–22, 284
Madura, 66, 75
Maetsuyker, John, 136
Maistre, 107
Malaboch, 2
Malaysia, 194
Manchus, 33, 55, 274, 275, 280

Mani family, 78
Maoriland, 260–5
Martillat, P. de, 120, 121, 125
martyrs, 10–12, 14, 15, 18, 19, 25–6, 29, 42, 49, 70, 101, 106, 113. *See also* Uganda
Marxism, *see* Communism
Massachusetts, 87, 90
Mayhew, Experience, 87, 90–1
Mead, Margaret, 235
Melanesian people, 10, 232, 234, 235, 237
Menezes, Manoel de Souza de, 133
Metge, Dr. Joan, 265
Methodism, 3, 10, 176, 179, 180, 183–5, 231, 261, 264, 276, 284
Mexico, 242–5
Miao-Chi, 153–71, 316
Middleton, Rev. Thomas Fanshaw, 74
Miller, Dr. Walter, 319–20
Ming Emperor, 55
Missions Étrangères, Société des, 104, 106, 116, 117, 119–20
Miti, James, 28
Miwake, 47, 48
Mokwaë, Queen, 78–86
monastic life, 214–15, 293
Movelos, José, 244–5
Mott, Dr. John R., 275
Mukasa, Joseph, 24–6, 27
Mulla-zadé, 'Paul' Mehmet-ali, 196–201
Mullener, Mgr., 119, 125
Muslims, 22, 24, 30, 32, 196–201, 318–19
Mutesa, King, 22–4, 29–30
Muttathupadathu, Sister Alphonsa, 190
Muzeyi, Jean-Marie, 25
Mwanga, King, 22, 25–6, 29–30

Nag, Rev. B. A., 221
Nagaï, Dr. Paul Takahashi, 201–9, 320
Nagasaka, 149
Nagasaki, 13, 15, 16, 201–9
Nambu, 49
Namugongo, 26
Nanking, 269, 270, 272–3

Native American Church, 290
Neill, Bishop Stephen, 230–1
Nestorian Tablet, 155–6
New Zealand, 260–5
Niger Mission, 227, 228–9, 231
Nigeria, 7, 226–32
Nikolai, Fr., 148, 149, 152
Nilakandam-Pillay, *see* Pillai, Devasagayam
Nobili, Robert de, 65, 66, 215
North American Indians, 2, 86–99
Nsenkoto, Fr. François Xavier, 259–60
Nuku'alofa, 176, 181
Nyasaland, 251–4

Olichon, Père, 130
Ongaravadono, 42
Orthodox Churches, Eastern, 31, 143, 144, 147, 149, 151–3
Ôshu mission, 47
Oxford Mission to Calcutta (O.M.C.), 211

Padroado, 104, 113, 131–3, 140, 285
Pai Shang-ti Hui, 268
Pakalita, 80
Panikkar, Dr. K. M., 55
Paris Evangelical Mission, 64, 84
Parkman, Francis, 86–7, 91–2
Paul V, Pope, 48, 115
Paul VI, Pope, 28
Peace conferences, 223, 224
Peking, 103, 104, 115
Pentecostal movement, 178, 184, 274
Petitjean, Père, 16
Philippines, 245–50
Philippine Independent Church, 249–50
Pierron, Fr., 94
Pillay, Devasagayam, 66–71
Pius X, Pope, 192
Pius XI, Pope, 201
Polynesia, 1, 3, 10, 171, 174, 284
Pompallier, Bishop, 180
Porrès, Martin de, 190
Port-au-Prince (privateer), 172–3
Portuguese, 13, 65–6, 78, 115, 130–2, 139, 140
Pottier, Fr., 127–8, 129
Presbyterians, 7, 251, 253

Propaganda, *see* Sacred Congregation de Propaganda Fidei
Protestantism, 22–4, 27–8, 71, 78, 90, 284
Providence Industrial Mission (Ajawa), 251–2
P'u-Yi, 276, 277

Rachinsky, S. A., 153
Radama, King, 16–17
Rae, Rev. Colin, 2–3
Rafaravavy, 18, 19
Rakotobe, Prince, 17
Rakotondradama, Prince, 20
Ramakrishna, 211
Ramonja, Prince, 20
Ranavalona, Queen, 17–18, 20
Rasalama, 19
Rasoamanarivo, Victoire, 284
Ratana, Tahupoteki Wiremu, 260–5
Reichelt, Dr. Karl, 156, 166, 167–70, 316
Ren, Pastor, 292
Ricci, Fr. Matteo, 49, 50–4, 102, 115
Rickaby, Fr., Joseph, 221
Rikirangi, Te Kooti, 261
Ringatu Church, 261
Ringeltaube, 71
Rites, Chinese, 105, 116–17, 315–16, 324
Rizal, José, 246–50
Roberts, Archbishop, 130
Roberts, Rev. Issacher J., 268, 270–2
Roman Catholicism, 9, 11–12, 22–5, 27–8, 33, 65, 71, 78, 87, 102, 140, 201–9, 219, 281, 284, 292. *See also* Franciscans, Jesuits
Roots, Bishop L. H., 162, 167
Rosalie, 59
Rossi, Commandant de, 257–9
Rowe, J. A., 28–9
Roxas, Manuel, 250
Russell, Bertrand, 287
Russell, Lord John, 266
Russia, 223
Russian Orthodox Mission, 31, 143–4, 149, 151, 152

Sacred Congregation de Propaganda Fidei, 104, 106, 119, 132, 285

Sadhu Sundar Singh, 210
Salinger, Fr., 213
Samoa, 185
Sandhya (journal), 220
Sato, Fr., Paul, 147
Satsuma, 12
Sattianaden, 71–7
Schall, Fr. Adam, 54–6, 102, 126–7
Schön, Rev. F. J., 226
Schwartz, Frederick, 71–2
Scotland, Church of (in Nyasaland), 251, 253–4
Scbulimba, 'Lakeri' Rachel, 293
Sen, Keshub Chunder, 211
Seodzi, Sergei, 142–53
Shanghai, 56
Shensi, 276
Shiba, Colonel, 32
Shingon School, 155
Shwang-Shu-Tze, 34
Simeon, Bishop, 151
Siu, Jacques, 55, 60–1
Siu, Stephen, 124–5
Soames, Joseph, 261
smallpox epidemic (Ceylon), 139
Société des Missions Étrangères, 16, 104, 116, 117, 119, 120, 315
Society for Promoting Christian Knowledge (S.P.C.K.), 71, 73–4
Society for the Propagation of the Gospel (S.P.G.), *see* United Society, etc.
Sonntag, Rev. C., 2
Sophia (journal), 213, 215
Sôtau, Abbot Kanyeisô, 44
Sotelo, Fr., 46
Sottomayor, Antonio, 137–8
Souza, Fr. de, 66
Steward, Bishop John Mainwaring, 233, 234
Subhan, J. A., 198
Surugadai, 143, 149, 150
Sun Yat-Sen, Dr., 1, 162, 223, 276, 277, 280, 315
Sung, Ju-Ju (John), 193–4
Suzuki, Prof. D. T., 156
Szechwan, 116, 118, 119, 121, 127, 128

Tagore, Debindranath, 216
Tahitian people, 5

T'ai-Hsü, 162–4
Taiping movement, xiii, 266, 268–9,
  273, 285
Takahashi, 155–6
Takayama Ukon, 38
Tamatave, 21
Tegaquitha, Kateri, 91–9, 290, 302
Tekawitha, Catherine, *see* Tega-
  quitha, Kateri
Tao-Ying, *see* Miao-Chi
Tenko Nishida, 156–7, 165
Thailand, 115, 194
Thakombau, 182–3
Thomas, John, 176, 177, 179, 184
Thomson, Sir Basil, 7–8, 181, 184,
  185, 186–7, 317
Thoonen, Fr., 28
'Three-Self Movement', 194
Thury, Fr., 4
Tikhomirov, Sergius, 152
Tikopia, 235–6
Tilak, Lakshmibai, 210
Tilak, Narayan Vama, 210
Tinnevelly, 71, 75–7
Tji-tchoung, Paul Youn, 105
Tokugawa Iyeyasu, 38, 42–3, 45, 49
Tonga, 3–4, 171–88
Torres, Fr. Camilo, 245n.
Tournon, Mgr. Charles Thomas
  Maillard de, 116, 117–18, 139,
  140
Townsend, Fr. Henry, 230
Toyotomi Hideyoshi, 12–14, 38, 40
Triem, Pierre Huu ('Father Six'),
  191–3, 308
Trigault, Fr., 51
Tucker, Bishop, 293
Tu'i Tonga (priest king), 173–4,
  179, 180–1
Tupou, Taufa'ahau, *see* George,
  King of Tonga
Turkey, 196–201
Twentieth Century (journal), 216, 219

Uganda martyrs, 22–30
Ukalala, Finau, 174–5, 176
United Society for the Propagation
  of the Gospel (U.S.P.G.), xvii
Upadhyay Brahmabandhav, 211–
  22, 321–2

Ursis, Fr. de, 54

Valignano, Fr. Alessandro, 45, 53,
  65
Van Rheede, Hendrick Adriaan,
  136
Vaughan, Cardinal, 219
Vava'u, 178, 180
Vaz, Joseph, 130–41
Vedanta, 215, 216, 218
Vellozo, Jacques, 105–6
Venn, Henry, 194, 229–31
Verthamon, 121
Vi, Peter, 176–7, 317
Vietnam, 191–3
Vivekananda, Swami, 211
Vladimir, Fr., 148, 149

Waitangi, treaty of, 260–1, 264
Wei-Shih School, 161, 163
Wên Ch'ing, Dr., 283
Wesleyan Methodist Society, 3
West Africa, 292
White Fathers, 24–5, 43, 194–5
White Lotus sect, 34
Williams, John B., 182
Williams, Canon W., 263
Winthrop, John, 2
Wu, John C., 225
Wu P'ei-fu, General, 278
Wuchang Academy, 163–4

Yang, Michael, 55
Yang Kuang-hsien, 61
Yang, Wen-Hui, 161
Yan-shan, 31
Yi Piek, 102–3
Yi Seung-houn, 102–4
Yonekawa, 49
Yüan Shih-kai, 162, 224, 275–6
Yuang-Kuang, 160
Yu-lan, 31–2
Yun Chun-hsi, 50

Zaleski, Mgr. L. M., 215
Zambia, 78
Zamora, Fr. Jacinto, 245, 247, 249–
  50
Ziya Gökalp, 198